PROGRESS IN BEHAVIOR MODIFICATION

Volume 24

CONTRIBUTORS TO THIS VOLUME

Keith D. Allen

David O. Antonuccio

Donald H. Baucom

Janet Woodruff Borden

George A. Clum

Norman Epstein

Eleonora Gullone

Jeffrey A. Kelly

Neville J. King

James K. Luiselli

Janet S. St. Lawrence

Trevor F. Stokes

Blake H. Tearnan

Clay H. Ward

PROGRESS IN BEHAVIOR

MODIFICATION

EDITED BY

Michel Hersen

University of Pittsburgh School of Medicine
Pittsburgh, Pennsylvania

Richard M. Eisler

Department of Psychology
Virginia Polytechnic Institute and State University
Blacksburg, Virginia

Peter M. Miller

Hilton Head Health Institute
Hilton Head Island, South Carolina

Volume 24

1989

SAGE PUBLICATIONS
The Publishers of Professional Social Science
Newbury Park   London   New Delhi

For information address:

SAGE Publications, Inc.
2111 West Hillcrest Drive
Newbury Park, California 91320

SAGE Publications Ltd.
28 Banner Street
London EC1Y 8QE
England

SAGE Publications India Pvt. Ltd.
M-32 Market
Greater Kailash I
New Delhi 110 048 India

Printed in the United States of America

Library of Congress: 75-646720
ISBN 0-8039-3212-X
FIRST PRINTING, 1989

CONTENTS

Behavioral Assessment and Treatment
of Pediatric Feeding Disorders
in Developmental Disabilities

James K. Luiselli

Acceptability of Behavioral Interventions:
Child and Caregiver Perceptions

Eleonora Gullone and Neville J. King

The Behavioral Treatment of
Unipolar Depression in Adult Outpatients

David O. Antonuccio, Clay H. Ward, and Blake H. Tearnan

Etiology and Treatment of Panic Disorders

George A. Clum and Janet Woodruff Borden

The Role of Cognitive Variables in the Assessment and Treatment of Marital Discord

Donald H. Baucom and Norman Epstein

CONTRIBUTORS

KEITH D. ALLEN is in the Department of Psychology, Meyer Children's Rehabilitation Institute, University of Nebraska Medical Center, Omaha. His research interests include the assessment and treatment of children's distress during invasive medical and dental procedures and the management of chronic pain in children.

DAVID O. ANTONUCCIO, Ph.D., is Coordinator of the Mental Hygiene Clinic, V.A. Medical Center, and in the Department of Psychiatry and Behavioral Sciences, University of Nevada School of Medicine, Reno. He is an ABPP Diplomate in Clinical Psychology, and his clinical and research interests are in the areas of depression and smoking cessation.

DONALD H. BAUCOM is in the Psychology Department at the University of North Carolina, Chapel Hill. His research interests are in the areas of marital discord and treatment of marital distress from a cognitive-behavioral orientation.

JANET WOODRUFF BORDEN is affiliated with the Western Psychiatric Institute and Clinic, University of Pittsburgh School of Medicine. Her research interests include physiological and cognitive dimensions of anxiety disorders and cognitive-behavioral treatment of panic.

GEORGE A. CLUM is in the Department of Psychology, Virginia Polytechnic Institute and State University. He is the Director of the Anxiety Disorders Clinic and conducts research in anxiety and affective disorders.

NORMAN EPSTEIN is in the Department of Family and Community Development, University of Maryland, College Park. His research interests and publications focus on assessment and treatment of marital and family dysfunction, particularly within a cognitive-behavioral framework.

ELEONORA GULLONE is in the Department of Psychology, Phillip Institute of Technology, Victoria, Australia. Her clinical and research interests include the behavioral assessment and treatment of children's problems, and social validation. Of particular interest are children's phobias and toilet training of intellectually disabled preschool-aged children.

JEFFREY A. KELLY is Professor of Psychology (Psychiatry) and Chief of the Division of Psychology at the University of Mississippi Medical Center, Jackson. He currently conducts research and provides services to persons who are at risk for or are already affected by AIDS.

NEVILLE J. KING is a member of the Faculty of Education, Monash University, Victoria, Australia. His research interests and publications are focused on child behavior therapy, childhood fears and anxieties, and health psychology.

JAMES K. LUISELLI is a clinical psychologist affiliated with Psychological and Educational Resource Associates, Concord, Massachusetts. His primary clinical and research interests include child and adolescent behavior therapy, developmental disabilities, childhood psychopathology, and pediatric behavioral medicine.

JANET S. St. LAWRENCE is Associate Professor of Psychology at Jackson State University and Clinical Associate Professor of Psychiatry (Psychology) at the University of Mississippi Medical Center, Jackson. Her research and clinical practice emphasize AIDS prevention and counseling HIV-affected persons.

TREVOR F. STOKES is Professor and Clinical Director in the Department of Child and Family Studies, Florida Mental Health Institute, University of South Florida, Tampa. His research interests include child behavior management, self-management, and generalization of behavior changes.

BLAKE H. TEARNAN, Ph.D., is Director of Psychological Services, Sierra Pain Institute, and in the Psychology Department, University of Nevada, Reno. His clinical and research interests include anxiety management, chronic pain, and the treatment of depression.

CLAY H. WARD, Ph.D., is Coordinator of the Consultation-Liaison Service, V.A. Medical Center, and in the Department of Psychiatry and Behavioral Sciences, University of Nevada School of Medicine, Reno. His clinical and research interests are in the areas of behavioral medicine, health psychology, and psychological assessment and interventions for medical and surgical patients.

AIDS PREVENTION: COMMUNITY AND BEHAVIORAL INTERVENTIONS[1]

JANET S. St. LAWRENCE
Jackson State University

JEFFREY A. KELLY
University of Mississippi Medical Center

Authors' Note: Preparation of this chapter was supported by National Institutes of Mental Health Grant R01-MH41800.

I. INTRODUCTION

Less than a decade has passed since acquired immune deficiency syndrome (AIDS) was first identified in a small number of patients with unusual opportunistic illnesses who presented themselves for medical care in New York, San Francisco, and Los Angeles (Centers for Disease Control, 1981a, 1981b). Public health authorities and medical specialists became alarmed by the rise in what had formerly been rare conditions and initiated close surveillance efforts. As researchers attempted to find some meaningful pattern behind these atypical illnesses, one common denominator emerged. All of the patients displayed underlying immune system compromise.

Within two years, the human immunodeficiency virus (HIV), a virus that compromises immune system integrity, was identified as the cause of AIDS. Continuing medical investigations assembled information into a disconcerting picture that suggested a health crisis of unprecedented proportions. It is now apparent that such a health crisis exists, posing a challenge to public health that transcends national boundaries and is worldwide in its scope. While the continuing escalation of the epidemic is discouraging, the health care professions, including psychology, face a greater challenge than has existed for centuries and an opportunity to adapt their professional skills to make a substantial impact—both in the saving of human lives and in the compilation of knowledge that can benefit vast numbers of people now and in the future.

The principal facts of the AIDS health crisis are well known. Epidemiological research documents steadily increasing projections regarding the numbers of people at risk for HIV infection and ever worsening estimates of the eventual health progression of persons infected by HIV. As of late 1988, 1–2 million Americans were HIV-infected, nearly 80,000 persons within this country were diagnosed with AIDS, and from 365,000 to 380,000 Americans were expected to be diagnosed with AIDS by 1992 (Curran et al., 1988).

Despite intensive biomedical research, it is increasingly clear that an effective vaccine cannot be anticipated within the foreseeable future and the only immediately available hope for stemming future cases of HIV infection and AIDS lies in developing effective education and prevention programs (Ada, 1988; Kelly & St. Lawrence, 1988a, 1988b; Osborne,

1988). Even in the absence of a vaccine, new cases of HIV infection are preventable if people can make specific behavioral changes that will preclude exposure to the virus (Kelly & St. Lawrence, 1988a, 1988b). This chapter will review the epidemiological and medical literature about AIDS that is relevant to psychology, describe service delivery and research on AIDS prevention, discuss barriers to education and prevention efforts, and identify areas where psychological intervention and research are particularly needed at this time.

II. AIDS EPIDEMIOLOGY AND TRANSMISSION

AIDS is a collection of end-stage illnesses resulting from HIV infection. AIDS is diagnosed when a person exhibits specific opportunistic illnesses that reflect immune system compromise and meets the Centers for Disease Control's (CDC) definitional criteria for an AIDS diagnosis, and when there are no other causes for the underlying immune system failure (Centers for Disease Control, 1986b). Although persons with AIDS exhibit a variety of bacterial, fungal, viral, neurological, and neoplastic illnesses, pneumocystic *carinii* pneumonia, Kaposi's sarcoma, constitutional wasting, and lymphomas are the most common life-threatening conditions that affect persons with AIDS (DeVita, Hellman, & Rosenberg, 1985; Ebbesen, Biggar, & Melbye, 1984). Some 80% of persons diagnosed with AIDS die within two years following their diagnosis (Curran, Morgan, Starcher, Hardy, & Jaffe, 1985). For reasons that are not yet well understood, persons diagnosed with Kaposi's sarcoma survive longer than persons with pneumocystic *carinii* pneumonia, intravenous drug users have a shorter survival than homosexual men, and racial minorities have a shorter life expectancy following an AIDS diagnosis (Mulleady, 1987; Peterson & Bakeman, 1988; Saltzman et al., 1988).

AIDS develops in a person with HIV infection after the virus invades and destroys a sufficient number of T-4 lymphocytes ("Helper T cells"), which mediate the body's immune responses. T-4 cell reductions leave the body unable to resist diseases and vulnerable to opportunistic infections (Boyko et al., 1985; Groopman et al., 1985). A substantial drop in the number of T-4 lymphocytes reliably precedes or accompanies AIDS onset (Goedert et al., 1987). AIDS patients often experience recurrent debilitating illnesses interspersed with periods of relatively good health before they die. Because HIV is neurotropic as well as lymphotropic and directly invades central nervous system cells, neuropsychological impairments are common and may be the earliest clinical predictor of worsening health in an otherwise asymptomatic person with HIV infection (Eisdorfer, 1987a, 1987b; Marshall et al., 1988; van Wielink et al., 1988; Wolcott, 1986).

Persons who are HIV-infected can develop a host of symptoms reflecting immune system compromise, but that do not meet the definitional criteria for a diagnosis of frank AIDS. These conditions are often loosely grouped into a pattern referred to as AIDS-related complex (ARC). Current estimates suggest that the number of persons with ARC is ten times higher than the number of persons diagnosed with clinical criterion AIDS (Fauci, 1986). ARC illnesses are highly variable, ranging from mild to severe, from transient to persistent, and from life-compromising to life-threatening. Over the short term, some persons with ARC deteriorate from ARC to frank AIDS, while others experience at least a temporary improvement in their general health or continue to have symptoms without any immediate worsening in their overall health.

An even larger number of persons are currently HIV-infected, asymptomatic, and in good clinical health. Estimates of the number of HIV-infected persons suggest their numbers may be 30 to 50 times higher than the number of diagnosed AIDS cases (Fauci, 1986). Asymptomatic HIV infection is inferred from the presence of viral antibodies to HIV, and a person who is healthy but HIV seropositive is capable of transmitting the virus to others. Originally, it was thought that only a small proportion of those who were HIV seropositive would eventually develop ARC or AIDS, but those early estimates now appear incorrect. The likelihood of developing AIDS increases with the length of time a person has been HIV-infected. From 4% to 5% of HIV-infected individuals develop AIDS each year following the time when HIV exposure first occurred (Hessol et al., 1988; Schechter et al., 1988). Recent estimates predict that from 65% to 100% of HIV-infected persons will, in the absence of medical advances, develop AIDS within 16 years following their HIV exposure (Lemp et al., 1988). If these projections are correct, the demand on health care resources already strained by AIDS in many areas of the country will dramatically increase.

Extensive clinical trials are under way to develop agents that can successfully reverse the progression of HIV-related illnesses or restore immune system integrity. To date, a limited number of medications reduce the severity, frequency, and mortality of the illnesses that affect persons diagnosed with AIDS. However, no currently available agent reverses the underlying immune system impairment resulting from HIV infection, and the available treatments prolong survival but are not curative.

Unlike viral infections responsible for the common cold or influenza, the human immunodeficiency virus is transmitted only in very narrow and specific ways. Body fluids high in HIV concentration (blood, semen, vaginal secretions, and possibly breast milk) must gain direct access to the bloodstream of an uninfected person for viral transmission to take place (Bucene, Armstrong, & Stuckey, 1988; Centers for Disease Control, 1986b; Ziegler, Stewart, Penny, Stuckey, & Good, 1988). All current AIDS cases can be attributed to specific behavioral practices that permit one of these bodily fluids to gain direct bloodstream entry routes. Although very low concentrations of HIV have been found in tears and saliva, it is rarely present in these fluids and, even when present, is at very low concentrations (Ho et al., 1985). No AIDS cases have ever been linked to transmission by either saliva or tears. HIV is not transmitted through physical proximity to an infected person, and AIDS has never resulted from casual social contact in the home, school, or workplace. Family members who live with and care for persons with AIDS in their homes are at no risk for HIV infection (Friedland et al., 1986, 1987). Even in developing countries where family members live in close proximity to an AIDS patient under unsanitary living conditions, viral transmission does not occur in the absence of sexual or blood contact. Despite public misconceptions, it is exceedingly clear that HIV is not transmitted by insects, shared living facilities, coughs, or touch. If the virus were transmitted through airborne or insect-borne vectors, few preventive steps could curtail the future course of the epidemic. However, since transmission is clearly linked to specific behavioral routes, effective prevention of future cases is a reasonable and achievable goal. If persons who are currently uninfected make self-protective behavioral changes that preclude viral transmission, primary prevention efforts can succeed.

Table 1 shows the distribution of adolescent and adult AIDS cases in mid-1988. Hemophiliacs and transfusion recipients acquired HIV-infection following the administration of contaminated blood or clotting factor agents. Most cases of HIV transmission through blood and blood products occurred before 1985, when laboratory tests to detect HIV antibodies became available and were rapidly introduced for wide-scale screening of blood bank supplies. Because hemophiliacs require frequent infusions and because blood clotting factors combine sera from multiple donors, many hemophiliacs became HIV-infected before blood screening programs were available (Curran, Lawrence, & Jaffe, 1984). New cases of HIV infection attributable to transfusions or clotting factor agents have decreased since 1985 and are likely to continue to diminish in the future.

Intravenous drug users (IVDUs) are at risk for HIV infection because of the common practice of sharing needles. When a needle with HIV in blood from a previous user is inserted into the bloodstream of an uninfected person, HIV transmission can occur. IV drug users constitute a substantial and increasing proportion of AIDS patients. Depending upon the particular area of the country being surveyed, HIV seroprevalence among intravenous drug users ranges from 15% to 60% (Des Jarlais, 1988a). In the New York City area, where HIV prevalence is high, HIV infection rates among IV drug users may be as high as 60%, and approximately 25% of current American AIDS cases are current or former drug users (Centers for Disease Control, 1987a). There are an estimated 1.1 million IVDUs in the United States, most concentrated in large, economically depressed urban

TABLE 1
Distribution of Adult and
Adolescent AIDS Cases in the United States (in percentages)

Homosexual and bisexual men	63
Intravenous drug users	19
Homosexual male intravenous drug users	7
Heterosexuals	4
Undetermined	3
Transfusion, blood components	2
Hemophilia/coagulation disorders	1

SOURCE: *AIDS Weekly Surveillance Report* (Centers for Disease Control, June 6, 1988).

areas, and three-quarters of whom are male (Centers for Disease Control, 1987a). Most have their primary sexual relationships with women who do not inject drugs (Office of Technology Assessment, 1988). The number of women who do not inject drugs, but who are regular sexual partners of male IV drug users, is estimated to be at least half as large as the number of IV drug users, or about 550,000 women (Des Jarlais, 1988a). Thus the potential for further spread of HIV infection to intravenous drug users, their sexual partners, and their children is high.

HIV-infected mothers give birth to infants who are seropositive at the time of delivery 20% to 50% of the time (Mok et al., 1987). While infants have constituted a small proportion of American AIDS cases up to the present, pediatric AIDS is increasing rapidly in urban areas with large populations of drug users. In New York City, 1 of every 61 infants is now HIV-infected at birth ("AIDS & Infants," 1988). Recent research has also documented HIV transmission through breast-feeding, and mothers infected with HIV are advised to use alternate methods of infant feeding (Bucene et al., 1988; Ziegler et al., 1988). Given the increase in cases due to intravenous drug use and heterosexual transmission, the number of pediatric AIDS cases is likely to increase in the future.

Racial minorities and the urban poor are disproportionately represented among American AIDS cases (Krueger, Wood, Diehr, & Maxwell, 1988; Rutherford, Barnhart, & Lemp, 1988). Cumulative incidence rates (cases per million population) are 2.6 times higher for black men and 2.5 times higher for Hispanic men than the rates for white males. The cumulative incidence rates for black and Hispanic women are 12.2 and 8.5 times, respectively, higher than for white women (Bakeman, McCray, Lumb, Jackson, & Whitley, 1987). While this disparity is in part due to drug use patterns, even among AIDS cases not attributable to IV drugs, the cumulative incidences for blacks and Hispanics are still higher than for whites (St. Lawrence, Betts, Hogan, & MacDonald, 1988).

Most AIDS cases are due to practices that permit the virus to be transferred between sexual partners. In this country, homosexual men constitute 70% of current AIDS cases. Although estimates of HIV prevalence vary among cities and regions of the country, current estimates suggest that from 20% to 65% of nonmonogamous gay men are already HIV-infected (Anderson & Levy, 1985; Jaffe et al., 1985). To the best of our knowledge, there is only one population-based estimate of HIV infection prevalence among gay and bisexual men. Winkelstein, Samuel, and Padian (1987) report that HIV seropositivity rates within a San Francisco research sample rose from 22.8% in 1982 to 48.6% by 1984 and then stabilized. This suggests that approximately half of the gay men in San Francisco are HIV-infected. Selected sample studies reflect even higher prevalence. The San Francisco City Clinic Cohort recruited homosexual and bisexual men from sexually transmitted disease (STD) clinics and assessed HIV infection prevalence at five intervals spanning the time between 1978 and 1985. HIV infection prevalence increased from 4% in 1978 to 69% by mid-1985. A multicity cohort (the MACS cohort) reported that 45% of the sample was seropositive when they entered the study (Kingsley et al., 1987), and Martin (1987) reported the seroprevalence of a New York City sample to be 36%. The prevalence rates reported from the widely studied cohort samples may not reflect overall prevalence rates among the population of gay and bisexual men for several reasons. It is possible that reports from narrow samples, such as persons treated in STD clinics, overestimate the actual prevalence of HIV infection. Participating in a longitudinal epidemiological investigation may also have reactive effects, and all of the cities represented in the much-studied cohorts have a high to moderate AIDS prevalence.

Base-rate estimates of HIV prevalence for heterosexuals also vary widely depending upon the area of the country that is sampled and the subgroups represented within a sample, but are substantially lower than for gay and bisexual men. Recent research suggests that from 0.0002% to 3.7% of the general population is currently HIV-infected in this country and that prevalence is steadily increasing (Gordon, Gilbert, Hawley, & Willoughby, 1988; Hoff et al., 1988). In central and western Africa, where AIDS has reached epidemic proportions, AIDS is a heterosexually transmitted disease, and the overrepresentation of homosexual men in this country's AIDS cases is different from the pattern in some other areas of the world. The most likely explanation for the high prevalence of AIDS among American gay and bisexual men is that the virus appeared relatively early in this country's homosexual male population and then spread between persons who had multiple sexual partners and who engaged in practices that permitted efficient viral transmission. Recently, the proportion of AIDS patients who are gay or bisexual men has shown a slight decrease (Starcher, Dondero, Noa, Efird, & Curran, 1988), although it is unclear whether this is due to an increasing proportion of IVDU and heterosexually transmitted cases, to infection rates having reached natural ceiling levels among homosexual men in some large cities, to risk-reduction changes in sexual behavior by homosexual men, or to other factors. Gay and bisexual men are most immediately affected by HIV, with cases attributable to intravenous drug use and heterosexual transmission increasing substantially. Although the absolute numbers are still relatively small, heterosexual women account for the most rapidly increasing proportion of AIDS cases (Starcher et al., 1988), and many of the cases reported in Table 1 as having "undetermined" causes are probably individuals who were infected heterosexually without their knowledge.

Although past discussions concerning AIDS have focused on "risk groups," it is now more productive to direct our attention to the specific behavioral practices that transmit HIV (Kelly & St. Lawrence, 1988b). Persons are not at risk for AIDS because of their personal identity characteristics, but because they engage in specific practices that allow HIV transmission to take place. A gay man is no more likely to become HIV-infected simply because he is homosexual than a heterosexual is risk free simply because of his or her sexual preference. The distinction between risk *groups* and risk *behaviors* is important. Focusing on risk practices allows precise behavior change goals to be identified as the targets for education and prevention efforts (Kelly & St. Lawrence, 1988b). Since there is a long latency between HIV exposure and the onset of any physical disease symptoms, current AIDS cases reflect the demography of HIV infection from literally years ago. By the time a population subgroup shows an increase in AIDS cases, HIV infection prevalence is already likely to be high. Since the aim of AIDS prevention efforts is to prevent infection, changes in risky behavior must occur before AIDS cases become prevalent in a population subgroup (Kelly & St. Lawrence, 1988b). Taken together, this suggests that it is more productive to emphasize risk practices than current AIDS risk groups.

A. Risk Practices for Sexual Transmission

Sexual risk practices are similar for heterosexuals and for homosexual men. Unprotected intercourse without the barrier protection of condoms carries high risk if one partner is infected. Unprotected vaginal intercourse permits viral transmission from female-to-male or from male-to-female partners (Calabrese & Gopalakrishna, 1986; Fischl et al., 1987; Redfield et al., 1987). Unprotected anal intercourse carries extremely high risk because the rectal trauma associated with this practice permits ready bloodstream access for the viral transmission. Gay men who engage in unprotected receptive anal intercourse with a single partner over 12 months' time are three times more likely to seroconvert than gay males who do not engage in anal intercourse, and the same practice with five sexual partners over a year's time results in an 18-fold increase in the probability of becoming HIV-infected (Kingsley et al., 1987). A heterosexual female who is the receptive partner during anal intercourse is 300 times more likely to seroconvert than a woman who refrains from this practice (Greenblatt et al., 1988; Sion et al., 1988). The risk associated with oral/ genital intercourse is less clear. Some epidemiological studies have not found oral/genital intercourse to be a significant independent risk predictor, but this may be because oral intercourse can rarely be disentangled from other risk practices such as also engaging in vaginal or anal intercourse. The consensus of most public health authorities is that any sexual practice that allows the exchange of semen, blood, or vaginal secretions should be considered risky if one partner is HIV-infected. Other sexual practices such as rectal or vaginal finger or fist insertion, oral/anal contact, or the sharing of sexual stimulation devices between partners may also carry transmission risk.

Early in the health crisis, large numbers of different sexual partners was a strong predictor of HIV infection risk, but may be a less relevant predictor for gay and bisexual men today. The specific activities that occur between partners are probably a stronger determinant of risk. When the base-rate prevalence for HIV infection was low, large numbers of partners were required before an individual encountered a partner who carried the virus. Because the base-rate prevalence among sexually active gay and bisexual men is much higher today, there is a substantial likelihood that any nonmonogamous gay male's partner is already HIV exposed. At present, the number of different sexual partners is a more relevant risk predictor for heterosexuals, since the base-rate prevalence is still relatively lower among this population (Brundage et al., 1987).

B.   Risk Practices Associated with Intravenous Drug Use

Intravenous drug users are at risk for HIV infection because of the common practice of sharing needles between drug users, as well as from sexual transmission. A person who becomes infected through contaminated needles is then capable of transmitting the virus to subsequent sexual partners through any of the sexual practices described earlier as well as by needle sharing. Most IV drug users are male heterosexuals, whose adherence or lack of adherence to safer sexual practices has direct implications for HIV transmission to female partners (Des Jarlais, 1988b). Some evidence suggests that IV drug users are more cautious about sexual practices during casual sexual contacts than in long-term relationships, a finding of serious concern since it is within long-term relationships that children are most likely to be conceived and the potential for increasing prevalence of pediatric infection is centered (Des Jarlais, 1988b).

III.   BEHAVIORAL OBJECTIVES TO CURTAIL AIDS RISK

The only absolute protections from sexually transmitted diseases, such as AIDS, are celibacy or maintaining a lifelong monogamous relationship with an uninfected partner and avoiding intravenous needle sharing. While these alternatives preclude any risk for HIV infection, it is not sufficient to limit prescriptive advice to these alternatives. It is unrealistic to expect that millions of sexually active individuals will cease all sexual activity or commit themselves to lifelong monogamy. There are several reasons for recommending a broader approach to prevention efforts. Many adolescents and adults become sexually active before marriage (Hein, 1987). Persons who are committed to a monogamous relationship may see that relationship end through separation, divorce, or death, to be succeeded by subsequent relationships, and infidelity does occur. Thus, if HIV infection is to be curtailed, risk-reduction information is urgently needed by those who remain, resume, or soon will become sexually active as well as by those who do not maintain monogamous life-styles. Although substance abuse treatment programs were available long before AIDS, substance abuse has not been eradicated and nearly 90% of persons who seek to enter drug treatment programs cannot be accommodated by existing resources (Des Jarlais, 1988a). Since the specific risk practices that enable HIV transmission have been identified, education and prevention programs can assist persons to change the specific practices that confer HIV exposure risk. Risk behaviors for gay and bisexual men, heterosexual men and women, and intravenous drug users are shown in Table 2.

A.   Behavioral Risk-Reduction Objectives for Homosexual Men and Heterosexual Men and Women

Risk-reduction changes for nonmonogamous heterosexuals are similar to the changes recommended for homosexual men. These include the consistent adoption of low-risk practices between partners and condom use during sexual activities that permit fluid exchange (Francis & Chin, 1987). Mutual masturbation or frottage (body rubbing) pose very little risk so long as fluids do not come into contact with skin breaks or if condoms are used (Francis & Chin, 1987). The barrier protection afforded by condoms is unlikely to permit viral transmission during oral/genital contact. Numerous laboratory studies have established that the use of high-quality latex condoms in combination with a water-based lubricant containing nonoxynol-9, a spermicide in some over-the-counter contraceptives that effectively kills HIV, greatly reduces transmission likelihood (Fineberg, 1988; Kaplan, 1988). Even though condoms afford greater protection, condom use is not entirely safe, because condom failures occur due to breakage, incorrect use, age, or slippage. Because condom failure rates may be higher during

TABLE 2
Risk Behaviors for HIV Infection for Homosexual Men,
Heterosexual Men and Women, and Intravenous Drug Users

Homosexual and bisexual men, heterosexual men, and heterosexual women	Any sexual practice involving fluid exchange, such as unprotected vaginal, oral, or anal intercourse. Unprotected anal intercourse is the practice most strongly predictive of HIV infection, but any form of unprotected intercourse—oral/anal, digital/anal, and fist/rectal—practices also carry risk. Number of different sexual partners is no longer a relevant risk predictor for gay and bisexual men given the high prevalence of HIV infection among nonmonogamous homosexual and bisexual men, but is still an independent risk factor for heterosexuals since the base rate prevalence is lower among heterosexuals at present.
Intravenous drug users	Sharing nonsterile needles. Once an individual is HIV-infected, viral transmission can occur during any of the sexual practices described above.

anal intercourse than during vaginal intercourse, both homosexuals and heterosexuals are most prudently advised to avoid anal intercourse entirely (Kelly & St. Lawrence, 1987). Valdiserri et al. (1988a) studied condom failure rates reported by a sample of 955 homosexual men who engaged in anal intercourse and found that 7% to 14.6% of the participants reported at least one occurrence of condom failure.

B.   Behavioral Risk-Reduction Objectives for Intravenous Drug Users

While persons at risk for sexually transmitted HIV face the immediate need to change sexual behavior, intravenous drug users are simultaneously faced with the need to change substance use patterns and to modify sexual practices. Drug use changes may be to discontinue substance use entirely, to disinfect needles consistently after each use with a substance that neutralizes HIV, or to employ sterile needles when drugs are injected. The needed sexual practice changes are the same as the changes described above.

IV.   AIDS RISK BEHAVIOR CHANGE STRATEGIES

Grass-roots organizations in the gay community have pioneered vigorous AIDS prevention programs. These organizations intervened with only limited resources and an emphasis on service delivery rather than empirical evaluation. Only rarely have AIDS prevention efforts employed research designs that permitted a controlled evaluation of intervention effects. This is not surprising since the immediate concern of community organizations was to curtail the spread of HIV infection. However, as a result, knowledge about the relative effectiveness of different approaches with various populations has been slow to accumulate. It is important to evaluate the effectiveness of different educational programs and identify which methods work best for whom if we are to use resources in the most cost-effective manner and with the maximum public health impact.

Research on health marketing strategies and on attitude change suggests that information is most effective when it is frequently repeated, presented in a variety of formats (i.e., visual, auditory, and so on), presented by sources that are credible to the message's intended recipient, and include behaviorally specific information regarding how to implement needed changes (Leventhal, Safer, & Panagis, 1983; Siegel, Grodsky, & Herman, 1986). Adapted to AIDS outreach education, specific, explicit, and behaviorally prescriptive information should be provided on a sustained basis, through a variety of outlets, and the content and delivery should be tailored to the message's intended recipients.

Based on what is already known from marketing research, health promotion research, and attitude change literature, desirable characteristics for AIDS prevention programs can be specified. First, they should present clear information that AIDS is a serious health threat, and should indicate how the virus is transmitted and why behavior change now can prevent future illness. High-risk practices should be identified in clear and specific language along with a rationale for why these practices are risky. Lower-risk alternatives should be described, with practical suggestions for putting these alternatives into practice. In addition, written materials should emphasize that changes can be implemented successfully and should stress the positive outcomes from protecting oneself and others from AIDS (Kelly & St. Lawrence, 1988b). Written materials are useful in AIDS education because they are relatively inexpensive and can be mass produced and distributed in locations where they will be readily available to the targeted population. The content and language can also be tailored to the specific audience for which they are intended. For example, the San Francisco AIDS Foundation has developed different brochures for gay men, heterosexuals, Hispanics, IV drug users, adolescents, employers, parents, and women with content specific to their intended audiences. This is effective and appropriate because the information or language relevant to one group may not be effective or equally appropriate for other audiences. However, existing informational brochures sometimes are inconsistent in meeting these characteristics. When researchers reviewed 22 AIDS informational brochures and examined their content according to existing criteria for effective public health communication (Siegel et al., 1986), most of the pamphlets conveyed a sense of immediate health threat, discussed the causes of AIDS, and provided information on high-risk sexual practices, but fewer than half offered information about why a particular practice was risky. The brochures often lacked any description of lower-risk practices, failed to convey that the needed changes could be successfully made, and rarely advised their readers how to put lower-risk behaviors into effect (Siegel et al., 1986).

Informational messages are effective only when they reach and have impact upon persons vulnerable to HIV infection. In many large cities, grass-roots organizations have implemented comprehensive outreach programs using a variety of methods to disseminate information and to incorporate visible prompts for lowered risk conduct into settings where gay men meet and socialize. The following sections will describe AIDS prevention approaches that have been employed with gay and bisexual men, intravenous drug users, and heterosexual adults and adolescents, as well as efforts to promote AIDS prevention through HIV testing programs and legislative mandates.

A.   Prevention Research with Gay and Bisexual Men

1. COMMUNITY-BASED EDUCATION AND OUTREACH PROGRAMS

Organizations in several large cities have developed creative AIDS outreach and education programs. These programs provide information and create a supportive social environment for AIDS risk reduction. Although the range of activities differs from one program to another, common elements among different programs often include information about HIV infection and transmission, educational brochures and posters, making materials available in social settings where gay men meet and socialize, and condom distribution programs.

The Gay Men's Health Crisis (GMHC) in New York City was among the first organizations to mobilize a response to the AIDS epidemic and has taken a leading role in public education and outreach campaigns. A description of their services illustrates the breadth and variety of services that are being provided (D'Eramo, 1987). Ongoing programs of GMHC are organized into three areas: educational services, patient services, and research support. Educational services include disseminating emerging information on diagnosis, treatment, and long-term management of AIDS, publishing a newsletter that is used as a training manual by many hospitals and universities, conducting open forums for persons at risk for HIV infection, and providing training seminars for physicians, psychologists, and social workers. GMHC has also shared its experience with other regions of the country by helping to establish similar organizations in Atlanta, Philadelphia, Houston, Los Angeles, and several other cities. GMHC also operates a 24-hour telephone hotline for public education. In addition to these individual and group services, GMHC works closely with city, state, and federal agencies to promote AIDS-related research, participates in a multicity task force to coordinate resources, and sponsors fund-raising for research projects in the New York City area.

In San Francisco, the STOP AIDS Project adopted in-home marketing strategies used to sell household products to provide safer sex seminars for gay and bisexual men. The STOP AIDS Project was developed to motivate participants to reexamine their personal behavior and create a normative shift within the San Francisco gay community (Bye, 1987). The in-home group sessions are informal, but structured. Participants consent in advance to meet with professional facilitators and discuss concerns about AIDS and its impact on their sexual behavior and life-styles. Information about safer sex is distributed and discussed, and the group process is used to encourage participants to confront beliefs that may act as barriers to the successful adoption of safer practices. After the seminar, the project continues to support participants through a newsletter, follow-up activities, and by enlisting participants themselves to become peer educators.

AIDS Atlanta also uses social networks to disseminate risk-reduction information (Smith, 1987). A highly visible media campaign organized by AIDS Atlanta includes slogans and logos on bar napkins, cups, and matchbooks to reinforce the idea of risk reduction, posters placed in bars and businesses in metropolitan Atlanta, publicly displayed decals and stickers, flyers distributed on cars in the parking lots of gay businesses, direct mailings of safer sex pamphlets, and advertisements in local gay publications. In addition, AIDS Atlanta adapted the format successfully employed by STOP AIDS in San Francisco to recruit trainers and provide in-the-home "parties" that present risk-reduction information through informational "games," demonstrations, and question-and-answer sessions. During the parties, risk-reduction trainers and hosts for future parties are identified and recruited. Like many of the organizations already described, AIDS Atlanta also has developed outreach subgroups for youth, minorities, and IV drug abusers.

Such community outreach programs have their greatest overall impact through changing community norms and creating peer social supports for lowered risk behavior. While different methods are used to implement outreach programs in different communities, Coates (1988) describes six common outcome objectives that characterize effective programs: increasing knowledge of HIV and its transmission, facilitating recognition of one's personal susceptibility to AIDS, generating positive outcome expectations that behavior change now can prevent HIV infection and future illness, providing training in social skills to negotiate safer life-styles, creating personal efficacy beliefs that changes can be made successfully, and changing the social norms within the subcommunity.

Even though it is difficult to identify the program elements responsible for changes in risk behavior, several surveys in these same geographic areas clearly document dramatic behavioral changes and increases in AIDS risk knowledge. These surveys make it possible to describe the cumulative effects that have resulted from community outreach efforts and changing community norms. In several large cities such as New York and San Francisco, there have been measurable changes in sexual risk behavior, lowered rates of new HIV seroconversion, reductions in the mean number of different sexual partners, and shifts from sexual practices high in AIDS risk to those low in risk (Martin, 1987; McKusick, Horstman, & Coates, 1985; McKusick, Wiley, et al., 1985). Other studies in the same urban areas document reductions in sexually transmitted diseases among gay men and reduced bathhouse patronage, providing further evidence of behavior changes (Golubjatnikov, Pfister, & Tillotson, 1983; Schechter et al., 1988).

Several intensively studied cohorts of gay and bisexual men in different areas of the country attest to the changes in sexual behavior that have taken place in areas where community outreach campaigns are well organized. In New York City, Martin (1987) reported on the sexual behavior of a well-educated sample of gay and bisexual men. The interview format in this study collected information about sexual behavior for the past year and, retrospectively, for sexual behavior from the year before participants learned about AIDS. Participants who engaged in sexual activity outside the home setting reported a reduction in the number of sexual partners from 36 to 8. The median number of sexual partners in the home declined from 8 to 3, the frequency of receptive anal intercourse declined by 75%, and condom use during insertive anal intercourse increased from 2% to 19% during the same interval. A total of 40% of the sample had decreased their risk behavior, 49% had not changed, and 8.3% were at increased risk. Becker and Joseph (1988), in a comprehensive review of the AIDS risk behavior change literature, note that Martin's data are a highly conservative estimate of risk behavior change, since a man who decreased the number of different sexual partners from 20 to 2 would remain classified as having multiple sexual partners despite a marked reduction in the number of total partners.

Three research cohorts have been reported from San Francisco. In one study, randomly sampled telephone numbers listed to a male name were contacted and those who identified themselves as gay or bisexual were asked to participate in an interview survey; 81.4% consented to be interviewed. A total of 500 men identified in this way were interviewed in 1984 and again nine months later. Unprotected anal intercourse outside a primary relationship decreased from 17% to only 7%; the proportion of men reporting celibacy, monogamy, or no sexual activities involving fluid exchange outside a primary relationship rose from 69% to 81%; and the number of persons reporting sex with more than one partner in the preceding month declined by 27% (Centers for Disease Control, 1985).

Biannual assessments since January 1984 have followed the San Francisco Men's Health Study, a cohort recruited by stratified sampling within the San Francisco census tracts with the highest cumulative AIDS incidence rates (Winkelstein et al., 1987). At the time of initial recruitment into the study, seropositivity rates within the cohort were 48.6% and stabilized within six months to 49.3% of the cohort. During the same interval, seronegative participants reported major declines in the prevalence of receptive anal intercourse, seropositive subjects reported major reductions in the frequency of insertive anal intercourse, and the prevalence of sexual activity with ten or more partners and anal/genital contact with two or more partners declined by 60%.

McKusick, Horstman, and Coates (1985) recruited a third San Francisco cohort from gay bathhouses, gay bars, advertisements recruiting gay men who did not frequent either bars or bathhouses, and stable couples who had participated in earlier research. Of the total sample recruited, 42% (N = 655) completed and returned the survey. Changes in sexual behavior were evaluated by asking the participants to recall their sexual activity a year earlier and to describe their present behavior. In the initial assessment, McKusick, Horstman, and Coates indicated that exclusively monogamous relationships increased from 35% to 41% in one year, and unprotected receptive anal intercourse became less frequent in nonmonogamous relationships. Although condom use increased during receptive anal intercourse, only 3.6% to 8.1% of the participants were using condoms. When the same sample was resurveyed six months later (McKusick, Wiley, et al., 1985), the average number of sexual partners had decreased 13.5%, the frequency of unprotected anal intercourse had decreased by 46.2%, and the average number of different sexual partners in one month had decreased by 20.4%. Several other sexual behavior changes also reflected substantive changes: oral/anal contact declined by 50%, receptive oral intercourse to orgasm declined by 27.3%, and the average number of visits to a sex club or bathhouse declined by 60%.

Cohorts in other large cities reflect similar changes. In the MACS cohort of 1,000 homosexual/bisexual men in several large cities, 80.5% reported making some behavior changes in response to the AIDS crisis. Slightly over 76% reduced the number of different sexual partners and 20.2% of those who continued to engage in receptive anal intercourse had modified their behavior by asking partners either to use a condom or to withdraw prior to ejaculation (Emmons et al., 1986). When the same cohort was reevaluated six months later, 51.4% were no longer engaging in receptive anal intercourse and among those who continued to do so, 61.8% were using condoms or withdrawal to prevent semen exchange.

A cohort of 488 homosexual men seen at a clinic for treatment of sexually transmitted diseases and screened for STDs in gay bars was surveyed in Wisconsin, an area less heavily affected by HIV infection and AIDS (Golubjatnikov et al., 1983). Reports of sexual activity for two 6-month intervals separated by one year reflected sharp declines in the number of men reporting ten or more different partners, twice as many men reporting one sexual partner, and an increase in the number of participants who chose celibacy.

It is important to note that each of these large-scale surveys reports risk reductions that are relative rather than absolute. In geographic areas where HIV infection is prevalent, even infrequent high-risk behavior carries substantial risk for HIV transmission. Safety is contingent on consistently adapting safer sex alternatives with *all* partners. Studies of recidivism following initial risk-reduction behavior changes offer ample evidence of inconsistency in maintaining behavioral risk reduction (Becker & Joseph, 1988). When retrospective analyses of one of the San Francisco samples compared participants who were originally at no risk with those originally at high risk one year later, 54% of those originally at no risk had engaged in behavior that placed them at greater risk, while 45% of those originally at high risk were engaging in safer behavior (Stall, McKusick, Wiley, Coates, & Ostrow, 1986). Although high relapse rates are also frequently reported from health promotion areas, such as cigarette smoking and obesity, in the case of AIDS any relapse is potentially lethal. For maximum effectiveness, community outreach programs will need to reinforce sustained behavior change and develop programs enhancing maintenance as well as initiating lowered-risk behavior.

Few studies have evaluated behavior change outside the urban setting where AIDS prevention services are most plentiful. This makes it difficult to determine whether the risk reductions of gay men in these urban areas result from the intensive educational programs, reactive effects of participating in a longitudinal study, higher levels of fear when so many participants personally have friends with AIDS, or a combination of these and other factors. When AIDS risk knowledge and sexual practices of gay men in an urban AIDS epicenter were compared with men in moderate-size cities that had lower AIDS prevalence rates, significant differences were found (St. Lawrence, Hood, Brasfield, & Kelly, 1988). Gay men in the epicenter city obtained significantly higher AIDS risk knowledge scores and most frequently engaged in sexual activities characterized by low-risk practices, such as mutual masturbation and frottage. In the low AIDS-prevalence areas, unprotected oral and anal intercourse were the most common sexual activities and overall knowledge levels were lower. It is not clear whether the higher frequency of risk behavior among gay men outside the AIDS epicenter was due to less accurate AIDS knowledge, to having fewer educational resources, to the lower prevalence of AIDS cases, to lower levels of perceived personal vulnerability, or to other factors, but several recent studies confirm that gay men in low-incidence areas remain at significantly higher risk than counterparts who live in the urban areas hardest hit by AIDS (Becker, Howe, & Zielinski, 1988; Messiah, Pollack, LaPorte, & Brunet, 1988). Taken together, these results attest to the urgent

need for broader, well-organized community intervention outside AIDS
epicenters as a primary prevention priority.

2. FOCUSED GROUP BEHAVIOR CHANGE INTERVENTIONS

Most behavioral studies to date have concentrated on determining predictors of HIV seroconversion and behavioral consequences following antibody testing. Relatively few controlled outcome studies have evaluated
psychological interventions to reduce AIDS risk. However, those that have
been reported suggest that focused psychological interventions are effective in assisting at-risk individuals to lower their risk for AIDS.

Kelly, St. Lawrence, Hood, and Brasfield (1989) recruited 104 healthy
gay men who engaged in high-risk sexual activities with multiple partners to
participate in a behavioral prevention program. Participants were individually assessed using biweekly self-monitoring of sexual behavior, self-
reported sexual behavior over four-month periods, role plays of assertion
when verbally coerced to engage in high-risk activities, and a test of practical AIDS risk knowledge. The sample was then randomly divided into an
intervention group and a delayed-treatment control group.

The intervention group received a series of 12 weekly small group sessions concerning AIDS risk behavior, risk-reduction methods, self-
management training, sexual assertion, and skills for developing steady
relationships characterized by low-risk practices. The first three sessions
focused on education and reviewed basic medical and virological characteristics of HIV, its transmission, and the specific sexual practices high, moderate, and low in risk. Misconceptions about AIDS, HIV infection, and risk
practices were also identified and corrected. Three group sessions then
taught participants to identify and alter functional antecedents to personal
high-risk behavior patterns. Participants identified past high-risk situations
and patterns, such as setting, intoxicant use, mood, cognitive intentions,
and self-talk that contributed to high-risk behavior. Participants and group
leaders together developed self-management strategies to alter the identified risk antecedents. Some self-management strategies used practical environmental rearrangement, such as keeping condoms readily available
where sexual activity might occur or avoiding settings associated with casual sex in the past. Others emphasized cognitive modification strategies,
such as self-reinforcement for lower-risk activity or generating AIDS-
related visual images when particularly vulnerable to coercion. Three additional group sessions focused on sexual assertion training using standard
assertion training paradigms. Participants learned and rehearsed ways to
initiate discussions regarding the need for safety and practiced refusing
unsafe coercions from a sexual partner. Finally, the last three sessions
addressed life-style goals, developing affirmative and health-conscious personal relationships and social supports, self-pride, and self-efficacy that
needed changes could be made. Problem-solving training, communication

skills, conflict resolution skills, and relationship skills were incorporated into these final sessions. In the final session, each participant identified the specific steps he had taken to reduce risk and how this had been accomplished. This provided multiple coping models from within the group and social support from the other group members affirming the risk-reduction efforts.

After the intervention and again at an eight-month follow-up, experimental participants had reduced the frequency of unprotected anal intercourse, were more effective in refusing pressures to engage in risk activities during role-play simulations, increased the adoption of safer sexual activities, and had higher scores on the measure of AIDS risk knowledge than control subjects. Roffman, Gilchrist, Stephens, and Kirkham (1988) evaluated a similar broad-spectrum intervention that included risk education, safer sex guidance, self-management training, and assertion training for persons who had difficulty changing aspects of their sexual behavior that were creating continued AIDS risk. They found that the intervention was highly effective in assisting subjects who had been unsuccessful in modifying risk behavior before the intervention.

Valdiserri and his colleagues (1988b) compared two risk-reduction interventions provided to 588 gay and bisexual men who were randomly assigned to the interventions. One group attended a peer-led small group lecture on HIV infection and risk reduction. A second group received the same lectures plus skills training promoting "safer sex." Self-reports of sexual behavior were collected before and after the intervention and at 6- and 12-month follow-up assessments. The results indicated that subjects in both conditions lowered risk behavior, but the men who received skills training showed greater changes than those who received lecture information alone.

Another project evaluated the comparative effectiveness of four interventions in changing the sexual risk behavior of gay and bisexual men (D'Eramo, Quadland, Shattls, Shumann, & Jacobs, 1988). The four experimental conditions included (1) standard printed materials describing safer sex guidelines, (2) printed materials plus lectures on HIV transmission and safer sex guidelines, (3) lecture plus erotic verbal and printed safer sex information, and (4) lecture plus explicit safer sex videos. Participants (N = 619) met for four weekly sessions and completed an extensive assessment battery preintervention and two months following the program. The results showed that the second condition was effective in motivating participants to reduce risk behavior, but did not motivate them to have safer sex when sexual activity did occur. The fourth condition (lecture information plus explicit safer sex videos) was most effective in promoting both lowered risk behavior and safer practices when sexual activity did occur.

Coates and McKusick (1987) provided stress management training to a sample of HIV antibody positive men and evaluated the effects of the intervention on behavior and immune system functioning. The eight-week intervention emphasized meditation, relaxation, positive health habits, and stress coping strategies. A total of 64 subjects were initially assessed and then divided into an experimental group and a waiting-list control group. After intervention, experimental subjects were significantly lower in risk behavior than at preintervention, while control subjects remained unchanged. The outcome data further suggested beneficial effects on immune system functioning for those who participated in stress management training.

Taken together, these studies indicate that if sufficient intervention assistance is made available, and the intervention is based on sound psychological principles, even persons at extremely high risk can make behavior changes that lower their risk for HIV infection. In order for such programs to be most effective, it is essential that therapists who provide them are knowledgeable about AIDS risk behavior, sensitive to life-style issues, and, as with all effective therapies, understanding and affirmative toward the person being counseled (Kelly & St. Lawrence, 1988a).

B. Prevention Research with Intravenous Drug Users

Several studies of AIDS knowledge in subpopulations of drug users suggest the need for educational and outreach programs. Williams (1986) surveyed participants in a Detroit methadone maintenance program and found that only 62% were even aware that intravenous drug users are at risk for contracting AIDS, 57% were unconcerned about becoming exposed to AIDS, and only 11.2% were "very worried" that they might develop AIDS. When New Jersey addicts entering drug treatment centers were surveyed, almost 87% knew the virus was spread through needle sharing and 81% were aware that never sharing needles would reduce AIDS risk, but fewer than 30% could correctly identify needle disinfection strategies (Ginzburg et al., 1986). Within the same group, one-third of the participants were unaware that an HIV-infected drug user could transmit the virus to a heterosexual partner and 43% were unaware that infants born to intravenous drug users and their partners were at increased risk for AIDS. There was also considerable misinformation among the sample: More than 16% believed that AIDS could be transmitted by sharing a home or work site with an AIDS patient and 15% believed that simply wiping off a needle was sufficient to prevent HIV transmission. Friedman, Des Jarlais, and Southern (1986) found that although New York City addicts in methadone maintenance programs were highly knowledgeable about the risk of sharing needles, inaccurate information was also widespread. For example, a majority of their sample believed that AIDS could be transmitted by sharing a drinking cup.

Reaching IV drug users with information about AIDS risk is a challenge. Unlike the gay community, which is relatively well organized and characterized by educational and socioeconomic advantage, intravenous drug users are more often minority group members, and their average educational levels are lower. Communication within the drug subculture is more often oral than written, largely because of literacy problems (Becker & Joseph, 1988). In addition, the majority culture and the drug subculture tend to be distrustful of each other. There is a general impression that drug users are disinterested in health or behavior change, while drug users often view public health authorities with suspicion.

Whether prevention of HIV infection is even possible with currently addicted intravenous drug users has been the subject of controversy (Des Jarlais, Friedman, & Stoneburner, 1988). The belief that drug use is self-destructive behavior, as well as past difficulties enlisting drug users in treatment programs, leads some to suggest that successful prevention is not a realistic goal. However, substantial changes in knowledge and behavior began to take place among drug users even before any AIDS prevention programs were developed. As early as the fall of 1983, many intravenous drug users in New York City who were not in treatment programs were aware that IV drug use was associated with higher AIDS risk (Des Jarlais, 1988a). By 1984, more than half of the patients in New York City methadone maintenance programs had made changes in their injecting behavior, usually by increasing their use of sterile needles, cleaning needles more frequently between uses, and reducing the number of persons with whom they would share equipment, although only 14% reported changing their sexual behavior (Friedman et al., 1987). A survey of intravenous drug users who were not involved in treatment programs found that 41% reported making changes in their needle use patterns (Kleinman et al., 1987). These risk-reduction efforts were primarily the result of information received through the mass media and through oral communication channels within the drug-use subculture, rather than the result of specific prevention programs. Evidence supporting the validity of these self-reported behavior changes comes from information about the marketing of illicit sterile drug injection equipment. Interviews with intravenous drug users in storefront centers and on the streets indicated a dramatically increased demand for new needles. This was corroborated by street interviews with 22 needle sellers, 18 of whom confirmed an increased demand for sterile needles (Des Jarlais, Friedman, & Hopkins, 1985). Unfortunately, 10 of these sellers also reported that they had fraudulently resold used needles as new, and 7 indicated they had resealed used needles in order to do so.

Educational programs targeting IV drug users tend to be concentrated in drug treatment and methadone maintenance populations, or when drug users come into contact with the criminal justice system. Although entering a treatment program often leads to immediate reductions in IV drug use, single treatment encounters are often insufficient to lead to permanent cessation (Office of Technology Assessment, 1988). An innovative AIDS outreach program in New Jersey effectively increased drug users' access to treatment facilities through a treatment voucher program. More than 80% of the first 1,000 vouchers distributed by AIDS outreach workers were redeemed for free detoxification treatment, and over 25% of those who entered treatment through the voucher program continued into longer-term treatment (Jackson & Rotkiewicz, 1987). Since the length of time a person remains in treatment is associated with greater reductions in intravenous drug use, the voucher program may well have had a significant effect on long-term drug use in that area (Office of Technology Assessment, 1988).

However, not all drug users seek treatment, the number of existing drug treatment facilities is inadequate to serve all who seek treatment, and treatment is not equally effective for everyone who is admitted (Des Jarlais, 1988b). Therefore, AIDS education efforts for intravenous drug users have incorporated strategies for safer drug injection through street outreach programs, teaching addicts the necessary social skills to refuse sharing equipment, providing information on needle sterilization techniques, providing bleach or alcohol to decontaminate used equipment, or providing sterile needle exchange programs.

In an attempt to reach drug users who were not in drug treatment programs, one New York City program employed former addicts to provide street outreach in drug "shooting galleries," providing on-the-spot information and instruction regarding AIDS risk and needle disinfection methods (Buning, 1987; Wodak et al., 1987). Street outreach workers in San Francisco distributed more than 15,000 vials of bleach to addicts along with instructions on how to use it to clean drug paraphernalia. Posters and billboards were also used to promote the use of bleach. While the proportion of addicts enrolling in treatment programs remained stable, the number of persons who reported usually or always cleaning needles with bleach increased from 6% in 1985 to 47% by 1987 (Chaisson, Moss, Onishi, Osmond, & Carolson, 1987). During this same period, the proportion who reported never using bleach fell from 76% to 36%.

When street outreach programs are provided by persons who are sensitive to the life-style issues of the population targeted for counseling, and who are tolerant, nonjudgmental, and credible, they offer several advantages. Information can be specifically tailored to the at-risk population, understanding and misconceptions can be clarified and corrected on the spot, and the information has immediacy since it is being disseminated in the settings where change will need to be implemented. Another advantage of using street educators is that the same persons who provide the outreach services become visible prompts for reduced risk conduct, serve as peer models for implementing safer behavior changes, provide visible evidence that change can be successful, and become a social support system for maintaining lower risk conduct.

Since needle sharing, rather than drug use per se, is the practice that transmits HIV, proposals have been advanced in this country and implemented abroad to make sterile needles available to drug users through needle exchange programs. Needle exchange has been politically controversial in this country, since it is often perceived as promoting drug use. However, such programs in other countries have proven beneficial, and no adverse outcomes have resulted from their use (Des Jarlais, 1988a). Before the AIDS crisis, Amsterdam had already established a needle exchange program to reduce the spread of hepatitis B. Concern about contracting AIDS led to an increased demand for sterile needles and the program was expanded. The proportion of IV drug users participating in the exchange system increased from less than 10% to more than 50%, and the program did not produce any overall increase in the number of people who injected drugs (Van den Hoek, Coutinho, Van Zadelhoff, Van hass Trecht, & Goudsmit, 1987). In fact, drug users decreased their injection frequency after becoming involved in the needle exchange program; the proportion of drug users who injected more than once a day dropped from 90% of drug users to less than 50% (Van den Hoek et al., 1987). Needle exchange programs in this country have been delayed as the result of public controversy (D. C. Des Jarlais, personal communication, August 12, 1988).

While these programs indicate that risk-reduction changes do occur among intravenous drug users, several problems remain. The amount of risk-reduction achieved has not been sufficient to stop the spread of HIV infection among intravenous drug users (Des Jarlais, Friedman, & Stoneburner, 1988). Existing drug treatment programs are inadequate to meet the increased demand for their services and, in the New York City area, nearly 90% of persons seeking to enter drug treatment facilities cannot be accommodated by existing resources (Des Jarlais, 1988a). Clearly, reductions in the reuse of contaminated needles have followed community outreach programs (Buning, 1987; Wodak et al., 1987) and increased demands for new, sterile needles signal heightened AIDS awareness (Des Jarlais et al., 1985). Yet it is difficult to produce substantial, consistent reductions in needle sharing between addicts, and reuse is higher when a sterile needle supply is unavailable.

Even when changes can be effected in needle sharing, few intravenous drug users implement reduced-risk sexual practices (Des Jarlais, Tross, Abdul-Quader, & Friedman, 1988). Virtually every study examining both drug use and sexual behavior among IV drug users has shown that sexual behavior is not changing as much as needle use patterns. Studies evaluating behavior change among intravenous drug users find that 55% to 85% report changing their needle use, while only 15% to 30% report changes in sexual behavior (Des Jarlais, 1988b). While figures vary somewhat from study to study, it is clear that few drug users are taking steps to preclude sexual HIV exposure and transmission. Typically, only 10% to 15% of intravenous drug users report they have started or increased condom use during sexual activities (Battjes & Pickens, 1988; Flynn et al., 1988). Among heterosexual intravenous drug users, 65% of the males and 71% of the females continue to engage in unprotected vaginal intercourse (Des Jarlais, 1988b).

C. Prevention Research with Heterosexual Adults and Adolescents

Few studies have formally evaluated interventions with a general population of heterosexuals or with high-risk subpopulations, such as hemophiliacs and their partners, heterosexuals treated for other sexually transmitted diseases, and persons employed in the sex industry. The few that have been completed suggest educational interventions can improve knowledge and attitudes toward behavior change, but it is less clear whether actual behavior change has occurred.

1. INTERVENTIONS WITH HETEROSEXUAL ADULTS

The sexual transmission of HIV from infected hemophiliacs to their sexual partners is well documented (Centers for Disease Control, 1987b), and the National Hemophilia Foundation provides information on behavioral risk reduction to hemophiliacs and their spouses (Becker & Joseph, 1988). However, the limited research in this area emphasizes the psychological consequences of being in a high-risk subgroup rather than empirical evaluation of programs to change behavior. A survey of 116 hemophiliacs from several treatment centers revealed an increased reluctance to receive blood clotting factor agents and decreased sexual frequency between hemophiliacs and their wives because of their concerns about AIDS (Agle, Cluck, & Pierce, 1987).

Recognizing that women of childbearing age can be reached through family planning clinics, Title X funds are available to support AIDS education activities in federally funded clinics (Office of Technology Assessment, 1988). A needs assessment survey conducted in a San Francisco clinic revealed that nearly 90% of the women who were being served had some risk history factor and 55% reported that their sexual partners never used condoms (Olivia & DiClemente, as cited in Office of Technology Assessment, 1988). To date, evaluation research has not yet accumulated from interventions within family planning clinics.

Women employed in the sex industry are at high AIDS risk. A creative community outreach program in San Francisco used mobile outreach vans and former prostitutes to provide AIDS education to prostitutes (Cohen et al., 1988). Educational sessions were provided in the community through medical, women's, and drug treatment clinics, and in motel rooms near areas where prostitution was centered. In this way, the program staff were able to reach 90% of non-street-solicitation prostitutes and 44% of the street prostitutes in San Francisco. In other countries, government-sponsored programs have enlisted and trained prostitutes to become peer educators with considerable success (Lacking, 1988). Such community-based educational programs are an effective way to reach persons employed in the sex industry and who are at high risk for incurring and transmitting the virus. Some survey research indicates that in the absence of such focused educational programs, condom use by prostitutes is uncommon (Darrow et al., 1988), while other research has produced different findings. Des Jarlais et al. (1987) surveyed 67 incarcerated street prostitutes, and 92% reported they "usually" required clients to use condoms. However, this behavior was adopted in the early 1970s in response to concerns about sexually transmitted diseases in general, rather than as a consequence of the AIDS health crisis. Even when education produces safer on-the-job sexual practices, prostitutes are less likely to use condoms in steady relationships with boyfriends and husbands than with paying clients (Darrow et al., 1988).

Research addressing heterosexual behavior change generally reveals increased awareness of AIDS risk, but little reduction in risk behavior. Condom use remains rare between heterosexuals, even among heterosexual males and females who have multiple partners (Klonoff, Cargill, & Gayle, 1988; Leishman, 1987). A San Francisco survey found that 59% of heterosexuals who engaged in unprotected intercourse and had two or more sexual partners in the preceding year were no more likely to use condoms now than in the past and that 22% actually had decreased their condom use (Research and Decisions Corporation, 1986). Thus, although heterosexuals are aware of AIDS and even knowledgeable about risk reduction, they often have not personalized their risk sufficiently to embark on behavioral changes.

2. INTERVENTIONS WITH CHILDREN AND ADOLESCENTS

Risky sexual behavior is widespread among adolescents (Office of Technology Assessment, 1988). Several surveys of adolescent sexual behavior have reported that approximately 60% of adolescents are engaging in risky behavior (D. Rugg, personal communication, August 12, 1988; St. Lawrence, Betts, Hogan, & MacDonald, 1988). As a result, by March 1988 eighteen states had developed and implemented school-based AIDS education and prevention programs for children and adolescents, although the effectiveness of school-based efforts on behavior has not been formally evaluated (Office of Technology Assessment, 1988). Because AIDS education in the schools is quite recent, there is little specific information yet available regarding content, optimal ages for intervention, and effectiveness. When educational counseling is available to children before the onset of sexual activity, the primary prevention goal is to reduce the likelihood that high-risk activities will take place when the child becomes sexually active. School-based education offers a uniform setting in which to reach youth who are already sexually active before high-risk practices become established.

In several states, "train the trainers" programs have been implemented with teachers and with health care professionals to prepare a cadre of AIDS educators—a cost-effective strategy for disseminating information quickly. Such programs are usually organized in a hierarchical fashion. A small cadre of trainers educates a larger group, who then become the trainers for a subsequent group. For example, in California, education was quickly provided to all of the states' teachers in this way. Several "train the trainers" sessions were held across the state. In each area, a representative from each school system was designated to become that school's trainer and attended "train the trainers" sessions. These teachers returned to their individual school systems and provided the same training to all of the teachers and administrators there. The California Nurses Association developed a two-day workshop training nurses to provide AIDS classes in their communities. A total of 1,350 nurses were trained over a two-year period. In turn, they provided classes to more than 33,000 in their communities (Schietzinger, 1988).

A number of studies indicate that adolescents are fairly knowledgeable about AIDS, but that few have initiated behavioral change in response to AIDS (Office of Technology Assessment, 1988; St. Lawrence, Betts, Hogan, & MacDonald, 1988). Some surveys indicate there are important knowledge deficits among teenagers. For example, one San Francisco survey showed that although 92% of the students knew sexual intercourse transmitted AIDS, only 60% were aware that condoms lowered risk (DiClemente, Zorn, & Temoshok, 1986). A similar survey in Connecticut found that only half the students were aware that intravenous drug users were at risk for AIDS (Helgersen et al., 1988). Other studies have shown that even when sexually active adolescents are aware that condom use reduces AIDS risk, the actual use of condoms and the intention to use them in the future are low (Kegeles, Allen, & Irwin, 1988). A random-digit telephone survey of 16- to 19-year-old adolescents (N = 863) found that 70% were sexually active, but that only 15% took any precautions against AIDS and that 80% of the precautions the teenagers described were ineffective in preventing HIV infection (Strunin & Hingson, 1987).

Whether or not educational initiatives will influence adolescents' AIDS risk behaviors is still uncertain, and there is an urgent need to develop and evaluate preventive programs for youth and adolescents. There are a number of reasons informational programs alone may be insufficient with this population, since many factors other than knowledge influence adolescent sexual behavior and contraception use (Office of Technology Assessment, 1988). It would be worthwhile to evaluate whether programs that incorporate sexual assertion skills training and the social skills to initiate conversations about AIDS risk or contraception use would offer an incremental benefit over the effects of education alone. There is some evidence from other health promotion areas, such as cigarette smoking, that when programs are implemented early, they may be more effective than when they are delayed until after the targeted behavior is frequent (Office of Technology Assessment, 1988). Another reason for initiating early educational programs in school-based settings is that nationally about 25% of youth do not remain in school until high school graduation (Office of Technology Assessment, 1988), and these young people will become more difficult to access with preventive information once they have departed from the school setting. However, sex education in the schools is still controversial in many areas of the country and, when a community is reluctant to incorporate sex education into the curriculum, the likelihood of implementing effective AIDS prevention programs from within the school setting is correspondingly reduced.

D.   AIDS Prevention Through HIV Testing Programs

HIV testing programs are a widely advocated prevention strategy. In the following section we will briefly review characteristics of the tests and behavioral outcome effects from HIV testing programs. It would be helpful if there were a single test that definitively showed whether or not the HIV virus was present, but no such test currently exists. However, the immune system produces antibodies to the virus, and it is possible to test for the presence of these antibodies. Usually, blood samples are first screened with the enzyme-linked immunosorbent assay (ELISA) technique. When the ELISA detects no antibodies, the sample is regarded as seronegative (i.e., showing that the person whose blood was tested is not infected with HIV). When the initial ELISA is positive, it is usually repeated. If it then turns out negative, the first test is judged to have been faulty. When ELISA tests are antibody positive several times in succession, the blood is then tested by a second method, known as the Western blot test. Instead of detecting antibodies as the ELISA does, the Western blot detects specific antibodies that the immune system produces in response to each of HIV's main proteins. This means the test is less likely to react to the wrong antibodies and produces fewer "false positive" results than the ELISA. Thus the Western blot test is more accurate than the ELISA. However, the Western blot is more expensive, more time-consuming to conduct, more difficult to perform, and harder to interpret than the ELISA. Moreover, even the results of a Western blot test can be indeterminate for as many as 26% of the samples analyzed (Agius et al., 1988).

As with most clinical laboratory tests, both the ELISA and the Western blot can produce a relatively small number of false positive and false negative results. A false positive incorrectly indicates that uninfected blood is infected. A false negative incorrectly identifies infected blood as HIV free. Most false negatives can be attributed to characteristics of HIV. Months may elapse between the time the virus enters a person's body and when the immune system produces a response that is detectable by the existing tests. Between 5% and 10% of the samples that actually contain HIV receive a false negative result for this reason (Saxinger, Wantzin, & Gallo, 1988). However, the problem of false negatives is relatively small in comparison with the high false positive rate when the ELISA is used alone (Saxinger et al., 1988). ELISAs are particularly likely to give a false positive result for pregnant women, for people who have had several blood transfusions, and following some infections unrelated to AIDS (Myrmel & Haukenes, 1988; Ujhelyi, Bohn, Fust, Meretey, & Hollan, 1988). While HIV tests are sensitive in detecting antibodies for populations at high AIDS risk, such as nonmonogamous gay men or intravenous drug users living in AIDS epicenters, they are less useful for groups that have low infection rates or persons who live in places where AIDS is not yet prevalent (Cook & Sherlock, 1988). Many people in low-prevalence groups who obtain a positive result on the ELISA are actually uninfected. The need to confirm any positive ELISA result makes testing low-risk groups quite costly. It is estimated that wide-scale screening of low-risk populations would cost more than $50,000 for each genuinely positive result obtained ("Testing for AIDS," 1988).

Persons who have engaged in high-risk behavior are often urged to undergo testing so they will know if they are HIV-infected. This recommendation can disguise issues that are less clear-cut than it might seem on the surface. Although HIV antibody testing is helpful and necessary in evaluating patients with symptoms that may be AIDS related, testing healthy individuals is controversial. Advocates of HIV testing claim that such testing motivates reduction in risk behavior, while others emphasize that the risks of discrimination, ostracism, loss of confidentiality and civil rights, and psychological distress must be taken into account. In addition, research shows that individuals high in risk can be motivated to reduce dangerous behavior even without knowing their personal HIV serostatus. An emerging body of research evaluates the behavior outcomes from HIV testing. The results of learning that one is seropositive or seronegative are complex and the outcome effects are not uniformly predictable across individuals. These studies, conducted with gay and bisexual men and with intravenous drug users, will be reviewed in the following sections.

1. BEHAVIORAL EFFECTS FROM HIV ANTIBODY TESTING PROGRAMS WITH
GAY AND BISEXUAL MEN

Investigators have studied changes in the sexual behavior among gay and bisexual men who requested HIV antibody testing and learned that they were either seropositive or seronegative (Coates, Morin, & McKusick, 1987; Doll et al., 1988; Fife et al., 1988; Hoff et al., 1988; Joseph, Montgomery, Emmons, et al., 1987; Morlett, Gold, Guinan, & Cooper, 1988; Tindall & Cooper, 1988; Willoughby et al., 1987). Several of these studies have shown that gay men who know they are HIV-infected display greater reductions in high-risk behavior than gay men who learn they are seronegative (Coates et al., 1988; Tindall & Cooper, 1988). McCusker et al. (1988) studied the effects of HIV antibody testing in a sample of 270 homosexual men in Boston. They found that levels of all risk activities declined, whether or not the men knew of their antibody status. Seropositive men who learned of their test results more often discontinued unprotected insertive anal intercourse, while seronegative men more often reported decreased frequencies of unprotected receptive anal intercourse. These findings attest to the fact that most gay men who seek testing and learn they are HIV-infected react responsibly so as not to transmit infection to others.

Other research conducted in the same geographic areas found that significant reductions in risk behavior by gay men were not related to knowledge of HIV status, but were taking place regardless of whether or not persons knew their antibody status (Doll et al., 1988; Ostrow et al., 1988). Gay men who knew their HIV status and those who did not were both lowering AIDS risk behavior at comparable rates. Several studies also found that risk behavior change precedes, rather than follows, the decision to obtain HIV testing (Farthing, Jesson, Taylor, Lawrence, & Gazzard, 1987; Pollack & Schiltz, 1988), suggesting the decision to undergo an HIV test often is made *after* an individual has already taken steps to reduce risk, rather than serving as a stimulus for change. Thus the decision to seek testing and to engage in safer sex may be initiated by the same factors. Much of the research evaluating risk behavior following HIV testing has been generated from intensively studied longitudinal cohorts of gay men. These cohorts may be atypical, in that they have been much studied, undergo medical evaluation and laboratory testing at regular intervals, benefit from extensive counseling, and are located in geographic areas where AIDS is most prevalent. This makes it difficult to know whether behavioral shifts are due to testing or to other factors.

Not all studies document a desirable outcome effect following HIV antibody testing. While many persons who are seropositive take steps to prevent transmitting the virus, this is not uniformly true. Some persons who learn they are seropositive continue to engage in risk behavior with the same frequency after receiving their test results (Coates et al., 1988; Miller, Goldberg, Wright, & Ogg, 1988; Pollack & Schiltz, 1988; Witkor, Biggar, Melbye, Ebbesen, & Goedert, 1988). One study of 74 homosexual men in Chicago found that men who were seropositive and learned their test results increased their frequency of receptive anal intercourse more than men who were seropositive and chose not to learn their HIV status (Office of Technology Assessment, 1988). A finding of considerable concern is that persons who learn that they are seronegative often fail to reduce their frequencies of engaging in risky practices that, if continued, may result in HIV exposure (Fife et al., 1988; Morlett et al., 1988). An individual who engages in high-risk behavior and learns that he or she is seronegative may be more likely to conclude, incorrectly, that he or she is somehow protected from HIV infection and may misinterpret the negative result as a license to continue past behavior.

Persons who learn they are seropositive, but who are healthy and symptomless, frequently experience severe emotional distress (Ostrow et al., 1988). This is understandable since the HIV-infected individual must cope with literally years of uncertainty about future health, has few definitive answers available to the many questions that arise, and may become preoccupied by future uncertainties so that present adjustment is negatively affected. Reactive adjustment disorders have been reported in 75% of the persons who learn they are seropositive (Tross, Hirsch, Rabkin, Berry, & Holland, 1987). On standard psychological distress inventories, HIV positive individuals who are in good clinical health score two to three standard deviations above the norm for the general population (Jacobsen, Perry, Scavuzzo, & Roberts, 1987). More than 50% of those who test positive for HIV antibodies experience significant anxiety, depression, insomnia, and memory problems after they learn their test results.

2. BEHAVIORAL EFFECTS FROM HIV ANTIBODY TESTING PROGRAMS WITH INTRAVENOUS DRUG USERS

The behavioral impact of HIV antibody status on the actions of intravenous drug users is unclear. Some studies have shown that drug users who learn they are seropositive display greater risk reduction than those who are seronegative (Des Jarlais, 1988b). The risk-reduction steps undertaken included reducing or eliminating drug use and needle sharing, as well as increasing adherence to safer sexual practices. However, participants' attempts to change sexual practices within long-term relationships often precipitate dissolution of the relationships, and negative emotional consequences of seropositivity were also documented in this population. It is unclear whether antibody testing was responsible for the behavioral changes that took place in this sample. When comparison groups of tested and untested intravenous drug users were compared, both groups showed comparable risk reduction (Des Jarlais, 1988b). Thus the observed reductions may have resulted from general AIDS awareness and educational campaigns, rather than reflecting a specific outcome effect from antibody testing. Some preliminary evidence suggests that this may be the case. When risk behavior of drug users in treatment who received AIDS education was compared with a group that was tested and learned they were seropositive and a group that was tested and learned they were seronegative, one year later all three groups exhibited comparable and positive changes in risk behavior (Black, Dolan, & DeFord, 1986).

The availability of voluntary HIV testing under anonymous conditions and when accompanied by substantial pretest, posttest, and follow-up counseling is almost universally recommended. However, the findings of research on the behavioral effects of test result feedback are not clear-cut, in part because intensive education and prevention campaigns also produce substantial, and often comparable, reductions in high-risk sexual behavior in populations such as gay men. While access to voluntary HIV antibody testing is important, there is no evidence that testing alone constitutes a practical, cost-efficient, and effective approach to community primary prevention of AIDS. The outcome studies reviewed earlier more strongly support the efficacy of aggressive education-prevention programs based on behavioral principles.

E.   Efforts to Mandate AIDS Prevention Through Legislation

Behavioral and epidemiological research have already produced solid data on which to base public health policies. For perhaps the first time in history, basic science has provided policymakers with an opportunity for rational action in response to a crisis. Social scientists can aid policymakers in translating that knowledge into sound policies, rather than precipitating reactions that reflect prejudice or panic. It would be regrettable to invest so much in scientific knowledge and then fail to use that knowledge to develop public health measures based on sound behavioral principles (Osborne, 1988).

Legislation and bills related to AIDS are proliferating in this country. In 1986, 51 AIDS-related bills were introduced and passed by state legislatures. Within just the first eight months of 1987, 550 such bills were introduced (Dickens, 1988). Many of the bills reflect little understanding of behavior change principles and are largely irrelevant to any practical management of the health crisis (Dickens, 1988). Legislative mandates that are not well grounded in practical behavioral principles or cost-effective program evaluation, or that are not sensitive to ethical and civil rights issues, may have consequences diametrically opposed to what the legislation was intended to accomplish.

A number of bills have proposed mass testing programs for a variety of populations. For example, marriage license applicants in several states must undergo an HIV antibody test before a marriage license will be issued. The intent is to protect infants from being born with HIV infection, *but most infected babies are born to unwed mothers* (Cleary et al., 1987). The cost of such mass screening among low-risk populations is also prohibitively high. If universal premarital screening were required of all marriage license applicants for one year, screening would detect less than one-tenth of 1% of all HIV-infected individuals at a cost of more than $100 million, more than 100 individuals erroneously would be told they were not infected, and hundreds of persons would be told incorrectly that they were infected (Cleary et al., 1987). While discretionary voluntary testing can be a tool for reducing the spread of HIV infection, mandatory screening programs in populations with very low HIV prevalence are a relatively ineffective and inefficient use of limited resources.

Other proposals require reporting the identity of persons who receive positive HIV antibody test results to public health authorities, tracing their past sexual partners, and sometimes releasing the results of the tests of all HIV seropositive individuals to police, courts, health care providers, and others. Proponents of this approach justify mandatory identity reporting as a "time-proven" method for controlling sexually transmitted diseases, but there is considerable evidence to suggest it is a method that has never worked well (Osborne, 1988). While syphilis and some strains of gonorrhea have been curtailed, it is probably due to the discovery of penicillin rather than to partner tracing or identity reporting. Presumably this is due to fears of discrimination, confidentiality abridgements, or even eventual quarantine. The ineffectiveness of partner tracing is also suggested by the steadily increasing rates of penicillin-resistant gonorrhea and other difficult-to-treat STDs (Holmes, 1988).

When the identity of persons who obtain positive HIV test results is reportable and recorded, persons who are at highest risk tend to avoid testing (Dickens, 1988; Fehrsi et al., 1988; Gostin & Curran, 1987; Gostin, Curran, & Clark, 1987; Johnson, Su, & Jackson, 1988; Meachem & Milliken, 1988; Ohi et al., 1988; Wood, Leonard, & Krueger, 1988). Most studies have found a marked decrease in requests for HIV testing when public health policy changes made anonymous testing unavailable. Thus mandatory identity-reporting laws drive underground the persons who are most likely to be HIV-infected and produce the paradoxical effect of distancing from public health authorities the persons they most wish to reach.

In addition, and in contrast to sexually transmitted diseases that produce symptoms quickly and are treatable, the long latency of asymptomatic infection means that seropositive individuals would need to be able (and willing) to identify all sexual partners over a period of many years for contact tracing to be useful. This is unlikely to prove feasible and is expensive. One San Francisco study found that contact tracing cost $2,203 for each seropositive person identified (Woo et al., 1988). Given that millions of Americans are already HIV positive and given the deterrent effect of identity reporting and contact tracing on requests for voluntary testing, attempts to curtail AIDS through such methods seem both wasteful and ineffective as a primary prevention approach.

V.   OBSTACLES TO AIDS EDUCATION AND PREVENTION

A number of barriers impede education and prevention efforts in this country: outdated knowledge and research about sexuality, negative attitudinal biases, fragmentary knowledge about cofactors that influence HIV susceptibility or disease progression, incomplete understanding of how persons perceive and then personalize their health risk, and personal characteristics that inhibit risk behavior change. Each of these obstacles will be examined with particular attention to psychology's potential role in resolving these issues.

A.   Knowledge and Attitudes Regarding Sexuality

Although we know a great deal about the molecular structure of HIV, scientific knowledge of human sexual behavior is less complete (Gagnon, 1988). The basic references for sexual behavior, still cited in articles about the AIDS epidemic, are the Kinsey studies completed more than 40 years ago. Much more research is needed on human sexual behavior, attitudes concerning sexuality, factors that influence sexual compulsivity, the adoption of contraception use, and decision making concerning sexual activity.

B.   Incomplete Understanding of Personalization of Health Risk

Current evidence indicates that many individuals who are at high risk for HIV infection significantly underestimate their personal vulnerability (Bauman & Siegel, 1988; Coates et al., 1987; Joseph, Montgomery, Kessler, et al., 1987; Olin, Giesecke, Hallqvist, Lagergren, & Lidman, 1988). Differing subsets within risk populations also do not respond uniformly to prevention interventions. There is an urgent need to identify the cultural, social, and psychological factors that influence whether or not a person at risk accurately estimates his or her health risk. The primary prevention literature attests to the necessity of recognizing personal susceptibility as a prerequisite of effective preventive action, yet we have little grasp of how to facilitate that recognition.

Other factors relevant to risk reduction also need to be better understood. One is the tendency to underestimate personal threat so as to avoid the anxiety that would follow a realistic appraisal of one's vulnerability. In some cases, the manner in which health authorities communicate about a health threat can be misleading (Siegel & Gibson, 1988). The emphasis on anal intercourse, an extremely dangerous practice, may inadvertently contribute to the incorrect conclusion that sexually active heterosexuals or homosexuals who refrain from this practice are not at risk. Similarly, emphasizing large numbers of sexual partners may lead persons who have fewer partners to minimize their personal concern, even though the possibility of HIV transmission exists with any infected partner during unprotected sexual activity. Emphasizing homosexuals and IV drug users may mislead people who do not identify with one of these groups to believe they are not at risk, even when their actual behavior indicates otherwise (Glaser, Strange, & Rosati, 1988). In these ways, some messages may inadvertently contribute to misappraisals of personal risk (Siegel & Gibson, 1988).

C. Inadequate Knowledge Regarding Cofactors Governing Illness Development

Cofactors affecting the variable health course of persons with HIV infection have been inadequately studied. Some persons quickly develop AIDS and die, others remain asymptomatic and in good clinical health for years, and still others develop symptoms of immune system compromise that do not immediately proceed to AIDS. Even persons with AIDS show variations in health course. Many quickly worsen and die, others alternate between periods of remission and illness, and there are reports of long-term survivors. If research can identify cofactors that influence these differential outcomes, such knowledge could have inestimable value and might preserve the health of literally millions of people while basic biomedical research continues. It is possible, for example, that behavioral triggers may activate dormant HIV infection (Bentwich, Burstein, Berner, & Handzel, 1988). It is already well known that stress and some chemical substances produce immunosuppression and reduce the absolute numbers of T-4 lymphocytes (Dax, Adler, Nagel, Lange, & Jaffe, 1988; Kemeny et al., 1988). It would be helpful to investigate whether there are similar behavioral factors that compromise immune functioning or precipitate illness in persons who are HIV-infected.

D. Predictors of Risk Behavior Change and Failure to Change

Several longitudinal studies have attempted to identify factors that distinguish those who implement risk behavior change from those who fail to change. A number of common factors recur from studies conducted with gay men in different areas of the country. Continued alcohol and drug use in association with sex is associated with higher levels of risk behavior (Stall et al., 1986), possibly because the behavioral disinhibition associated with these substances undermines safe intentions. Persons who successfully lower risk tend to be older and report being able to visualize the physical deterioration that accompanies AIDS (McKusick, Wiley, et al., 1985). Numerous studies have noted that youth are less likely to change. Analysis of the data from the MACS cohort found that knowledge about AIDS, perceived risk of AIDS, the perceived value of risk-reduction behavior change, and supportive peer norms were all related to successful risk reduction (Emmons et al., 1986). The same study found that reliance on medical technology to develop a cure for AIDS and sexual impulsivity predicted failure to change. When the same cohort was later restudied, the availability of social support was the single strongest predictor for initial risk behavior change and maintenance, while knowledge no longer showed a significant relationship to risk behavior reduction. This latter finding may have been a function of relatively high knowledge levels within the sample, though it is consistent with other research that has found little relationship between cognitive risk knowledge and actual risk behavior (Kelly, St. Lawrence, Brasfield, & Hood, 1987). After surveying the literature regarding HIV infection risk, Coates (1988) identified several variables that predict continued risk: geographic location, poverty, lower educational levels, youth, racial minority status, continued use of drugs and/or alcohol, cigarette smoking, not engaging in other health-promoting regimens such as taking vitamins, lower risk knowledge levels, denial of the threat of AIDS, low self-efficacy expectations, and not knowing one's serostatus (Coates, 1988).

E. Attitudinal Barriers Affecting Prevention Efforts

From the very beginning of the health crisis, attitudinal biases have confounded AIDS prevention efforts. Responses to HIV infection and AIDS are inextricably interwoven with preexisting attitudes toward sexuality, toward sexually transmitted diseases, and toward gay men, intravenous drug users, and others at greatest risk for the disease. We will consider several aspects of these issues as they affect prevention efforts.

1. ATTITUDES TOWARD CONDOMS

High-quality latex condoms, in combination with a spermicide containing nonoxynol-9, are 90% effective in impeding HIV transmission during sexual intercourse (Fineberg, 1988; Kaplan, 1988), and condom use is one of the few defenses for preventing HIV transmission during intercourse (Feldblum & Fortney, 1988; Francis & Chin, 1987; Voeller & Potts, 1985). However, despite condoms' efficacy and minimal cost, resistance to condom use is considerable. Even among populations at high risk for sexually transmitted diseases, condom use remains uncommon. Only 8% to 20% of patients treated in an STD clinic were found to use condoms, and it is estimated that fewer than 25% of adult males use condoms during sexual activity (Siegel & Gibson, 1988). Attitudinal barriers to condom use include belief that condoms lower sensitivity during intercourse; belief that condom use is unnatural; belief that condoms are only for birth control; failure to anticipate that sexual activity might occur; concern that a sexual partner would be offended; hope that effective AIDS treatment will become available soon and render condom protection unnecessary; overuse of behavioral disinhibitors such as alcohol or drugs, leading to unplanned sexual activity; improper usage; beliefs that condoms are used only by persons who are promiscuous, by prostitutes, or by those who engage in extramarital sex; belief that condoms are ineffective or unreliable; embarrassment about purchasing condoms; and the belief that condoms compromise spontaneity and make sex seem artificial or premeditated (Martin, Dean, Garcia, & Hall, 1988; Siegel & Gibson, 1988). Availability of condoms also influences their use. When condoms were freely distributed to inner-city adolescent males at risk for STDs, one study found that usage increased from 19% to 68%, and use in the most recent sexual encounter increased from 20% to 91% (Arnold, 1972; Arnold & Cogswell, 1971). Because women purchase 40% of condoms that are sold (Siegel & Gibson, 1988), AIDS prevention efforts directed toward women may be especially important.

2. ATTITUDES TOWARD AIDS

Sexually transmitted diseases have always been stigmatized in our society, and AIDS is no exception. In large part because of its association with homosexuality and intravenous drug use, AIDS elicits harsh stigmatizing attitudes. Public opinion polls confirm that negative attitudes concerning persons with AIDS are common ("AIDS," 1985; Fisher, 1986; Siegel, 1986), and since the beginning of the AIDS health crisis, violence against persons suspected of being gay has doubled and tripled in some large cities (National Gay and Lesbian Task Force, 1987). This suggests that at least a part of the stigma associated with AIDS is based on disdain and prejudice toward the life-styles of persons so afflicted. AIDS is an emotional and political disease that is not viewed impartially by most people (Kelly & St. Lawrence, 1988b).

A number of empirical investigations have established the presence of harsh prejudicial attitudes toward patients with AIDS and persons at risk for the syndrome among college students, physicians, medical students, and nurses (Kelly, St. Lawrence, Hood, Smith, & Cook, 1987a, 1987b, 1988; St. Lawrence, Husfeldt, Kelly, Hood, & Smith, in press). It appears that the origins of stigma, prejudice, and avoidance concerning AIDS are due to a combination of fear of the disease, especially unfounded but persistent fears of casual transmission, preexisting negative biases toward people at risk, especially homosexual males, and perhaps lack of experience in areas related to AIDS. This latter point remains problematic even given the increasing scope of AIDS. A recent survey of graduate and internship programs in clinical psychology found that more than 75% of programs do not offer any training in AIDS, and most still do not train students in behavioral topics related to AIDS prevention (Campos, Brasfield, & Kelly, 1988).

Attitudes about AIDS carry a number of public health, research, and intervention ramifications that affect AIDS prevention. It has proven difficult to establish political, community, and public health policy consensus concerning fundamental aspects of AIDS prevention. Disagreements exist regarding the explicitness of content in AIDS prevention materials, advocacy of condom use by the sexually active, needle distribution or exchange programs for drug addicts, the most effective strategies to limit the spread of HIV infection, and steps needed to protect persons from unwarranted civil rights abridgements (see Shilts, 1987). Although these are social and political issues, they also bear on the implementation of AIDS prevention programs and on behavioral research related to prevention.

VI.   SUMMARY AND DIRECTIONS FOR FUTURE RESEARCH

Although prevention through behavior change is widely acknowledged as the only available means to curtail the AIDS epidemic, there is still a paucity of experimental outcome research on behavioral prevention programs. At the Fourth International Conference on AIDS, more than 3,600 research papers were presented by scientists from throughout the world. Less than 4% of the papers addressed education or prevention, and fewer still, less than 1%, reported empirical data on prevention interventions. Budgetary allocations for AIDS research to date reflect a similar pattern, with a relatively small proportion of total monies directed to behavioral prevention research. There is no doubt that greatly expanded, vigorous, basic, and ethical biomedical research on HIV infection is urgently needed to develop effective medical treatments for those who currently have HIV illnesses. At the same time, and given the poor outlook for the quick development of a vaccine, increased behavioral research on the primary prevention of HIV infection is also essential.

One of the few bright spots in the AIDS area is evidence of substantial reductions in high-risk sexual behavior by gay men in San Francisco, New York, and other epicenters. Although the occurrence of these behavior changes have been repeatedly documented, the factors that prompted them remain unclear. It appears that the greatest risk behavior changes have occurred in geographical areas and in populations after AIDS cases became common and, unfortunately, after HIV seroprevalence reached very high levels. From a primary prevention standpoint, an important objective is promoting risk-reduction changes in populations where HIV infection prevalence is still lower. Community-based interventions are especially needed for intravenous drug users, gay or bisexual men who live in areas outside the nation's largest cities, the urban poor, adolescents, heterosexuals with multiple partners, and racial minorities.

Education is a necessary foundation for AIDS prevention efforts. While it appears that public knowledge about general aspects of AIDS has increased considerably over the past several years, focused educational efforts are needed for special segments of the population. Examples include detailed needle cleaning information for drug users, safer sex practice information for gay or bisexual men, and information about correct use of condoms. Because the content of educational messages must be highly specific and "prescriptive" concerning necessary risk behavior changes, and because the same information is not equally relevant or appropriate for all populations, focused campaigns are warranted. In addition, different educational approaches and modalities may be needed for different racial, ethnic, and age groups.

Research from other health promotion areas indicates that information provision and education alone are often insufficient to promote risk behavior change, especially when the behavior that confers risk is long-standing, highly reinforced, and temporally distant from the negative health outcome. Research is needed on ways to redefine social norms within at-risk populations so that safer conduct is socially reinforced and risky behavior is socially discouraged (see Coates, 1988). To the extent that peer group norms can be modified to sanction only health-conscious behavior by gay men, drug users, sexually active adolescents, and heterosexuals with multiple partners, natural contingencies favoring safer conduct will be strengthened. An important challenge for behavioral interventions at community levels is the development of mechanisms and strategies to promote these changes.

Finally, the proliferation of local grass-roots programs to prevent further spread of HIV infection in the gay community is impressive. Rarely if ever before has a community so directly hard-hit by an epidemic also taken the lead in developing ways to prevent its spread, often with minimal funding or outside support. Applied researchers with expertise in community behavioral interventions, health promotion, and program design and assessment methods are in a position to assist in the application, refinement, and evaluation of effective AIDS prevention programs. Even our best efforts carry no guarantee of success, but to do anything less invites a national tragedy of unprecedented proportions.

REFERENCES

Achilli, G., Cattaneo, E., Danesino, M., & Rondanelli, E. G. (1988, June). *Western blot analysis of HIV-1 lgG in sera of asymptomatic carriers for the evaluation of six ELISA kits.* Paper presented at the Fourth International Conference on AIDS, Stockholm.

Ada, J. L. (1988, June). *Prospects for HIV vaccines.* Paper presented at the Fourth International Conference on AIDS, Stockholm.

Agar, M. H. (1973). *Ripping and running: A formal ethnography of urban heroin addicts.* New York: Seminar.

Agius G., Biggar, R. J., Alexander, S. S., Waters, D. J., Drummond, J. E., Murphy, E. L., Weiss, S. H., Levine, P. H., & Blattner, W. A. (1988, June). *Problems with HTLV-1 antibody detection by ELISA, p24-RIA, & Western blot tests.* Paper presented at the Fourth International Conference on AIDS, Stockholm.

Agle, D., Cluck, H., & Pierce, G. F. (1987). The impact of AIDS: Psychologic impact on the hemophiliac population. *General Hospitalization in Psychiatry, 9,* 11–17.

AIDS: A growing threat. (1985, August 12). *Newsweek,* pp. 40–47.

AIDS & infants. (1988, March). *AIDS Report, 1,* 2.

Anderson, R. E., & Levy, J. A. (1985). Prevalence of antibodies to AIDS-associated retrovirus in single men in San Francisco. *Lancet, 1,* 217.

Arnold, C. B. (1972). The sexual behavior of inner city adolescent condom users. *Journal of Sex Research, 8,* 298–309.

Arnold, C. B., & Cogswell, B. E. (1971). A condom distribution program for adolescents: The findings of a feasibility study. *American Journal of Public Health, 61,* 739–750.

Bakeman, R., McCray, E., Lumb, J. R., Jackson, R. E., & Whitley, P. N. (1987). The incidence of AIDS among blacks and Hispanics. *Journal of the National Medical Association, 79,* 921–928.

Battjes, R. J., & Pickens, R. (1988, June). *AIDS transmission risk behaviors among intravenous drug abusers (IVDAs).* Paper presented at the Fourth International Conference on AIDS, Stockholm.

Bauman, L. J., & Siegel, K. (1987). Misperception among gay men of the risk for AIDS associated with their sexual behavior. *Journal of Applied Social Psychology, 17,* 329–350.

Becker, C., Howe, H., & Zielinski, M. (1988, June). *Gay male sexual behavior change in a low incidence area for AIDS.* Paper presented at the Fourth International Conference on AIDS, Stockholm.

Becker, M. H., & Joseph, J. G. (1988). AIDS and behavioral change to reduce risk: A review. *American Journal of Public Health, 78,* 394–410.

Bentwich, Z., Burstein, R., Berner, Y., & Handzel, C. (1988, June). *Preexisting immune impairments in male homosexuals: Predisposing factors for HIV infection.* Paper presented at the Fourth International Conference on AIDS, Stockholm.

Black, J. L., Dolan, M. P., & DeFord, H. A. (1986). Sharing of needles among users of intravenous drugs. *New England Journal of Medicine, 314,* 446–447.

Boyko, W. J., Schechter, M. T., Jeffries, E., Douglas, B., Maynard, M., & O'Shaughnessy, M. (1985). The Vancouver Lymphadenopathy AIDS study III: Relation of HTLV-III seropositivity, immune status, and lymphadenopathy. *Canadian Medical Association Journal, 133,* 28–32.

Brundage, J. F., Burke, D. S., Gardner, L. I., Herbold, J., Boskovitch, J., & Redfield, R. R. (1987, June). *Temporal trend of prevalence and incidence of HIV infection among civilian applicants for US military service: Analysis of 18 months of serological screening data.* Paper presented at the Third International Conference on AIDS, Washington, DC.

Bucene, M., Armstrong, J., & Stuckey, M. (1988, June). *Virological and electron microscopic evidence for postnatal HIV transmission via breastmilk.* Paper presented at the Fourth International Conference on AIDS, Stockholm.

Buning, E. C. (1987, June). *Prevention policy on AIDS among drug addicts in Amsterdam.* Paper presented at the Third International Conference on AIDS, Washington, DC.

Bye, L. (1987). "Stop AIDS" community-based health education project in San Francisco, California. In D. G. Ostrow (Ed.), *Biobehavioral control of AIDS* (pp. 166–170). New York: Irvington.

Calabrese, L. H., & Gopalakrishna, K. V. (1986). Transmission of HTLV-III infection from man to woman to man. *New England Journal of Medicine, 314,* 987.

Camerson, D. W., D'Costa, L. J., Ndinya-Achola, J. O., Piot, P., & Plummer, F. A. (1988, June). *Incidence and risk factors for female to male transmission of HIV.* Paper presented at the Fourth International Conference on AIDS, Stockholm.

Campos, P. E., Brasfield, T. L., & Kelly, J. A. (1988). *Psychology training related to AIDS: A survey of graduate and internship training programs.* Unpublished manuscript, University of Mississippi Medical Center.

Carlson, J. R., Hinrichs, S. J., Levy, N. B., Gardner, M. B., Holland, P., & Pedersen, N. C. (1985). Evaluation of commercial AIDS screening test kits. *Lancet, 1,* 1388.

Carlson, J. R., Yee, J. L., Watson-Williams, E. J., Jennings, M. B., Mertens, S. C., Gardner, M. B., Ghrayer, J., & Biggar, R. J. (1987, February 14). Rapid, easy, and economical screening test for antibodies to human immunodeficiency virus. *Lancet,* pp. 361–362.

Centers for Disease Control. (1981a). Pneumocystis pneumonia—Los Angeles. *Morbidity and Mortality Weekly Report, 30,* 250–252.

Centers for Disease Control. (1981b). Kaposi's sarcoma and pneumonia among homosexual men—New York City and California. *Morbidity and Mortality Weekly Report, 30,* 305–308.

Centers for Disease Control. (1985). Self reported behavioral changes among homosexual and bisexual men—San Francisco. *Journal of the American Medical Association, 254,* 2537–2538.

Centers for Disease Control. (1986a, November 17). *Acquired immunodeficiency syndrome (AIDS) weekly surveillance report: United States AIDS program.* Atlanta, GA: Author.

Centers for Disease Control. (1986b). Classification system for human T-lymphotropic virus type III/lymphadenopathy associated virus infection—United States. *Morbidity and Mortality Weekly Report, 34,* 507–514.

Centers for Disease Control. (1987a). Human immunodeficiency virus infection in the United States: A review of current knowledge. *Morbidity and Mortality Weekly Report, 36,* 1–48.

Centers for Disease Control. (1987b). HIV infection and pregnancies in sexual partners of HIV seropositive hemophiliac men—United States. *Morbidity and Mortality Weekly Report, 35,* 593–595.

Centers for Disease Control. (1988, June 6). *AIDS Weekly Surveillance Report.* Atlanta, GA: Author.

Chaisson, R. E., Moss, A. R., Onishi, R., Osmond, D., & Carolson, J. R. (1987). Human immunodeficiency virus infection in heterosexual intravenous drug users in San Francisco. *American Journal of Public Health, 77,* 169–172.

Cleary, P. D., Barry, M. J., Mayer, K. H., Brandt, A. M., Goslin, L., & Fineberg, H. V. (1987). Compulsory premarital screening for the human immunodeficiency virus: Technical and public health considerations. *Journal of the American Medical Association, 258,* 1757–1762.

Coates, T. J. (1988, August). We need community-based interventions to prevent more HIV infection. In J. A. Kelly (Chair), *Outcomes of AIDS prevention programs: What works best with whom.* Symposium conducted at the meeting of the American Psychological Association, Atlanta, GA.

Coates, T. J., & McKusick, L. (1987, June). *The efficacy of stress management in reducing high risk behavior and improving immune function in HIV antibody positive men.* Paper presented at the Third International Conference on AIDS, Washington, DC.

Coates, T. J., Morin, S. F., & McKusick, L. (1987, June). *Consequences of AIDS antibody testing among gay men: The AIDS Behavioral Research Project.* Paper presented at the Third International Conference on AIDS, Washington, DC.

Coates, T. J., Morin, S. F., McKusick, L., Hoff, C., Catania, J., Kegeles, S., & Pollock, L. (1988, June). *Long-term consequences of AIDS antibody testing on gay and bisexual men.* Paper presented at the Fourth International Conference on AIDS, Stockholm.

Cohen, J. B., Poole, L. E., Lyons, C. A., Lockett, G. J., Alexander, P., & Wofsy, C. B. (1988, June). *Sexual behavior and HIV infection risk among 354 sex industry women in a participant based research and prevention program.* Paper presented at the Fourth International Conference on AIDS, Stockholm.

Cook, D., & Sherlock, C. H. (1988, June). *Performance of commercial ELISA test kits for HIV antibody testing in problem sera.* Paper presented at the Fourth International Conference on AIDS, Stockholm.

Curran, J. W., Jaffe, H. W., Hardy, A. M., Morgan, W. M., Selik, R. M., & Dondero, T. J. (1988, June). *The epidemiology of HIV infection and AIDS in the United States.* Paper presented at the Fourth International Conference on AIDS, Stockholm.

Curran, J. W., Lawrence, D. N., & Jaffe, H. (1984). Acquired immunodeficiency syndrome (AIDS) associated with transfusions. *New England Journal of Medicine, 310,* 69–75.

Curran, J. W., Morgan, W. M., Starcher, E. T., Hardy, A. M., & Jaffe, J. W. (1985). Epidemiological trends of AIDS in the United States. *Cancer Research, 45,* 4602–4604.

Darrow, W. W. (1988, August). Potential spread of HIV infection in female prostitutes. In L. S. Doll (Chair), *Behavioral research and AIDS at the Centers for Disease Control.* Symposium conducted at the meeting of the American Psychological Association, Atlanta, GA.

Darrow, W. W., Bigler, W., Deppe, D., French, J., Gill, P., Potterat, J., Ravenholt, O., Schable, C., Sikes, R. K., & Wofsy, C. (1988, June). *HIV antibody in 640 U.S. prostitutes with no evidence of intravenous (IV) drug abuse.* Paper presented at the Fourth International Conference on AIDS, Stockholm.

Dax, E. M., Adler, W. H., Nagel, J. E., Lange, W. R., & Jaffe, J. H. (1988, June). *Immunosuppression persists during chronic volatile nitrite exposure.* Paper presented at the Fourth International Conference on AIDS, Stockholm.

D'Eramo, J. E. (1987). The AIDS prevention education program of GMHC (NYC). In D. G. Ostrow (Ed.), *Biobehavioral control of AIDS* (pp. 183–189). New York: Irvington.

D'Eramo, J. E., Quadland, M. E., Shattls, W., Shumann, R., & Jacobs, R. (1988, June). *The 800 men project: A systematic evaluation of AIDS prevention programs demonstrating the efficacy of erotic, sexually explicit safer sex education on gay and bisexual men at risk for AIDS.* Paper presented at the Fourth International Conference on AIDS, Stockholm.

Des Jarlais, D. C. (1988a, June). *HIV infection among persons who inject illicit drugs: Problems and progress.* Paper presented at the Fourth International Conference on AIDS, Stockholm.

Des Jarlais, D. C. (1988b, August). Intravenous drug use and the heterosexual transmission of AIDS. In J. A. Kelly (Chair), *Outcomes of AIDS prevention programs: What works best with whom.* Symposium conducted at the meeting of the American Psychological Association, Atlanta, GA.

Des Jarlais, D. C., Friedman, S. R., & Hopkins, W. (1985). Risk reduction for the acquired immune deficiency syndrome among intravenous drug users. *Annals of Internal Medicine, 103,* 755–759.

Des Jarlais, D. C., Friedman, S. R., & Stoneburner, R. L. (1988). HIV infection and intravenous drug use: Critical issues in transmission dynamics, infection outcomes, and prevention. *Reviews of Infectious Diseases, 10,* 151–158.

Des Jarlais, D. C., & Hopkins, W. (1985). Free needles for intravenous drug users at risk for AIDS: Current developments in New York City. *New England Journal of Medicine, 313,* 1476.

Des Jarlais, D. C., Tross, S., Abdul-Quader, A., & Friedman, S. R. (1988, August). Intravenous drug users and the heterosexual transmission of AIDS. In J. A. Kelly (Chair), *Outcomes of AIDS prevention programs: What works best with whom.* Symposium conducted at the meeting of the American Psychological Association, Atlanta, GA.

Des Jarlais, D. C., Wish, F., Friedman, S. R., Stoneburner, R., Wildvan, D. E., El-Sadr, W., Brady, E., & Cuadrado, M. (1987). Intravenous drug use and the heterosexual transmission of the human immunodeficiency virus: Current trends in New York City. *New York State Journal of Medicine, 20,* 283–296.

DeVita, W. T., Hellman, S., & Rosenberg, S. A. (1985). *AIDS: Etiology, diagnosis, treatment, and prevention.* Philadelphia: J. B. Lippincott.

Diaco, R. (1988, June). *Use of chromium dioxide particles for HIV testing.* Paper presented at the Fourth International Conference on AIDS, Stockholm.

Dickens, B. M. (1988). Legal rights and duties in the AIDS epidemic. *Science, 239,* 580–585.

DiClemente, R., Zorn, J., & Temoshok, L. (1986). Adolescents and AIDS: A survey of knowledge, attitudes, and beliefs about AIDS in San Francisco. *American Journal of Public Health, 76,* 1443–1445.

Doll, L. S., O'Malley, P. O., Pershing, A., Hessol, N., Darrow, W., Lifson, A., & Cannon, L. (1988, June). *High-risk behavior and knowledge of HIV antibody status in the San Francisco City Clinic cohort.* Paper presented at the Fourth International Conference on AIDS, Stockholm.

Ebbesen, P., Biggar, R. J., & Melbye, M. (1984). *AIDS: A basic guide for clinicians.* Philadelphia: W. B. Saunders.

Eisdorfer, C. (1987a, June). *Neuropsychiatric aspects of AIDS.* Paper presented at the Third International Conference on AIDS, Washington, DC.

Eisdorfer, C. (1987b, June). *CNS complications of AIDS.* Paper presented at the Third International Conference on AIDS, Washington, DC.

Emmons, C. S., Joseph, J. C., Kessler, R. C., Wortman, C. B., Montgomery, S. B., & Ostrow, D. G. (1986). Psychosocial predictors of reported behavior change in homosexual men at risk for AIDS. *Health Education Quarterly, 13,* 331–345.

Farthing, C. F., Jesson, W., Taylor, H.-L., Lawrence, A. G., & Gazzard, B. G. (1987, June). *The HIV antibody test: Influence on sexual behavior of homosexual men.* Paper presented at the Third International Conference on AIDS, Washington, DC.

Fauci, A. S. (1986). Current issues in developing a strategy for dealing with the acquired immunodeficiency syndrome. *Proceedings of the National Academy of Science, 83,* 9278–9283.

Fehrsi, L. J., Fleming, D., Foster, L. H., McAlister, R. O., Fox, V., & Conrad, R. (1988, June). *Anonymous vs. confidential human immunodeficiency virus (HIV) testing: Results of a trial in Oregon.* Paper presented at the Fourth International Conference on AIDS, Stockholm.

Feldblum, P. J., & Fortney, J. A. (1988). Condoms, spermicides, and the transmission of human immunodeficiency virus: A review of the literature. *American Journal of Public Health, 78,* 52–53.

Fife, K. H., Jones, H. B., Marrero, D. G., Katz, B. P., Serpe, R. T., & Scott, J. (1988, June). *Behavioral changes among sexually active homosexual men after learning they are negative for HIV antibody.* Paper presented at the Fourth International Conference on AIDS, Stockholm.

Fineberg, H. V. (1988). Education to prevent AIDS: Prospects and obstacles. *Science, 239,* 592–596.

Fischl, M. A., Dickinson, G. M., Scott, G. B., Klimas, N., Fletcher, M. A., & Parks, W. (1987). Evaluation of heterosexual partners, children, and household contact of adults with AIDS. *Journal of the American Medical Association, 257,* 640–644.

Fisher, E. J. (1986, March). How to combat the AIDS and FRAIDS epidemic. *Michigan Medicine*, pp. 93–102.

Flynn, N., Jain, S., Bailey, V., Siegel, B., Bahles, V., Nassar, N., Lindo, J., Harper, S., & Ding, D. (1988, June). *Characteristics and stated AIDS risk behavior of IV drug users attending drug treatment programs in a medium sized U.S. city.* Paper presented at the Fourth International Conference on AIDS, Stockholm.

Francis, D. P., & Chin, J. J. (1987). The prevention of acquired immunodeficiency syndrome in the United States: An objective strategy for medicine, public health, business, and the community. *Journal of the American Medical Association, 257*, 1357–1366.

Friedman, S. R., Des Jarlais, D. C., & Southern, J. L. (1986). AIDS health education for intravenous drug users. *Health Education Quarterly, 13*, 383–393.

Friedman, S. R., Des Jarlais, D. C., Southern, J. L., Garber, J., Cohen, H., & Smith, D. (1987). AIDS and self organization among intravenous drug users in New York City. *International Journal of the Addictions, 22*, 201–219.

Friedland, G. H., Saltzman, B. R., Rogers, M. F., Kahl, P. A., Lesser, M. L., Mayer, M. M., & Klein, R. S. (1986). Lack of transmission of HTLV-III/LAV infection to household contacts of patients with AIDS or AIDS-related complex with oral candidiasis. *New England Journal of Medicine, 314*, 344–349.

Friedland, G. H., Saltzman, B. R., Rogers, M. F., Kahl, P. A., Weiner, C., & Mayers, M. (1987, June). *Additional evidence of lack of transmission for HIV infection to household contacts of AIDS patients.* Paper presented at the Third International Conference on AIDS, Washington, DC.

Gagnon, J. H. (1988, June). *Sexual conduct and sex research.* Paper presented at the Fourth International Conference on AIDS, Stockholm.

Ginzburg, H. M., French, J., Jackson, J., Hartsock, P. I., MacDonald, M. G., & Weiss, S. H. (1986). Health education and knowledge assessment of HTLV-III diseases among intravenous drug users. *Health Education Quarterly, 13*, 373–382.

Glaser, J. B., Strange, T. J., & Rosati, D. (1988, June). *Heterosexual HIV transmission among the middle class.* Paper presented at the Fourth International Conference on AIDS, Stockholm.

Goedert, J. J., Biggar, R. J., Melbye, M., Mann, D. L., Wilson, S., Gail, M. H., Grossman, R. J., Digioia, R. A., Sanchez, W. C., Weiss, S. H., & Blattner, W. A. (1987). Effects of T4 count and cofactors on the incidence of AIDS in homosexual men infected with human immunodeficiency virus. *Journal of the American Medical Association, 257*, 331–334.

Gold, J.W.M., Hollinger, F. B., van der Horst, C., Myers, L., Makuch, R., Parks, W., & NIH-NIAD Treatment Branch. (1988, June). *Establishing quality assessment in AIDS treatment evaluation units (ATEU) in the USA: Virus isolation from peripheral blood.* Paper presented at the Fourth International Conference on AIDS, Stockholm.

Golubjatnikov, R., Pfister, J., & Tillotson, T. (1983). Homosexual promiscuity and the fear of AIDS, *Lancet, 2*, 681.

Gordon, F., Gilbert, C., Hawley, H., & Willoughby, A. (1988, June). *Seroprevalence of HIV infection in unselected hospital admissions.* Paper presented at the Fourth International Conference on AIDS, Stockholm.

Gostin, L., & Curran, W. J. (1987). Legal control measures for AIDS: Reporting requirements, surveillance, quarantine, and regulation of public meeting places. *American Journal of Public Health, 77*, 214–218.

Gostin, L. O., Curran, W. J., & Clark, M. E. (1987). The case against compulsory casefinding in controlling AIDS-testing, screening, and reporting. *American Journal of Law and Medicine, 12*, 7–53.

Greenblatt, R. M., Osmond, D., Moss, A., Samuel, M., Shabosky, S., & Winkelstein, W. (1988, June) *Behaviors associated with incident HIV infection among homosexual men in*

San Francisco. Paper presented at the Fourth International Conference on AIDS, Stockholm.

Groopman, J. E., Darngadharan, M. D., Salahuddin, S. Z., Buxbaum, R., Huberman, M. S., Linnigurgh, J., Sliski, A., Melane, M. F., Essex, M., & Gallo, R. C., (1985). Apparent transmission of human T-cell leukemia virus type III to a heterosexual woman with the acquired immunodeficiency syndrome. *Annals of Internal Medicine, 102,* 63–66.

Hein, K. (1987, May). AIDS in adolescents: A rationale for concern. *New York State Journal of Medicine,* pp. 290–295.

Helgersen, S. D., Petersen, L. R., & the AIDS Education Study Group. (1988). Acquired immunodeficiency syndrome and secondary school students: Their knowledge is limited and they want to learn more. *Pediatrics, 8,* 350–355.

Hendee, W. R., Schwarz, M. R., Rinaldi, R. C., Henning, J. J., & Rapoza, N. P. (1988, June). *Health education in AIDS: Development of a U.S. strategy.* Paper presented at the Fourth International Conference on AIDS, Stockholm.

Hessol, N. A., Rutherford, G. W., Lifson, A. R., O'Malley, P. M., Doll, L. S., Darrow, W. W., Jaffe, H. W., & Werdegar, D. (1988, June). *The natural history of HIV infection in a cohort of homosexual and bisexual men: A decade of follow up.* Paper presented at the Fourth International Conference on AIDS, Stockholm.

Ho, D. D., Byington, R. E., Schooley, R. T., Flynn, T., Rota, T. R., & Hirch, M. S. (1985). Infrequency of isolation of HTLV-III virus from saliva in AIDS. *New England Journal of Medicine, 313,* 1606.

Hoff, R., Berardi, V. P., Weiblen, B. J., Mahoney-Trout, L., Mitchell, M. L., & Grady, G. L. (1988). Seroprevalence of human immunodeficiency virus among childbearing women: Estimation by testing samples of blood from newborns. *New England Journal of Medicine, 318,* 525–530.

Holmes, K. K. (1988, June). *Heterosexual transmission of HIV: Current evidence and future prospects.* Paper presented at the Fourth International Conference on AIDS, Stockholm.

Jackson, J., & Rotkiewicz, L. (1987, June). *A coupon program: AIDS education and drug treatment.* Paper presented at the Third International Conference on AIDS, Washington, DC.

Jacobsen, P. B., Perry, S. W., Scavuzzo, D., & Roberts, R. B. (1987, June). *Psychological reactions of individuals at risk for AIDS during an experimental drug trial.* Paper presented at the Third International Conference on AIDS, Washington, DC.

Jaffe, H. W., Darrow, W. W., Echenberg, D. F., O'Malley, P. M., Getchell, G. P., Kalyanarain, V. S., Byers, R. H., Drennan, D. P., Braff, E. H., Curran, J. N., & Francis, D. P. (1985). The acquired immunodeficiency syndrome in a cohort of homosexual men. *Annals of Internal Medicine, 103,* 210–214.

Johnson, W. D., Su, F. S., & Jackson, K. L. (1988, June). *The impact of mandatory reporting of HIV seropositive persons in South Carolina.* Paper presented at the Fourth International Conference on AIDS, Stockholm.

Joseph, J. G., Montgomery, S. B., Emmons, C. A., Kessler, R. C., Ostrow, D. G., Wortman, C. B., O'Brien, K., Eller, M., & Eshleman, S. (1987). Magnitude and determinants of behavioral risk reduction: Longitudinal analysis of the cohort at risk for AIDS. *Psychology & Health, 1,* 73–96.

Joseph, J. G., Montgomery, S. B., Kessler, R. C., Ostrow, D. G., Emmons, C. A., & Phair, J. P. (1987, June). *Two-year longitudinal study of behavioral risk reduction in a cohort of homosexual men.* Paper presented at the Third International Conference on AIDS, Washington, DC.

Kaplan, L. L. (1988, June). *Biological assessment of nonoxynol-9 formulated in a tissue and latex compatible hydrocolloid gel.* Paper presented at the Fourth International Conference on AIDS, Stockholm.

Kegeles, S. M., Allen, N. E., & Irwin, C. E. (1988). Sexually active adolescents and condoms:

Changes over one year in knowledge, attitudes, and use. *American Journal of Public Health, 78*, 460–461.

Kelly, J. A., & St. Lawrence, J. S. (1986). Behavioral intervention and AIDS. *Behavior Therapist, 6*, 121–125.

Kelly, J. A., & St. Lawrence, J. S. (1987). The prevention of AIDS: Roles for behavioral intervention. *Scandinavian Journal of Behaviour Therapy, 16*, 5–19.

Kelly, J. A., & St. Lawrence, J. S. (1988a). *The AIDS health crisis: Psychological and social interventions.* New York: Plenum.

Kelly, J. A., & St. Lawrence, J. S. (1988b). AIDS prevention and treatment: Psychology's role in the health crisis. *Clinical Psychology Review, 8*, 255–284.

Kelly, J. A., St. Lawrence, J. S., Brasfield, T., & Hood, H. V. (1987, June). *Relationship between knowledge about AIDS risk and actual risk behavior in a sample of homosexual men: Implications for prevention.* Paper presented at the Third International Conference on AIDS, Washington, DC.

Kelly, J. A., St. Lawrence, J. S., Brasfield, T., & Hood, H. V. (1988, July). *Group intervention to reduce AIDS risk behaviors in gay men: Application of behavioral principles.* Paper presented at the Vermont Conference on the Primary Prevention of Psychopathology, Burlington.

Kelly, J. A., St. Lawrence, J. S., Hood, H. V., & Brasfield, T. (1988). *The AIDS risk knowledge test: Psychometric characteristics and validation.* Paper presented at the Fourth International Conference on AIDS, Stockholm.

Kelly, J. A., St. Lawrence, J. S., Hood, H. V., & Brasfield, T. (1989). Behavioral intervention to reduce AIDS risk activities. *Journal of Consulting and Clinical Psychology, 67*, 60–67.

Kelly, J. A., St. Lawrence, J. S., Hood, H. V., Smith, S., & Cook, D. J. (1987a). Medical students' attitudes toward AIDS: Stigma associated with the disease and with patients' sexual preference. *Journal of Medical Education, 62*, 549–556.

Kelly, J. A., St. Lawrence, J. S., Hood, H. V., Smith, S., & Cook, D. J. (1987b). Stigmatization of AIDS patients by physicians. *American Journal of Public Health, 77*, 789–795.

Kelly, J. A., St. Lawrence, J. S., Hood, H. V., Smith, S., & Cook, D. J. (1988). Nurses' attitudes toward AIDS. *Journal of Continuing Education in Nursing, 19*, 78–83.

Kemeny, M. E., Fahey, J. L., Schneider, S., Weiner, H., Taylor, S., & Visscher, S. (1988, June) *Bereavement associated alterations in phenotypes of lymphocytes in HIV+ and HIV− homosexual men.* Paper presented at the Fourth International Conference on AIDS, Stockholm.

Kingsley, J., Detels, R., Kaslow, R., Polk, B. F., Rinaldo, C. R., Jr., Chmiel, D. K., Kelsey, S. F., Odaka, K., Ostrow, D., Van Raden, M., & Visscher, B. (1987). Risk factors for seroconversion to human immunodeficiency virus among male homosexuals. *Lancet, 1*, 345–349.

Kleinman, P. H., Friedman, S. R., Mauge, C. E., Goldsmith, D. S., Des Jarlais, D. C., & Hopkins, W. (1987, June). *Beliefs and behaviors regarding AIDS: A survey of street intravenous drug users.* Paper presented at the Third International Conference on AIDS, Washington, DC.

Klonoff, E. A., Cargill, V. A., & Gayle, J. (1988, August). AIDS education and prevention in an urban minority population. In J. A. Kelly (Chair), *Outcomes of AIDS prevention programs: What works best with whom.* Symposium conducted at the meeting of the American Psychological Association, Atlanta, GA.

Krueger, L., Wood, R., Diehr, P., & Maxwell, C. (June, 1988). *Poverty and HIV seropositivity: The poor are more likely to be infected.* Paper presented at the Fourth International Conference on AIDS, Stockholm.

Krupka, U., & Wiebhaar, D. (1988, June). *Reliable detection of low titre anti HIV-1 with a new ultrasensitive ELISA procedure.* Paper presented at the Fourth International Conference on AIDS, Stockholm.

Lacking, K. C. (1988, June). *Prostitutes as AIDS educators*. Paper presented at the Fourth International Conference on AIDS, Stockholm.

Leishman, K. (1987, February). Heterosexuals and AIDS. *Atlantic Monthly*, pp. 39–58.

Lemp, G. F., Hessol, H. A., Rutherford, G. W., Payne, S. F., Chen, R. T., Winkelstein, W., Wiley, W. A., Moss, A. R., Feigal, D., & Werdergar, D. (1988, June). *Projections of AIDS morbidity and mortality in San Francisco using epidemic models*. Paper presented at the Fourth International Conference on AIDS, Stockholm.

Leventhal, H., Safer, M. A., & Panagis, D. M. (1983). The impact of communication on the self regulation of health benefits, decisions, and behavior. *Health Education Quarterly, 10*, 3–31.

Marshall, D. W., Brey, R. L., Cahill, W. T., Zajac, R., Houk, R., & Boswell, R. (1988, June). *CSF findings in asymptomatic individuals infected by HIV*. Paper presented at the Fourth International Conference on AIDS, Stockholm.

Martin, J. L. (1987). The impact of AIDS on gay male sexual behavior patterns in New York City. *American Journal of Public Health, 77*, 578–581.

Martin, J. L., Dean, L., Garcia, M., & Hall, M. (1988, June). *The influence of drug use and lover status upon gay male sexual behavior patterns: 1981–1987*. Paper presented at the Fourth International Conference on AIDS, Stockholm.

McCusker, J., Stoddard, A. M., Mayer, K. M., Zapka, J., Morrison, C., & Saltzman, S. P. (1988). Effects of HIV antibody test knowledge on subsequent sexual behaviors in a cohort of homosexually active men. *American Journal of Public Health, 78*, 462–467.

McKusick, L., Horstman, W., & Coates, T. J. (1985). AIDS and sexual behavior reported by gay men in San Francisco. *American Journal of Public Health, 75*, 493–496.

McKusick, L., Wiley, J. A., Coates, T. J., Stall, R., Saika, G., Morin, S., Charles, K., Horstman, W., & Conant, M. A. (1985). Reported changes in the sexual behavior of men at risk for AIDS: San Francisco 1982–1984: The AIDS Behavior Research Project. *Public Health Reports, 100*, 622–629.

McNeil, J. G., Wann, F., Burke, D., Brundage, J., & Peterson, M. (1988, June). *A direct estimation of the rate of new HIV infections in U.S. Army personnel*. Paper presented at the Fourth International Conference on AIDS, Stockholm.

Meachem, S., & Milliken, N. (1988, June). *AIDS screening: Who is willing to be tested*. Paper presented at the Fourth International Conference on AIDS, Stockholm.

Messiah, A., Pollack, M., LaPorte, A., & Brunet, J. B. (1988, June). *From Paris middle classes to small towns and blue collar workers: Sociodemographic trends of AIDS epidemic among French homosexual men*. Paper presented at the Fourth International Conference on AIDS, Stockholm.

Miller, M., Goldberg, D., Wright, R., Ogg, D. (1988, June). *Relationship between knowledge about AIDS and actual risk behavior in a sample of homosexual men*. Paper presented at the Fourth International Conference on AIDS, Stockholm.

Mok, J. Q., Giaquinto, C., DeRossi, A., Grosch-Worner, I., Ades, A. E., & Peckham, C. S. (1987). Infants born to mothers seropositive for human immunodeficiency virus. *Lancet, 1*, 1164–1168.

Morlett, A., Gold, J. Guinan, J. J., & Cooper, D. (1988, June). *Continued risk taking behaviour and seroconversion in HIV tested individuals*. Paper presented at the Fourth International Conference on AIDS, Stockholm.

Mulleady, G. (1987). A review of drug abuse and HIV infection. *Psychology and Health, 1*, 149–163.

Myrmel, H., & Haukenes, G. (1988, June). *False positive reaction with HIV-1 envelope protein (GP41) in the Western blot*. Paper presented at the Fourth International Conference on AIDS, Stockholm.

National Gay and Lesbian Task Force. (1987). *Anti-gay violence: Victimization and defamation in 1986*. New York: Author.

Office of Technology Assessment. (1988). *How effective is AIDS Education?* Washington DC: Government Printing Office.

Ohi, G., Hasegawa, T., Hirano, W., Terao, H., Urano, N., Kai, I., & Kobayashi, Y. (1988, June). *Change in acceptance rate for HIV testing when AIDS is notifiable: An attempt for assessment.* Paper presented at the Fourth International Conference on AIDS, Stockholm.

Olin, R., Giesecke, J., Hallqvist, J., Lagergren, M., & Lidman, K. (1988, June). *Reasons for seeking HIV testing: Results from a Swedish anonymous questionnaire.* Paper presented at the Fourth International Conference on AIDS, Stockholm.

Oliva, G., & DiClemente, R. J. (1988, November). *A survey of risk behaviors associated with HIV transmission in a family planning clinic population in San Francisco.* Paper presented at the American Association of Public Heath.

Osborne, J. (1988). AIDS: Politics and science. *New England Journal of Medicine, 318,* 444–447.

Ostrow, D. C., Joseph, J., Soucey, J., Eller, M., Kessler, R., Phair, J., & Chmiel, J. (1988, June). *Mental health and behavioral correlates of HIV antibody testing in a cohort of gay men.* Paper presented at the Fourth International Conference on AIDS, Stockholm.

Peterson, J., & Bakeman, R. (1988). The epidemiology of adult minority AIDS. *Multicultural Inquiry and Research on AIDS, 2,* 1–2.

Pollack, M., & Schiltz, M. (1988, June). *Does voluntary testing matter? How it influences homosexual safer sex.* Paper presented at the Fourth International Conference on AIDS, Stockholm.

Quinn, T. C., Glasser, D., Cannon, R. O., Matuszak, D. L., Dunning, R. W., Kline, R. L., Campbell, C. H., Israel, E., Fauci, A. S., & Hock, E. W. (1988). Human immunodeficiency virus infection among patients attending clinics for sexually transmitted diseases. *New England Journal of Medicine, 318,* 1987–2023.

Redfield, R. R., Markham, P. D., Salahuddin, S. Z., Wright, D. C., Sarugadharan, M. G., & Gallo, R. C. (1987). Heterosexually acquired HTLV-III/LAV disease (AIDS related complex and AIDS): Epidemiologic evidence for female-to-male transmission. *Journal of the American Medical Association, 254,* 2094–2096.

Research and Decisions Corporation. (1986). *Designing an effective AIDS risk reduction program for San Francisco: Results from the first probability sample of multiple/high-risk partner heterosexual adults.* San Francisco: Author.

Roffman, R. A., Gilchrist, L. D., Stephens, R. S., & Kirkham, M. A. (1988, November). Relapse prevention with gay or bisexual males at risk of AIDS due to ongoing unsafe sexual behavior. In J. A. Kelly (Chair), *Behavioral intervention to prevent AIDS: Current status and future directions.* Symposium conducted at the meeting of the Association for the Advancement of Behavior Therapy, New York.

Rosen, J. C., & Solomon, L. J. (1985). *Prevention in health psychology.* Hanover, NH: University Press of New England.

Rutherford, G. W., Barnhart, J. L., & Lemp, G. F. (1988, June). *The changing demographics of AIDS in homosexual and bisexual men.* Paper presented at the Fourth International Conference on AIDS, Stockholm.

St. Lawrence, J. S., Betts, R., Hogan, I. G., & MacDonald, G. (1988). A survey of Jackson State University students' knowledge of AIDS, attitudes toward persons with AIDS, and AIDS-risk behavior: Implications for campus prevention. *Jackson State University Researcher,* pp. 17–30.

St. Lawrence, J. S., Hood, H. V., Brasfield, T., & Kelly, J. A. (1988, June). *Patterns and predictors of risk knowledge and risk behavior across high- and low-AIDS prevalence cities.* Paper presented at the Fourth International Conference on AIDS, Stockholm.

St. Lawrence, J. S., Husfeldt, B. A., Kelly, J. A., Hood,, H. V., & Smith, S. (in press). The stigma of AIDS: Fear of disease and prejudice toward gays. *Journal of Homosexuality.*

St. Lawrence, J. S., Kelly, J. A., Owens, A. D., Hogan, I. G., & Wilson, R. A. (1988, June).

Psychologists' attitudes toward AIDS. Paper presented at the Fourth International Conference on AIDS, Stockholm.

Saltzman, B. R., Friedland, G. H., Klein, R. S., Vileno, J., Freeman, K., & Cutello, P. (1988, June). *Comparison of AIDS clinical manifestation between men and women in a primarily heterosexual population.* Paper presented at the Fourth International Conference on AIDS, Stockholm.

Saxinger, C., Wantzin, L., & Gallo, R. C. (1988, June). *ELISA confirmatory test for HIV antibody more sensitive and specific than Western blot.* Paper presented at the Fourth International Conference on AIDS, Stockholm.

Schechter, M. T., Craib, K.J.P., Willoughby, B., Sestak, P., Weaver, M. S., & Douglas, B. (1988, June). *Progression to AIDS in a cohort of homosexual men: Results at 5 years.* Paper presented at the Fourth International Conference on AIDS, Stockholm.

Schietzinger, H. (1988, June). *AIDS Train the Trainer program for health care.* Paper presented at the Fourth International Conference on AIDS, Stockholm.

Shih, J., Allen, R., Webber, S., Donoghue, S., Pawlowski, J., Fico, R., & Dawson, G. (1988, June). *Envacor II: An improved competitive enzyme immunoassay for diagnosis of exposure to HIV.* Paper presented at the Fourth International Conference on AIDS, Stockholm.

Shilts, R. (1987). *And the band played on.* New York: St. Martin's.

Siegel, K. (1986). AIDS: The social dimension. *Psychiatric Annals, 16,* 168–171.

Siegel, K., & Gibson, W. C. (1988, February). Barriers to the modification of sexual behavior among heterosexuals at risk for acquired immunodeficiency syndrome. *New York State Journal of Medicine,* pp. 66–70.

Siegel, K., Grodsky, P. B., & Herman, A. (1986). AIDS risk-reduction guidelines: A review and analysis. *Journal of Community Health, 11,* 233–243.

Sion, F. S., Sa Ca, M., Lacerda, R., Quinhoes, E. P., Perei, R. A., Balvao-Castro, B., & Castilho, E. A. (1988, June). *The importance of anal intercourse in transmission of HIV to women.* Paper presented at the Fourth International Conference on AIDS, Stockholm.

Smith, D. (1987). Barriers to risk reduction in a southern community. In D. G. Ostrow (Ed.), *Biobehavioral control of AIDS* (pp. 121–124). New York: Irvington.

Stall, R., McKusick, L., Wiley, J., Coates, T. J., & Ostrow, D. G. (1986). Alcohol and drug use during sexual activity and compliance with safe sex guidelines for AIDS: The AIDS Behavioral Research Project. *Health Education Quarterly, 13,* 359–371.

Starcher, E. T., Dondero, T., Noa, M., Efird, J., & Curran, J. (June, 1988). *A trend analysis of the first 50,000 AIDS cases reported in the United States.* Paper presented at the Fourth International Conference on AIDS, Stockholm.

Stoneburner, R., Guigli, P., & Kristal, S. (1986, June). *Increasing mortality in intravenous drug users in New York City and its relationship to the AIDS epidemic: Is there an unrecognized spectrum of HTLV-III/LAV related disease?* Paper presented at the Second International Conference on AIDS, Paris.

Strunin, L., & Hingson, R. (1987). Acquired immunodeficiency syndrome and adolescents: Knowledge, beliefs, attitudes, and behaviors. *Pediatrics, 79,* 825–828.

Testing for AIDS. (1988, July 2). *Economist,* pp. 14–19.

Tindall, B., & Cooper, D. A. (1988, June). *High risk sexual practices and condom usage in a group of homosexual men according to HIV antibody status.* Paper presented at the Fourth International Conference on AIDS, Stockholm.

Tross, S., Hirsch, D., Rabkin, B., Berry, C., & Holland, J.C.B. (1987, June). *Determinants of current psychiatric disorders in AIDS spectrum patients.* Paper presented at the Third International Conference on AIDS, Washington, DC.

Ujhelyi, E., Bohn, U., Fust, G., Meretey, K., & Hollan, S. R. (1988, June). *E. coli antibodies do not cause false positivity in recombinant anti-HIV essays.* Paper presented at the Fourth International Conference on AIDS, Stockholm.

Valdiserri, R. O., Lyter, D. W., Leviton, L. C., Callahan, C., Kingsley, L. A., & Rinaldo, C. R. (1988a). Variables influencing condom use in a cohort of gay and bisexual men. *American Journal of Public Health, 78*, 801–805.

Valdiserri, R. O., Lyter, D. W., Leviton, L. C., Callahan, C., Kingsley, L. A., & Rinaldo, C. R. (1988b, June). *AIDS prevention in gay men.* Paper presented at the Fourth International Conference on AIDS, Stockholm.

Van den Hoek, J.A.R., Coutinho, R. A., Van Zadelhoff, A. W., Van hass Trecht, H. J., & Goudsmit, J. (1987, June). *Prevalence, incidence, and risk factors of HIV infection among drug addicts in Amsterdam.* Paper presented at the Third International Conference on AIDS, Washington, DC.

van Wielink, G., McArthur, J. C., Farzadegan, H., Moench, T., Johnson, R. T., & Polk, B. F. (1988, June). *Changes in cerebrospinal fluid with increasing duration of HIV-1 infection and neurological findings: The Multicenter AIDS Cohort Study.* Paper presented at the Fourth International Conference on AIDS, Stockholm.

Voeller, B., & Potts, M. (1985). Has the condom any proven value in preventing the transmission of sexually transmitted viral disease—for example, acquired immune deficiency syndrome? *British Medical Journal, 2891*, 1196.

Williams, L. S. (1986). AIDS risk reduction: A community health education intervention for minority high risk group members. *Health Education Quarterly, 13*, 407–421.

Willoughby, B., Schechter, M. T., Boyko, W. J., Craib, K.J.P., Weaver, M. S., & Douglas, B. (1987, June). *Sexual practices and condom use in a cohort of homosexual men: Evidence of differential modification between seropositive and seronegative men.* Paper presented at the Third International Conference on AIDS, Washington, DC.

Winkelstein, W., Lyman, D. M., & Padian, N. (1987). Sexual practices and risk of infection by the human immunodeficiency virus. *Journal of the American Medical Association, 257*, 321–325.

Winkelstein, W., Samuel, M., & Padian, N. S. (1987). The San Francisco Men's Health Study III: Reduction in human immunodeficiency virus transmission among homosexual/ bisexual men: 1982–1986. *American Journal of Public Health, 77*, 685–589.

Witkor, S., Biggar, R., Melbye, M., Ebbesen, P., & Goedert, J. (1988, June). *Effect of knowledge of HIV status upon sexual activity among homosexual men.* Paper presented at the Fourth International Conference on AIDS, Stockholm.

Wodak, A. D., Dolan, K., Imrie, A., Gold, J., Whyte, B. M., & Cooper, D. A. (1987, June). *HIV antibodies in needles and syringes used by intravenous drug users.* Paper presented at the Third International Conference on AIDS, Washington, DC.

Wolcott, D. L. (1986). Neuropsychiatric syndromes in AIDS and AIDS-related diseases. In L. McKusick (Ed.), *AIDS and mental health: Policy, administration, treatment* (pp. 46–62). (Preprint draft of L. McKusick [Ed.], *What to do about AIDS: Physicians and mental health professionals discuss the issues.* Berkeley: University of California Press, 1986.)

Woo, J. M., Neal, D. P., Geoghegan, C. M., Rauch, K. J., Barnhart, J. L., Lemp, G. F., & Rutherford, G. W. (1988, June). *Evaluation of heterosexual contact tracing of partners of AIDS patients.* Paper presented at the Fourth International Conference on AIDS, Stockholm.

Wood, R., Leonard, J., & Krueger, L. (1988, June). *Anonymous participation in a longitudinal cohort study of gay and bisexual men.* Paper presented at the Fourth International Conference on AIDS, Stockholm.

Zeugin, P., Lehmann, P., Dubois-Arber, F., & Hausser, D. (1988, June). *Sexual behavior and attitudes of young people in Switzerland: Before the start of the campaign "Stop AIDS" and 8 months later.* Paper presented at the Fourth International Conference on AIDS, Stockholm.

Ziegler, J. B., Stewart, G. H., Penny, R., Stuckey, M., & Good, S. (1988, June). *Breast feeding and transmission of HIV from mother to infant.* Paper presented at the Fourth International Conference on AIDS, Stockholm.

PEDIATRIC BEHAVIORAL DENTISTRY

KEITH D. ALLEN
Meyer Children's Rehabilitation Institute
University of Nebraska Medical Center

TREVOR F. STOKES
Florida Mental Health Institute
University of South Florida

I. INTRODUCTION

Over the past 20 years, dental researchers have found that serious progressive dental disease can be arrested and controlled provided that plaque and calculus are thoroughly removed (Linde et al., 1982; Lovdal, Arno, Schei, & Waerhaug, 1961; Suomi et al., 1971). That is, developing good dental hygiene, especially at an early age, obtaining periodic prophylactic treatment, and obtaining restorative treatment, when needed, can aid in preventing serious dental health problems. While there has been a general decline in the prevalence and intensity of dental caries (i.e., cavities) in the United States (Burt, 1982), the presence of dental caries is the most prevalent disease of children in the United States today (Public Health Service, 1980, p. 28). Consequently, dentists have acknowledged that they must be more than technicians who focus only on the technical precision needed to repair or remove diseased teeth effectively. They must be able to promote continued oral hygiene behaviors and ensure patient cooperation during prophylactic and restorative treatment.

According to Cohen (1981), the management of these patient compliance problems can best be accomplished through the control of relevant conditions within the patient's environment. In addition, Milgrom, Weinstein, and Smith (1984) note that dentists should choose as collaborators those who are able to identify the role of learning in conceptualizing and understanding behavior change. As a result, dentists have begun to collaborate with behavioral psychologists (e.g., Melamed, Hawes, Heiby, & Glick, 1975; Stokes, Stark, & Allen, in press; Williams, Hurst, & Stokes, 1983) in the study of behaviors related to the maintenance of oral health and prevention of serious oral disease (Ingersoll, 1982). The result has been the development of behavioral technology designed to motivate children to engage in those behaviors that will prevent oral disease and maintain a clinically healthy mouth. In addition, technology has been developed to assist the dentist with the management of children's behaviors that can effect the successful completion of quality preventive procedures. That is, patients who are disruptive or noncompliant while receiving restorative dental treatment may increase the likelihood of their own injury, increase the intrusiveness of procedures, delay the completion of treatment, or disrupt the concentration of the dentist, and, perhaps, affect the quality of dental work.

We will review current behavior management technology available to oral health professionals in motivating and maintaining the oral health behavior of children. We will also examine techniques that have been employed to manage children's behavior during restorative dental treatment.

II. STRENGTHENING ORAL HEALTH BEHAVIOR

The Health Belief Model has been proposed as a model for understanding why it is difficult to motivate children to engage in preventive oral health behaviors (Haefner, 1974). It is likely, however, that a child's beliefs are the product of the same contingencies that currently maintain (or fail to maintain) oral health behaviors.

Because the consequences for failure to comply with primary preventive oral health practices are so remote, these delayed consequences do not maintain oral health behaviors by themselves, leading to "beliefs" of insusceptibility. To enhance the salience and benefits of complying with preventive oral health recommendations, rules are often used to describe the delayed consequences of current behavior. But the success of these rules depends upon a history of reinforcement for rule-following behavior. To a much greater extent, a rule's success depends upon the absence of immediate reinforcement for competing behaviors, since reinforcing events maintain behavior much more effectively when they follow the behavior closely in time (Skinner, 1938). Thus, given a statement (or rule) by a dentist, parent, or teacher about prevailing contingencies (e.g., you should brush your teeth so you won't get cavities and you will have nice breath), the likelihood of taking action is dependent upon the following: (1) the extent to which rules, in the past, have accurately predicted the consequences of noncompliance and the severity of those consequences, (2) the extent to which the child, in complying with the rules, has indeed avoided or suffered the described consequences, and (3) the extent to which there are concurrently operating contingencies maintaining behaviors that compete or are incompatible with the prescribed oral health behaviors. This suggests that investigators of primary prevention may want to rely less on the rule-following behaviors of their child patients and more on shaping and maintaining primary preventive oral health behaviors through the management of current contingencies. This means arranging more immediate, reinforcing consequences for primary preventive oral health behaviors.

III.   PRIMARY PREVENTION TECHNOLOGY

A.   Instruction

A child's failure to engage in certain desirable behaviors may be due to a skill deficit or a motivational deficit. A motivational deficit occurs when a child is able but does not perform the behavior (i.e., the behavior has been observed to be in the child's repertoire). Some of the procedures described in the primary prevention literature are better designed for eliminating skill deficits than motivational deficits, although nearly all of the procedures have been used to try to motivate children to practice oral health behaviors reliably (see Horner & Keilitz, 1975; Poche, McCubbrey, & Munn, 1982). For example, instructional strategies have typically combined information about why oral health is important (e.g., Evans, Rozelle, Noblitt, & Williams, 1975) with demonstrations (modeling) of appropriate oral health behaviors. Some studies have looked at information alone (e.g., Albino, Juliano, & Slakter, 1977; Evans et al., 1975; Fodor & Ziegler, 1966), and others have looked at modeling alone (e.g., Murray & Epstein, 1981; Pinkham & Stacey, 1975), although most have combined the two and called it instruction.

Two studies have found instruction to improve oral health in children, but both of these studies had methodological problems. Beedle, Henderson, Field, and Karagan (1976) did not use a control group and Clark, Fintz, and Taylor (1974) included a peer reinforcement system and the charting of dental plaque. In both studies, it is unclear whether the reductions were a result of the instructions. In addition, Clark et al. (1974) did not control for the amount of time spent with the children across groups.

Controlled studies have indicated that instruction may be useful in the acquisition of toothbrushing skills in both normal (e.g., Murray & Epstein, 1981; Poche et al., 1982) and mentally retarded children (e.g., Horner & Keilitz, 1975), but that simply providing instruction may not be sufficient to motivate changes in oral health behaviors (see Albino, 1978; Albino et al., 1977; Podshadley & Schweikle, 1970; Podshadley & Shannon, 1970). Poche et al. (1982) found that instruction, modeling, and some physical guidance were effective in teaching three preschool children to brush their teeth properly. Toothbrushing was divided into 16 component steps within four criteria groupings: angle, motion, surface, and duration. They found that as the children mastered the brushing criteria across 20 to 30 days, plaque levels scored via the Patient Hygiene Performance Index (PHP; Podshadley & Haley, 1968) decreased. One of the children continued to use nearly all of the steps at an 8-week follow-up, and another used 75% of the steps. No measure of plaque was conducted at follow-up, so it is unclear whether the children maintained low plaque scores. While it was clearly demonstrated that even young children can acquire adequate brushing skills, the amount of time required to teach the skill may prove prohibitive for many oral health professionals. In addition, the small sample size does not adequately address the value of the procedure in supporting the maintenance of toothbrushing over time.

Murray and Epstein (1981) addressed this issue directly when they evaluated the effectiveness of an instructional package in maintaining oral hygiene improvements over a six-week period. They presented a group of preschool children with a 14-minute videotape demonstration of proper brushing techniques and then asked the children to imitate the behaviors they had just viewed. A feedback group was not given specific instructions on how to brush, but were awarded stars for low scores on the PHP plaque measure (Podshadley & Haley, 1968). A control group was simply told to brush their teeth as usual following their morning meal. In fact, all children were prompted to brush their teeth after breakfast each day. To assess the durability of any improvement found in oral health, Murray and Epstein compared plaque levels (PHP) for the three groups over a six-week period. Results from this experiment indicate that, although all of the scores deteriorated across the six-week period, the experimental group maintained lower PHP scores than either the control or the feedback group.

Although these results support the use of instruction in teaching oral health skills, conclusions about the durability of these skills should be drawn cautiously. As all children were prompted each day to brush, the improvement in the experimental group may have been due to the fact that they had been taught the skills they needed to remove plaque. The success of the experimental group compared to the others over time, however, might better be attributed to the prompting that occurred on a daily basis than to the modeling. Even the modeling group did not maintain low PHP scores across the posttreatment period.

In a representative study investigating the efficacy of instructional packages for promoting the maintenance of oral health behavior, Albino (1978) first assessed baseline levels of plaque (Kobayashi & Ash, 1976) and gingival inflammation (Ramfjord, 1959) in 12-year-old students from three different schools. A control group was not contacted again until the first posttreatment assessment 24 weeks later. An experimental group received two 20- to 30-minute instructional sessions concerning plaque control, along with demonstrations of toothbrushing and flossing. The children then practiced removing disclosed stains. A "booster" session was also administered 9 weeks later. During this session, the format followed that of the original session, but the focus was on perfecting brushing and flossing procedures. Results indicate that the instruction group, even with the booster, did not differ significantly from the control group on either of the posttreatment measures of plaque or gingival inflammation.

In summary, there is little evidence to suggest that providing knowledge about or instruction in oral health behaviors influences children's oral health practices. Results from controlled studies using standard measures of scoring plaque and gingivitis have indicated that instruction in dental health concepts and in the techniques of disclosing, brushing, and flossing are insufficient to produce reliable improvements in oral health behaviors. This is not surprising, however, since children's instruction-following behavior, like most other behaviors, must be reinforced to be maintained (Baer, Rowbury, & Baer, 1973). If instructional strategies are to be successful, it is likely that positive consequences will have to be arranged for following these rules.

B. Supervision

Supervision is one method of ensuring that children engage in efficient oral hygiene activities, both through the use of instructional control (i.e., prompts) and the arrangement of immediate and often negative consequences (e.g., reprimand) for behaviors other than those prescribed. Since most children attend school, the classroom provides an ideal setting within which supervision of group plaque-reduction measures can be provided. Not surprisingly, a number of school dental health programs have been promoted that involve supervision (Heifetz, Bagramian, Suomi, & Segreto, 1973; Masters, 1972), yet only a few studies have investigated the effectiveness of a supervisory dental health program (Graves, McNeal,

Haefner, & Ware, 1975; Horowitz, Suomi, Peterson, Vogelsong, & Mathews, 1976; Koch & Linde, 1965; Leske, Ripa, & Soposato, 1982; Ripa, Leske, & Levinson, 1978).

Graves et al. (1975) conducted a comparison of a traditional dental health education program involving instruction techniques and the Toothkeeper Program, which combines instructional procedures with the daily supervised removal of plaque. About 500 children, ages 5 through 12, were randomly assigned by classroom to one of the two programs. Baseline examinations for plaque and gingivitis were scored by two calibrated observers using methods developed by Loe and Silness (1963). Children in the traditional instructional program received a lecture intended to improve knowledge about functional and anatomical considerations of teeth, read books, saw films about the importance of oral health, and observed demonstrations on proper brushing and flossing techniques. Children in the Toothkeeper Program received the same instructions, but, on a daily basis, also participated in 16 weeks of supervised brushing and flossing. That is, rather than simply showing and telling the children what to do, the children in the Toothkeeper Program were shown and then expected to do the actual brushing and flossing in class, under supervision, to ensure that it was done.

Results indicated that after four months, the Toothkeeper children exhibited a significantly greater reduction in plaque and gingivitis scores than children in the traditional program. Although statistically significant, however, the absolute differences were small and the clinical significance may be questioned. In addition, these differences were not maintained at the four-month follow-up.

Similar effects were found by Horowitz et al. (1976) using 10- to 12-year-old students. The children in the experimental group received 10 sessions of intensive instruction in plaque removal (brushing and flossing). Then, each day, the children spent 15 minutes in supervised plaque removal. After brushing and flossing, disclosing solution was applied to identify any remaining plaque. A supervisor examined each child's mouth for plaque, requested rebrushing or flossing if any plaque was found, and then checked again. Horowitz et al. found that children who participated in this daily supervised staining, brushing, and flossing during the school year reduced their plaque scores by 14% and their gingivitis scores by 29%. Children in a control group who received no supervision showed no changes. However, when follow-up measures were taken at the end of summer vacation, the children who had been in the supervised group exhibited plaque scores 2% higher than their own baseline scores.

Results of these studies suggest that while supervision of oral health regimens by itself may be sufficient to produce reductions in plaque and gingival inflammation, the failure to program for the maintenance of those skills will lead to lack of generalization and maintenance of those skills in nonschool settings. Those interested in the further development of supervised school dental health programs should focus on the development and evaluation of programs that plan for the maintenance of those skills over time (e.g., Blount, Baer, & Stokes, 1987) and for the generalization of those skills across a variety of settings, individuals, and occasions (Stokes & Baer, 1977).

C. Contingency Management

As early as 1969, investigators were exploring different ways of providing positive reinforcement for dental health behaviors without the aid of supervision, but through the management of prevailing contingencies (e.g., Lattal, 1969; Stacey, Abbott, & Jordan, 1972; Talsma, 1975). However, in these early studies, the absence of some control conditions and the inclusion of subtle supervisory aspects make it difficult to assess the role of the reinforcement procedures. More recently, researchers have continued to investigate the applicability of contingency management to the development and maintenance of regular toothbrushing (Blount et al., 1987; Blount & Stokes, 1984; Swain, Allard, & Holborn, 1982), to brushing and flossing (Claerhout & Lutzker, 1981; Greenberg, 1977), to the use of fluoride rinses (Kegeles, Lund, & Weisenberg, 1978; Lund & Kegeles, 1982), and even to seeking restorative and prophylactic dental treatment (Reiss, Piotrowski, & Bailey, 1976).

In 1977, Lund and associates began a series of studies in which they sought to increase compliance among 12- and 13-year-old children with a fluoride mouth-rinse program. In their first study they found that age-appropriate rewards (ranging in cost from \$.25 to \$1.00) provided contingent upon the children receiving three treatments over an 11-month period was superior to either an information group or a discussion group. In the discussion group, topics focused on health beliefs about susceptibility to tooth decay, seriousness of decay, and the likely effectiveness of oral health behavior. A total of 76% of the reward group children completed all three treatments, compared to 61% for the information group and 50% for the discussion group. In an effort to extend this success to a daily mouth-rinse program, a second experiment was conducted in which 12- and 13-year-old children earned small rewards (\$.25-\$.55) varying in value depending upon the number of doses finished during a 2-week period (Kegeles et al., 1978). Every 2 weeks, the children were to return their empty bottles of fluoride mouth rinse to school and obtain new ones. They were also told that they could earn bonus prizes for a high level of compliance over the 20-week program. The researchers found that nearly 50% of the reward group obtained the final bottle of rinse; only 31% of a control group and 18% of a discussion group obtained the final bottle.

Seeking to reduce the 50% attrition rate in the reward group, the investigators conducted a third study in which children in contingency management groups received either a postcard to remind them of upcoming appointments or "action instructions" detailing plans for carrying out the health recommendations made during the initial instructional sessions (Lund & Kegeles, 1982). Results indicated that the postcards had no impact on compliance and that action instructions added minimally to the contingency management procedures. In fact, while the action instructions improved compliance in urban populations, they actually had a detrimental effect on suburban populations. This evidence is consistent with studies cited earlier suggesting that instructions do not reliably produce changes in primary preventive health behavior. One issue that the authors fail to address is the impact of their rinsing program on oral health. That is, they provide no empirical evidence that the 50% who complied with the rinsing program throughout the 20-week study had any better oral health than children who did not complete the program or who participated in the control group. In addition, no attempt was made to ensure or assess the maintenance of rinsing at the termination of the program.

Lund and Kegeles (1984) set out to address the maintenance issue by examining the effects of an intermittent schedule of reinforcement and the effects of the introduction of self-management instruction. Seventh-grade children placed in an intermittent schedule group received rewards after weeks 2, 4, 8, and 14, rather than every two weeks, and they also received no bonuses. Children in a "saturated schedule" group received rewards every two weeks and had bonuses available. Half of the children in each group were also instructed to use self-management techniques to promote continued oral health behavior. They were asked to graph their rinse use at home and to think about taking care of their teeth while rinsing and plotting their performance. Follow-ups were conducted over a two-year period.

While contingent rewards were effective in initiating new oral health habits among adolescents, neither the intermittent reward schedule nor the self-management program contributed to long-term maintenance. The establishment of behaviors that will be maintained in the absence of external rewards in children and youth is certainly desirable but may prove to be a practical difficulty. The consequences for failure to comply on a regular basis are too far removed, while the benefits are minimal. In addition, there are often well-established behaviors that are incompatible and compete with the desired oral health behaviors. It may prove more fruitful to develop reward programs that can be established as a regular feature of the environment, yet are inexpensive and practical.

Blount and Stokes (1984) addressed this issue when they evaluated the effectiveness of posting the photographs of children aged 6–8 contingent on decreased plaque levels, a program significantly less expensive than other programs that delivered prizes to large numbers of children (e.g., Lund & Kegeles, 1982; Martins, Frazier, Hirt, Maskin, & Proshek, 1973). A multiple baseline design across two classrooms was used to assess the effectiveness of a feedback condition alone, where the children were told the location of plaque on their teeth, compared with a feedback plus photo condition. In this latter condition, Simplified Oral Hygiene Index (OHI-S) plaque scores were taken on the average of every two days. Children whose plaque scores were below a 1.0 criterion had their pictures posted on a "Better Brushers" poster board in the front of the class.

Results indicated that the contingent posting of the children's photographs was a powerful and inexpensive reinforcer that could be implemented with minimal disruption of classroom activities. The mean OHI-S scores for both classrooms fell below the 1.0 criterion when photos were being posted. Unfortunately, no follow-up was conducted to see how well these scores were maintained at the conclusion of the program.

Cipes (1985) extended the concept of providing regular feedback and rewards into the home when he compared the effectiveness of self-monitoring with parent-mediated rewards in supporting the use of a fluoride rinse in second-grade children. In a ten-week program, children either monitored their own use of the rinse and delivered stickers to themselves for compliance or had their parents monitor use and praise them for compliance. He found that compliance with the rinse program was significantly improved over a control group, whether it was the self-management group, the parental involvement group, or a combination of the two. Already high compliance levels in the control group (71%) were further increased to approximately 85% compliance with the oral rinse program. There were no differences between the experimental groups. The limited duration of the program (10 weeks) raises questions about the durability of the high compliance rates, however, the study provides a sound demonstration of the efficacy of a relatively inexpensive intervention such as self-monitoring.

Blount et al. (1987) extended the use of parental involvement in the home when they trained 15 parents to instruct, prompt, and then reward their 4- and 5-year-old children for brushing. Feedback in the form of the child's plaque level measured at school using the Simplified Oral Hygiene Index (Greene & Vermillion, 1964) was provided every day to encourage the parents to prompt their children to brush and then to praise them for brushing correctly. During a "thinning" phase, this feedback was given less frequently or sometimes more frequently over an 11-month period depending upon the plaque scores of the children. For example, if the plaque score was below a specified criterion for three consecutive days, then feedback was provided only three of the next four days. Each time the criterion was met, another day of feedback was dropped. Failure to meet the criterion for five consecutive days resulted in adding a day of feedback.

Blount et al. found that plaque levels could be reduced to low levels after a single training session. More important, they found that these low levels were being maintained at follow-ups conducted 3 to 12 months later, without feedback. Thus a relatively inexpensive form of feedback was utilized to promote the maintenance of important oral health skills within the home. The impact on dental caries was more difficult to determine.

Claerhout and Lutzker (1981) used a multiple baseline design across brushing and flossing behavior for each of four different children (aged 7 to 9) to assess the efficacy of individualized contingency management procedures to increase the frequency and quality of prescribed brushing and flossing regimens. The frequency of brushing and flossing was recorded daily by one parent while the other parent conducted reliability checks once every week. The quality of oral health was rated on a scale of poor to excellent using the Simplified Oral Hygiene Index and with Snyder's test, a measure of cavity-causing bacteria in the saliva. After varying numbers of days in baseline, each child was exposed to one or more of the following conditions: disease control, which involved one-to-one discussions of the rationale for good dental hygiene, causes of cavities, and skills of brushing and flossing; stars, which involved awarding different colored stars contingent on brushing and flossing; or token economy, which involved awarding stars contingent on brushing twice a day and flossing once a day. The stars awarded in the last condition could be exchanged at the end of the week for items or activities from a menu of rewards designed by the family and one of the authors.

Results indicated that the contingency management programs effectively produced large increases in the frequency of both flossing and brushing, with improvements found in both oral health measures. In addition, one youth maintained high rates of brushing and flossing when the reinforcement programs were first removed (100% flossing), while a follow-up with another youth revealed continued high rates of meeting the brushing (90%) and flossing (100%) criteria one year later. Note that while the individualized nature of each child's program may have contributed significantly to the impressive long-term compliance achieved, the cost of providing such an individualized program to large numbers of children may be prohibitive in some settings.

Interestingly, Claerhout and Lutzker (1981) found that they could achieve increases in brushing and flossing as well as low plaque and bacteria scores simply by targeting the frequency of the behaviors. Dahlquist et al. (1985), on the other hand, found that when teaching three 9-year-olds to floss, targeting the frequency of flossing was insufficient to sustain low plaque scores, independent of how often the children flossed. In a multiple baseline design across subjects, the children were exposed first to instructions and demonstrations of flossing, then prompts, rewards, and self-monitoring of flossing, and finally corrective feedback and criterion-based rewards based on scores on the PHP-M (Martins & Meskin, 1972).

Dahlquist et al. (1985) found that the rewards and corrective feedback for proper flossing were effective in producing substantial reductions in plaque scores. Without targeting the plaque, however, two of the children reported flossing 100% of the time with minimal plaque reductions. Since monitoring plaque levels requires more effort than simply monitoring the frequency of compliance, future studies should continue to explore the importance of checking plaque levels to the success of a contingency management program.

In general, contingency management programs have proven quite effective in producing reliable and somewhat durable changes in oral health behavior. In addition, these changes have been demonstrated across a variety of oral health behaviors, including toothbrushing, flossing, and rinsing with topical fluoride. Several of the programs appear to offer extremely practical and cost-efficient (e.g., Blount & Stokes, 1984; Cipes, 1985) means of achieving these changes, although the long-term maintenance of oral health behavior remains an area in need of continued investigation. In addition, the application of some of these programs on a larger, schoolwide scale may be needed to evaluate the most cost-effective means of ensuring long-term maintenance of oral health behavior.

In summary, information, instruction, and supervision have proven to be unreliable means of producing sustained changes in oral health behavior and subsequent measures of oral health. Instruction packages have proven valuable in establishing the requisite oral health behaviors, while contingency management programs have added the features critical to the maintenance of behaviors. More specifically, those programs that have established reward features within the home environment, mediated by either the parents or the children themselves, and that have targeted both the frequency and the quality of the oral health behaviors have been particularly effective. Apparently, strengthening oral health behaviors within the natural environment with both corrective and positive feedback is a critical feature in the development of important lifelong habits.

While the quality of the primary preventive studies in this area have improved over the past decade, additional improvements would benefit the field. Until it is proven unnecessary, investigators should measure changes in plaque and gingivitis scores, since changes in the frequency of oral health behaviors may not necessarily produce qualitative changes in oral health. Blount and Stokes (1986) note that standard plaque scales such as the PHP or OHI-S should be used in order to facilitate communication of the meaning of the results. Interobserver agreement reliability should also be conducted with all dependent measures (Allard & Stokes, 1980; Blount & Stokes, 1984). Finally, within-subject designs would help determine what variables are important in the control of individual behavior. On occasions where within-subject designs are not possible, appropriate control groups should be carefully planned to isolate the independent variable(s) of interest.

IV. DISTRESS DURING DENTAL TREATMENT

A national survey found that dentists cite the noncompliant child as one of the most frequent problems in clinical work (Ingersoll, Ingersoll, Seime, & McCutcheon, 1978). In addition, there is evidence to suggest that this disruptive behavior actually increases with additional visits to the dentist (Allen & Stokes, 1987; Stokes & Kennedy, 1980; Venham, Bengston, & Cipes, 1977; Venham & Quatrocelli, 1977). Traditionally, restorative treatment procedures were thought by many to produce anxiety in a child, which then resulted in subjective, behavioral, and physiological distress. The distress is typically assessed via overt, covert, and physiological components (Leventhal & Nerenz, 1983; Neitzel & Bernstein, 1981). Overt responses include directly observable behaviors, which may be assessed via global rating scales (e.g., Frankl, Shiere, & Fogels, 1962; Venham, Gaulin-Kremer, Munster, Bengston-Audia, & Cohen, 1980) or interval recording procedures (e.g., Allard & Stokes, 1980; Melamed, Hawes, Heiby, & Glick, 1975). Covert responses include thoughts and feelings that are determined through self-report ratings of distress (e.g., Melamed, Yurcheson, Fleece, Hutcherson, & Hawes, 1978). Physiological responses include muscle tension, increased heart rate and blood pressure, and palmar sweating.

It is likely, however, that this complex of observed "anxiety" behaviors is a function of specific antecedent or consequent stimuli (Allen & Stokes, 1987; Neitzel & Bernstein, 1981). For example, some of the sensations of restorative treatment may function as unconditioned aversive stimuli (i.e., stimuli whose removal may be reinforcing). Through as few as one pairing with the unconditioned aversive stimuli, the sights and sounds of the dental operatory become conditioned aversive stimuli. These stimuli may occasion disruptive behaviors that, in the past, have resulted in the termination or avoidance of contact with dental situations (Allen & Stokes, 1987).

Within this analysis, physiological and subjective events would not be thought of as the cause of disruptive behavior, but rather as a product of the same kind of conditioning history. While previous research has indicated that the three response systems are not highly correlated (Borkovic, Weerts, & Bernstein, 1977; Lang, 1968), it may be of heuristic value to monitor collateral changes in physiological and subjective conditions. However, it is the disruptive behaviors that interfere with the successful delivery of restorative treatments that are of primary concern to dentists.

V.   IN-OPERATORY BEHAVIOR MANAGEMENT TECHNOLOGY

A.   Information Strategies

Children have been provided with information about upcoming dental procedures on the assumption that they become anxious when confronted with the unknown and that they gain comfort and security or view the procedure as less threatening if they know what to expect. Information can include sensory aspects of the visit such as the sights, sounds, smells, and sensations one may encounter, or procedural aspects, concerning the actual steps that will be taken throughout the visit. There is, however, very little research to suggest that providing information is of value. The paucity of research concerning this strategy in preparation for dental treatment is surprising, given that the tell-show-do approach (Adleston, 1959) is currently one of the most widely used procedures in dentistry (Ingersoll, 1982). Yet, most of the research investigating the effects of information has been done with children facing invasive medical procedures. Reviews of this literature (e.g., Melamed, 1977; Siegel, 1976) have concluded that methodological flaws make conclusions about the efficacy of information impossible. In one of the few empirical studies investigating the effects of dental information, Siegel and Peterson (1980) looked at the impact of sensory information on the responses of school-aged children to their initial dental visits. Children in a sensory information group were provided with information describing the typical procedures, physical sensations, and sights and sounds that they would be experiencing. The authors measured disruptive behavior during successive time intervals via the Behavior Profile Rating Scale (Melamed, Hawes, Heiby, & Glick, 1975). Dependent measures also included 7-point rating scales of anxiety and cooperation, a self-report measure of dental anxiety (Venham & Gaulin-Kremer, 1979), and measures of heart rate. The children were seen on two occasions. The first visit was prophylactic and radiographic. Before the next visit, the children were exposed to the sensory information. The second visit included an injection and restorative work. The results indicated that children provided with information were less anxious and more cooperative than control children, who were read a story about Winnie the Pooh. Children provided with information also showed lower heart rates immediately following treatment; however, there were no treatment effects of the self-report measure.

Although this study suggests the efficacy of providing sensory information, the information actually included procedural descriptions, making it difficult to separate the role of procedure from sensory information. In addition, there was no evidence that the children actually retained the information that was provided or that the observed changes held any clinical significance. Finally, because only one treatment visit was evaluated, there is no evidence that improvements would be maintained across multiple visits.

Overall, there is inadequate research supporting the use of sensory or procedural information to reduce distress behaviors in children visiting the dentist. This is consistent with the findings by Schultheis, Peterson, and Selby (1987), who found conflicting support for the use of the informational strategies in preparation for stressful medical procedures. They conclude that support for information presentation rests more in clinical experience than in published research findings. One might predict a minimal response to information strategies, particularly with children, since the effectiveness of information seems to rely on rules or descriptions of contingencies to control behavior (e.g., "While you are here X will happen and you will feel Y"). If the child has formulated incorrect rules, based perhaps on what peers have said, then providing information may be effective. Note, however, that because of a briefer learning history, rule-following behavior may be less well established in young children, making information ineffective. In addition, if disruptiveness is more strongly under the control of other, past negative experiences in dental or medical settings, then simply telling children what to expect will be ineffective. It may be more fruitful to explore interventions that directly address the control by prevailing contingencies.

B. Modeling

A preponderance of the research investigating methods of reducing disruptive and uncooperative behavior during secondary preventive treatment visits has looked at modeling procedures. At least nine different studies have shown that, in one form or another, watching another child undergo dental treatment may benefit the observer (Adelson & Goldfried, 1970; Gordon, Terdal, & Sterling, 1974; Klingman, Melamed, Cuthbert, & Hermecz, 1984; Klorman, Hilpert, Michael, LaGana, & Sveen, 1980; Machen & Johnson, 1974; Melamed et al., 1978; Melamed, Weinstein, Hawes, & Katin-Borland, 1975; Stokes & Kennedy, 1980; Williams et al., 1983). The fact that the observer emits the behavior that has been modeled may be primarily a function of the observer's conditioning history (Deguchi, 1984; Gerwitz, 1971). That is, modeling effects depend upon an already established imitative repertoire, where the child has been reinforced for similarity between the form of his or her own behavior and the form of the model's behavior (Bijou & Baer, 1978). In addition, there is evidence that the similarity between the model and the observer and the prestige of the model are important features of the model (Bandura, 1968; Bandura, Ross, & Ross, 1963).

A representative modeling study was conducted by Melamed, Hawes, Heiby, and Glick (1975) in which the effects of filmed modeling were investigated in reducing children's uncooperative behavior during dental treatment. Children 5 to 11 years old who had never seen the dentist before were shown either a 13-minute film of a 4-year-old boy model "coping" with a typical dental visit or a 13-minute film unrelated to dentistry. Dependent measures included the Behavioral Profile Rating Scale (BPRS), a physiological measure of palmar sweating, the Children's Fear Survey Schedule (CFSS; Scherer & Nakamura, 1967), and ratings of fear and cooperativeness by the dentist and an observer.

Results indicated that the group that observed the model had significantly lower BPRS scores than did the control group that viewed the unrelated film. Interestingly, scores on the palmar sweat index, the CFSS, and the ratings of cooperativeness did not differentiate the two groups. While these results are consistent with many of the other modeling studies, several design features found throughout these studies make it difficult to draw firm conclusions about important parameters of modeling. First, many of these studies either did not conduct baseline visits (e.g., Green, Meilman, Routh, & McIver, 1977; Machen & Johnson, 1974) or conducted baseline visits that differed significantly from the intervention visits (e.g., Melamed, Weinstein, Hawes, & Katin-Borland, 1975). For example, in the study just described, the first two baseline visits consisted only of prophylaxis and visual exams by the dentist, while the third intervention visit consisted of actual restorative procedures. Although statistical analyses have typically indicated no pretreatment group differences, the introduction of changes in the dental procedures at the same time modeling is introduced confounds the results. Second, the use of group designs raises the question as to whether the data actually provide a true picture of the individual behavioral processes the dentist will experience on a day-to-day basis. Within-subject designs, on the other hand, avoid problems introduced by intersubject variability while strengthening the likelihood that the design will detect actual functional relationships.

At least two recent studies were designed to eliminate these problems in the investigation of the effectiveness of modeling in reducing children's disruptive behavior. Stokes and Kennedy (1980) and Williams et al. (1983) used children (ages 5 through 9) who had a history of disruptive behavior during restorative dental treatment. An intensive analysis of each child's behavior and responses to live peer modeling, using a modified version of the interval recording system developed by Allard and Stokes (1980), was conducted within a multiple-baseline design across subjects. In both studies, each child observed the appointment of the child scheduled immediately before, and was observed during his or her appointment by the child scheduled next. The Stokes and Kennedy study included reinforcement delivery contingent on cooperative behavior in addition to the modeling, whereas the Williams et al. (1983) study looked at the effects of modeling alone. Both studies found large reductions in the disruptive behavior of the children who observed and were observed. These reductions were considered significant by the dentist and the dental assistant.

Interestingly, Williams et al. (1983) also found that the disruptive behavior of the models, while relatively low in frequency from the outset, decreased further when the children were observed by peers. Thus, at least for mildly disruptive children, being observed was an effective intervention. It is unclear whether reductions in the other subjects' disruptiveness was due to observing, being observed, or a combination. Regardless, the results suggest that a dentist may decrease disruptive behavior by encouraging children to observe each other while undergoing treatment.

While most researchers have focused on demonstrating that modeling works, a few have studied the parameters critical to the success of modeling interventions. For example, an imitative behavior is more likely to occur if the modeled behavior includes some components the observer has already learned (Bandura, 1965). This supports the use of coping models, who present complex behaviors in small steps as they overcome difficulties similar to those to be experienced by the observer. Models who demonstrate mastery of a desired yet complex response without the benefit of this shaping may not be as effective.

Only one study has investigated coping versus mastery models in reducing the disruptiveness of pedodontic patients (Klorman et al., 1980). In a three-experiment study, the effectiveness of a filmed coping model was compared with that of a filmed mastery model and a control film. In the mastery tape, the model appeared happy and cooperative throughout. In the coping tape, the model appeared anxious and hesitant initially, and became less fearful throughout. In Experiment 1, 60 children with an average age of 8 were divided into the three experimental groups and shown the corresponding film. During a subsequent standard restorative treatment visit, disruptive behavior was evaluated using the BPRS. At the end of treatment, the dentist, blind to film assignment, rated each child on a 5-point scale of nervousness during treatment. Surprisingly, no differences were found among the groups.

Suspecting that the differences between the mastery and coping tapes may not have been adequate, a posttreatment interview was added to the modeling tapes so the models could describe what they had experienced. The coping model described his initial fear and efforts to cope via a counting exercise. Although the children reported being sensitive to the differences between the two types of models, again no differences were found among any of the three groups.

Finally, the researchers repeated the second experiment with children never before exposed to restorative dental treatment. Under these conditions, exposure to the mastery and coping models significantly reduced uncooperative behavior during the first restorative visit. In addition, the children who observed the coping model were less disruptive (though non-significant) than those who observed the mastery model.

The results, which suggest that modeling may be effective only for those children lacking previous experience, are consistent with those of Melamed et al. (1978). However, Melamed et al. used mastery models exclusively. In preparation for invasive medical procedures, research showing that coping models effectively reduced distress used coping models who described feelings and concerns at each stage of the experience, and how these concerns were overcome (Melamed, Meyer, Gee, & Soule, 1976; Melamed & Siegel, 1975). The coping model in this study made no comments about concerns or how to cope with them during the actual procedure. In addition, while the children reported perceiving the model as being better at the end of the film, there was no evidence that the children who observed the model learned to cope. Perhaps the "shaping" that appears critical to the success of coping models was not adequately exploited.

Another parameter of modeling explored by Klingman et al. (1984) involves the contribution of active participant modeling. Children between 8 and 13 years old watched a coping model using controlled deep breathing and imagery techniques during dental treatment. Half of the children were encouraged to practice these very techniques as they watched. These children were found to be more cooperative and less anxious, and to have obtained more information from the model than the other children, suggesting that active practice of the coping model's techniques can strengthen the effectiveness of a coping model. Whether the active participation is critical to the success of a coping model remains unclear, as do the long-term effects of participant modeling. The critical parameters of coping models, as well as value of coping versus mastery models should continue to be explored.

Finally, Zachary, Friedlander, Huang, Silverstein, and Leggott (1985), concerned that informational and modeling aspects of films are often confounded, explored the impact of the type of stressful situation to which the model is exposed. They suggested that if the functional feature in modeling is the opportunity to observe how someone else copes with a stressful situation, then the type of situation should be irrelevant. A sample of 53 children ranging from 4 to 9 years old watched (1) a coping model undergoing dental treatment, (2) a coping model undergoing orthopedic cast removal, or (3) a control film of a boy playing. They found that neither model had any effect on the children's ability to cope with dental treatment. There were no differences between the control group and children who saw a model on observational measures, global ratings or BPRS, self-report measures, or the Palmer Sweat Measure of physiological arousal (Johnson & Dabbs, 1967).

The failure to replicate previous research showing the effectiveness of coping models is intriguing. Note, however, that the subjects in this study were observed to be generally cooperative prior to intervention. The failure to replicate may have been due to the fact that there was little room for improvement in any of the groups. So while coping models may be of little use to children only mildly distressed, they may still offer important coping benefits to more distressed children.

In summary, although research has generally found modeling to be effective, there remain a number of unanswered questions about a variety of different parameters that may affect the power and generalizability of modeling techniques. For example, there are still unresolved issues surrounding the efficacy of coping versus mastery models, the importance of different model characteristics in a dental setting including degree of disruptiveness exhibited by the model, the effects of stress-irrelevant settings, the maintenance of modeling effects across multiple restorative visits, and the effectiveness of modeling procedures with age groups ranging from preschool to junior high.

C.   Desensitization/Distraction

Since some of a child's disruptive behavior may be a function of "emotional" arousal, desensitization has been proposed as a promising procedure. Typically, relaxation is taught as the competing response and is then paired with increasingly aversive conditioned stimuli. Two studies have looked at desensitization procedures, one conducted by Machen and Johnson (1974) and one by Gordon et al. (1974). Machen and Johnson (1974) exposed a group of preschool children to a predetermined hierarchy of anxiety-evoking dental stimuli during three 30-minute sessions prior to the first dental visit and appeared to use social interaction as the competing response to anxiety. They found that the desensitization group exhibited less negative behavior than a control group. However, much like Gordon et al. (1974), they provided no pretreatment baseline data, had an inadequate control group, and used global ratings of cooperative behavior rather than objective, direct observation measures that might be more sensitive to important moment-to-moment disruptive behavior changes.

Another procedure similar to desensitization has been traditionally called an attention diversion or distraction task. In this procedure, rather than teaching incompatible responses to aversive stimuli, nonaversive, pleasant stimuli are presented in the hope that they will have more control than the aversive stimuli, thereby setting the occasion for more cooperative behaviors. Researchers have tried presenting such nonaversive stimuli as videotaped cartoons (Ingersoll, Nash, Blount, & Gamber, 1984), television shows (Venham et al., 1981), audiotapes with music or stories (Ingersoll, Nash, & Gamber, 1984), and, in some cases, visual imagery (Ayer, 1973). For example, Ingersoll, Nash, and Gamber (1984) looked at the use of audiotaped children's stories and videotaped cartoons to produce coopera-tive behavior, as measured by the Allard and Stokes (1980) interval record-ing system, in children 4 to 9 years old. They also had the children assess their own anxiety (Venham Picture Test) and fear on a modified CFSS (Melamed, Hawes, Heiby, & Glick, 1975). Results from both studies indi-cated that distraction by itself was not sufficient to reduce uncooperative behavior of children during dental treatment compared to a control group who experienced no distraction.

One disadvantage of the distraction procedure is that it relies on the fact that control by the stimulus has already been established or that the stimu-lus has more powerful control than other contingencies operating in the dental environment. In an effort to establish control rather than rely on uncertain conditioning history, Stark, Allen, Hurst, Nash, and Stokes (in press) presented children with pretaped stories about posters suspended over the dental chair. After each session, the children were asked ques-tions about the story. A prize was provided contingent on being able to respond correctly to least 80% of the questions. While the distractions helped to reduce disruptive behavior initially, Stark et al. found that effects began to diminish on subsequent appointments, even though a new poster and story were presented with each visit. Unfortunately, there were insuffi-cient data to determine whether the reward contingency would have en-hanced the control by the distractions over time, thereby recovering the original reductions.

In summary, there are currently no adequate investigations of the effec-tiveness of desensitization procedures with children. While the procedure may require a greater time investment than other management techniques, desensitization may prove useful with children who, for example, are a serious management problem but are found to fear just one of the dental procedures intensely. Desensitization awaits further evaluation as a reason-able addition to the in-operatory management repertoire.

Presenting "interesting" stimuli as "distractions," on the other hand, is unlikely to provide an effective means of improving cooperation in a pediat-ric dental population. There is some preliminary evidence that the effective-ness of distractions can be enhanced by making attention to them "valu-able," however, it remains to be seen whether such an addition can be made effective, practical, and manageable.

D. Coping Skills

The recent interest in the use of self-control techniques has led to the application of coping skills packages with children during dental treatment. These coping packages have typically included some combination of relaxa-tion and deep breathing, pleasant imagery, and calming self-talk (Nelson, 1981; Noccella & Caplon, 1982; Siegel & Peterson, 1980; Treiber, Seidner,

Lee, Morgan, & Jackson, 1985). The rationale for these treatments is that a child's cognitions about an invasive event mediate the distress the child experiences. It may be, however, that the conditions that set the occasion for negative self-talk and images also evoke distress responses. Therefore, changing the conditions that lead to negative "cognitions" also produces changes in distress responses. For example, calming self-talk and pleasant imaging also function as distractions and introduce behavior alternatives incompatible with distress.

In a representative study, Siegel and Peterson (1980) taught a group of children general body relaxation, deep and regular breathing, and pairing of relaxing cue words such as *calm* and *nice*. In addition, each child was instructed to think about a pleasant or favorite scene. Finally, the children were instructed to repeat the phrase, "I will be all right in just a little while. Everything is going to be all right." It was found that, compared with a no-treatment control group, the self-control coping skills group exhibited greater reduction in disruptive behavior, ratings of anxiety and discomfort, and physiological arousal. No differences were noted on a self-report assessment of distress.

While these results are certainly encouraging, several methodological problems in this study and the other coping skills studies raise questions about the efficacy of packaged coping skills treatments. For example, in the Siegel and Peterson (1980) study, dental professionals rated the control group children one full point lower on a seven-point scale of cooperation and anxiety than children in the experimental group prior to the treatment. That is, the professionals perceived the children to be less cooperative and more anxious prior to the intervention, suggesting the groups were not comparable. In the studies by Nocella and Caplon (1982) and Treiber et al. (1985), no baseline comparisons were made between experimental and control groups. Again, it is difficult to know whether differences between the groups were a function of the coping skills package or whether they existed prior to the intervention. Finally, none of these studies provided measures that indicated whether the children actually used the skills taught during training. Siegel and Peterson (1980) asked the children to demonstrate recall after the training sessions, but there is no evidence that the children actually practiced the relaxation or deep breathing, utilized images of pleasant events or places, or rehearsed the self-talk statements during dental treatment. Evidence of the efficacy of coping skills packages such as these should provide demonstrations that changes in disruptive behavior and distress are indeed a function of children utilizing these skills during treatment.

While coping skills training is relatively low in preparation and implementation costs, future research should focus not only on well-controlled studies of coping skills packages that assess the demonstrated use of the skills, but also on which components of these packages are critical to their success. It may be that simply providing children with the coping skills of calming self-talk or instructions in deep and regular breathing would be sufficient to provide significant improvements. Researchers should also seek to demonstrate the maintenance of effects across repeated restorative dental visits, since children may need to make return visits.

E. Contingency Management

In spite of the evidence that the effects of punishment are short-lived and may result in undesirable side effects (such as aggression, withdrawal, and imitation of aversive procedures), aversive procedures such as the hand-over-mouth technique receive widespread use in dentistry (Davis & Rombom, 1979). The use of punishment will undoubtedly continue in the absence of more desirable, positive reductive techniques, yet there is a paucity of studies investigating positive techniques. Although several studies have looked at the use of reinforcement in combination with other procedures (Christen, 1972; Hill & O'Mullane, 1976; Stokes & Kennedy, 1980), only three studies have looked exclusively at the use of rewards contingent on cooperative child behavior during dental treatment (Ingersoll, Nash, Blount, & Gamber, 1984; Ingersoll, Nash, & Gamber, 1984; Melamed et al., 1983), and one study explored the use of reinforcement during nondental training visits (Allen & Stokes, 1987).

Melamed et al. (1983) matched children 4 to 12 years old across four treatment groups on disruptiveness (BPRS), self-reported fear (CFSS), previous experience, age, sex, and race. Preliminary assessments for group assignment were conducted during an exam involving no restorative procedures. Children in a social reinforcement condition were praised by the dentist when compliant, and disruptive behavior was ignored. Children in a punishment group were criticized for noncompliance and disruptiveness. Children in a neutral group received no praise or reprimands, while children in a combined group received both.

Interestingly, the results indicate that all of the children who underwent repeated exposure to dental treatment showed improved behavior regardless of the type of feedback. However, children in the punishment condition were significantly more disruptive and reported more fear than any of the other children. Across the other groups, children who received clear feedback about the appropriateness of their behavior, through praise or criticism, were more likely to exhibit beneficial effects. While it would have proven valuable to have included some check on the dentists' implementation of the conditions as prescribed, the evidence suggests the importance of including positive feedback in managing children during dental treatment.

In the studies by Ingersoll and colleagues previously discussed, when audio- and videotaped material was presented contingently as a reward for cooperative behavior, reductions in disruptive behavior were significantly greater for the contingent reward group than for a control or distraction alone group. However, the mean disruptive behavior for each group prior to intervention was at or below 30%. According to Ingersoll, Nash, Blount, and Gamber (1984), 30% disruptive behavior or less was considered within an acceptable range by a group of practicing dentists who rated videotapes of children during dental treatment. In other words, contingent audiotaped and videotaped material was found to be effective with children whom a group of dentists would not have considered to be disruptive in the first place.

Allen and Stokes (1987) developed a reinforced practice procedure based on work done with older mentally retarded patients by Kohlenberg, Greenberg, Reymore, and Hass (1972). The procedure was modified and designed to facilitate the development of cooperative behavior in young children during dental treatment. In a multiple-baseline design across subjects, five 3- to 6-year-old children were rewarded for demonstrating cooperative behavior during a practice visit conducted just prior to the actual dental treatment. The children were exposed to the sights, sounds, and some sensations of each dental procedure and rewarded with escape from the ongoing procedures as well as with small stickers and praise for exhibiting cooperative behavior. Following each treatment visit in baseline and intervention, the children were awarded inexpensive prizes for low levels (less than 30%) of disruptive behavior during treatment.

Observations of four classes of disruptive behavior using a 15-second interval recording system indicated that the disruptive behavior of each child was reduced more than 70% following several practice visits. The children also exhibited lower heart rates and blood pressures during treatment. In addition, the dentist and the dental assistant rated the children as more cooperative and less anxious. Unfortunately, an average of over 20 minutes of practice was required with each child prior to each visit. Since dentists are typically paid by the procedure rather than on the basis of time, this sort of time investment may prove unreasonable for most dentists.

While simply offering a prize at the end of treatment was not an effective intervention, the results of this study along with those reported by Ingersoll and colleagues suggest the importance of continued investigation of the systematic presentation of positive consequences contingent on cooperative and compliant behavior during treatment. Investigators should continue to explore how dentists can best manage the immediate contingencies in the dental operatory to increase the probability of cooperative behavior of children during restorative dental treatment. Perhaps reinforcement needs to be provided more often than at the end of a session, especially with very young children who have not yet learned to tolerate long delays in reinforcement. In addition, it may prove valuable to explore programs for instructing dentists in behavior management skills. Like parent training, dentist training could provide dentists with experience in the use of empirically derived principles of learning in the management of children's disruptive behavior, both in preparation for treatment (Allen & Stokes, 1987) and during treatment.

VI. CONCLUSIONS AND FUTURE DIRECTIONS

The promotion of oral health behavior and the effective management of children's behavior during dental treatment have become areas of serious concern for pediatric dentists. In a growing body of research, oral health professionals now have empirical support for the inclusion of recent advances in behavioral technology into their behavior management armamentarium. Investigations of the promotion of oral health behavior have demonstrated the value of combined instructional and contingency management programs in the development and maintenance of brushing, flossing, and oral fluoride rinses. Those using self- or parent-delivered rewards have proven more effective, while preliminary results support the value of making the rewards contingent upon low plaque scores. Future research will need to explore larger applications of these programs as well as means of ensuring maintenance over time.

Investigations exploring in-operatory behavior management technology have found a variety of both cost-effective and powerful strategies for managing a wide range of distressed children. Filmed modeling appears to be most effective when inexperienced children observe and then actively rehearse the techniques demonstrated by a coping model. Filmed modeling presents obvious practical advantages, since it can be presented to children without additional staff present and can be used repeatedly once it has been made. As a general preparation procedure, filmed modeling may be the most cost-effective management technique available. Live modeling offers a unique variation and one with equally cost-effective potential, since the children merely need to observe and/or be observed by a peer. This technique has not been sufficiently studied at this point, however, to know exactly who can successfully serve as models. While modeling may not meet the needs of all children, its potential remains unmatched as a standard preparation procedure.

Once in the operatory, contingent audio- or videotapes appear to offer a relatively simple means of reducing distress in children during dental treatment. The efficacy of this strategy with very disruptive children remains to be seen. However, as a standard feature of the dental operatory, it may provide the most practical means of managing most children. For those children who are particularly difficult to manage, evidence has been provided demonstrating that children as young as 3 years old can be effectively managed without physical restraint or sedation. Although still in the early stages of development, the "reinforced-practice" procedure provides encouragement for those seeking less restrictive means of managing difficult children.

Future investigations in all areas of pediatric behavioral dentistry should assess the extent to which new or modified technology ensures the maintenance of newly acquired oral health skills or cooperative behavior. For example, evidence indicates that the maintenance of oral hygiene may be enhanced through the provision of immediate feedback, by the self or parent. Perhaps children could be taught to monitor each other's as well as their own behavior and deliver positive consequences themselves across a variety of different settings. In addition, the maintenance of these skills may be strengthened through the use of increasingly lean schedules of intermittent reinforcement or through the planned use of natural rather than arbitrary rewards (Ferster, 1967) from the onset of the treatment. Maintenance of cooperative behavior in the dental operatory may require actually targeting dentists' ongoing management behavior across visits, an area that has been neglected in the past. Useful interventions must be demonstrated to be effective over time, since children have been observed to become more disruptive across multiple treatment visits and since many children require more than two restorative treatment visits.

Future research in this area would also benefit from research designs that provide a detailed analysis of the individual behavioral processes of interest. Toward this end, within-subject designs provide particularly sensitive analyses of individual treatment effects. Designs should include objective, direct observations of behavior in addition to or in place of more subjective measures and should also include reliability assessments of dependent measures. Recent improvements in direct observation measures of disruptive behavior during dental treatment have produced systems that now offer several advantages over self-report measures and older, more global ratings of disruptiveness (Frankl et al., 1962; White, Akers, Green, & Yates, 1974). Melamed, Weinstein, Hawes, and Katin-Borland (1975) introduced the Behavior Profile Rating Scale, and Allard and Stokes (1980) introduced a direct observation scale. Both scales have high interobserver reliability (Melamed, Weinstein, Hawes, & Katin-Borland, 1975; Williams et al., 1983) and allow for detailed comparisons between subjects. The observation method by Allard and Stokes (1980) has an added advantage in that it avoids inferences about unobservable events with operationalized behaviors and scoring criteria.

In building a useful behavior management technology for the dental clinic, investigators would do well to explore the effects of the age of the dental patient. Procedures effective with 10- to 12-year-old children may not be equally effective with 2- to 4-year-olds. For example, very young children may have more limited imitative repertoires than older children. In fact, several of the modeling studies have found differential effectiveness depending upon the age of the child. In addition, behaviors that are topographically similar in different age children (e.g., disruptiveness) may actually be under the control of very different variables, suggesting the efficacy of different procedures at different ages.

Investigators should also look at the social validity of their procedures. Problems of social importance are determined through value judgments made by relevant consumers. In pediatric dentistry, the consumers are the dentists, dental assistants, and oral health educators who have identified disruptiveness and/or noncompliance with dental health regimens as important problems. Consequently, researchers should be determining the validity of the behavior change introduced by their procedures by assessing the relationship between those changes (measured via direct observation methods or observed changes in oral health) and value-judgment ratings of the dental health professionals.

It is encouraging that behavioral technology has been and continues to be applied successfully to the management of children in pediatric dentistry (Ingersoll, 1982). Behavior analysis has much more to offer, however, providing investigators conduct functional analyses of the target behaviors they have selected. In addition, behavioral investigators should provide a conceptual framework within which the technology they have examined can be understood. These strategies will promote the development and application of new and contextually appropriate technology to pediatric dentistry management needs.

REFERENCES

Adelson, R., & Goldfried, M. R. (1970). Modeling and the fearful child patient. *Journal of Dentistry for Children, 37*, 476–489.

Adleston, H. K. (1959). Child patient training. *Fortnightly Review of the Chicago Dental Society, 38*, 7.

Albino, J. E. (1978). Evaluation of three approaches to changing dental hygiene behaviors. *Journal of Preventive Dentistry, 5*(6), 4–10.

Albino, J. E., Juliano, D. B., & Slakter, M. J. (1977). Effects of an instructional-motivational program on plaque and gingivitis in adolescents. *Journal of Public Health Dentistry, 37* (4), 281–289.

Allard, G. B., & Stokes, T. F. (1980). Continuous observation: A detailed record of children's behavior during dental treatment. *Journal of Dentistry for Children, 46*, 246–250.

Allen, K. D., Stark, L. J., Rigney, B. A., Nash, D. A., & Stokes, T. F. (1988). Reinforced practice of children's cooperative behavior during restorative dental treatment. *Journal of Dentistry for Children, 55*(4), 273–277.

Allen, K. D., & Stokes, T. F. (1987). The use of escape and reward in the management of young children during dental treatment. *Journal of Applied Behavior Analysis, 20*(4), 381–390.

Ayer, W. A. (1973). Use of visual imagery in needle phobic children. *Journal of Dentistry for Children, 40*, 125–127.

Baer, A. M., Rowbury, T., & Baer, D. M. (1973). The development of instructional control over classroom activities of deviant preschool children. *Journal of Applied Behavior Analysis, 6,* 289–298.

Bailit, H. L., & Silversin, J. B. (Eds.). (1981). National research conference on oral health behavior [Special issue]. *Journal of Behavioral Medicine, 4*(3).

Bandura, A. (1965). Vicarious processes: A case of no-trial learning. In L. Berkowitz (Ed.), *Advances in experimental social psychology* (Vol. 2, pp. 1–55). New York: Academic Press.

Bandura, A. (1968). Social learning theory of identificatory processes. In D. A. Goslin & D. C. Glass (Eds.), *Handbook of socialization theory and research.* Chicago: Rand McNally.

Bandura, A., Ross, D., & Ross, S. A. (1963). Imitation of film-mediated aggressive models. *Journal of Abnormal and Social Psychology, 66,* 3–11.

Beedle, G. L., Henderson, W. G., Field, H. M., & Karagan, N. J. (1976). Psycho-social variables as predictors of an improved oral health state. *Journal of Preventive Dentistry, 3*(4), 17–28.

Bijou, S. W., & Baer, D. M. (1978). *Behavior analysis of child development.* Englewood Cliffs, NJ: Prentice-Hall.

Blount, R. L., Baer, R. A., & Stokes, T. F. (1987). Promoting maintenance of effective tooth brushing by Head Start children. *Journal of Pediatric Psychology, 12*(3), 363–378.

Blount, R. L., & Stokes, T. F. (1984). Contingent public posting of photographs to reinforce dental hygiene. *Behavior Modification, 8*(1), 79–92.

Blount, R. L. & Stokes, T. F. (1986). A comparison of the simplified oral hygiene index and the patient hygiene performance method in an oral hygiene program. *Journal of Dentistry for Children, 53,* 53–56.

Borkovic, T. D., Weerts, T., & Bernstein, D. (1977). Assessment of anxiety. In A. Ciminero, K. Calhoun, & H. Adams (Eds.), *Handbook of behavioral assessment.* New York: John Wiley.

Burt, B. A. (1982). New priorities in prevention of oral disease. *Journal of Public Health Dentistry, 42*(2), 170–179.

Christen, A. G. (1972). Improving the child's dental behavior through mental rehearsal. *Northwest Dentistry, 51,* 223–225.

Cipes, M. H. (1985). Self-management versus parental involvement to increase children's compliance with home fluoride mouthrinsing. *Pediatric Dentistry, 7*(2), 111–118.

Claerhout, S., & Lutzker, J. R. (1981). Increasing children's self-initiated compliance to dental regimes. *Behavior Therapy, 12,* 165–176.

Clark, C. A., Fintz, J. B., & Taylor, R. (1974). Effects of the control of plaque on the progression of dental caries: Results after 19 months. *Journal of Dental Research, 53,* 1468–1474.

Cohen, L. K. (1981). Dentistry and the behavioral/social sciences: An historical overview. *Journal of Behavioral Medicine, 4*(3), 247–456.

Dahlquist, L. M., Gil, K. M., Hodges, J., Kalfus, G. R., Ginsberg, A., & Holborn, S. W. (1985). The effects of behavioral intervention on dental flossing skills in children. *Journal of Pediatric Psychology, 10*(4), 403–412.

Davis, M. J., & Rombom, H. M. (1979). Survey of the utilization of and rationale for hand-over-mouth (HOM) and restraint in postdoctoral pedodontic education. *Pedodontic Dentistry, 1,* 87.

Deguchi, H. (1984). Observational learning from a radical-behavioristic viewpoint. *Behavior Analyst, 7*(2), 83–95.

Evans, R. I., Rozelle, R. M., Noblitt, R., & Williams, D. L. (1975). *Journal of Applied Social Psychology, 5*(2), 150–156.

Ferster, C. B. (1967). Arbitrary and natural reinforcement. *Psychological Record, 17,* 341–347.

Fodor, J. T., & Ziegler, J. E. (1966). A motivational study in dental health education. *Journal of the Southern California State Dental Association, 34,* 203–216.

Frankl, S. N., Shiere, F. R., & Fogels, H. R. (1962). Should the parent remain with the child in the dental operatory? *Journal of Dentistry for Children, 29*, 150–163.

Gallagher, E. B., & Moody, P. M. (1981). Dentists and the oral health behavior of patients: A sociological perspective. *Journal of Behavioral Medicine, 4*(3), 283–295.

Gerwitz, J. L. (1971). Conditional responding as a paradigm for observational, imitative learning and vicarious learning. In H. W. Reese (Ed.), *Advances in child development and behavior* (Vol. 6, pp. 273–304). New York: Academic Press.

Gordon, D. A., Terdal, L., & Sterling, E. (1974). The use of modeling and desensitization in the treatment of a phobic child patient. *Journal of Dentistry for Children, 41*, 102–105.

Graves, R. C., McNeal, D. R., Haefner, D. P., & Ware, B. G. (1975). A comparison of the effectiveness of the "Tooth-keeper" and a traditional dental health education program. *Journal of Public Health Dentistry, 35*(2), 85–90.

Green, R. V., Meilman, P., Routh, D. K., & McIver, F. T. (1977). Preparing the preschool child for a visit to the dentist. *Journal of Dentistry, 5*(3), 321–336.

Greenberg, J. S. (1977). A study of behavior modification applied to dental health. *Journal of School Health, 47*, 594–596.

Greene, J. C., & Vermillion, J. R. (1964). The simplified oral hygiene index. *Journal of the American Dental Association, 68*, 25–31.

Haefner, D. P. (1974). School dental health programs. *Health Education Monographs, 2*(3), 212–219.

Heifetz, S. B., Bagramian, R. A., Suomi, J. D., & Segreto, V. A. (1973). Programs for the mass control of plaque: An appraisal. *Journal of Public Health Dentistry, 33*, 91–95.

Hill, F. J., & O'Mullane, D. M. (1976). A preventive program for the dental management of frightened children. *Journal of Dentistry for Children, 43*, 326–330.

Horner, R. D., & Keilitz, I. (1975). Training mentally retarded adolescents to brush their teeth. *Journal of Applied Behavior Analysis, 8*, 301–309.

Horowitz, A. M., Suomi, J. D., Peterson, J. K., Vogelsong, R. H., & Mathews, B. L. (1976). Effects of supervised daily dental plaque removal by children: First-year results. *Journal of Public Health Dentistry, 36*(3), 193–200.

Ingersoll, B. (1982). *Behavioral aspects in dentistry*. New York: Appleton-Century-Crofts.

Ingersoll, B. D., Nash, D. A., Blount, R. L., & Gamber, C. (1984). Distinction and contingent reinforcement with pediatric dental patients. *Journal of Dentistry for Children, 51*, 203–207.

Ingersoll, B. D., Nash, D. A., & Gamber, C. (1984). The use of contingent audiotaped material with pediatric dental patients. *Journal of the American Dental Association, 109*, 717–720.

Ingersoll, T. G., Ingersoll, B. D., Seime, R. S., & McCutcheon, W. R. (1978). A survey of patient and auxiliary problems as they relate to behavioral dentistry curricula. *Journal of Dental Education, 42*, 260.

Johnson, J. E., & Dabbs, J. M. (1967). Enumeration of active sweat glands: A simple physiological indicator of psychological changes. *Journal of Nursing Research, 16*(3), 273–276.

Kegeles, S. S., Lund, A. K., & Weisenberg, M. (1978). Acceptance by children of a daily home mouth rinse program. *Social Science Medicine, 12*, 199–210.

Keys, A. (Ed.). (1970). *Coronary heart disease in seven countries.* (Monograph No. 29). New York: American Heart Association.

Klingman, A., Melamed, B. G., Cuthbert, M. I., & Hermecz, D. A. (1984). Effects of participant modeling on information acquisition. *Journal of Consulting and Clinical Psychology, 52*(3), 414–422.

Klorman, R., Hilpert, P. L., Michael, R., LaGana, C., & Sveen, O. B. (1980). Effects of coping and mastery modeling on experienced and inexperienced pedodontic patients' disruptiveness. *Behavior Therapy, 11*, 156–168.

Kobayashi, L., & Ash, M. (1976). A clinical evaluation of an electric tooth brush used by orthodontic patients. *Angle Orthodontology, 34,* 209–219.

Koch, G., & Linde, J. (1965). The effects of supervised oral hygiene on the gingiva of children. *Odontologisk Revy, 16,* 327–336.

Kohlenberg, R., Greenberg, D., Reymore, L., & Hass, G. (1972, January-February). Behavior modification and the management of mentally retarded dental patients. *Journal of Dentistry for Children,* pp. 61–67.

Lang, P. (1968). Fear reduction and fear behavior: Problems in treating a construct. In J. Schlien (Ed.), *Research in psychotherapy.* Washington, DC: American Psychological Association.

Lattal, K. A. (1969). Contingency management of tooth-brushing behavior in a summer camp for children. *Journal of Applied Behavior Analysis, 2,* 195–198.

Leske, G. S., Ripa, L. W., & Soposato, A. L. (1982). Post-treatment benefits from participation in a school-based fluoride mouth rinsing program: Results after three to five years of rinsing. *Journal of Public Health Dentistry, 42*(3), 222–227.

Leventhal, H., & Nerenz, D. R. (1983). A model for stress research with some implications for the control of stress disorders. In D. Meichenbaum & M. E. Jaremko (Eds.), *Stress reduction and prevention.* New York: Plenum.

Levy, G. F. (1984). A survey of preschool oral health education programs. *Journal of Public Health Dentistry, 44*(1), 10–18.

Linde, J., Westfelt, E., Nyman, S., Socransky, S. S., Heijl, L., & Bratthall, G. (1982). Healing following surgical/non-surgical treatment of periodontal disease: A clinical study. *Journal of Clinical Periodontology, 9,* 115–128.

Loe, H., & Silness, J. (1963). Periodontal disease in pregnancy. *Acta Odontology Scandinavica, 21,* 533.

Lovdal, A., Arno, A., Schei, D., & Waerhaug, J. (1961). Combined effect of subgingival bacteria as an aid in selecting recall intervals: Results after 18 months. *Journal of Clinical Periodontology, 9,* 537–555.

Lund, A. K., & Kegeles, S. S. (1979, October). *Partial reward schedules and self-management techniques in children's preventive dental programs.* Paper presented at the Second National Conference on Behavioral Dentistry, Morgantown, WV.

Lund, A. K., & Kegeles, S. S. (1982). Increasing adolescents' acceptance of long-term personal health behavior. *Health Psychology, 1*(1), 27–43.

Lund, A. K., & Kegeles, S. S. (1984). Rewards and adolescent health behavior. *Health Psychology, 3*(4), 351–369.

Lund, A. K., Kegeles, S. S., & Weisenberg, M. (1977). Motivational techniques for increasing acceptance of preventive health measurers. *Medical Care, 15*(8), 678–692.

Machen, J. B., & Johnson, R. (1974). Desensitization, model learning, and the dental behavior of children. *Journal of Dental Research, 53,* 83–87.

Martins, L. V., Frazier, P. J., Hirt, K. J., Maskin, L. H., & Proshek, J. (1973). Developing brushing performance in second graders through behavior modification. *Health Services Reports, 88*(9), 818–823.

Martins, L. V., & Meskin, J. H. (1972). An innovative technique for assessing oral hygiene. *Journal of Dentistry for Children, 39,* 12–14.

Masters, D. H. (1972). The classroom teacher: effective dental health education. *Journal of School Health, 42,* 257–261.

Melamed, B. G. (1977). Psychological preparation for hospitalization. In S. Rachman (Ed.), *Contributions to medical psychology* (Vol. 1). New York: Pergamon.

Melamed, B. G., Bennett, C. G., Jerrell, G., Ross, S. L., Bush, J. P., Hill, C., Courts, F., & Ronk, S. (1983). Dentists' behavior management as it affects compliance and fear in pediatric patients. *Journal of the American Dental Association, 106,* 324–330.

Melamed, B. G., Hawes, R. R., Heiby, E., & Glick, J. (1975). Use of filmed modeling to reduce uncooperative behavior of children during dental treatment. *Journal of Dental Research, 54,* 797–801.

Melamed, B. G., Meyer, R., Gee, C., & Soule, L. (1976). The influence of time and type of preparation on children's adjustment to hospitalization. *Journal of Pediatric Psychology, 1*(4), 31–37.

Melamed, B. G., & Siegel, L. J. (1975). Reduction of anxiety in children facing hospitalization and surgery by use of filmed modeling. *Journal of Counseling and Clinical Psychology, 43,* 511–521.

Melamed, B. G., Weinstein, D., Hawes, R., & Katin-Borland, M. (1975). Reduction of fear-related dental management problems with use of filmed modeling. *Journal of the American Dental Association, 90,* 822–826.

Melamed, B. G., Yurcheson, R., Fleece, E. L., Hutcherson, S., & Hawes, R. (1978). Effects of film modeling on the reduction of anxiety-related behaviors in individuals varying in level of previous experience in the stress situation. *Journal of Consulting and Clinical Psychology, 46,* 1357–1367.

Milgrom, P., Weinstein, P., & Smith, T. (1984). The union of dental behavioral and clinical science: Educational and research prospectives. *Journal of Dental Education, 48,* 192–195.

Murray, J. A., & Epstein, L. H. (1981). Improving oral hygiene with videotape modeling. *Behavior Modification, 5*(3), 360–371.

Neitzel, M. T., & Bernstein, D. A. (1981). Assessment of anxiety and fear. In M. Hersen & A. S. Bellack (Eds.), *Behavioral assessment: A practical handbook* (2nd ed.). New York: Pergamon.

Nelson, W. M. (1981). A cognitive-behavioral treatment for disproportionate dental anxiety and pain: A case study. *Journal of Clinical Child Psychology, 10,* 79–82.

Nocella, J., & Caplon, R. (1982). Training children to cope with dental treatment. *Journal of Pediatric Psychology, 7,* 175–178.

Pinkham, J. R., & Stacey, D. C. (1975). Using classroom leaders as models for teaching tooth brushing. *Journal of Public Health Dentistry, 35*(2), 91–94.

Poche, C., McCubbrey, H., & Munn, T. (1982). The development of correct toothbrushing technique in preschool children. *Journal of Applied Behavior Analysis, 15*(2), 315–320.

Podshadley, A. G., & Haley, J. V. (1968). A method for evaluating oral hygiene performance. *Public Health Reports, 83,* 259.

Podshadley, A. G., & Schweikle, E. S. (1970). The effectiveness of two educational programs in changing the performance of oral hygiene by elementary school children. *Journal of Public Health Dentistry, 30*(1), 17–20.

Podshadley, A. G., & Shannon, J. H. (1970, July-August). Oral hygiene performance of school children following dental health education. *Journal of Dentistry for Children,* pp. 298–302.

Public Health Service. (1980). *Healthy children: Children's oral health* (U.S. DHHS). Washington, DC: Government Printing Office.

Ramfjord, S. (1959). Indices for prevalence and incidence of periodontal disease. *Journal of Periodontology, 30,* 51–58.

Reiss, M. L., & Bailey, J. S. (1982). Visiting the dentist: A behavioral community analysis of participation in a dental health screening and referral program. *Journal of Applied Behavior Analysis, 15,* 353–362.

Reiss, M. L., Piotrowski, W. D., & Bailey, J. S. (1976). Behavioral community psychology: Encouraging low-income parents to seek dental care for children. *Journal of Applied Behavior Analysis, 9,* 387–397.

Ripa, L. W., Leske, G. S., & Levinson, A. (1978). Supervised weekly rinsing with a 0.2% neutral NaF solution: Results from a demonstration program after two school years. *Journal of the American Dental Association, 97,* 793–798.

Scherer, M. W., & Nakamura, C. Y. (1967). A fear survey for children (FSS-FC): A factor analytic comparison with manifest anxiety. *Behavior Research and Therapy, 68,* 173–182.

Schultheis, K., Peterson, L., & Selby, V. (1987). Preparation for stressful medical procedures and person – treatment interactions. *Clinical Psychology Review, 7,* 329–352.

Siegel, L. J. (1976). Preparation of children for hospitalization: A selected review of the research literature. *Journal of Pediatric Psychology, 1,* 26–30.

Siegel, L. J., & Peterson, L. (1980). Stress reduction in young dental patients through coping and sensory information. *Journal of Consulting and Clinical Psychology, 48,* 785–787.

Skinner, B. F. (1938). *The behavior of organisms.* New York: Appleton.

Stacey, D. C., Abbott, D. M., & Jordan, R. D. (1972). Improvement in oral hygiene as a function of applied principles of behavior modification. *Journal of Public Health Dentistry, 92*(4), 234–242.

Stark, L. J., Allen, K. D., Hurst, M., Nash, D. A., & Stokes, T. F. (in press). Decreasing children's disruptive behavior during restorative dental procedures through the use of a distraction task. *Journal of Applied Behavior Analysis.*

Stokes, T. F. (1985). Contingency management. In A. S. Bellack & M. Hersen (Eds.), *Dictionary of behavior therapy techniques* (pp. 74–78). New York: Pergamon.

Stokes, T. F., & Baer, D. M. (1977). An implicit technology of generalization. *Journal of Applied Behavior Analysis, 10,* 349–367.

Stokes, T. F., & Kennedy, S. (1980). Reducing child uncooperative behavior during dental treatment through modeling and reinforcement. *Journal of Applied Behavior Analysis, 13,* 41–50.

Stokes, T. F., Stark, L. J., & Allen, K. D. (in press). Behavioral dentistry. In A. Gross & R. Drabman (Eds.), *Handbook of clinical behavioral pediatrics.* New York: Plenum.

Suomi, J. D., Greene, J., Vermillion, J., Doyle, J., Chang, J., & Leatherwood, E. C. (1971). The effect of controlled oral hygiene procedures on the progression of periodontal disease in adults: Results after third and final year. *Journal of Periodontology, 42,* 152–160.

Swain, J. J., Allard, G., & Holborn, S. W. (1982). The good tooth brushing game: A school-based dental hygiene program for increasing the tooth brushing effectiveness of children. *Journal of Applied Behavior Analysis, 15,* 171–176.

Talsma, E. S. (1975). Contingency management of tooth-brushing with an 11 year old boy. In B. Van Zoost (Ed.), *Psychological readings for the dental professional* (pp. 169–175). Chicago: Nelson-Hall.

Treiber, F. A., Seidner, A. F., Lee, A. A., Morgan, S. F., & Jackson, J. (1985). The sex of a group cognitive-behavioral treatment on preschool children's responses to dental treatment. *Children's Health Care, 13*(3), 117–121.

Venham, L., Bengston, D., & Cipes, M. (1977). Children's response to sequential dental visits. *Journal of Dental Research, 56,* 454–459.

Venham, L., & Gaulin-Kremer, E. (1979). A self-report measure of situational anxiety for young children. *Pediatric Dentistry, 1,* 19.

Venham, L., Gaulin-Kremer, E., Munster, E., Bengston-Audia, D., & Cohen, J. (1980). Interval rating scales for children's dental anxiety and uncooperative behavior. *Pediatric Dentistry, 2,* 195–202.

Venham, L., Goldstein, M., Gaulin-Kremer, E., Peteros, K., Cohen, J., & Fairbanks, J. (1981). Effectiveness of a distraction technique in managing young dental patients. *Pediatric Dentistry, 3*(1), 7–11.

Venham, L., & Quatrocelli, S. (1977). The young child's response to repeated dental procedures. *Journal of Dental Research, 56*(7), 734–738.

White, W. C., Akers, J., Green, J., & Yates, D. (1974). Use of imitation in the treatment of dental phobia in early childhood: A preliminary report. *Journal of Dentistry for Children, 41,* 106–110.

Williams, J. A., Hurst, M. K., & Stokes, T. F. (1983). Peer observation in decreasing unco-
    operative behavior in young dental patients. *Behavior Modification, 7,* 225–242.
Zachary, R. A., Friedlander, S., Huang, L. N., Silverstein, S., & Leggott, P. (1985). Effects of
    stress-relevant and irrelevant filmed modeling on children's responses to dental treatment.
    Journal of Pediatric Psychology, 10, 383–401.

BEHAVIORAL ASSESSMENT AND TREATMENT OF PEDIATRIC FEEDING DISORDERS IN DEVELOPMENTAL DISABILITIES

JAMES K. LUISELLI
Psychological and Educational Resource Associates

I. INTRODUCTION

Picture the following scenario: John, a 6-year-old child with multiple developmental disabilities, sits down at a table located in the feeding area of a specialized day-treatment program. His teacher positions herself in a chair at the same table and begins to prepare John's meal. Other children are present in the area and begin eating their meals. John has arrived at school, as he does every day, with food prepared by his mother. The foods include several pureed meat and vegetable items that the teacher must warm slightly before serving. John has a history of consuming only these pureed foods and rejecting other products. Today, John's teacher has decided to place small, bite-size pieces of bread into his meal, in the hope of getting him to eat something different. Because John refuses to feed himself, the teacher presents spoonfuls of food to him while sitting at his side. John reacts today by screaming, crying, and pushing the teacher's hand away each time the bread and pureed mixture is brought to his lips. On several occasions, the teacher tries to open John's mouth and deposit the food. These attempts lead to even more disruption and agitation. After numerous rejections by John, the teacher withdraws the food and prepares a new portion of puree, this time without the bread. She subsequently presents this to him, and he consumes it without difficulty.

Although it is a fictional example, the preceding description depicts one of many feeding problems commonly observed in developmentally disabled children. In fact, some investigators have estimated that 80% or more of severely handicapped individuals present some type of feeding disorder that can deleteriously affect development (Perske, Clifton, McLean, & Stein, 1977). In severe cases, the physical well-being of the child may be threatened due to malnourishment, dehydration, and the like. Since mealtimes provide many opportunities to promote social and language skills, the child with a feeding problem usually fails to benefit from such interactions. Because food consumption is such a basic human response, a condition of inadequate feeding is extremely anxiety-provoking for professionals and parents who must care for the child. Finally, some children may be denied access to special education and therapeutic service settings because such programs are ill equipped to treat those with difficult feeding disorders.

The effective management of feeding problems, like other maladaptive behaviors, requires a determination of the causes of the presenting disorder and implementation of a systematic, individually tailored treatment plan. Over the past decade, behavior analysis and therapy techniques have been utilized with increasing frequency as a methodology to assess and treat feeding disorders of developmentally disabled children. Overall, a behavioral therapeutic approach may be viewed from three preventive perspectives (Luiselli, 1987b; Masek, Epstein, & Russo, 1981). In the area of *tertiary prevention*, procedures are applied to manage a present affliction or pathological condition. For example, children who are underweight and malnourished due to problems of food refusal or chronic rumination require therapeutic intervention to overcome these physical maladies and restore health. *Secondary prevention* may be conceptualized as behavioral risk reduction. Efforts in this regard seek to eliminate behaviors that are health-threatening. As related to feeding disorders, examples of secondary prevention would include increasing the quantity and variety of foods consumed by children who eat small amounts or display extreme selectivity. The third area, *primary prevention*, consists of interventions designed to prevent the development of illness or pathological risk factor. Teaching parents proper feeding techniques for children who have been sustained initially at birth via parenteral hyperalimentation and enteral feedings represents one focus of primary prevention.

This chapter provides a critical review of the behavioral assessment and treatment of pediatric feeding disorders in developmental disabilities. It begins with a description of several feeding difficulties commonly encountered among disabled children and the undesirable effects associated with these problems. This is followed by a discussion of organic and nonorganic influences on maladaptive feeding behavior. The importance of determining these controlling influences through functional assessment methodology is stressed. Research studies are then examined relevant to five consummatory disorders: (1) food refusal and selectivity, (2) self-feeding deficits, (3) improper pacing, (4) mealtime behavior problems, and (5) rumination and vomiting. Obesity in developmentally handicapped persons, although a food-related problem, is not covered in the chapter since it has been examined extensively in several exemplary reviews (Fox, Meyer, & Rotatori, 1989; Fox, Switzky, Rotatori, & Vitkus, 1982).

II. CLASSIFICATION OF FEEDING DISORDERS

The third edition of the *Diagnostic and Statistical Manual of Mental Disorders* (DSM-III; American Psychiatric Association, 1980) lists anorexia nervosa, bulimia, pica, rumination disorder of infancy, and atypical eating disorder under the category of "Eating Disorders." Failure-to-thrive, a condition of "inappropriately slow weight gain in infancy without obvious cause" (Mitchell, Gorrell, & Greenburg, 1980, p. 971), is included under the DSM-III category of "Reactive Attachment Disorder in Infancy." The categories of "Specific Developmental Disorders" and "Pervasive Developmental Disorders" do not include diagnostic criteria related to feeding problems.

The developmental syndrome of failure-to-thrive deserves additional comment. A diagnosis of failure-to-thrive is commonly applied to an infant who falls below the third percentile in weight (but not necessarily in height or head circumference) during the span of birth to two years (Roberts & Maddux, 1982). A distinction is usually made between organic and nonorganic failure-to-thrive, although questions as to the clinical relevance of this dichotomy have arisen in recent years (Bithoney, 1987). Organic etiologies consist of food allergies, endocrine dysfunction, malabsorption, and chronic infections. Nonorganic influences include neglect, maternal deprivation, and other disturbances in the nurturing relationship between infant and caregivers. In effect, failure-to-thrive represents an *outcome* stemming from behavioral excesses and deficits, which may be a function of physical and/or psychosocial causes.

Feeding disorders among developmentally handicapped children can be defined by response typography and the resulting detrimental effects. Specific categories of dysfunction are described below.

Food refusal and selectivity. The problem of *food refusal* is characterized by near-total rejection of edible substances. The child presenting with food refusal may ingest only liquid from a bottle or a single food item such as pureed baby food. All other foods are avoided and attempts to induce consumption of these items usually result in extreme agitation, distress, and tantrumous behavior. Many children with a refusal problem will mouth nonedible objects but virtually never do so with a food product. Food acceptance, when it does occur, tends to be under very restricted stimulus control. To illustrate, a child who ingests baby food from a bottle may refuse consumption of the same product if it is presented on a spoon.

The child who displays *food selectivity* eats only certain types of food. Some children may consume substances such as cottage cheese, macaroni, and pureed vegetables but reject foods of greater texture and composition. Conversely, other children may refuse soft foods and show a preference for "crunchy" items such as chips and fried potatoes. Selectivity can also extend to certain classes of foods, as in the case of a child who readily consumes all varieties of vegetables but avoids meat products. Finally, some children may even evince selectivity within a food group. For example, I have seen children who will consume only one type of cold cereal or a particular brand of cold cuts.

The primary ill effect from refusal and selectivity problems is chronic malnourishment. Since the child does not consume a sufficient variety of foods, many essential nutrients are missing from the diet. As a result, physical growth and development is compromised. Bowel functioning may also be adversely affected, particularly when only dairy products or semisoft substances are ingested.

Limited food intake. Children presenting with limited food intake consume small portions of their meals. A child with this problem may readily accept a variety of foods with varying textures but only eats a small amount of each item. Thus the difficulty is not one of selective eating, but rather very limited consumption. Like the problems of food selectivity and refusal, the major ill effect from limited food intake is potential malnourishment. Overall, growth and weight gain can be seriously affected as a result of poor nutritional consumption.

Self-feeding deficits. Palmer and Horn (1978) report that out of 500 patients seen at a nutrition clinic over a four-year period, 8% had self-feeding deficiencies. The definition of self-feeding used herein is that the child locates, transports, and inserts food into the mouth independently, using an appropriate utensil or hands (for "finger foods" such as chips, pieces of fruit, or sandwiches). In some cases, a self-feeding deficit can present itself in combination with food selectivity, for example, a child who self-feeds only when preferred food is presented. Other children never feed themselves, regardless of the type of food made available to them. Still others will accept and consume most food items if they are fed by another person; if required to self-feed, these children will not eat. Another subgroup of self-feeding deficits includes children who attempt to feed themselves, and do not evince selective food preferences, but lack requisite feeding skills. These children may eat with their hands instead of utensils, place their mouths directly onto plates, or spill liquids from glasses.

Children who do not self-feed or who do so infrequently or under select conditions must be fed by others to ensure proper food intake. This requirement places demands on caregivers and makes it difficult to integrate the child into group mealtime arrangements. Frequently, the meal format for the child who does not self-feed becomes one in which spoonful after spoonful of food is presented in rapid succession, with minimal social interaction or attempts to encourage desirable eating behaviors.

Improper pacing. Children with pacing problems are generally capable of self-feeding and do not demonstrate food aversion. Instead, it is the *rate* of consumption that is problematic. The pacing difficulties may present themselves as either excessively rapid or slow feeding. In cases of rapid eating, the child "shovels" food into his or her mouth in repetitive fashion, often without regard to utensil use. Food is frequently swallowed without adequate chewing. Extremely slow feeding occurs as prolonged latencies between bites.

Pacing problems as a whole present a major difficulty with regard to caregiver supervision, since an attending adult must usually be present at meals to prompt an acceptable rate of consumption. Very rapid eaters who do not chew properly can choke on their food and, at times, induce vomiting. When children eat at a very slow pace, they ingest only a limited amount of food if time constraints are placed on their meals. When such limitations are not imposed, the time to complete a meal is usually quite lengthy. This effect, in turn, makes it difficult to schedule meals, ensure consistent supervision, and arrange group mealtime formats.

Mealtime behavior problems. The occurrence of problem behaviors during meals is often a secondary feature of children who present with many of the aforementioned feeding disorders. Tantrumous behavior is perhaps the most frequently encountered problem and is usually manifested by the child crying, screaming, and becoming highly agitated. Aggression and self-injury may also occur within the context of a tantrum. Other common responses include the child's throwing utensils, spilling food, tipping furniture, and getting out of his or her seat. In many cases, such behaviors are displayed when a child is confronted with a change in some previously established routine (e.g., being presented with a different type of food) or if particular demands are introduced.

Problem behaviors during meals obviously interfere with the implementation of feeding programs. Furthermore, the occurrence of highly disruptive behavior severely limits opportunities to encourage useful social and language skills. The management of problem behaviors within the context of meals is often a necessary first step before actual feeding intervention is initiated.

Rumination and vomiting. Rumination is defined typically as the *deliberate* regurgitation of previously consumed food into the mouth. Singh (1981) indicates that it is the volitional inducement of rumination that differentiates it from involuntary regurgitation, in which a physical cause is usually implicated. Developmentally disabled persons who ruminate usually do so by inserting fingers into the mouth or engaging in thrusting tongue movements. When emesis occurs, the vomitus is then reswallowed or allowed to drool from the mouth. Vomiting, in contrast to rumination, consists of bringing up ingested food without attempts to reconsume the gastric contents. This disorder is sometimes referred to as "psychogenic" or projectile vomiting.

Rumination and vomiting can lead to numerous ill effects, including dehydration, weight loss, electrolyte imbalance, and malnutrition. Mortality rates among ruminating infants ranges from 12% to 50% (Gaddini & Gaddini, 1959; Kanner, 1957; Sajwaj, Libet, & Agras, 1974). In addition to these physical maladies, social development can also be affected adversely. It is common, for example, for peers and adults to avoid a child who vomits due to the presence of vomitus and its unappealing sensory features. As a result, the child fails to benefit from desirable social interactions.

III. ETIOLOGY OF FEEDING DISORDERS

Both organic and nonorganic factors can influence the emergence and maintenance of a feeding disorder. As discussed subsequently in this section, many feeding problems are multiply determined by the interaction of organic and nonorganic variables.

A. Organic Influences

Neuromuscular causes. Certain congenital disorders such as cerebral palsy involve various types of oral-motor dysfunction that can affect feeding responses. Problems of pathological tongue and jaw thrusting make it difficult to insert food or a utensil into the mouth. Similarly, an abnormal tonic bite reflex causes a strong closure of the jaw during oral stimulation. Children with weak or insufficient sucking responses are unable to maintain closure around a nipple in addition to demonstrating an arrhythmic sucking pattern. The ability to swallow effectively can also be affected by neuromuscular deficits. In cases of very slow swallowing, the latency between bites is quite prolonged, as the child tends to store food in the mouth without active chewing. With passive swallowing, food is maintained in the mouth and allowed to flow into the esophagus. Passive swallowers usually extend their heads in an upward direction to facilitate the swallowing motion.

Congenital dysfunction of the neuromuscular system can also affect postural responses and fine-motor hand skills that, in turn, interfere with self-feeding. Hypotonia within the neck and upper torso produces an inability to maintain an erect body position so that food cannot be transported into, or contained within, the mouth. The presence of flaccid muscle tone in the extremities makes the grasping and holding of utensils difficult. Similarly, spasticity in arms and hands results in motor incoordination that can impede voluntary movements.

Other neuromuscular deficiencies related to oral-motor functioning can occur as the sequelae to prolonged periods of artificial feeding during neonatal development. Many infants who are sustained through central line and/or gastrostomy tube feedings fail to develop sufficient suck/swallow responses. Because of inadequate strength in the oral musculature, later acceptance of liquids and solid foods is severely compromised. Another common view is that when infants are exposed to extended periods of nonoral feeding, they do not experience certain critical and sensative developmental milestones related to oral ingestion (Illingworth & Lister, 1964). As a result, these children never learn to eat or experience eating as a pleasurable event.

Anatomical causes. Various physiological or "structural" anomalies represent another common organically based determinant of feeding disorders. Children with cleft lip and/or palate, as an example, are unable to control the intake of food and liquid effectively during feeding due to problems of sucking and swallowing (Blackman, 1983). Cleft disorders are complicated further by the presence of faulty tooth alignment (malocclusion). Youngsters afflicted with short-gut syndrome must usually undergo surgical repair before sufficient oral ingestion can be established (Linscheid, Tarnowski, Rasnake, & Brams, 1987). My own clinical experiences include several pediatric feeding disorders related to distinct physical abnormalities. One case involved a 3-year-old child who was born with a very small opening in her esophagus (esophageal stricture) and whose only form of oral ingestion was liquid. A second child presented with food refusal stemming from a congenital malformation in which a large vein was wrapped around her esophagus. In a third case, a 2-year-old child rejected most solid foods prior to surgery for the removal of chronically enlarged adenoids, a condition that seriously impeded her breathing. Following the initial postsurgical recovery, she began consuming a wide variety of solid foods and eventually learned to feed herself.

Physical disease and metabolic disorders. Feeding difficulties are often associated with conditions such as congenital heart disease and cystic fibrosis. Various food allergies and intolerances are similarly involved. The large number of other possible medical factors includes malabsorption, chronic infection, renal dysfunction, and endocrine disturbances (Roberts & Maddux, 1982).

B. Nonorganic Influences

Nonorganic etiologies relate to dysfunctional interpersonal interactions and behavioral mismanagement that occur during meals. One such illustration is the concept of environmentally based growth failure or nonorganic failure-to-thrive (NOFTT). Several authors, for example, have reviewed various environmental, social, maternal, and familial factors commonly associated with a diagnosis of NOFTT (Drotar, Malone, Negray, & Dennstedt, 1981; Roberts & Maddux, 1982). *Physical/emotional* problems such as depression, a sense of loneliness, and low self-esteem can affect how a parent responds to and nurtures the child during feeding. These and similar personality characteristics often cause the parent to misperceive important infant cues or to fail to provide sufficient stimulation. *Educational* influences generally consist of improper feeding techniques that stem from a parent's poor or limited understanding of the child's developmental needs. Thus some parents may lack knowledge of nutritional requirements, make poor food choices, or engage in undesirable strategies such as forced-feeding efforts. Among *environmental* factors are a host of familial stressors that affect the feeding situation. These include chronic family illness, separation, financial constraints, and an impoverished home environment. Some children, therefore, may not receive nutritionally adequate meals or may have their meals terminated abruptly due to time demands of other family members. It should be noted that although the preceding discussion has focused on nonorganic determinants of failure-to-thrive and the particular involvement of parental (primarily maternal) influences, these nonorganic variables play a role in many other feeding disturbances and the behavior of various caregivers (e.g., therapy aides in a residential treatment facility).

Behavioral mismanagement during meals concerns the relationship between child feeding responses and the contingent consequences of caregivers. The study of operant contingencies, of course, is the foundation of applied behavior-analytic methodology. Within the feeding situation, the contingent response to mealtime behaviors can be *positively or negatively reinforcing* (Iwata, Riordan, Wohl, & Finney, 1982). Positive reinforcement operates in situations such as those in which a child is given preferred foods when he or she refuses to eat less preferred meals or a parent constantly attends to a child's misbehavior at the table. With negative reinforcement, the particular behavior results in the termination or avoidance of an undesired situation. A child who resists the requirements of self-feeding by throwing utensils or pushing the plate away may eventually be fed by another person. The feeding problems in this example are reinforced because being fed by another person removes the undesired (demand) condition.

C. Interaction of Organic and Nonorganic Influences

Many feeding disorders develop initially and/or are maintained subsequently by the interaction between organic and nonorganic factors. This interplay is perhaps best demonstrated by the concept of *conditioned aversion*. Consider, for example, a young handicapped child whose neonatal history included a prolonged period of gastrostomy tube feeding. Later efforts to feed this child orally result in choking and vomiting. Each time attempts are made to remove the system of enteral feeding, the child reacts with extreme agitation, crying, resistance, and rejection of orally presented foods or liquid. Artificial feedings must then be reinstated to ensure proper nourishment.

In the preceding example, the physical distress associated with oral ingestion for this child (choking, vomiting) establishes the feeding situation as an extremely aversive event. Food presentation, normally a neutral stimulus, acquires conditioned aversive properties and, as a result, elicits fear, anxiety, and emotional disturbance whenever it is encountered. Removal of the provoking stimulus upon distress subsequently reinforces the preceding food refusal. In this and similar cases, both respondent and instrumental learning interact concurrently.

IV. ASSESSMENT

The behavioral assessment of feeding disorders entails several interrelated functions: (1) pretreatment screening, (2) objective clinical measurement, (3) determination of functionally controlling variables, and (4) evaluation of treatment process and outcome.

A. Pretreatment Screening

Gathering information concerning the history of a child's feeding problem is the initial step toward designing a formalized assessment protocol. The primary goal is to determine the natural history of the disorder and its present status. The most common method in this regard is for the clinician

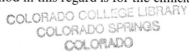

to interview the child's parents or caregivers. Linscheid and Rasnake (1986) suggest use of a standardized inventory that poses a series of objective questions aimed at defining the existing problem. For example, asking the respondent to list foods the child currently consumes and those he or she regularly rejects will identify difficulties of food selectivity and refusal. These authors also recommend obtaining information on the location and duration of meals. Details such as seating arrangements, persons present, and time allotted for feeding can reveal important sources of stimulus control possibly associated with the problem behavior.

A screening inventory should also ask the respondent to check off specific overt behaviors that occur regularly during meals. Various problem responses (throwing food, tantrums), emotional reactions (crying, screaming), and feeding "styles" (use of utensils, "finger feeding") should be included. Estimates of the amount of food consumed at daily meals will help determine whether differences in the child's levels of hunger account for within- or between-meal variability (Iwata et al., 1982). Finally, those responsible for feeding the child should be asked to specify previous and ongoing strategies employed during meals.

B. Objective Clinical Measurement

In order to verify the therapeutic effects from a feeding intervention, objective measurement of relevant clinical behaviors must be undertaken. Ideally, multiple measures should be obtained across several categories of assessment.

Indirect measures. Indices such as body weight, caloric intake, or grams of food consumed serve as indirect outcome measures of treatment (Iwata et al., 1982). Determining the weight of a malnourished child with chronic food refusal before, during, and following intervention may show that the child's physical health has improved, but it does not account for the actual behaviors that led to the positive result. Likewise, the measurement of consumption by weighing food or converting meals into caloric content are not behavior-specific strategies. These procedures are additionally too time-consuming to warrant implementation by most practitioners. This difficulty has been remedied somewhat by the design of more efficient nutritional rating systems (see Traughber, Erwin, Risley, & Schnelle, 1983).

Direct measures. Direct measurement strategies focus on recording of the actual feeding problem and associated behavioral components. Responses such as bites of food consumed, placement of food into the mouth from a utensil, and expulsion of food past the lips represent dependent measures that are relatively simple to define operationally, quantify, and record during meals. Many measurement formats utilize a frequency-count method of data collection. A measurement of frequency is useful when the target behavior(s) can be quantified into discrete units and is generally adaptable to most clinical situations. Figure 1 shows a feeding assessment form used with children who feed themselves but demonstrate selective food preferences and problem behaviors during meals. The therapist specifies the time (to the nearest minute) each meal begins and ends and, within this time frame, records the number of bites taken of individually listed food items. Occurrences of designated problem behaviors are also scored. By dividing the duration of the meal in minutes into the cumulative frequency of target behaviors, a rate per minute measure is obtained per behavior. Differences in rate of consumption by food item provide an objective appraisal of selective eating and suggest possible treatment strategies (e.g., use of preferred foods as reinforcement for consumption of nonpreferred foods).

When behaviors cannot be categorized into standard response units, other measurement techniques are required. A problem such as mealtime tantruming can be measured by recording the duration of such behavior using a stopwatch. The watch would be activated whenever a tantrum begins and stopped when it terminates. When meals are scheduled for a fixed amount of time (e.g., 30 minutes), the cumulative duration of tantruming can be plotted per meal. If meal duration fluctuates from session to session, a percentage measure would be calculated (cumulative duration of tantruming divided by the total duration of the meal). With the method of interval recording, observation periods are sequenced into brief segments such as consecutive 15-second durations and the occurrence/nonoccurrence of selected behaviors during each interval are scored. Thus an observer might record the occurrence or nonoccurrence of chewing movements by a child receiving treatment for early food acceptance. The data obtained from interval recording are converted to a percentage occurrence per interval measure.

Assessment of child and caregiver interaction. The assessment of child and caregiver interactions during meals enables the clinician to pinpoint interpersonal variables that may account for the development and maintenance of a feeding disorder. The general methodology used to carry out such assessment is to delineate the relevant child feeding behaviors and specific antecedent and consequence responses on the part of the caregiver. The occurrence of these responses preceding and following the child's behavior are then scored, usually via time sampling or interval recording procedures. Data can be collected during analog feeding situations or within natural mealtime settings.

Iwata et al. (1982) cite several caregiver behaviors that should be assessed during mealtime interactions. Important *antecedents* include verbal prompts to eat (e.g., "Open your mouth!"), physical guidance (e.g., holding the child's hand on a utensil), and rate of food presentation. *Consequence* responses include verbal (praise, approval) and physical (pats on

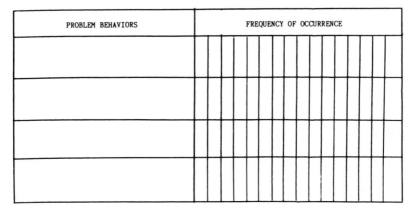

Figure 1. Example of an assessment form used to record the frequency of self-feeding responses and problem behaviors during meals.

the back) reinforcement, punishment (reprimands, disapproval), and presentation of preferred or nonpreferred foods. The basis of an interaction analysis, of course, is to evaluate how these and similar responses are functionally related to problematic feeding behavior. Results of this assessment, in turn, assist in the selection of a treatment strategy. Thus in a case where high rates of caregiver demands preceded food refusal, intervention would be geared toward reducing or eliminating such instructions. The continued assessment of child-caregiver interactions would show subsequently whether the particular treatment manipulation was responsible for improved feeding behavior.

C. Functional Behavior Analysis

The information gleaned from pretreatment screening and direct observational assessment forms the basis of a functional behavior analysis. The task for the clinician is to isolate contingencies that *currently maintain* the child's feeding problem. In Table 1, the five primary feeding disorders highlighted in this review form the column heads, and organic/ physiological, positively reinforcing, and negatively reinforcing categories are the row descriptors. The controlling relationships associated with each disorder appear in the appropriate columns. Selecting rumination and vomiting as an illustration, possible organic/physiological influences include gastric distress, esophageal reflux, food intolerance, and stomach overloading. Positive reinforcement may operate as a function of reconsumption of vomitus or contingent social attention from caregivers. Negatively reinforcing contingencies would affect rumination and vomiting through avoidance or escape from the feeding situation. It should be emphasized again that these disorders frequently have multiple sources of control and, as such, necessitate a very thorough analysis of the child's feeding behavior.

D. Evaluation

The empirical assessment of feeding disorders preceding, during, and following treatment is essential for documenting the therapeutic effects of an intervention plan. One of the major contributions of applied behavior analysis in this regard is single-case research methodology (Hersen & Barlow, 1984; Kazdin, 1982). Single-case experimental designs utilize each client or research participant as his or her own control. Repeated measurement of clinically relevant target behaviors is performed while one or more independent variables are manipulated systematically. Functional control of variables is demonstrated by showing that changes in behavior are associated with these manipulations.

As applied to the study and treatment of feeding disorders, several single-case strategies are available to the researcher-clinician. An *ABAB reversal design* consists of an initial baseline phase followed by the introduction, removal, and reinstatement of treatment. The effects of preferred foods as reinforcement, for example, could be evaluated by alternately presenting and removing these items during meals. With a *multiple-baseline design*, two or more dependent measures are recorded initially under baseline conditions and treatment is introduced sequentially and cumulatively at different points in time for each measure. These measures may include

TABLE 1
Functional Behavior Analysis

Area	Food Selectivity and Refusal	Deficits in Self-Feeding	Improper Pacing	Behavior Problems	Vomiting and Rumination
Organic/Physiological	Oral-motor dysfunction Anatomical deficits	Motor impairment Sensory impairment	*Slow/rapid*: motor/sensory impairment	Response to discomfort or pain	Gastric distress, esophageal reflux, food intolerance, stomach overloading
Positively reinforcing	Exposure to restricted range of food items Permitted to eat only certain foods	Undesired responses lead to increased consumption	*Slow*: sensory pleasurable ("savoring"); social attention (instructions) *Rapid*: increased consumption	Contingent social attention Contingent presentation of preferred foods	Reconsumption of vomitus Social attention
Negatively reinforcing	Avoidance of nonfamiliar foods	Avoidance of response requirements	*Slow*: Avoidance of nonpreferred foods *Rapid*: avoidance of delays in consuming preferred foods	Avoidance/escape from feeding situation	Avoidance/escape from feeding situation

several behaviors of one child, several children with similar disorders, or one child within different settings. The across-settings multiple-baseline design is particularly well suited for evaluating feeding interventions since the daily sequence of breakfast, lunch, and supper meals provides a natural arrangement for experimental implementation. Finally, the *alternating treatment design* is useful for comparing the differential effectiveness from two or more interventions. Different treatments are counterbalanced across stimulus conditions (e.g., a different procedure during breakfast, lunch, and supper meals) and levels of responding associated with each treatment indicate comparative differences or similarities between them. The incorporation of single-case designs in pediatric feeding research within developmental disabilities will be highlighted in the review of clinical and experimental studies that follows.

V. TREATMENT

Many behavioral treatment procedures have been utilized to modify feeding disorders of developmentally disabled children. For the most part, these procedures have consisted of shaping, reinforcement, punishment, and stimulus control techniques. Unfortunately, many practitioners view behavioral treatment as a "cookbook" approach whereby strategies are applied one after another until desired change hopefully emerges. Choice of treatment, however, should be based upon an intervention plan that is functionally determined by the controlling variables of the presenting problem. Failure to do so usually results in a poorly conceived program and unsuccessful clinical outcome.

Following the format presented in Table 1, Table 2 delineates suggested functional treatments for the five categories of feeding disorders based upon suspected controlling variables. Selecting rumination and vomiting as an example once again, possible interventions for organic/physiological influences include dietary restriction, spaced mealtimes, and portion control. Positive reinforcement that operates through the reconsumption of vomitus could be addressed by a food satiation approach. For situations in which attention from caregivers functions as reinforcement, various differential reinforcement of other behavior (DRO) strategies would be programmed to rearrange social contingencies. If rumination or vomiting are reinforced negatively through avoidance or escape from the feeding situation, relevant management techniques would include escape extinction, DRO, and overcorrection. For feeding disorders that have multiple sources of control, several techniques would be combined in a multicomponent treatment package.

TABLE 2
Functional Treatment Strategies

Area	Food Selectivity and Refusal	Deficits in Self-Feeding	Improper Pacing	Behavior Problems	Vomiting and Rumination
Organic/physiological	Oral-motor desensitization Texture fading	Adaptive equipment and environments	*Slow:* paced prompting *Rapid:* portion control	Medical evaluation and treatment	Diet restriction "minimeal" scheduling Portion control
Positively reinforcing	Food sampling Preferred foods as reinforcement for nonpreferred consumption Texture fading	Behavior shaping Stimulus control	*Slow:* paced prompting *Rapid:* brief interruption time-out; graduated guidance	Planned ignoring DRO Time-out Overcorrection	Food satiation DRO
Negatively reinforcing	Food sampling Preferred foods as reinforcement for nonpreferred consumption Texture fading	Behavior shaping Stimulus control	*Slow:* Paced prompting *Rapid:* brief interruption time-out; graduated guidance	Escape extinction DRO Communication training	Escape extinction Overcorrection

VI. REVIEW OF TREATMENT RESEARCH

A. Food Refusal and Selectivity

The problems of food refusal and selectivity have been addressed in a variety of clinical and experimental studies. Research on preferential eating has typically targeted children who engaged in self-feeding or responded compliantly when fed by another person but only with specific food types and/or textures. The primary treatment component has been to utilize these preferred foods to reinforce consumption of nonpreferred items. In other cases, social and material reinforcers have been programmed contingently.

Linscheid, Oliver, Blyer, and Palmer (1978, Study 1) reported the case of a 4-year-old female with spina bifida. Before intervention, her diet consisted of peanut butter and jelly sandwiches, chocolate milk, and french fries. The goals of treatment were to increase the variety of foods accepted and the overall amount of food consumed. The treatment program, applied within a specialized hospital environment, consisted of informing the girl that she could have the preferred edibles only if she consumed all of the nonpreferred food presented to her during a 30-minute meal. The amount of nonpreferred food offered was very small initially and was increased gradually over time. Prompts to eat (e.g., "Eat some [name of a nonpreferred food]") were delivered every minute. In addition to the availability of preferred foods, the girl was allowed to play with toys and watch television if the entire meal was consumed within the time limit. These rewards were withheld if the meal was not completed. An ABAB reversal design demonstrated that when first instituted, the treatment program produced a substantial increase in consumption over the initial baseline phase. However, when baseline conditions were reinstated, the rate of feeding did not revert to pretreatment levels. Therefore, although obvious clinical improvement was attained with this child, it is not possible to determine unequivocally the controlling effects of the program.

Riordan, Iwata, Wohl, and Finney (1980) employed an alternative method to evaluate the treatment of selective feeding through a multiple-baseline design across food groups. A multiple-baseline strategy does not require the withdrawal of treatment and, as such, does not have to contend with potential irreversibility of behavior noted in the previous case. The participants were two girls (ages 6 and 9), diagnosed as moderately retarded, who possessed self-feeding skills but displayed chronic food selectivity. The weights and heights for each child were below the fifth percentile and nutritional evaluations indicated pronounced dietary deficiencies. All assessment and treatment procedures were performed within a hospital setting for developmentally handicapped children. During meals, the girls were presented with several foods from various food groups (e.g., vegetables, fruits, meats) and their rates of self-feeding were recorded. One of the three food groups was treated sequentially according to the multiple-baseline format. During an initial treatment phase, each bite of nonpreferred food was reinforced with praise and a bite of preferred food. The ratio of bites to reinforcement was increased gradually. A second treatment phase was programmed subsequently and consisted of the same reinforcement strategy but this time contingent upon *bites and swallows* of the nonpreferred food. This variation was introduced because it was observed that each child would "hoard" bites of food and later expel the contents. For both children, the procedures of contingent reinforcement for bites and, later, bites plus swallows, were associated with dramatic increases in self-feeding responses and grams of food consumed. Follow-up assessment for one child (6–9 weeks) revealed continued improvement.

The studies by Linscheid et al. (1978) and Riordan et al. (1980) were conducted within tightly controlled hospital environments. One of the concerns with any behavior-change methodology is the capacity to apply treatment in less controlled settings under "naturalistic" conditions. Luiselli, Evans, and Boyce (1985) report a clinical case study describing the multicomponent behavioral treatment of an 11-year-old boy in a residential school program. This child was moderately retarded, visually and hearing impaired, and below the third percentile for height and the tenth percentile for weight. At the time of referral, his range of food consumption consisted primarily of white bread, macaroni, bananas, peanut butter and jelly sandwiches, and milk. He actively resisted introduction of other foods and engaged frequently in mealtime problem behaviors such as stereotyped hand movements, playing with food, and whining vocalizations. The assessment and treatment procedures were implemented by the child's regular caregivers during daily meals. Each meal was timed for a 25-minute duration and upon conclusion the percentage of the meal consumed was rated on a precoded recording form. Under baseline conditions, formal contingencies were not in effect. The treatment program allowed the child to preselect one of three preferred edibles from a picture-cue "menu card" and to receive this item if he completed the entire meal within the allotted time. In addition, he was provided with an interval timer to provide visual feedback on the passage of time during the meal. Finally, staff were trained to withhold attention upon the display of problem behaviors. As evaluated in an ABAB reversal design, this treatment package produced large increases in mealtime consumption when contrasted to no-treatment conditions. At a one-month follow-up, nearly 100% consumption was recorded and the child had gained weight.

The behavioral treatment of food refusal is similar to the problem of food selectivity, with two notable exceptions. First, children who exhibit food refusal rarely feed themselves, and therefore procedures must be designed to prompt acceptance of feeding from another person. And second, the opportunity to use preferred foods as contingent reinforcement is usually not applicable in cases of severe refusal since edibles are not pleasurable to the child. This requires the identification of functional reinforcers that can be integrated into the feeding situation.

Since virtually all children with chronic food refusal display extreme agitation and resistance when food is presented to them, prompt procedures must be chosen carefully so as not to increase the aversion already associated with feeding interactions. A generally effective strategy is to identify conditions that produce nonagitation and then gradually shape approximations toward consumption until consistent acceptance of food is achieved. One method employed by Linscheid et al. (1978, Study 2) involved the graduated presentation of a spoon with a 2-year-old severely retarded boy who accepted soy formula only from a bottle. Access to the bottle was initially made contingent upon the child sitting quietly, facing forward, and keeping his fingers out of his mouth for 1-, 3-, and eventually 5-second durations. Next, he was reinforced for successively tolerating a spoon with food held near his face, the spoon close to his lips, the spoon maintained in front of his open mouth, and finally acceptance of food from the spoon.

Another prompting strategy is to begin food presentation with a substance the child will readily accept and then alter the composition of the food very gradually through texture fading. Typically, the child may ingest only one item and often it is either a liquid or puree mixture. An example of this technique was reported by Luiselli and Gleason (1987), who treated chronic food refusal in a 4-year-old deaf-blind girl with rubella syndrome. Before intervention, she consumed only milk and, occasionally, pureed baby food. The texture-fading sequence, shown in Table 3, began with baby food that was thickened progressively through the addition of coarser food items. Another stimulus control intervention was applied with a 2-year-old sensory-impaired multihandicapped girl who would ingest milk and finely pureed foods from a bottle but refused to accept these same substances if presented on a spoon or from a cup. A stimulus shaping procedure was instituted whereby the opening in the nipple of her bottle was enlarged through a series of very gradual steps. The nipple was eventually cut from the bottle to form a ridge similar to the tip of a spoon. An actual spoon was then substituted and the child was able to accept food from this utensil without agitation or rejection.

Not all prompting strategies to overcome food refusal have relied on a "shaping" approach to intervention. A program designed by Duker (1981), for example, included an overcorrection functional movement training procedure to treat food refusal of a 10-year-old severely retarded quadriplegic boy. Before intervention, he consumed only cereal or baby food and usually engaged in mealtime resistance, such as turning of his head, grabbing the plate, biting the spoon, and spitting out food. Contingent on these

TABLE 3
Example of a Texture-Fading Sequence Used in the Treatment of Chronic
Food Refusal

Level	Food Items Presented per Meal	Foods
1	1	strained baby food (meat or fruit)
2	1	strained baby food (meat or fruit) thickened with yogurt
3	2	thickened baby food mixed with pureed fruit, pureed meat/poultry, or mashed potato
4	2–3	mashed potato mixed with pureed meat/vegetable combinations (chicken and peas; ham and carrots; squash; finely diced fruit cocktail; cooked apricot)
5	3	squash; cottage cheese/fruit combinations; scrambled egg; tuna; hamburger; creamed spinach; elbow macaroni with tomato sauce; fish; diced vegetables with butter

SOURCE: Luiselli and Gleason (1987).

refusal responses, the child's arms were physically guided through four positions (e.g., arms above head, arms at sides of body), each position sustained for 5 seconds, for a total of 2 minutes. Results indicated a significant reduction in food refusal and increase in the amount of food consumed. Ives, Harris, and Wolchik (1978) incorporated a forced-feeding procedure within a multicomponent treatment program for food refusal in a 5-year-old autisticlike boy with rubella syndrome. To implement forced feeding, the "child was placed on his back on a thick mat with a pillow under his head and straddled by the therapist so that he could not escape" (p. 62). Food was placed into his mouth and chewing motion was prompted if necessary. As greater acceptance of foods was established, the forced-feeding procedure was used as a consequence for refusal that was encountered during subsequent training phases to promote self-feeding.

To their credit, both the Duker (1981) and Ives et al. (1978) studies carefully evaluated outcome from the therapy programs by way of reversal and multiple-baseline designs, respectively. It is my contention, however, that extreme physical prompting and consequence control techniques such as overcorrection should not be recommended for the management of severe food aversion. Forced feeding, in particular, is a highly restrictive procedure that is difficult to implement and can produce gagging and choking. In fact, many children who present with extreme food refusal have a history of attempted forced feeding. A primary treatment objective should be to attenuate the aversion associated with feeding, and this can be accomplished best through methods of graduated presentation, texture fading, and stimulus shaping.

For cases of chronic food refusal in which food does not serve as a functional reinforcer, events such as access to toys or preferred free-time activities have been programmed contingently (Linscheid et al., 1978; Riordan, Iwata, Finney, Wohl, & Stanley, 1984). In some situations, the clinician must be quite resourceful to discover and arrange reinforcing stimuli. For example, in the previously cited study by Luiselli and Gleason (1987), only light stimulation and rocking movement could be identified as pleasurable activities for the child. These sensory events were utilized as reinforcers by feeding the child in a swing and, following consumption of specified foods, allowing the swing to move back and forth while bright incandescent lights were illuminated. Eventually, the swing and lights were withdrawn through a standardized fading sequence. Combined sensory stimulation in the forms of contingent illumination and music were also employed by Luiselli (1988c) to treat the self-feeding deficits of a visually impaired multihandicapped boy (this study is described more fully below).

Food aversion is also encountered frequently in infants and young children who have been sustained via enteral support in the forms of nasogastric, gastrostomy, and jejunostomy tubes. Handen, Mandell, and Russo (1986) and Blackman and Nelson (1987) describe intensive hospital-based programs to induce oral ingestion in multihandicapped children with protracted histories of tube feeding. These programs shared several common elements: (1) specification of consistent staff trainers, (2) identification of target foods based upon texture and digestibility, (3) standardization of food presentation, (4) gradual shaping of oral acceptance, (5) precise scheduling of feeding sessions, (6) presentation of child-specific reinforcement, and (7) implementation of consequences for nonconsumption and interfering behaviors. The initial clinical outcome from these programs appears promising, but results must be qualified by the fact that the method of evaluation in each case was a descriptive analysis of pre- and posttreatment feeding behavior without objective assessment data. Clearly, more methodologically controlled evaluations of programs to wean children from tube to oral feeding are warranted.

B. Self-Feeding Deficits

In a review of dressing and feeding skills training with mentally retarded persons (both children and adults), Reid (1983) summarizes the research on self-feeding as falling into three general categories. One group of studies has evaluated methods to establish rudimentary utensil skills, such as eating with a spoon or fork. The second category includes training programs to develop more advanced feeding behaviors, for example, multiple utensil use, wiping with a napkin, and proper chewing. The third area consists of teaching independent and multicomponent feeding skills in public dining locales such as restaurants or "fast-food" establishments

(Marholin, O'Toole, Touchette, Berger, & Doyle, 1979; van den Pol et al., 1981). Among pediatric developmentally disabled populations, the bulk of treatment research has focused on the first two categories, and, as with adults, the primary diagnostic group has been children who are mentally retarded.

The general methodology to promote basic self-feeding responses has consisted of prompt, prompt-fading, and contingent reinforcement procedures. In most instances, *physical prompting* is utilized because appropriate self-feeding is almost never displayed prior to training. O'Brien, Bugle, and Azrin (1972) describe a now-typical application of prompting strategies in a study with a 6-year-old severely retarded girl. When meals were presented to her before intervention, "she reached into the food with either one or both hands, crushed the food in the palms of her hands with her fingers, and with her hand in an open position, brought the food to her mouth, invariably spilling food on herself and her immediate surroundings" (p. 68). The child was taught to grasp a spoon, scoop food from a bowl, and bring food to her mouth by having a trainer guide her manually through each composite step of the feeding response and then gradually withdraw assistance in a backward chaining format. Interestingly, this approach did not produce correct, independent feeding until it was combined with an "interruption-extinction" procedure. That technique entailed stopping the child from grabbing food with her free hand and placing it in her mouth. This combined intervention resulted in a steady increase to nearly 100% correct self-feeding. Subsequently, independent eating was maintained through the use of interruption-extinction alone. However, when this procedure was discontinued, appropriate self-feeding was not sustained.

Several large-scale programs have examined different training methods to develop basic self-feeding. Stimbert, Minor, and McCoy (1977) evaluated the Azrin and Armstrong (1973) "mini-meal" feeding program for adults with six moderately to severely retarded children. The children were prompted to eat with a spoon through physical assistance that was faded gradually from wrist, to forearm, to elbow, to upper arm, and finally to shoulder. Other procedures included social reinforcement for correct responses, overcorrection for feeding errors, and brief interruption of meals (time-out) contingent upon disruptive behaviors. Results revealed that the program was primarily effective in reducing inappropriate behaviors to near-zero levels for all children. Rates of proper self-feeding were variable for each child and were difficult to interpret in that acquisition data during the initial training phase were not recorded. Another feature of this program was that it was extremely time-consuming, requiring two trainers and an average of 173 sessions for each child.

Nelson, Cone, and Hanson (1975) compared the effects from physical guidance and modeling procedures on the acquisition of correct utensil use by 24 mentally retarded boys ($\overline{X}$ age = 13.5 years). Correct utensil use was defined as proper holding of a fork for eating/cutting (with edge) and a knife for spreading. During Part 1 of the study, the children were divided into three groups: (1) *control* (no training), (2) *physical guidance* (a trainer provided assistance through appropriate utensil responses), and (3) *modeling* (a trainer demonstrated appropriate utensil responses). Within Part 1, the procedures were implemented *before* meals were served. In Part 2, procedures remained the same except that they were introduced during the actual meals. Overall, data indicated that physical guidance during meals or physical guidance combined with additional social reinforcement was more effective than modeling in increasing correct utensil use. Premeal training was not effective for either methodology. A subsequent follow-up phase incorporated intermittent physical guidance and token reinforcement, a strategy that was associated with maintenance of utensil skills acquired as a result of initial training.

Problems of "sloppy" eating, messiness, and food spillage generally occur in children with poorly developed feeding skills. Therefore, the most parsimonious treatment approach to overcome these difficulties is to train the functional motor responses involved in locating, transporting, and handling food. The various shaping, prompting, and guidance procedures outlined previously can be utilized for such training. Another strategy has been to implement decelerative consequences when undesired behaviors occur during the process of self-feeding. A very early study in the feeding literature by Barton, Guess, Garcia, and Baer (1970) employed time-out procedures (removal from meal, withdrawal of plate) contingent on behaviors such as spilling food off of utensils, eating food off of table or clothing, pushing food off of plate with utensil, and placing mouth directly onto plate. Programming was evaluated with severely to profoundly retarded institutionalized residents and produced dramatic reductions in target problems with a concurrent increase in appropriate self-feeding. More recently, Cipani (1981) reduced chronic food spillage in a 16-year-old severely retarded female though a combination of differential reinforcement for nonspillage and response-contingent brief time-out (30-second plate removal). It is worth noting that since self-feeding deficiencies involve a *deficit* in behavior, decelerative consequences should be used only in conjunction with shaping and reinforcement techniques to promote skill acquisition.

For the training of advanced and multiple self-feeding behaviors with mentally retarded children, Sisson and Dixon (1986a, 1986c) reported two methodologically elegant studies. The participants in one study were four mildly to moderately retarded youngsters ($\overline{X}$ age = 11 years); in the second study, six children ($\overline{X}$ age = 12 years) who were mildly to profoundly retarded were included. All children displayed behavior disorders in addition to their skill deficits and all were hospitalized on an inpatient psychiatric unit. Four behaviors were targeted for intervention: (1) appropriate utensil use, (2) proper use of napkin, (3) chewing with mouth closed, and (4) good sitting posture. A training program was conducted within a classroom setting, with meals served to the children in a group, family-style dining format. Generalization data were assessed several times weekly during meals in the hospital dining room. The training program, applied in a multiple-baseline design across behaviors, incorporated instructions and modeling of appropriate target skills, physical prompts, and contingent token reinforcement. This intervention was extremely effective in increasing self-feeding behaviors of all children, many of whom demonstrated total skill deficiencies during baseline assessment phases. For many of the children, skills acquisition generalized to the nontraining setting. Only one of the studies reported maintenance data (Sisson & Dixon, 1986a), and in it, behavioral improvements were sustained at levels achieved during training.

As noted previously, the bulk of research on self-feeding acquisition in pediatric developmental disabilities has been conducted with mentally retarded children. Another clinical population that has received recent research attention includes children who are blind, significantly visually impaired, or afflicted with combined vision and hearing loss (deaf-blind). Self-feeding is typically delayed in such children (Van Hasselt, 1987), but behavioral intervention programs to address this problem have been evaluated experimentally only within the past five years (Luiselli, 1987a). Like many of the studies reviewed previously, various physical prompting procedures have been a common element in training programs. Luiselli and Evans (1988), for example, taught a 5-year-old blind child (optic nerve hypoplasia) with multiple developmental delays to eat with a spoon through graduated guidance applied to scooping, transporting, and inserting food into the mouth. In a second study, a 9-year-old deaf-blind girl with rubella syndrome was also taught to feed herself with a utensil by providing hand-over-hand physical assistance through the feeding response and then withdrawing guidance following a backward chaining sequence. In both studies, baseline probe sessions (absence of physical prompts) were instituted during training to assess each child's rate of acquisition. Using a multicomponent program of manual guidance, instructions, contingent reinforcement, and brief time-out, Sisson and Dixon (1986b) successfully trained appropriate utensil and napkin use in a 10-year-old blind and severely retarded girl. Functional control in this case was demonstrated in a multiple-baseline experimental design.

Luiselli (1989a) conducted feeding research with two deaf-blind multihandicapped boys, one of whom did not feed himself independently. He was 10 years old, had a diagnosis of retrolental fibroplasia (RLF), and possessed functional skills within a 17–23-month level. This child readily consumed all foods but only when he was prompted by another person. His rate of independent self-feeding was recorded during a daily lunch meal, first during a baseline phase and then during conditions in which he was physically prompted to eat based upon a predetermined pacing schedule

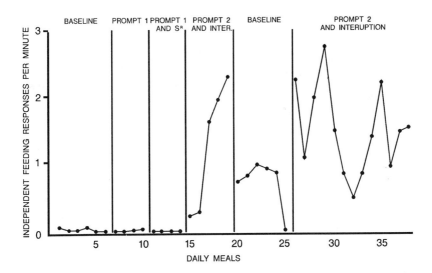

Figure 2. Frequency of independent feeding responses per minute displayed by a 10-year-old deaf-blind multihandicapped boy during daily lunch meals. During the Prompt 2 and Interruption phases, physical guidance to initiate feeding was combined with contingent redirection of interfering behaviors. Source: Luiselli, J. K., "Behavioral Feeding Intervention with Deaf-Blind, Multihandicapped Children," *Child & Family Behavior Therapy*, 1989, Vol. 10, pp. 49–62. Reprinted by permission.

and then with contingent reinforcement plus prompting. Figure 2 shows that these interventions did not increase the rate of self-feeding. However, observations during these phases indicated that the child engaged frequently in stereotypic hand movements during the intervals between prompts (e.g., shaking and tapping utensil), behaviors that seemed to interfere with feeding responses and attention to task. Treatment procedures were then changed to include contingent interruption of these behaviors (see O'Brien et al., 1972) and an accelerated rate of prompting. As depicted in Figure 2, this program produced an immediate increase in self-feeding.

Finally, a second study by Luiselli (1988c) treated a 9-year-old visually impaired boy with Lowe's syndrome (occulo-cerebral-renal syndrome). Children with this disorder must receive daily supplemental nutrients, such as phosphorous and sodium bicarbonate, in their food due to the loss of these substances in the body as a result of tubular renal dysfunction and aminoaciduria. If supplements are not ingested regularly, a life-threatening condition will develop. In this case, the child accepted only spoon-feeding from another person and actively refused all prompts and suggestions to feed himself. Given the described medical irregularities, the child had to be fed to ensure his health. The treatment program incorporated shaping and stimulus fading procedures that required the child initially to hold a trainer's hand while being fed and then, gradually, to grasp the utensil from the trainer, pick up the utensil from a marker on the table, and, finally, scoop food from a plate. The fading sequence avoided agitated behavior and food refusal by slowly introducing self-feeding requirements. Essential to the program was the presentation of incandescent light and music (highly pleasurable stimuli for the child) as contingent reinforcement for compliance and consumption. The outcome was 100% acquisition of self-feeding, which was subsequently maintained following the withdrawal of sensory reinforcement.

C. Improper Pacing

In contrast to food refusal/selectivity and self-feeding deficits, few studies have addressed the problem of improper pacing. However, the research to date is encouraging, particularly since methodologically sound experimental designs have been employed consistently. Essentially all of this treatment research has focused on rapid eating.

Favell, McGimsey, and Jones (1980) studied four residents in an institutional setting with an average age of 14.2 years. Each client was able to self-feed with a spoon, but ate at excessively rapid rates ($\overline{X}$ = 10.5 bites per 30 seconds). The treatment program was composed of two components: (1) physical prompts to initiate pauses between bites, and (2) reinforcement contingent upon pauses of a specified duration. The prompting intervention included the verbal instruction, "Wait," and physical guidance of the client's utensil hand onto the table. Each pause was reinforced with a bite of preferred food. Pauses of 1–2 seconds were reinforced initially (either independently or following a prompt) and then increased to a 5-second duration. Eventually, only independent pauses were reinforced. Subsequent fading of the program entailed "thinning" of reinforcement to a variable ratio schedule, gradually removing the trainer from the meal, and transferring responsibility for the program to on-line staff. A multiple-baseline design across clients demonstrated that pretreatment rates of 10–12 bites per 30 seconds were reduced to an average of 3–4 bites per 30 seconds with programming in effect. The authors speculated that since rapid eating was most likely reinforced by increased contact with food, intervention was successful because it prevented rapid responding while providing reinforcement for the alternative behavior of pausing between bites. Recently, Lennox, Miltenberger, and Donnelly (1987) applied a similar methodology to decrease rapid consumption by older-age mentally retarded persons. Their treatment included reinforcement for specific interresponse durations (spaced-responding DRL) combined with physical prompting of utensil-to-plate and hand-on-lap responses between bites. Although evaluated with an adult population, this approach could be replicated easily with children.

The effects of teacher-paced instruction on rapid eating were reported by Knapczyk (1983) in a study with a 10-year-old severely retarded boy within a special education classroom. The child displayed a pattern of repetitive eating with few or no delays between bites. Proper pacing was established by having a teacher place an individual spoonful of food on an empty plate, verbally instruct the child in the appropriate sequence of feeding responses (pick up spoon, scoop food, bring utensil to mouth, and so on), and provide manual guidance to complete these responses if necessary. Treatment was applied in a one-to-one mealtime setting and evaluated in a reversal design. The results indicate that a near-zero frequency of appropriate pauses between bites observed during baseline phases increased to a 100% level with treatment in effect. In an effort to maintain these results during regular classroom meals, a fading strategy was introduced that consisted of gradually introducing more food onto the child's plate and eventually having him eat with his peers. Appropriate pacing was maintained throughout the fading process and at a one-month follow-up assessment.

Variations of paced prompting were evaluated by Luiselli (1988a) in two single-case studies. One study addressed the problem of rapid eating by an 8-year-old girl who was deaf and mentally retarded. She typically scooped food rapidly from her plate with a utensil while simultaneously grasping food items and consuming them with her free hand. Two treatment phases were introduced in a reversal design. In the first phase, she was prompted to keep her left hand on her lap during the meal and to place her right hand (holding utensil) onto the table following each independent bite. As soon as she swallowed the previous mouthful of food, the trainer waited 5 seconds and then released the child's hand, thereby enabling her to initiate another feeding response. This pattern of independent feeding, guiding hand onto table, delaying 5 seconds after consumption, and releasing guidance continued until she completed her meal. During the second treatment phase, graduated guidance was withdrawn while maintaining an acceptable rate of eating. Now after each mouthful of food, the trainer observed whether the girl chewed, swallowed, and then waited a minimum of 5 seconds before responding again. If she did, all physical guidance was withheld. If she attempted another feeding response before 5 seconds elapsed, the trainer prompted her hand to the table as described previously. Figure 3 shows that both treatment phases were associated with a reduced rate of consumption and elimination of eating with hands.

The second study reported by Luiselli (1988a) differed from previous investigations in that the pacing problem was one of *excessively slow* consumption. The child was a 13-year-old female who was mentally retarded, deaf, and totally blind as a result of rubella syndrome. She possessed appropriate motor skills for self-feeding but typically required in excess of one hour to complete a meal. During baseline phases of an ABAB reversal

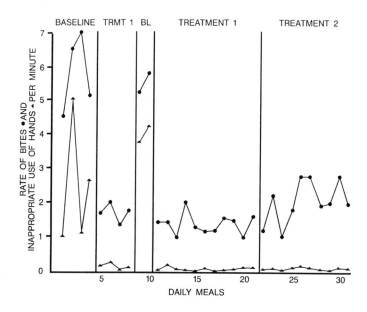

Figure 3. Rate of bites and inappropriate use of hands per minute displayed by an 8-year-old deaf mentally retarded girl during daily lunch meals. During treatment phases, graduated guidance (Treatment 1) and graduated guidance plus assistance fading (Treatment 2) were provided to establish an acceptable eating rate. Source: Luiselli, J. K., "Improvement of Feeding Skills in Multihandicapped Children Through Paced-Prompting Interventions," *Journal of the Multihandicapped Person,* 1988, Vol. 1, pp. 17–30. Reprinted by permission.

design, meals were served in the usual manner without intervention. With treatment in effect, a trainer physically guided the child to complete one feeding response whenever 40 seconds elapsed without independent consumption. As long as she ate independently (i.e., not exceeding 40 seconds between bites), prompting was not provided. This simple pacing strategy effectively increased the rate of independent feeding in contrast to baseline conditions. The frequency of prompting decreased steadily with a continuation of treatment.

D. Mealtime Behavior Problems

Intervention for mealtime behavior problems can take several forms. Since many children react initially to feeding programs with agitation and resistance regardless of the specific eating disorder, contingencies must usually be established during meals to respond to these behaviors. Some procedures require the therapist or caregiver to "ignore" occurrences of crying, screaming, and similar forms of distress by "working through" the behaviors. Other strategies consist of withholding attention, interrupting the availability of reinforcement, redirecting hands, and physically preventing interfering responses. Generally, these techniques can be integrated into meals as part of an overall feeding program. Some problem behaviors, however, are severe enough that they become the primary focus of intervention. For such situations, an individually designed treatment protocol is usually warranted.

Thompson (1977) treated a 6-year-old moderately retarded girl whose mealtime tantrums included crying, throwing food, and self-injury. Because tantrumous behavior appeared to be reinforced by contingent parental attention, a time-out consequence was programmed by either removing the child from the table or denying attention. This strategy, combined with differential reinforcement for alternative behaviors, was associated with reduced tantrums. However, the precise controlling effects from this program cannot be functionally determined due to limitations in experimental design. Sisson and Dixon (1986b) report a methodologically stronger study with a 10-year-old blind and severely retarded girl who engaged in severe self-injurious behavior during meals (hand-biting, skin-pinching, eye-poking). The goal of intervention was to reduce or eliminate self-injury by strengthening an incompatible response, in this case, appropriate sitting posture. An audiotape of preferred music was played continuously as long as the child's hands were maintained away from her face and her head was held upright. When self-injurious behavior or inappropriate sitting were exhibited, the music was interrupted. Under baseline conditions in a reversal design, appropriate sitting posture was infrequent and self-injury occurred at high rates. With treatment, appropriate sitting was quickly established throughout meals and self-injury decreased dramatically.

Luiselli (1988b) also evaluated a method of prompting an incompatible response to reduce mealtime problem behaviors. The child was a 7-year-old boy who was deaf and visually impaired. He possessed very proficient self-feeding skills and consumed all types of food but performed many interfering and disruptive behaviors with his hands during meals. Between bites he typically placed his elbows on the table, waved his hands in the air, moved his arms rhythmically, and flipped his utensil back and forth, usually while vocalizing loudly. In addition to being extremely disruptive, these behaviors interfered seriously with the child's attention during meals. Treatment was implemented by his teacher during the lunch meal in a special education classroom. Contingent upon the target behaviors, the child's hands were physically guided to a position approximately 5 inches above two colorful palm prints that were located on a place mat. As long as he maintained this position between bites, no other form of physical intervention was provided. Teacher praise—for example, "Good eating"—was delivered intermittently for compliant responding. Inappropriate hand positions that occurred during 90–100% of recording intervals within baseline phases of an ABAB reversal design were reduced immediately and eventually eliminated with treatment in effect. The behaviors remained absent when interruption/redirection was implemented without the visual cues and during monthly follow-up assessment.

The therapeutic effects of facial screening on disruptive mealtime behavior of an 8-year-old severely retarded girl were reported by Horton (1987). The child attended a public school special education classroom. During the lunch meal, she engaged in banging of her spoon against dish and table. Further consequences of this behavior included "flinging" food onto others and dropping the spoon on the floor. Intervention in the form of facial screening was implemented contingent upon spoon-banging. It consisted of pulling a terry cloth bib over the child's face and holding it there until the target behavior ceased for 5 seconds. As compared to baseline conditions in which physical interruption and redirection were applied contingently, facial screening eliminated spoon-banging rapidly. At 6- to 19-month follow-ups, the behavior failed to occur during meals even though treatment had been discontinued. Maintenance of suppression was most likely achieved because subjective reports indicated that the problem behavior had not appeared during the period following the study and preceding the follow-up phase.

E.   Rumination and Vomiting

There exists an extensive literature on the behavioral treatment of rumination and vomiting disorders in developmentally disabled persons. Since several in-depth reviews of the topic are available (Singh, 1981; Starin & Fuqua, 1987), only a cursory presentation of intervention strategies will be provided here. This discussion will focus primarily on techniques that have been empirically well documented. Although the efficacy of some procedures has been evaluated more extensively with adult populations, this information will be covered given its apparent applicability with children.

Food satiation. One conceptualization of the etiology and maintenance of rumination is that emesis occurs due to the reconsumption of vomitus. Food satiation approaches are intended to eliminate this source of reinforcement by providing large, and sometimes unlimited, quantities of food intake. Virtually all of the published research concerned with food satiation has been conducted with adolescent and adult populations. The general approach has been to allow the ruminator to consume additional portions of regular meals and, at times, supplemental items such as ice cream or milkshakes. Early reports by Jackson, Johnson, Ackron, and Crowley (1975), Libby and Phillips (1978), and Foxx, Snyder, and Schroeder (1979) all describe positive clinical effects from satiation interventions. These studies, however, are difficult to contrast and compare given variations in experimental design and satiation diets.

A series of well-controlled studies on food satiation have been conducted by Rast, Johnston, and associates. In one experiment, the postmeal rumination of three severely to profoundly retarded young adults was recorded under three conditions within a reversal design: (1) baseline (no intervention), (2) providing larger portions at meals, and (3) providing larger portions *plus* all the potatoes, unflavored instant grits, Cream of Wheat, and/or bread each client would consume freely (Rast, Johnston, Drum, & Corin, 1981). For all three cases, the frequency and duration of rumination incidents remained high during baseline and increased-portion conditions but decreased rapidly during satiation phases. Rast, Johnston, and Drum (1984) also extinguished rumination in mentally retarded adults through food satiation but found that therapeutic effects occurred only when full satiation quantities were presented at meals and not when meals were increased via gradual 10-ounce increments.

The effects of food satiation on rumination, although promising, must be interpreted cautiously. First, the actual source of control from this strategy has not been adequately determined. Rast, Johnston, Ellinger-Allen, and Drum (1985), for example, present data suggesting that the caloric value of satiation diets or possible oropharyngeal and esophageal stimulation may be influential variables. Another concern is that clients who receive food satiation treatment invariably gain weight. Although this may be a desirable initial outcome for ruminators due to chronic conditions of low weight and malnourishment, such interventions could not be recommended on a prolonged basis. As demonstrated by Lobato, Carlson, and Barrera (1986), the use of *low-calorie* satiation diets may be one method for reducing rumination without producing undesirable weight gain. Finally, satiation treatment has been studied only with adult ruminators, and its application with pediatric populations, although potentially effective, has yet to be documented empirically.

Reduced rate of consumption. Whereas satiation is predicated on providing increased amounts of food, an alternative and opposite approach for the treatment of *vomiting* is to reduce the rate of consumption. As indicated in an earlier section, it is important to distinguish between projectile vomiting, in which emesis is displayed without reconsumption of vomitus, and the repetitive regurgitation/reingestion that typifies rumination. The treatment rationale suggested by Azrin, Jamner, and Besalel (1986) is that "self-induced vomiting could be more simply a result of overly rapid eating and might represent an attempt to reduce the discomfort of stomach overloading. If so, slowing the food intake should decrease vomiting, even if the amount of food eaten remains the same" (p. 410).

Azrin et al. (1986) evaluated a "spaced eating" intervention with a 22-year-old severely retarded male who vomited regularly following meals. During treatment, each of his three daily meals was divided into five separate portions spaced 15 minutes apart. Physical guidance procedures were applied to pace a slow eating rate during the meals. This intervention virtually eliminated vomiting episodes. A second study by the same authors examined the identical spaced eating treatment with three profoundly retarded young adults (ages 21–24 years) and also compared this method with a program of food satiation (double portions at meals plus additional bread and milk) (Azrin, Jamner, & Besalel, 1987). For all three clients, the daily frequency of vomiting incidents recorded under baseline conditions increased dramatically during satiation conditions and decreased to near-zero rates while reduced eating rate was operative.

Although clinical control over vomiting was achieved in these studies by reducing the rate of consumption, the authors note that rumination was not similarly affected. That is, once the clients vomited, they tended to reconsume and regurgitate the ingested food. The induction of slower eating, therefore, might be viewed as an antecedent manipulation that reduces the likelihood that an initial vomiting incident, and subsequent rumination, will be encountered. However, whether this outcome is clearly related to stomach overloading awaits further experimental evaluation. Effective applications with children also must be demonstrated.

Differential reinforcement. Positive reinforcement for alternative behaviors should always be programmed when treating any clinical problem or health-threatening disorder (Luiselli, 1989b). Though there are limited examples of programs for rumination that have relied exclusively on the use of reinforcement methods, several studies have documented significant clinical effects and different procedures for delivering reinforcers. O'Neil, White, King, and Carek (1979) successfully treated rumination in a 26-month-old developmentally delayed child through a DRO procedure in the form of a honey-water solution that was dispensed whenever 15–30 seconds elapsed without a ruminating response. Mulick, Barbour, Schroeder, and Rojahn (1980) found that reinforcing a specific alternative behavior (toy-play) while concurrently ignoring rumination was an effective treatment for a 15-year-old profoundly retarded boy. An interesting finding from this study was that reinforcement for the absence of rumination without a designated alternative response (DRO) was less successful when compared to the previous strategy. Barmann (1980) also reduced rumination in a 6-year-old profoundly retarded boy through reinforcement of an alternative response. Because the child frequently induced rumination by placing hands into his mouth, reinforcement (vibration) was delivered contingently for behaviors such as maintaining hands on lap or playing with toys. This intervention decreased both hand-mouthing and rumination.

Because the therapeutic effects from positive reinforcement are often very gradual, careful consideration must be given to the *singular use* of this approach when a child's physical condition is at risk due to chronic, high-rate rumination and/or vomiting. It is likely that most reinforcement-based interventions will continue to be combined with other response-deceleration techniques or feeding manipulations such as food satiation and spaced eating.

Overcorrection. Overcorrection treatment of rumination and vomiting has consisted of two formats. *Restitutional* overcorrection requires the client to cleanse the environmental disturbance caused by the presence of vomitus. Thus Azrin and Wesolowski (1975) had a 36-year-old profoundly retarded woman clean up her vomitus and change her soiled clothing or bed sheets each time she engaged in ruminative vomiting. She was also required to rehearse proper vomiting responses by entering a bathroom and vomiting into a toilet. This combination of self-correction and positive practice produced complete suppression of vomiting within two weeks and therapeutic maintenance one year later. A similar method of restitution was instituted by Duker and Seys (1977) with a 19-year-old profoundly retarded ruminator. Positive results in this study were achieved by having her wash her face, clean the physical surroundings, and change into new clothing as a consequence of episodes of rumination.

The second method of overcorrection is termed *oral hygiene training* and usually entails the antiseptic cleansing of the teeth and gums contingent upon emesis. A well-conceived study by Singh, Manning, and Angell (1982) examined this strategy with 17-year-old profoundly retarded twins who engaged in high-rate ruminative vomiting. Overcorrection consisted of having the participants clean their teeth for 2 minutes with a toothbrush that had been soaked in mouthwash, followed by wiping the lips with a face cloth. Functional control of the treatment program was demonstrated in a multiple-baseline design across participants and daily meals. Foxx et al. (1979) incorporated an oral hygiene overcorrection procedure in combination with food satiation to suppress rumination in two profoundly retarded adults. The oral hygiene technique, like other forms of overcorrection, is made up of several separate components (e.g., graduated guidance, compliance training, response interruption) in addition to the response-contingent application of an aversive stimulus. Therefore, it is difficult to determine with certainty which procedure, or combination of procedures, is responsible for therapeutic control.

Aversive stimulation. The aversive treatment of developmentally handicapped persons remains a very controversial and hotly debated topic. The primary argument favoring such treatment is that aversive methods can produce immediate and long-lasting suppression, an outcome that is clinically desirable when health-threatening disorders such as rumination and vomiting are at issue. Problems associated with aversive treatment include the potential for abuse, possible negative side effects, and poor social acceptability by practitioners. As a result of these and similar concerns, most states have imposed strict guidelines regulating the utilization of aversive procedures.

The earliest reports on the aversive control of rumination and vomiting among developmentally handicapped persons employed electric shock as the noxious stimulus (Kohlenberg, 1970; Luckey, Watson, & Musick, 1968; Watkins, 1972; White & Taylor, 1967). Although the outcomes in these cases were positive, most of the studies were poorly executed, some lacked quantitative data, and most did not establish adequate methodological controls (Singh, 1981; Starin & Fuqua, 1987). With these limitations in mind, claims to the therapeutic efficacy of electric shock must be carefully considered. Furthermore, shock represents the most extreme form of aversive stimulation and, as such, many of the regulatory guidelines noted previously either limit severely or simply do not permit its use. As suggested by Luiselli (1989b), this may explain why, since approximately 1975, publications describing shock-based therapy programs have all but disappeared.

In response to both the restrictions imposed on electric shock stimulation and the quest for alternative strategies, researchers have identified other aversive conditioning methods. One of the first examples was provided by Sajwaj et al. (1974) with a 6-month-old infant who exhibited life-threatening rumination. Treatment entailed squirting 5–10 milliliters of lemon juice into her mouth contingent upon rumination or antecedent behaviors. This intervention eliminated rumination and resulted in desirable weight gain. Additional studies have replicated these earlier findings (Becker, Turner, & Sajwaj, 1978; Marholin, Luiselli, Robinson, & Lott, 1980) while also documenting reductive effects from other gustatory stimuli such as lime juice (Glasscock, Friman, O'Brien, & Christophersen, 1986) and pepper sauce (Marholin et al., 1980; Singh, 1979). Although perhaps less politically arousing when compared to electric shock, punishment via contingent taste aversion should still be considered a treatment of last resort because it is very intrusive and poses physical risks to the client (e.g., aspiration of liquid into the lungs, erosion of tooth enamel, mouth irritations). Such treatment should be attempted only if there is direct supervision provided by an experienced clinician and the inclusion of ongoing medical monitoring.

VII. CONCLUSIONS AND FUTURE DIRECTIONS

The behavioral assessment and treatment of feeding disorders has evolved into a primary area of clinical research in pediatric developmental disabilities. The intent of this chapter was to delineate the essential components that constitute a comprehensive therapeutic approach. Many advances have been realized in our understanding of the etiology of children's feeding problems and the complex interrelationships that typically exist between physiological and socioenvironmental influences. Improvements in assessment methodologies and strategies of functional behavior analysis have enabled clinicians to formulate treatment programs more effectively.

In turn, the variety of intervention techniques has expanded greatly and has been applied to a diverse range of feeding disorders. Overall, research appearing within the past five years has reflected a greater sophistication in the methods of assessment, intervention, and experimental evaluation. These achievements notwithstanding, continued progress in behavioral feeding intervention will require attention to additional therapeutic and research concerns.

Clearly, most feeding research has focused on children who do not present with organic deficits. Similarly, treatments are frequently instituted without concern for basic neurophysiological and sensorimotor processes. For example, children with a history of tube feeding may be conditioned to accept foods orally but without deliberate attempts to promote proper chewing or swallowing. One important goal for behavioral researchers, then, is to extend the application of our treatment technology to more medically based disorders and associated feeding responses. Although limited in number, several studies have obtained promising results in this regard. Sobsey and Orelove (1984) incorporated applied behavior-analytic experimental methodology to evaluate the effects of direct enteroceptive and proprioceptive stimulation on rotary chewing, lip closure, and food spillage of four multihandicapped children (ages 4–12 years). Oral-motor facilitation procedures are employed routinely by occupational and physical therapists, but empirical validation of clinical efficacy remains undetermined. In this study, notable improvements in target responses were achieved as a result of intervention. Pathological tongue thrust was treated by Thompson, Iwata, and Poynter (1979) in a 10-year-old severely retarded boy who had cerebral palsy and lacked efficient sucking, finger feeding, and lip closure. Thrusting was reduced and chewing increased through a program that combined differential reinforcement and mild punishment (gently pushing tongue back into mouth with a spoon). And Hyman et al. (1986) were able to increase oral acceptance of food in children with urea cycle and organic acid disorders, who required nasogastric or gastrostomy tube feeding. The design of specialized hospital programs for the treatment of feeding disorders in handicapped children should provide greater opportunities for collaboration between medical and behavioral psychology practitioners (Cataldo, Iwata, Page, & Parrish, 1988).

The studies presented in this review focused exclusively on tertiary and secondary prevention efforts. Programs to prevent the onset of chronic feeding problems are, unfortunately, in the minority. Much of the challenge rests with the organization of early-intervention settings that deliver clinical services to very young developmentally disabled children. A greater emphasis must be placed on the home-based training of parents by hospital clinics and public health agencies, since the establishment of proper parental feeding skills could avoid the appearance of subsequent problems. Currently, very few early-intervention programs are able to conduct such training.

Behavior therapists as a group have begun to focus more regularly on the assessment of social validity (Kazdin & Matson, 1981). One form of social validation is to measure the outcome behavior of a clinical population relative to that of a nonaffected comparison group. Thus Azrin and Armstrong (1973) found that the dining behavior of institutionalized mentally retarded adults following training was comparable to that displayed by hospital employees. Lennox et al. (1987) recorded the mealtime behavior of "socially acceptable eaters" to determine a criterion rate of consumption in a program to reduce rapid feeding by mentally retarded residents. Data of these types enhance the social significance of intervention by demonstrating how treatment outcome compares to the "population at large." A second objective of social validity assessment is to acquire measures of consumer satisfaction. This entails soliciting the subjective evaluation of clinical results and methods of behavior change from those responsible for treatment administration. In a study on paced prompting interventions for feeding disorders of multihandicapped children, Luiselli (1988a) had caregivers rate the effectiveness, practicality, and overall satisfaction associated with each child's program. Information gathered from such assessments is extremely desirable because it enables the clinician to identify procedures that are acceptable to practitioners and, therefore, have a greater likelihood of being implemented consistently.

Several issues relative to procedural and experimental methodology warrant attention. As revealed in the review of treatment research, most behavioral programs for feeding disorders encompass a multicomponent intervention approach. A combination of various treatment strategies is frequently required given the severity of many feeding problems and the attempt to produce the most robust clinical effect. Nevertheless, efforts to unravel the individual contributions from components of "packaged" interventions should be encouraged, since analyses of this type would suggest the most cost-efficient and therapeutically potent combination of treatment strategies.

Another concern is that very few studies have compared different behavioral techniques (see Nelson et al., 1975). Still other methods and therapy approaches have yet to be analyzed experimentally. Riordan et al. (1984), for example, comment that since many handicapped children with chronic food refusal are sustained via artificial feeding, oral consumption may not represent a very strong operant response. They suggest that restricting or otherwise altering the schedule of supplemental feeding may be one way to manipulate more natural contingencies to promote food intake. By conducting studies on this and other novel approaches, a wider range of treatment options will be made available to the clinician.

Concerning the issues of generalization and maintenance, continued emphasis must be placed on the analysis of clinical change beyond that achieved during the initial course of treatment. Many of the studies presented in this review included assessment of multiple dependent measures in order to ascertain generalization effects. More important, other studies described procedures to promote generalization purposefully through such tactics as multiple-meal training, transferring treatment from professional therapists to natural change agents (e.g., parents, teachers), and conducting intervention within "real-world" settings (e.g., homes, classrooms). With regard to maintenance, durable improvements in feeding behavior have been reported as much as one year posttreatment (Luiselli & Gleason, 1987). Due in part to the policy of many journal editors, more and more studies appearing in the behavioral literature are reporting extended follow-up data and describing deliberate attempts to enhance therapeutic maintenance. Such efforts should be an integral feature of feeding research.

Finally, the ultimate measure of success of behavioral intervention for pediatric feeding disorders in developmental disabilities will rest with the design and execution of methodologically rigorous experimental studies. It is only through the implementation of controlled research that assessment and treatment procedures can be tested adequately and empirically validated as methods to improve the feeding behavior and physical well-being of handicapped children.

REFERENCES

American Psychiatric Association. (1980). *Diagnostic and statistical manual of mental disorders* (3rd ed.). Washington, DC: Author.

Azrin, N. H., & Armstrong, P. M. (1973). The "mini-meal": A method for teaching eating skills to the profoundly retarded. *Mental Retardation, 11*, 9–13.

Azrin, N. H., Jamner, J. P., & Besalel, V. A. (1986). Vomiting reduced by slower food intake. *Applied Research in Mental Retardation, 7*, 409–413.

Azrin, N. H., Jamner, J. P., & Besalel, V. A. (1987). The rate and amount of food intake as determinants of vomiting. *Behavioral Residential Treatment, 2*, 211–221.

Azrin, N. H., & Wesolowski, M. D. (1975). Eliminating habitual vomiting in a retarded adult by positive practice and self-correction. *Journal of Behavior Therapy & Experimental Psychiatry, 6*, 145–148.

Barmann, B. C. (1980). Use of contingent vibration in the treatment of self-stimulatory hand-mouthing and ruminative vomiting behavior. *Journal of Behavior Therapy & Experimental Psychiatry, 11*, 307–312.

Barton, E. S., Guess, D., Garcia, E., & Baer, D. M. (1970). Improvement of retardate's mealtime behaviors by time-out procedures using multiple baseline techniques. *Journal of Applied Behavior Analysis, 3*, 77–84.

Becker, J. V., Turner, S. M., & Sajwaj, T. E. (1978). Multiple behavioral effects of the use of lemon juice with a ruminating toddler-age child. *Behavior Modification, 2*, 267–278.

Bithoney, W. G. (1987). Child and family attributes in failure-to-thrive. *Journal of Developmental and Behavioral Pediatrics, 8*, 32–36.

Blackman, J. A. (1983). *Medical aspects of developmental disabilities in children birth to three.* Iowa City: University of Iowa.

Blackman, J. A., & Nelson, C.L.A. (1987). Rapid induction of oral feedings in tube-fed patients. *Journal of Developmental and Behavioral Pediatrics, 8,* 63–67.

Cataldo, M. F., Iwata, B. A., Page, T. J., & Parrish, J. M. (1988). Behavioral-medical considerations for hospital inpatient services. In M. D. Powers (Ed.), *Expanding systems of service delivery for persons with developmental disabilities* (pp. 233–253). Baltimore: Paul H. Brookes.

Cipani, E. (1981). Modifying food spillage behavior in an institutionalized retarded child. *Journal of Behavioral Therapy & Experimental Psychiatry, 12,* 261–265.

Drotar, D., Malone, C. A., Negray, J., & Dennstedt, M. (1981). Patterns of hospital based care for infants with nonorganic failure-to-thrive. *Journal of Clinical Child Psychology, 10,* 16–22.

Duker, P. C. (1981). Treatment of food refusal by the overcorrective functional movement training method. *Journal of Behavior Therapy & Experimental Psychiatry, 12,* 337–340.

Duker, P. C., & Seys, D. M. (1977). Elimination of vomiting in a retarded female using restitutional overcorrection. *Behavior Therapy, 8,* 255–257.

Favell, J. E., McGimsey, J. F., & Jones, M. L. (1980). Rapid eating in the retarded: Reduction by nonaversive procedures. *Behavior Modification, 4,* 481–492.

Fox, R., Meyer, P., & Rotatori, A. F. (1989). Obesity and weight regulation. In J. K. Luiselli (Ed.), *Behavioral medicine and developmental disabilities.* New York: Springer-Verlag.

Fox, R., Switzky, H., Rotatori, A. F., & Vitkus, P. (1982). Successful weight loss techniques with mentally retarded children and youth. *Exceptional Children, 49,* 238–244.

Foxx, R. M., Snyder, W. S., & Schroeder, F. (1979). A food satiation and oral hygiene punishment program to suppress chronic rumination by retarded persons. *Journal of Autism and Developmental Disorders, 9,* 399–412.

Gaddini, R.D.B., & Gaddini, E. (1959). Rumination in infancy. In L. Jessner & E. Pavenstadt (Eds.), *Dynamic psychopathology in childhood.* New York: Grune & Stratton.

Glasscock, S. G., Friman, P. C., O'Brien, S., & Christophersen, E. R. (1986). Varied citrus treatment of ruminant gagging in a teenager with Batten's disease. *Journal of Behavior Therapy & Experimental Psychiatry, 17,* 129–133.

Handen, B. L., Mandell, F., & Russo, D. C. (1986). Feeding induction in children who refuse to eat. *American Journal of Diseases in Children, 140,* 52–54.

Hersen, M., & Barlow, D. H. (1984). *Single-case experimental designs: Strategies for studying behavior change.* New York: Pergamon.

Horton, S. V. (1987). Reduction of disruptive mealtime behavior by facial screening: A case study of a mentally retarded girl with long-term follow-up. *Behavior Modification, 11,* 53–62.

Hyman, S. L., Porter, C. A., Page, T. J., Iwata, B. A., Kissel, R., O'Brien, S., & Batshaw, M. L. (1986). *Behavior management of feeding disorders in children with urea cycle and organic acid disorders.* Paper presented at the meeting of the Society of Developmental Pediatrics, Williamsburg, VA.

Illingworth, R. S., & Lister, J. (1964). The critical or sensative period, with reference to certain feeding problems in infants and children. *Journal of Pediatrics, 65,* 839–848.

Ives, C. C., Harris, S. L., & Wolchik, S. A. (1978). Food refusal in an autistic type child treated by a multicomponent forced feeding procedure. *Journal of Behavior Therapy & Experimental Psychiatry, 9,* 61–64.

Iwata, B. A., Riordan, M. M., Wohl, M. K., & Finney, J. W. (1982). Pediatric feeding disorders: Behavioral analysis and treatment. In P. J. Accardo (Ed.), *Failure-to-thrive in infancy and early childhood* (pp. 297–329). Baltimore: University Park Press.

Jackson, G. M., Johnson, C. R., Ackron, G. S., & Crowley, R. (1975). Food satiation as a procedure to decelerate vomiting. *American Journal of Mental Deficiency, 80,* 223–227.

Kanner, L. (1957). *Child psychiatry*. Springfield, IL: Charles C Thomas.

Kazdin, A. E. (1982). *Single-case research designs: Methods for clinical and applied settings*. New York: Oxford University Press.

Kazdin, A. E., & Matson, J. L. (1981). Social validation in mental retardation. *Applied Research in Mental Retardation, 2*, 39–53.

Knapczyk, D. R. (1983). Use of teacher-paced instruction in developing and maintaining independent self-feeding. *Journal of the Association for the Severely Handicapped, 8*, 10–16.

Kohlenberg, R. J. (1970). The punishment of persistent vomiting: A case study. *Journal of Applied Behavior Analysis, 3*, 241–245.

Lennox, D. B., Miltenberger, R. G., & Donnelly, D. R. (1987). Response interruption and DRL for the reduction of rapid eating. *Journal of Applied Behavior Analysis, 20*, 279–284.

Libby, D. G., & Phillips, E. (1978). Eliminating rumination in a profoundly retarded adolescent: An exploratory study. *Mental Retardation, 16*, 57.

Linscheid, T. R., Oliver, J., Blyer, E., & Palmer, S. (1978). Brief hospitalization for the behavior treatment of feeding problems in the developmentally disabled. *Journal of Pediatric Psychology, 3*, 72–76.

Linscheid, T. R., & Rasnake, L. K. (1986). Behavioral approaches in failure-to-thrive. In D. Drotar (Ed.), *New directions in failure-to-thrive: Implications for research and practice* (pp. 279–294). New York: Plenum.

Linscheid, T. R., Tarnowski, K. J., Rasnake, L. K., & Brams, J. S. (1987). Behavioral treatment of food refusal in a child with short-gut syndrome. *Journal of Pediatric Psychology, 12*, 451–460.

Lobato, D., Carlson, E. I., & Barrera, R. D. (1986). Modified satiation: Reducing ruminative vomiting without excessive weight gain. *Applied Research in Mental Retardation, 7*, 337–347.

Luckey, R. E., Watson, C. M., & Musick, J. K. (1968). Aversive conditioning as a means of inhibiting vomiting and rumination. *American Journal of Mental Deficiency, 73*, 139–142.

Luiselli, J. K. (1987a). *Behavioral feeding intervention with sensory impaired children in applied settings*. Paper presented at the annual meeting of the Association for Advancement of Behavior Therapy, Boston.

Luiselli, J. K. (1987b). Behavioral medicine research and treatment in developmental disabilities. In R. P. Barrett & J. L. Matson (Eds.), *Advances in developmental disorders* (pp. 1–39). Greenwich, CT: JAI.

Luiselli, J. K. (1988a). Improvement of feeding skills in multihandicapped children through paced-prompting interventions. *Journal of the Multihandicapped Person, 1*, 17–30.

Luiselli, J. K. (1988b). *Behavioral intervention for feeding problems in multihandicapped children*. Manuscript submitted for publication.

Luiselli, J. K. (1988c). *"Errorless" acquisition of self-feeding in a child with Lowe's syndrome*. Manuscript submitted for publication.

Luiselli, J. K. (1989a). Behavioral feeding intervention with deaf-blind, multihandicapped children. *Child and Family Behavior Therapy, 10*, 49–62.

Luiselli, J. K. (1989b). Health threatening behaviors. In J. K. Luiselli (Ed.), *Behavioral medicine and developmental disabilities*. New York: Springer-Verlag.

Luiselli, J. K., & Evans, T. E. (1988). *Behavioral acquisition of self-feeding skills in deaf-blind children*. Manuscript submitted for publication.

Luiselli, J. K., Evans, T. E., & Boyce, D. A. (1985). Contingency management of food selectivity and oppositional eating in a multihandicapped child. *Journal of Clinical Child Psychology, 14*, 153–156.

Luiselli, J. K., & Gleason, D. J. (1987). Combining sensory reinforcement and texture-fading procedures to overcome chronic food refusal. *Journal of Behavior Therapy & Experimental Psychiatry, 18*, 149–155.

Marholin D., II, Luiselli, J. K., Robinson, M., & Lott, I. T. (1980). Response-contingent taste-aversion in treating chronic ruminative vomiting of institutionalized profoundly retarded children. *Journal of Mental Deficiency Research, 24,* 147–156.

Marholin, D., II, O'Toole, K. M., Touchette, P. E., Berger, P. L., & Doyle, D. A. (1979). "I'll have a Big Mac, large fries, large Coke, and apple pie" . . . or teaching adaptive community skills. *Behavior Therapy, 10,* 236–248.

Masek, B. J., Epstein, L. H., & Russo, D. C. (1981). Behavioral perspectives in preventive medicine. In S. M. Turner, K. S. Calhoun, & H. E. Adams (Eds.), *Handbook of clinical behavior therapy* (pp. 475–499). New York: John Wiley.

Mitchell, W. G., Gorrell, R. W., & Greenberg, R. A. (1980). Failure-to-thrive: A study in a primary care setting: Epidemiology and follow-up. *Pediatrics, 65,* 971–977.

Mulick, J. A., Barbour, R., Schroeder, S. R., & Rojahn, J. (1980). Chronic ruminative vomiting: A comparison of four treatments procedures. *Journal of Autism and Developmental Disorders, 10,* 203–213.

Nelson, G. L., Cone, J. D., & Hanson, C. R. (1975). Training correct utensil use in retarded children: Modeling vs. physical guidance. *American Journal of Mental Deficiency, 80,* 114–122.

O'Brien, F., Bugle, C., & Azrin, N. H. (1972). Training and maintaining a retarded child's proper eating. *Journal of Applied Behavior Analysis, 5,* 67–72.

O'Neil, P. M., White, J. L., King, C. R., & Carek, D. J. (1979). Controlling childhood rumination through differential reinforcement of other behaviors. *Behavior Modification, 3,* 342–355.

Palmer, S., & Horn, S. (1978). Feeding problems in children. In S. Palmer & S. Ekvall (Eds.), *Pediatric nutrition in developmental disorders.* Springfield, IL: Charles C Thomas.

Perske, R., Clifton, A., McLean, B. M., & Stein, J. I. (1977). *Mealtimes for severely and profoundly handicapped persons: New concepts and attitudes.* Baltimore: University Park Press.

Rast, J., Johnston, J. M., & Drum, C. (1984). A parametric analysis of the relationship between food quantity and rumination. *Journal of the Experimental Analysis of Behavior, 41,* 125–134.

Rast, J., Johnston, J. M., Drum, C., & Corin, J. (1981). The relation of food quantity to rumination behavior. *Journal of Applied Behavior Analysis, 14,* 121–130.

Rast, J., Johnston, J. M., Ellinger-Allen, J., & Drum, C. (1985). Effects of nutritional and mechanical properties of food on ruminative behavior. *Journal of the Experimental Analysis of Behavior, 44,* 195–206.

Reid, D. H. (1983). Trends and issues in behavioral research on training feeding and dressing skills. In J. L. Matson & F. Andrasik (Eds.), *Treatment issues and innovations in mental retardation* (pp. 213–240). New York: Plenum.

Riordan, M. M., Iwata, B. A., Finney, J. W., Wohl, M. K., & Stanley, A. E. (1984). Behavioral assessment and treatment of chronic food refusal in handicapped children. *Journal of Applied Behavior Analysis, 17,* 327–341.

Riordan, M. M., Iwata, B. A., Wohl, M. K., & Finney, J. W. (1980). Behavioral treatment of food selectivity and refusal in developmentally disabled children. *Applied Research in Mental Retardation, 1,* 95–112.

Roberts, M. C., & Maddux, J. E. (1982). A psychosocial conceptualization of non-organic failure-to-thrive. *Journal of Clinical Child Psychology, 11,* 216–226.

Sajwaj, T. E., Libet, J., & Agras, W. S. (1974). Lemon juice therapy: The control of life-threatening rumination in a six-month old infant. *Journal of Applied Behavior Analysis, 7,* 557–563.

Singh, N. N. (1979). Aversive control of rumination in the mentally retarded. *Journal of Practical Applications to Developmental Handicap, 3,* 2–6.

Singh, N. N. (1981). Rumination. In N. R. Ellis (Ed.), *International review of research in mental retardation* (Vol. 10, pp. 139–181). New York: Academic Press.

Singh, N. N., Manning, P. J., & Angell, M. J. (1982). Effects of an oral hygiene punishment procedure on chronic rumination and collateral behaviors in monozygous twins. *Journal of Applied Behavior Analysis, 15*, 309–314.

Sisson, L. A., & Dixon, M. J. (1986a). A behavioral approach to the training and assessment of feeding skills in multihandicapped children. *Applied Research in Mental Retardation, 7*, 149–164.

Sisson, L. A., & Dixon, M. J. (1986b). Improving mealtime behaviors of a multihandicapped child using behavior therapy techniques. *Journal of Visual Impairment and Blindness, 80*, 855–858.

Sisson, L. A., & Dixon, M. J. (1986c). Improving mealtime behaviors through token reinforcement: A study with mentally retarded, behaviorally disordered children. *Behavior Modification, 10*, 333–354.

Sobsey, R., & Orelove, F. P. (1984). Neurophysiological facilitation of eating skills in children with severe handicaps. *Journal of the Association for Persons with Severe Handicaps, 9*, 98–110.

Starin, S. P., & Fuqua, R. W. (1987). Rumination and vomiting in the developmentally disabled: A critical review of the behavioral, medical, and psychiatric treatment research. *Research in Developmental Disorders, 8*, 575–605.

Stimbert, V. E., Minor, J. W., & McCoy, J. F. (1977). Intensive feeding training with retarded children. *Behavior Modification, 1*, 517–530.

Thompson, G. A., Iwata, B. A., & Poynter, H. (1979). Operant control of pathological tongue thrust in cerebral palsy. *Journal of Applied Behavior Analysis, 12*, 325–334.

Thompson, R. J. (1977). Applied behavior analysis in the treatment of mealtime tantrums and delay in self-feeding in a multihandicapped child. *Journal of Clinical Child Psychology, 6*, 52–54.

Traughber, B., Erwin, K. E., Risley, T. R., & Schnelle, J. F. (1983). Behavioral nutrition: An evaluation of a simple system for measuring food and nutrient consumption. *Behavioral Assessment, 5*, 263–280.

van den Pol, R. A., Iwata, B. A., Ivancic, M. T., Page, T. J., Neef, N. A., & Whitley, F. P. (1981). Teaching the handicapped to eat in public places: Acquisition, generalization, and maintenance of restaurant skills. *Journal of Applied Behavior Analysis, 14*, 61–69.

Van Hasselt, V. B. (1987). Behavior therapy for visually handicapped persons. In M. Hersen, R. M. Eisler, & P. M. Miller (Eds.), *Progress in behavior modification* (Vol. 21, pp. 13–44). Newbury Park, CA: Sage.

Watkins, J. T. (1972). Treatment of chronic vomiting and extreme emaciation by an aversive stimulus: A case study. *Psychological Reports, 31*, 803–805.

White, J. C., & Taylor, D. J. (1967). Noxious conditioning as a treatment for rumination. *Mental Retardation, 5*, 30–33.

ACCEPTABILITY OF BEHAVIORAL INTERVENTIONS: CHILD AND CAREGIVER PERCEPTIONS

ELEONORA GULLONE
Phillip Institute of Technology

NEVILLE J. KING
Monash University

I. INTRODUCTION

In recent years, concern has been expressed by many authorities about the image of behavior modification (e.g., Deitz, 1978; Kazdin & Cole, 1981; O'Leary, 1984; Saunders & Reppucci, 1978; Turkat & Forehand, 1980; Turkat, Harris, & Forehand, 1979; Woolfolk & Woolfolk, 1979; Woolfolk, Woolfolk, & Wilson, 1977). Both the printed and electronic media have frequently portrayed an image of behavior modification that is inconsistent with freedom and dignity and associated with brainwashing and aversive control. Such an image is likely to create problems in the application of behavioral procedures (O'Leary, 1984; Turkat et al., 1979; Woolfolk & Woolfolk, 1979; Woolfolk et al., 1977). A solution to such problems has been postulated with the claim that there is a labeling and language bias against behavior modification (Barling & Wainstein, 1979; O'Leary, 1984; Woolfolk & Woolfolk, 1979; Woolfolk et al., 1977). According to this reasoning, if one alters the label and modifies the terminology of behavioral procedures, then an increased acceptance by the community should result. Kazdin and Cole (1981) refute this claim with their finding that when content and language of behavioral procedures were separated, content was found to be the critical determinant of unfavorable evaluations. Rather than relabeling existing treatments, they conclude that alternative procedures should be considered and/or treatment strategies should be modified so that they are evaluated more positively. Hence there is a need to identify those factors that make procedures more acceptable and to incorporate them into intervention programs as much as is practically feasible. This argument was first put forth by Wolf (1978), who coined the term "social validation." Researchers have subsequently acknowledged that when evaluating applied interventions, social validation is a criterion that must also be taken into consideration.

II.   SOCIAL VALIDATION

Various criteria have been suggested for evaluating behavioral interventions. First, there is the experimental criterion, which refers to requirements for establishing that behavior change is the result of the particular intervention applied. Second, the therapeutic criterion is considered. This criterion focuses on a comparison between behavior change that has resulted from intervention and the level of behavior change that is required so that there is an improvement in the client's everyday functioning (Kazdin, 1977). Wolf's more recent criterion postulates that applied interventions be *socially validated*. Social validation has been broadly defined as the process of assessing the social acceptability of intervention procedures (Kazdin, 1977).

According to Wolf (1978), if behavior modification is to achieve a role that is socially important, then it is society that must evaluate this role. Social validation must occur on three levels:

(1) The social importance of the goals: Are the specific behavioral goals really what society wants?
(2) The social appropriateness of the procedures: Do the ends justify the means? That is, do the participants, caregivers, and other consumers consider the treatment procedures acceptable?
(3) The social importance of the effects: Are consumers satisfied with the results? All the results, including any unpredicted ones? (p. 207)

The study of social validation of behavior therapy has been emphasized in the context of various consumer issues. Among these are the increasing public interest in accountability and cost-effectiveness. Also, there is a growing concern for the protection of consumers from procedures that have potentially iatrogenic consequences (Kiesler, 1983). Lebow (1982) maintains that research on consumer satisfaction is part of the trend toward a more consumer-oriented society. There has also been an increase in concern over the rights of individuals who are treated. Related to this issue are informed consent and ethical and legal considerations (Braun, 1975; Budd & Baer, 1976; Kazdin, 1977; Parloff, 1983; Wolf, 1978). Crowe, Marks, Agras, and Leitenberg (1972), among others, maintain that an acceptable intervention program is more likely to be implemented and adhered to than one that is less acceptable, although the latter may be potentially more effective. Wolf (1978) is in agreement with Crowe et al. when he states that "it may be that not only is it important to determine the acceptability of treatment procedures to participants for ethical reasons, it may also be that acceptability of the program is related to effectiveness, as well as to the likelihood that the program will be adopted and supported by others" (p. 210).

Another important issue addressed by social validation research is one that arises when a therapist is required to select an intervention procedure from a range of possible strategies. The research findings on social validation should be useful in assessing which intervention techniques are acceptable for use and also which techniques are perceived as being effective or potentially effective (Kazdin, 1977; Kazdin & Wilson, 1978; Norton, Allen, & Hilton, 1983; Singh & Katz, 1985; Van Houten, 1979; Wolf, 1978). However, instances where there are two or more equally effective treatments are rare. It is more likely that a therapist will be confronted with a situation in which more effective treatments are also more risky and costly (Yeaton & Sechrest, 1981). In such cases, choice of treatment is all the more complex and social validation may be the most valid and ethical method with which to make a decision. To be emphasized is the point that "if participants don't like the treatment then they may avoid it, or run away, or complain loudly, and thus, society will be less likely to use our technology, no matter how potentially effective and efficient it might be" (Wolf, 1978, p. 206).

Importance of all three levels proposed by Wolf (1978) is acknowledged. We focus, however, on the "acceptability" of behavioral interventions in clinical and educational settings. As expressed by Elliot (1986), although "the acceptability of intervention methods encompasses only a portion of the issues associated with social validity, it seems to capture the essence of social validity" (p. 26). An unacceptable treatment is likely to be avoided, resulting in no treatment at all. Acceptability, as defined by Kazdin (1980b) "refers to the judgments about the treatment procedures by non-professionals, lay persons, clients and other potential consumers of treatment" (p. 259). Several factors are likely to be assessed when considering judgments of acceptability. These include consideration about whether treatment is fair, reasonable, or intrusive, whether the treatment prescribed is appropriate for the particular problem, and whether the treatment is in accordance with conventional notions about what treatment should be (Kazdin, 1980a, 1980b).

Research on acceptability has, almost exclusively, examined treatment techniques implemented to suppress or reduce inappropriate behaviors (e.g., Fincham & Spettell, 1984; Kazdin, 1980a, 1980b, 1981; Mudford, 1987; Norton, Austen, Allen, & Hilton, 1983; Witt & Martens, 1983; Witt, Moe, Gutkin, & Andrews, 1984). Aversive procedures, because of their intrusiveness and because they are subject to abuse by increases in intensity, are of most concern (Brown & Bing, 1976; Koocher, 1976; Ross, 1980). The focus on children has occurred because children are often not given the opportunity to make decisions about treatment of which they are to be recipients. Children rarely have access to information about alternative treatments and are often unaware of their opportunities to refuse or terminate treatment (Kazdin, French, & Sherick, 1981). The presumption that minors are significantly less competent than the adults who are given the rights to make the decisions for them also contributes to their exclusion from decision-making processes that directly affect them (Taylor & Adelman, 1986). McMahon and Forehand (1983) maintain that for ethical reasons, children have the right to participate in treatment decisions and activities: "It is essential that the direct targets of our behavioral interventions be given an appropriate opportunity to evaluate their treatment" (p. 222).

According to Kaser-Boyd, Adelman, Taylor, and Nelson (1986), it is possible that children at the stage of formal operations are able to think about courses of action for psychological problems in a hypothetical manner. Formal operations, the most advanced stage of cognitive development, begins at approximately age 11 and consolidates by age 14 or 15. At this stage the individual is more likely to use a wider variety of cognitive operations and strategies in problem solving, becomes highly flexible in thought and reasoning, and can see things from a number of perspectives (Ginsburg & Opper, 1979; Inhelder & Piaget, 1958; Weithorn, 1982).

Further, Kaser-Boyd and her colleagues (1986) maintain that formal operations thinking is not essential to the treatment decision-making process. In previous work, Kaser-Boyd, Adelman, and Taylor (1985) found that children as young as 10 years of age could identify risks and benefits of treatment that were relevant to their situations and needs. In their 1986 study, Kaser-Boyd et al. found support for their previous work. They report that a substantial proportion of their sample of children, aged between 10 and 11 years and who had no previous experience of psychological treatment, were able to weigh the risks and benefits in a series of hypothetical treatment dilemmas. Other studies have also proposed that children in their early adolescence have the cognitive ability to be competent in their decisions about health care (McKinney, Chin, Reinhart, & Trierweiler, 1985; Taylor & Adelman, 1986).

Involvement of the child in treatment procedures is seen as being instrumental in obtaining the child's explicit cooperation (Ollendick & Cerny, 1981; Ollendick & Hersen, 1984). Research findings show that there are substantial risks and loss of benefits when youngsters are denied participation in treatment decisions. Also, it has been shown that many benefits are accrued if participation is allowed. Among the risks are minimum commitment and compliance to the prescribed treatment, reactivity against the treatment, increased probability of dropout, session absenteeism, and having the treatment terminated prematurely (Adelman, Kaser-Boyd, & Taylor, 1984; Melton, 1981). Commitment and increased motivation have been shown to be directly related to the ability to choose and to feel some control and self-determination over the situation. Other prominently mentioned benefits include improved understanding of the treatment process, a reduction of negative affect toward unpopular treatment decisions, improved relationships between the children and the adults involved in treatment decisions, and, most important, increased success (Adelman et al., 1984; Bastien & Adelman, 1984; Elliot, 1986; Elliot, Witt, Galvin, & Moe, 1986; Melton, 1981; Taylor & Adelman, 1986; Turco & Elliot, 1986).

Considering children's and adolescents' acceptability evaluations of treatment is desirable for ethical reasons as well as for facilitating therapeutic change (Bastien & Adelman, 1984; Elliot, 1986; Elliot et al., 1986; Melton, 1981; Turco & Elliot, 1986). While the measurement of parents', teachers', or other potential consumers' acceptability ratings of interventions is important, it cannot be presumed that the actual recipients' (i.e., the children's) perceptions of the treatment will be the same. Indeed, it seems logical to suspect that children will consider different variables in their evaluations of treatment procedures (Kiesler, 1983).

III.   RESEARCH FINDINGS ON ACCEPTABILITY EVALUATIONS

As it has been proposed that children and caregivers may differ in their evaluations of treatment procedures, this review will first focus on those studies that have examined caregivers' acceptability evaluations of treatment procedures, and, second, on those that have examined children's acceptability of treatment procedures.

A.   Perceptions of Adults and Caregivers

Kazdin, a major contributor in this field, has conducted a series of well-designed analog studies in which the acceptability of various child treatment techniques has been assessed. Kazdin (1980a, 1980b, 1981) utilized a case description methodology for the assessment of treatment acceptability, the basic approach being to present case descriptions of a child and his or her behavior problem to the participants. Also described are the treatment procedures employed. After listening to the audiotaped presentations, the respondents (undergraduate psychology students) were required to evaluate the treatment procedures by completing the Treatment Evaluation Inventory (TEI; Kazdin, 1980a). The TEI is a Likert-type survey that includes sixteen items to be rated on a seven-point scale. The participants were also required to complete a semantic differential scale measuring potency, activity, and evaluative dimensions of the treatment technique.

Kazdin's (1980a) study investigated the acceptability of reinforcement of incompatible behavior, time-out from reinforcement, drug therapy, and electric shock for deviant child behavior. It was found that the undergraduate students distinguished among treatments by their acceptability ratings. Further differential reinforcement of incompatible behavior was evaluated as the most acceptable procedure, followed in order by time-out from reinforcement, drug therapy, and electric shock. A third finding reported was that severity of the clinical problem to which the four treatments were applied significantly influenced the acceptability ratings. Each of the treatments was rated as more acceptable when related to a more severe case. Electric shock was evaluated as an unacceptable treatment and also as a very potent one.

Kazdin (1980b) examined the acceptability of nonexclusionary time-out (withdrawal of attention and contingent observation), exclusionary time-out (isolation in a time-out room), and reinforcement of incompatible behavior when applied to problem children. He also examined whether the manner in which a treatment is presented and implemented can increase its acceptability. A further analysis was conducted to ascertain whether the case description (i.e., gender of the child) to which the treatments were applied influenced acceptability ratings. Kazdin found that gender of the child in the case description did not alter acceptability ratings. Nonexclusionary forms of time-out were rated as more acceptable than exclusionary time-out. Also, it was found that positive reinforcement of incompatible behavior was rated as more acceptable than either of the punishment procedures. Kazdin demonstrated that the acceptability of procedures can be increased or altered by adding to the standard technique. For example, isolation was found to be markedly more acceptable when it was included as a backup to another form of time-out or when it was included in a contingency contract than when it was used on its own.

Kazdin's (1981) investigation evaluated reinforcement of incompatible behavior, positive practice, time-out from reinforcement, and medication. Reinforcement of incompatible behavior was rated as the most acceptable procedure, followed, in order, by positive practice, time-out, and medication. Efficacy of treatment was not found to be related to acceptability level, but adverse side effects were related to the level of acceptability such that the stronger the side effects, the lower the acceptability level.

Norton, Austen, Allen, and Hilton (1983) conducted a study in which they maintain that undergraduate students' view of acceptability (as obtained in the investigations of Kazdin, 1980a, 1980b, 1981) may differ from those of people who have direct experience with and responsibility for children (e.g., teachers, parents). Five behavioral procedures for reducing disruptive behavior were evaluated by parents and teachers. These included reinforcement, isolation, contingent observation, isolation and contractual agreement, and withdrawal of attention backed by isolation. Each treatment procedure was evaluated on two dimensions (acceptability and perceived effectiveness) using five-point Likert-type scales. The findings show that teachers evaluated the procedures as more acceptable and more effective than did parents. Reinforcement was rated as the most acceptable and the most effective treatment by teachers and parents. Overall, the findings are consistent with those of Kazdin (1980b); however, a major difference is reported by Norton and colleagues (1983). Whereas in Kazdin's study contingent observation was rated as highly acceptable, in Norton et al.'s study it was rated as least acceptable. The most important conclusion to be drawn from Norton, Austen, Allen, and Hilton's study is that different groups may have different perceptions of what is and what is not an acceptable treatment. Also, it is shown that different groups may vary in their comparative acceptability ratings of different intervention procedures.

Witt and Martens (1983) administered the Intervention Rating Profile (IRP) to preservice and student teachers in order to identify important factors contributing to teachers' evaluations of the acceptability of six classroom interventions. The intervention included praise, home-based reinforcement, token economy, ignoring, response cost, and time-out. The IRP consists of 20 items that are rated on a six-point Likert-type scale ranging from "strongly disagree" to "strongly agree." The findings indicated that the IRP measured several factors of acceptability ratings. The first factor appeared to consist of items reflecting a general concern that the intervention is appropriate and helpful to the child. Secondary factors appeared to reflect such aspects as amount of risk posed to the target child, the amount of time consumed by the teacher in applying the procedure, the effects of the procedure on other children in the classroom, and the amount of skill required by the teacher to implement the intervention procedure.

Witt, Moe, Gutkin, and Andrews (1984) utilized the IRP in their investigation that evaluated teachers' acceptability ratings of reinforcement of incompatible behavior with a backup token economy. Their findings are consistent with those of Kazdin (1980a) and Norton, Austen, Allen, and Hilton (1983). Teachers were found to rate the intervention as more acceptable when applied to a severe case, but different groups (i.e., highly experienced versus less experienced teachers) rated the intervention as differentially acceptable. The highly experienced teachers rated the intervention as less acceptable than the less experienced teachers.

Witt and Robbins (1985) conducted two studies on the acceptability of behavioral interventions. The first evaluated the acceptability of differential reinforcement of other behaviors, differential reinforcement of low rates of responding, reprimands, seclusion time-out, staying after school, and corporal punishment. A second independent variable that was included in the analysis was the severity of the behavior problem to which the treatment was applied. A third variable considered was experience level of teachers (the participants). A second study examined whether treatments are differentially acceptable depending upon who implements them (e.g., teachers themselves versus psychologists). Witt and Robbins's investigations yielded the findings that time-out, reinforcement of low rates of behavior, staying after school, and reprimands ranged from slightly unacceptable to slightly acceptable. Differential reinforcement of other behavior was found to be highly acceptable, and corporal punishment was found to be highly unacceptable. Also, teachers with fewer years of experience tended to rate all the treatments as more acceptable than did the highly experienced teachers. An interesting finding was that teachers rated the interventions more favorably if they were to implement them as opposed to someone else. Finally, case severity was found to influence acceptability ratings significantly only in the second investigation.

Witt, Martens, and Elliot (1984) investigated teachers' judgments concerning the acceptability of classroom interventions in an attempt to ascertain the salient factors of a treatment that may influence acceptability ratings. The effects of the type of intervention, the amount of teacher time, and the severity of the behavior problem on acceptability ratings were examined. Low levels of teacher involvement were viewed as less acceptable for severe, as opposed to mild and moderate, behavior problems. Also, positive intervention was perceived as most acceptable for low levels of teacher time; reductive intervention was perceived as most acceptable for medium amounts of teacher time. Thus it appears that teachers' judgments concerning the acceptability of classroom intervention techniques were highly influenced by the amount of time needed to plan and implement such interventions.

Elliot, Witt, Galvin, and Peterson (1984) conducted two studies. The first examined acceptability of positive intervention, while the second examined the acceptability of reductive intervention. Both studies included the manipulation of two independent variables. The first was intervention complexity, and the second was behavior problem severity. The findings revealed that, in general, positive interventions received more acceptable ratings than reductive interventions, for the same target behaviors. It was also found that those interventions that are relatively easy to implement and that require little time were rated as more acceptable than the more time-consuming and complex interventions, unless the target behavior was considered to be severe.

The work by Elliot et al. (1984), Norton, Austen, Allen, and Hilton (1983), Witt and Martens (1984), Witt, Martens, and Elliot (1984), Witt, Moe, Gutkin, and Andrews (1984), and Witt and Robbins (1985) is a valuable contribution to acceptability research, as it extends the investigation of acceptability of child treatment techniques (both by having teachers as the respondents and by extending the various interventions to those applicable in a typical classroom setting).

Fincham and Spettell's (1984) investigations further extend the parameters of acceptability research. They are concerned with the evaluation of acceptability ratings for dry bed training and urine alarm training as treatments of nocturnal enuresis. Parents and undergraduate students participated in the investigations. The authors found that the parents, who had actually implemented the treatments, rated the urine alarm procedure more favorably than the dry bed training on Kazdin's (1980a) TEI.

As in Fincham and Spettell's (1984) study, Hobbs, Walle, and Caldwell (1984) investigated the acceptability of treatment strategies following their actual use. A sample of 28 mother-child pairs were assigned to one of three treatment conditions or a no-treatment control group. The three treatment conditions were social reinforcement, time-out, and time-out plus social reinforcement. Following treatment implementation, the mothers completed the TEI. Time-out was found to receive the lowest acceptability ratings; however, all treatments were evaluated favorably. In comparison to previous research, the treatment strategies were rated as more acceptable. Also, unlike previous research, differences in acceptability were not found between time-out and reinforcement. Hobbs and his associates maintain that this difference is most likely to be accounted for by the mode of treatment presentation, that is, actual use of treatments as opposed to written descriptions.

Walle, Hobbs, and Caldwell (1984) examined the effects of different sequences of attention and time-out on acceptability ratings. A total of 25 mothers and their 38 children participated in the study. There were three different conditions to which the mothers were assigned: time-out followed by attention, attention followed by time-out, and attention and time-out concurrently. Following implementation of the procedures the mothers completed the TEI. Although acceptability ratings were not found to differ significantly for the different strategy sequences, acceptability for all of the treatments was found to be markedly higher than that reported for Kazdin's written descriptions of time-out and positive reinforcement. These findings, along with those of Hobbs et al. (1984), add support to the contention that actual use of treatment strategies increases their acceptability by consumers.

Singh and Katz (1985) investigated the extent to which acceptability ratings can be modified by educational means. They administered the TEI to 96 undergraduate psychology students who were divided into groups of 12 and assigned to one of eight conditions. Each condition was characterized by a different order (randomized) of two case descriptions and four treatments. The treatments were differential reinforcement of incompatible behavior, positive practice overcorrection, time-out, and humanistic parenting. The case descriptions were of hyperactivity and aggression. Following an initial evaluation of the four treatment strategies, the subjects were given three one-hour lectures on each of the first three treatment strategies, stressing positive effects and possible adverse effects. No information was provided on humanistic parenting. After the information sessions (four weeks later) the students were required to reevaluate the treatment strategies. Singh and Katz conclude, from their findings, that differential reinforcement was the most acceptable approach. However, should a more restrictive approach be required, according to Singh and Katz, it can be made more acceptable by providing educational information in advance.

A study by Mudford (1987) examined the acceptability of a visual screening procedure for the reduction of self-stimulation in severely retarded children. Included in the analysis were three treatment strategies: visual screening, visual screening and differential reinforcement of incompatible behavior, and differential reinforcement of incompatible behavior on its own. Nurses and training officers were required to complete the TEI. It was found that the two different occupational groups did not differ significantly in their ratings of the acceptability of differential reinforcement. However, the nurses were found to rate visual screening as more acceptable than did the training officers. For both groups, acceptability of visual screening was enhanced by the addition of reinforcement.

The research findings on acceptability thus far reviewed have shown that varied treatment strategies, when applied to children, are differentially acceptable to potential consumers. Generally, the least aversive strategies (e.g., differential reinforcement of incompatible behavior) have been found to be more acceptable than those that are more. potent or more aversive (e.g., time-out) (see, for example, Kazdin, 1980a, 1980b; Witt, Martens, & Elliot, 1984). Also, it has been demonstrated that acceptability is enhanced when treatment descriptions have been applied to cases of greater severity (Kazdin, 1980a; Norton, Austen, Allen, & Hilton, 1983; Witt, Martens, & Elliot, 1984). Another finding has been that, the stronger the side effects, the lower the acceptability level (Kazdin, 1981). Further, it has been found that different groups have different perceptions of the acceptability of treatment strategies (i.e., teachers versus parents or experienced teachers versus inexperienced teachers) (Norton, Austen, Allen, & Hilton, 1983; Witt & Martens, 1983; Witt, Martens, & Elliot, 1984). Treatments were found to be rated as more acceptable by the participants if they were to implement them as opposed to someone else (e.g., psychologist) (Witt & Martens, 1983). When evaluating teachers' judgments of acceptability for classroom interventions, it was demonstrated that interventions that are relatively easy to implement and that require little time were rated as more acceptable than the more time-consuming and complex interventions (e.g., Witt, Martens, & Elliot, 1984). With regard to the modification of acceptability ratings, a number of researchers (e.g., Fincham & Spettell, 1984; Hobbs et al. 1984; Kazdin, 1980b; Mudford, 1987; Singh & Katz, 1985; Walle et al., 1984) have demonstrated that the mode of presentation of treatment strategies (e.g., actual use as opposed to written descriptions) can alter acceptability ratings. Generally, acceptability has been shown to be enhanced if participants actually implement the procedures, if they receive detailed information about the strategies, or if components are added (e.g., reinforcement) to the standard technique.

Naifeh (1984) is one of the few researchers who has systematically evaluated potential consumers' acceptability of various treatments based on different theoretical models. A sample of 96 parents were required to complete a set of questionnaires in which they evaluated four major therapy approaches (nondirective individual play therapy, a strategic family systems therapy, behavioral parent training, and a psychoanalytic approach to family therapy) applied to the treatment of children referred for behavior problems. The findings indicate that the strategic family systems therapy was judged as the least acceptable of the treatments. The other three treatments received comparable judgments of acceptability. Also, in congruence with other acceptability studies (e.g., Elliot et al., 1984; Kazdin, 1980a; Witt, Martens, & Elliot, 1984; Witt, Moe, Gutkin, & Andrews, 1984; Witt & Robbins, 1985), acceptability ratings were significantly higher for the child case described as having more severe behavior problems than the less severe case description.

B.   Perceptions of Children

A number of researchers have examined children's perceptions of intervention acceptability in their studies (e.g., Dadds, Adlington, & Christensen, 1987; Elliot et al., 1986; Kazdin, 1984, 1986; Kazdin et al., 1981; Turco & Elliot, 1986). Kazdin et al. (1981) included children in their study focusing on the evaluations of actual consumers of treatment, since children are directly confronted with considerations that may affect views about alternative treatments. The treatments that were evaluated were positive reinforcement, positive practice, time-out from reinforcement, and medication. The participants in the study were 32 child psychiatric inpatients (aged 7 to 13 years), their parents, and staff. Kazdin et al. investigated whether alternative treatments were differentially acceptable and whether acceptability differed depending upon the persons providing the evaluations. The procedure followed was the same as that employed in Kazdin's previous investigations. It was found that (a) alternative treatments when applied to case descriptions of seriously disturbed children (e.g., severely aggressive or hyperactive behavior) were differentially acceptable; (b) reinforcement of incompatible behavior was found to be the most acceptable, followed in order by positive practice, medication, and time-out from reinforcement; (c) psychiatrically disturbed children were found to rate the alternative procedures as less acceptable than did their parents, and staff ratings were between those of parents and children; and (d) the relative ratings of alternative treatments were found to be the same across all three groups. An interesting finding was that reinforcement, although acceptable, was rated as being the least potent.

A further investigation by Kazdin (1984) examined whether treatment outcomes influence acceptability ratings. The alternative treatments included in the investigation were time-out from reinforcement, locked seclusion, and medication. It was found that the relative standing of alternative treatments varied between parents and their inpatient children. Parents rated time-out from reinforcement as the most acceptable treatment, while the children rated medication as the most acceptable. According to Kazdin, medication may be viewed by the children as a nonpunitive procedure, whereas time-out and locked seclusion may arouse associations with punishment. Overall, the effectiveness of treatment was found to influence the ratings of acceptability, for both parents and children, such that the treatments described as being more effective were more acceptable than those described as producing weaker effects.

In a 1986 study by Kazdin, 48 psychiatric inpatient children, aged 6 to 13, and their parents evaluated the acceptability of two modalities of treatment—outpatient psychotherapy and hospitalization in an inpatient children's unit. The treatments also varied in that some descriptions noted that the child was the focus of the intervention while others noted that the child and parents were both included in the treatment process. The treatments were applied to one of two case descriptions of seriously disturbed children. Treatments were evaluated by completion of the TEI. Parents were found to view the treatments as more acceptable than did the children. Also, parents viewed hospitalization as more acceptable than psychotherapy, whereas the opposite was found for the children. For the parents, acceptability was positively correlated with their perception of treatment strength. In contrast, for the children, the stronger the treatment the less acceptable it was rated. This finding is consistent with the findings of Kazdin's 1984 study, where an inverse relationship was found between locked seclusion and time-out and acceptability, for the children.

Elliot et al. (1986) utilized the Children's Intervention Rating Profile (CIRP; Witt & Elliot, 1985), a one-factor scale consisting of seven items, in one of the first attempts to evaluate "normal" children's acceptability ratings. A group of 79 sixth-grade children were required to rate the acceptability of 12 intervention procedures for classroom misbehaviors. The 12 treatments were classified as being a verbal, a reinforcement, or a traditional intervention strategy. Elliot and his associates found that the sixth-grade children rated the acceptability of 12 intervention strategies quite differently. Specifically, interventions were rated as relatively most acceptable when individual teacher-student interactions, group reinforcement, or negative sanctions for the target child were emphasized. Public reprimands and negative contingencies for a group when only one child misbehaved were rated as unacceptable. The four traditional interventions (i.e., quiet room, point system, staying in during recess, and principal's office) were generally rated as more acceptable when compared to the behaviorally oriented interventions (e.g., praise by the teacher). Finally, Elliot and associates found that acceptability ratings were not significantly affected by the severity of the problem behavior.

Following Elliot et al.'s (1986) study, Turco and Elliot (1986) examined CIRP acceptability ratings of 146 fifth-, seventh-, and ninth-grade children in response to eight teacher-initiated intervention methods (e.g., public reprimand, reprimand at home). The eight alternative interventions differed from one another on two dimensions: first, who was responsible for the implementation of the procedure, and, second, who was responsible for the monitoring of the consequences. The investigations found that self-monitored interventions were rated among the most unacceptable techniques (e.g., self-monitored reprimand), and home-monitored interventions were consistently rated as being among the most acceptable. It was also found that public reprimand was rated as the least acceptable intervention method among the eight.

A further investigation by Turco and Elliot (in press) examined the influence of children's developmental level and gender on their acceptability ratings of interventions for correcting classroom behavior problems. A sample of 693 fifth-, seventh-, and ninth-grade students completed the CIRP in response to 12 intervention methods. Turco and Elliot found that students' gender and grade, intervention method and grade, and intervention method, grade, and problem severity had main and interaction effects on acceptability ratings. The intervention preferences were found to be private and public praise for fifth-graders, but seventh- and ninth-graders rated private praise as an unacceptable method. Self-monitoring was found to be less acceptable for the younger as opposed to the older children. However, only the fifth-graders rated it as an acceptable intervention. Loss of recess or free time was rated as an unacceptable intervention for changing behavior by the fifth-grade students, but was rated as very acceptable by the seventh- and ninth-grade children. Finally, only ninth-grade children indicated a sensitivity to selecting intervention methods based upon the severity of the problem behavior and the respondent's gender.

Recent studies by Dadds et al. (1987) evaluated acceptability ratings of five maternal disciplinary techniques: permissiveness, physical punishment, directed discussion, quiet time, and time-out. These techniques were evaluated across four different situations: noncompliance with an initiating instruction, aggression toward others, noncompliance with a terminating instruction, and noncompliance with a known rule. A total of 20 children, aged 4 to 8 years, participated in the studies. They were classified as either behavior problem or nonproblem children. Comparisons were also made between the behavior problem children's perceptions of technique acceptability before and after behavioral treatment. Using a three-point "face rating scale" ranging from "very wrong" to "very right," Dadds et al. found that the children primarily discriminated between intervention and nonintervention rather than between the different techniques. Both clinical and nonclinical groups rated time-out as acceptable, supporting Turco and Elliot's (in press) findings that young children prefer more directive disciplinary strategies than do older children. Out of the five techniques only permissiveness was rated as unacceptable. A further finding, somewhat contradictory to previous research (e.g., Hobbs et al., 1984), was that exposure to behavioral disciplinary techniques (e.g., differential reinforcement, exclusionary and nonexclusionary time-out) did not alter children's acceptability ratings of the five disciplinary techniques.

The studies reviewed above share the belief that children are entitled to and capable of making judgments about the acceptability of various intervention strategies. In summary, the research findings concerning children's acceptability evaluations of alternative treatments, although not conclusive, have shown that (a) children are capable of differentiating treatments by their acceptability judgments; (b) younger children prefer positive interventions and interventions modeled by adults, while older children judge more aversive and nontraditional interventions as acceptable; (c) children's gender appears to affect their judgments of acceptability; and (d) while the severity of the target child's problem does not affect the acceptability judgments of younger children, it does influence adolescents' acceptability ratings.

IV.   METHODOLOGICAL AND THEORETICAL ISSUES

On reviewing the research findings on acceptability, several methodological shortcomings have become apparent. One major limitation of most acceptability studies (e.g., Fincham & Spettell, 1984; Kazdin, 1980a, 1980b, 1981; Norton, Allen, & Hilton, 1983; Singh & Katz, 1985) is the reliance on undergraduate students as the source of acceptability ratings. Although Witt and Martens (1983) had preservice and student teachers rate acceptability of treatment interventions, such a population can be argued to be comparable to undergraduate students. Research has shown that different groups rate acceptability of treatment procedures differently. Therefore, the generalizability of undergraduate students' ratings to those of potential consumers is questionable in view of the fact that many students may not have direct responsibility for the care of children. Kazdin (1980a) comments that students' ratings are likely to be different from those of people who have direct responsibility for children (e.g., teachers or parents).

On the other hand, research on clinical groups can present problems. Referring to his research on the acceptability ratings of children and parents, Kazdin (1986) notes that "the participants represent a very select group with severe clinical dysfunctions among the children and, often, the parents as well" (p. 339). With such a sample it is possible that because child dysfunction is particularly severe, more intrusive and restrictive alternatives may have a higher acceptability than would be the case for parents with less severely disturbed children. Another limitation is that such respondents may be biased in their ratings as they are experienced with at least one of the treatments they are required to rate. Also, research findings suggest that acceptability of treatment techniques is enhanced after implementation of treatment (e.g., Hobbs et al., 1984). Thus a sample population that combines subjects who have undergone a particular treatment and subjects who have not cannot be considered homogeneous, nor are the acceptability ratings representative of the group as a whole. A further limitation of acceptability research concerns the sample size of most subject groups, which has tended to be fairly small (e.g., Elliot et al., 1984, 1986; Hobbs et al. 1984; Norton, Allen, & Hilton, 1983; Walle et al., 1984).

It therefore becomes apparent that acceptability research should involve more representative and larger samples. Also, the incorporation of various consumer groups is essential if there is to develop an understanding of the way in which potential consumer groups differ in their perceptions of treatment acceptability. Inclusion of children's/adolescents' perceptions in such analyses is particularly desirable in view of the current emphasis on children's rights.

Another major limitation that applies to most of the acceptability research that has been conducted is the analog format. The acceptability of psychological treatments has mostly been conducted through analog design incorporating a problem-solution-evaluation format. It has been maintained by several researchers (e.g., Elliot, 1986; Reid & Whitman, 1983; Singh & Katz 1985; Witt, Martens, & Elliot, 1984) that the findings of analog studies may lack ecological validity. Thus subjects may respond differently to the relatively limited amount of information given in a written questionnaire or on audiotape than they would in a real-life situation. It follows that evaluations elicited through an analog format may not necessarily correspond with "actual" consumers' willingness to be recipients of a particular procedure or willingness of parents, teachers, and so forth to act as mediators of a procedure.

Another issue of concern pertains to the modes of problem and treatment presentation and the measures used to obtain consumers' evaluations of treatment procedures. As a result of the study-specific nature of acceptability research, different measures have been employed by researchers. This has the effect of limiting comparison of findings between studies. Even in studies where the same evaluation measure has been employed, variations among treatments, target behaviors, and format of presentation limit comparisons (Lebow, 1982, 1983; McMahon & Forehand, 1983). An example of such differences is the format of problem and treatment presentation in Kazdin's studies, which employed audiotaped presentations, compared to the written presentation employed in studies by Elliot and his colleagues.

Also relating to the instruments that have been used to obtain potential and actual consumers' evaluations of treatment acceptability is assessment of reliability and validity. There have been few attempts made to assess the reliability and validity of the measures used (Bornstein & Rychtarik, 1983; Lebow, 1982). There is, however, the exception of Kazdin's work that involved the validation of the TEI (Kazdin, 1980a), and hence has been described by other authors as a "reasonably well-validated acceptability measure" (McMahon & Forehand, 1983, p. 214). Elliot (1986) recommends the measurement of discriminant and convergent validity between acceptability measures and other instruments evaluating attitudes related to psychological treatments. He further argues that such data would contribute to the refinement of the acceptability concept. On a more positive note, however, the convergence of findings implies that the different instruments being used are measuring similar constructs, thus demonstrating some degree of validity. As with most research that relies on questionnaires, there are a number of more general problems, including social desirability and acquiescence. These problems can be minimized by guaranteeing anonymity to respondents and checking for response set (Lebow, 1982, 1983; McMahon & Forehand, 1983).

Finally, most of the research on acceptability has focused on operant procedures for conduct-disordered children (externalizing disorders). Other behavioral procedures and childhood disorders are in need of investigation in terms of their acceptability. For example, little is known about the reaction of consumers to fear-reduction procedures used to treat anxiety disorders of children and adolescents (internalizing disorders). School phobia has been successfully treated using systematic desensitization and its variants, such as emotive imagery (Garvey & Hegrenes, 1966; Lazarus & Abramovitz, 1962; Miller, 1972). In contrast to graduated approaches, flooding (forced return to school) also appears to be effective (Blagg & Yule, 1984; Kennedy, 1965). However, the reactions of children, caregivers, and professionals to these quite different procedures has yet to be determined (King, Hamilton, & Ollendick, 1988). As with other childhood disorders under treatment, acceptability should not be regarded as an automatic reaction. To conclude, further research is needed on the reactions of consumers and society to behavioral interventions with children and adolescents in both clinical and educational settings.

REFERENCES

Adelman, H. S., Kaser-Boyd, N., & Taylor, L. (1984). Children's participation in consent for psychotherapy and their subsequent response to treatment. *Journal of Clinical Child Psychology, 13,* 170–178.

Barling, J., & Wainstein, T. (1979). Attitudes, labeling bias and behavior modification in work organizations. *Behavior Therapy, 10,* 129–136.

Bastien, R. T., & Adelman, H. S. (1984). Noncompulsory versus legally mandated placement, perceived choice, and response to treatment among adolescents. *Journal of Consulting and Clinical Psychology, 52,* 171–179.

Blagg, N., & Yule, W. (1984). The behavioural treatment of school refusal: A comparative study. *Behaviour Research and Therapy, 22,* 119–127.

Bornstein, P. H., & Rychtarik, R. G. (1983). Consumer satisfaction in adult behavior therapy: Procedures, problems and future perspectives. *Behavior Therapy, 14,* 191–208.

Braun, S. H. (1975). Ethical issues in behavior modification. *Behavior Therapy, 6,* 51–62.

Brown, J. L., & Bing, S. R. (1976). Drugging children: Child abuse by professionals. In G. P. Koocher (Ed.), *Children's rights and the mental health professions.* New York: John Wiley.

Budd, K. S., & Baer, D. M. (1976). Behavior modification and the law: Implications of recent judicial decisions. *Journal of Psychiatry and Law, 4,* 171–244.

Crowe, M. J., Marks, I. M., Agras, W. S., & Leitenberg, H. (1972). Time-limited desensitization, implosion and shaping for phobic patients: A cross over study. *Behaviour Research and Therapy, 10,* 319–328.

Dadds, M. R., Adlington, F. M., & Christensen, A. P. (1987). Children's perceptions of time out and other maternal disciplinary strategies: The effects of clinic status and exposure to behavioral treatment. *Behaviour Change, 4,* 3–13.

Deitz, S. M. (1978). Current status of applied behavior analysis. *American Psychologist, 33,* 805–814.

Elliot, S. N. (1986). Children's ratings of the acceptability of classroom interventions for misbehavior: Findings and methodological considerations. *Journal of School Psychology, 24,* 23–35.

Elliot, S. N., Witt, J. C., Galvin, G. A., & Moe, G. L. (1986). Children's involvement in intervention selection: Acceptability of interventions for misbehaving peers. *Professional Psychology: Research and Practice, 17,* 235–241.

Elliot, S. N., Witt, J. C., Galvin, G. A., & Peterson, R. (1984). Acceptability of positive and reductive behavioral interventions: Factors that influence teachers' decisions. *Journal of School Psychology, 22,* 353–360.

Fincham, F. D., & Spettell, C. (1984). The acceptability of dry bed training and urine alarm training as treatments of nocturnal enuresis. *Behavior Therapy, 15,* 388–394.

Garvey, W. P., & Hegrenes, J. R. (1966). Desensitization techniques in the treatment of school phobia. *American Journal of Orthopsychiatry, 36,* 147–152.

Ginsburg, H., & Opper, S. (1979). *Piaget's theory of intellectual development* (2nd ed.). Englewood Cliffs, NJ: Prentice-Hall.

Hobbs, S. A., Walle, D. L., & Caldwell, H. S. (1984). Maternal evaluation of social reinforcement and time-out: Effects of brief parent training. *Journal of Consulting and Clinical Psychology, 52,* 135–136.

Inhelder, B., & Piaget, J. (1958). *The growth of logical thinking.* New York: Basic Books.

Kaser-Boyd, N., Adelman, H. S., & Taylor, L. (1985). Minors' ability to identify risks and benefits of therapy. *Professional Psychology: Research and Practice, 16*, 411–417.

Kaser-Boyd, N., Adelman, H. S., Taylor, L., & Nelson, P. (1986). Children's understanding of risks and benefits of psychotherapy. *Journal of Clinical Child Psychology, 15*, 165–171.

Kazdin, A. E. (1977). Assessing the clinical or applied importance of behavior change through social validation. *Behavior Modification, 1*, 427–452.

Kazdin, A. E. (1980a). Acceptability of time out from reinforcement procedures for disruptive child behavior. *Behavior Therapy, 11*, 329–344.

Kazdin, A. E. (1980b). Acceptability of alternative treatments for deviant child behavior. *Journal of Applied Behavior Analysis, 13*, 259–273.

Kazdin, A. E. (1981). Acceptability of child treatment techniques: The influence of treatment efficacy and adverse side effects. *Behavior Therapy, 12*, 493–506.

Kazdin, A. E. (1984). Acceptability of aversive procedures and medication as treatment alternatives for deviant child behavior. *Journal of Abnormal Child Psychology, 12*, 289–302.

Kazdin, A. E. (1986). Acceptability of psychotherapy and hospitalization for disturbed children: Parent and child perspectives. *Journal of Clinical Child Psychology, 15*, 222–240.

Kazdin, A. E., & Cole, P. M. (1981). Attitudes and labeling biases toward behavior modification: The effects of labels, content and jargon. *Behavior Therapy, 12*, 56–68.

Kazdin, A. E., French, N. H., & Sherick, R. B. (1981). Acceptability of alternative treatments for children: Evaluations by inpatient children, parents and staff. *Journal of Consulting and Clinical Psychology, 49*, 900–907.

Kazdin, A. E., & Wilson, G. T. (1978). Criteria for evaluating psychotherapy. *Archives of General Psychiatry, 35*, 407–416.

Kennedy, W. A. (1965). School phobia: Rapid treatment of fifty cases. *Journal of Abnormal Psychology, 70*, 285–289.

Kiesler, C. A. (1983). Social psychological issues in studying consumer satisfaction with behavior therapy. *Behavior Therapy, 14*, 226–236.

King, N. J., Hamilton, D. I., & Ollendick, T.H. (1988). *Children's phobias: A behavioural perspective*. Chichester: John Wiley.

Koocher, G. P. (1976). Bill of rights for children in psychotherapy. In G. P. Koocher (Ed.), *Children's rights and the mental health professions*. New York: John Wiley.

Lazarus, A. A., & Abramovitz, A. (1962). The use of 'emotive imagery' in the treatment of children's phobias. *Journal of Mental Science, 108*, 191–195.

Lebow, J. (1982). Consumer satisfaction with mental health treatment. *Psychological Bulletin, 91*, 244–259.

Lebow, J. L. (1983). Research assessing consumer satisfaction with mental health treatment. *Evaluation and Program Planning, 6*, 211–236.

McKinney, J. P., Chin, R. J., Reinhart, M. A., & Trierweiler, G. (1985). Health values in early adolescence. *Journal of Clinical Child Psychology, 14*, 315–319.

McMahon, R. J., & Forehand, R. L. (1983). Consumer satisfaction in behavioral treatment of children: Types, issues and recommendations. *Behavior Therapy, 14*, 209–225.

Melton, G. B. (1981). Children's participation in treatment planning: Psychological and legal issues. *Professional Psychology, 12*, 246–252.

Miller, P. M. (1972). The use of visual imagery and muscle relaxation in the counterconditioning of a phobic child: A case study. *Journal of Nervous and Mental Disease, 154*, 457–459.

Mudford, O. C. (1987). Acceptability of a visual screening procedure for reducing stereotypy in mentally retarded children: Evaluation by New Zealand institutional staff. *Behaviour Change, 4*, 4–13.

Naifeh, S. J. (1984). Acceptability of alternative treatment approaches: A comparative analysis of child and family therapies. *Dissertation Abstracts International, 46*, 1696-B.

Norton, G. R., Allen, G. E., & Hilton, J. (1983). The social validity of treatments for agoraphobia. *Behaviour Research and Therapy, 21*, 393–399.

Norton, G. R., Austen, S., Allen, G. E., & Hilton, J. (1983). Acceptability of time out from reinforcement for disruptive child behavior: A further analysis. *Child and Family Behavior Therapy, 5*, 31–41.

O'Leary, K. D. (1984). The image of behavior therapy: It is time to take a stand. *Behavior Therapy, 15*, 219–233.

Ollendick, T. H., & Cerny, J. A. (1981). *Clinical behavior therapy with children.* New York: Plenum.

Ollendick, T. H., & Hersen, M. (1984). *Child behavioral assessment.* New York: Pergamon.

Parloff, M. B. (1983). Who will be satisfied by "consumer satisfaction" evidence? *Behavior Therapy, 14*, 242–246.

Reid, D. H., & Whitman, T. L. (1983). Behavioral staff management in institutions: A critical review of effectiveness and acceptability. *Analysis and Intervention in Developmental Disabilities, 3*, 131–149.

Ross, A. O. (1980). *Psychological disorders of children: A behavioral approach to theory, research, and therapy* (2nd ed.). New York: McGraw-Hill.

Saunders, J. T., & Repucci, N.D. (1978). The social identity of behavior modification. *Progress in Behavior Modification, 6*, 143–158.

Singh, N. N., & Katz, R. C. (1985). On the modification of acceptability ratings for alternative child treatments. *Behavior Modification, 9*, 375–386.

Taylor, L., & Adelman, H. S. (1986). Facilitating children's participation in decisions that affect them: From concept to practice. *Journal of Clinical Child Psychology, 15*, 346–351.

Turco, T. L., & Elliot, S. N. (1986). Assessment of students' acceptability ratings of teacher-initiated interventions for classroom misbehavior. *Journal of School Psychology, 24*, 277–283.

Turco, T. L., & Elliot, S. N. (in press). Children's acceptability judgements of teacher-initiated interventions. *Journal of School Psychology.*

Turkat, I. D., & Forehand, R. (1980). The future of behavior therapy. *Progress in Behavior Modification, 9*, 1–47.

Turkat, I. D., Harris, F. C., & Forehand, R. (1979). An assessment of the public reaction to behavior modification. *Journal of Behavior Therapy and Experimental Psychiatry, 10*, 101–103.

Van Houten, R. (1979). Social validation: The evolution of standards of competency for target behaviors. *Journal of Applied Behavior Analysis, 12*, 581–591.

Walle, D. L., Hobbs, S. A., & Caldwell, H. S. (1984). Sequencing of parent training procedures. *Behavior Modification, 8*, 540–552.

Weithorn, L. A. (1982). Developmental factors and competence to make informed treatment decisions. In G. B. Melton (Ed.), *Legal reforms affecting child and youth services: Child and youth services.* New York: Hawthorn.

Witt, J. C., & Elliot, S. N. (1985). Acceptability of classroom management strategies. In T. R. Kratochwill (Ed.), *Advances in school psychology* (Vol. 4, pp. 251–288). Hillsdale, NJ: Erlbaum.

Witt, J. C., & Martens, B. K. (1983). Assessing the acceptability of behavioral interventions used in classrooms. *Psychology in the Schools, 20*, 510–517.

Witt, J. C., Martens, B. K., & Elliot, S. N. (1984). Factors affecting teachers' judgements of the acceptability of behavioral interventions: Time involvement, behavior problem severity, and type of intervention. *Behavior Therapy, 15*, 204–209.

Witt, J. C., Moe, G., Gutkin, T. B., & Andrews, L. (1984). The effect of saying the same thing in different ways: The problem of language and jargon in school-based consultation. *Journal of School Psychology, 22*, 361–367.

Witt, J. C., & Robbins, J. R. (1985). Acceptability of reductive interventions for the control of inappropriate child behavior. *Journal of Abnormal Child Psychology, 13*, 59–67.

Wolf, M. M. (1978). Social validity: The case for subjective measurement or how applied behavior analysis is finding its heart. *Journal of Applied Behavior Analysis, 11*, 203–214.

Woolfolk, A. E., Woolfolk, R. L., & Wilson, G. T. (1977). A rose by any other name . . . : Labeling bias and attitudes toward behavior modification. *Journal of Consulting and Clinical Psychology, 45*, 184–191.

Woolfolk, R. L., & Woolfolk, A. E. (1979). Modifying the effect of the behavior modification label. *Behavior Therapy, 10*, 575–578.

Yeaton, W. H., & Sechrest, L. (1981). Critical dimensions in the choice and maintenance of successful treatments: Strength, integrity, and effectiveness. *Journal of Consulting and Clinical Psychology, 49*, 156–167.

THE BEHAVIORAL TREATMENT OF UNIPOLAR DEPRESSION IN ADULT OUTPATIENTS

DAVID O. ANTONUCCIO, CLAY H. WARD

V.A. Medical Center and University of Nevada School of Medicine
Reno, Nevada

BLAKE H. TEARNAN

Sierra Pain Institute, Reno, Nevada

Authors' Note: We would like to thank Carol A. Vasso and Julie Anderson for their clerical assistance.

I. INTRODUCTION

The aim of this chapter is to review controlled research from the past decade on the behavioral treatment of unipolar depression in adult outpatients. This review is, of necessity, selective in nature and is in no way intended to cover every study conducted on depression. Any excursion into treatment must start with a definition of the problem, a technology for assessing the problem, and a theory that helps guide treatment. First, a review is presented of recent epidemiological research that has helped clarify the extent of this potentially serious but very treatable disorder. This is followed by a discussion of current issues and methods in assessment, because accurate assessment is an essential precursor to effective treatment. A brief summary of behavioral theory of depression is followed by an overview of the various treatment approaches that have been developed under the umbrella of behavior therapy. Cognitive therapies are included in this review because cognitions are often treated as learned covert behaviors, and this research is in the empirical tradition of behavioral analysis. An attempt is made to summarize the common elements and effectiveness of treatments with demonstrated efficacy. A special section has been included on the relative efficacy of drugs and behavioral interventions, a topic of some controversy and practical importance. We provide evidence that behavioral treatments are at least as effective as medications in the treatment of unipolar depression. Finally, some of the more common clinical problems are considered: relapse, compliance with "homework" assignments, handling suicidal behavior, and matching the most appropriate behavioral treatment to the patient's needs. It is hoped that this chapter will be a resource for the practicing clinician as well as a guidepost for future researchers in depression.

II. EPIDEMIOLOGY OF DEPRESSION

Depression, like the common cold, is a highly prevalent condition. Results of several major epidemiologic studies suggest that at any given time, from 3% to 9% of the adult population in the United States meets criteria for unipolar depression (Amenson & Lewinsohn, 1981; Aneshensel, 1985; Hirschfeld & Cross, 1982; Murphy, Sobol, Neff, Olivier, & Leighton, 1984; Myers et al., 1984; Noll & Dubinsky, 1985; Oliver & Simmons, 1985). As much as 20% of the adult population is experiencing at least some depressive symptoms (Oliver & Simmons, 1985). The lifetime incidence of unipolar depression is estimated to be 20% to 55% of all adults.

It is worth noting that epidemiological studies rely on the willingness of people to participate in extensive structured diagnostic interviews, to complete numerous forms, and to disclose highly detailed personal information. It is conceivable that many depressed people declined to participate in these studies, resulting in a selection bias and an underestimate of the prevalence of depression. For example, one study statistically corrected for selection bias and estimated that the prevalence of depression in community mental health center populations approaches 44% rather than the 25% derived from a censored sample (Frank, Schulberg, Welch, Sherick, & Costello, 1985).

These epidemiological studies consistently find rates of depression for women at least twice those for men, rates of unipolar depression at least four times greater than for bipolar disorder, an equal sex ratio for bipolar disorder, and a possible cohort effect (i.e., cohorts born after 1936 report earlier age of onset and higher rates of major depression). The sex difference appears cross-culturally and does not appear to be an artifact or a function of psychosocial role differences (Weissman, Leaf, Holzer, Myers, & Tischler, 1984). A recent review of the data on the sex difference proposes an explanation that men are more likely to engage in distracting behaviors that dampen their mood when depressed, but women are more likely to amplify their moods by ruminating about their depressed states and the possible causes of these states (Nolen-Hoeksema, 1987).

Depression also appears to be significantly correlated with less education, nonwhite racial status, younger age, less social support, and less than full-time employment (Noll & Dubinsky, 1985). Enduring strain in social roles, persistent losses, and the lack of gratifying emotional ties to others can influence depressive symptoms, resulting in their persistence over time (Aneshensel, 1985). The risk for developing an initial episode of unipolar depression is very low during childhood, increases dramatically during adolescence and young adulthood, peaks during the middle years, and decreases during the elderly years (Lewinsohn, Duncan, Stanton, & Hautzinger, 1986).

Several family studies of depression have been conducted. One study found that depressions associated with early onset, anxiety disorder, or alcoholism were independently related to increased risk of major depression in first-degree relatives (Weissman et al., 1986). After accounting for these variables, other factors (e.g., endogenous symptoms, history of hospitalization, suicidal ideation or attempts) were not associated with increased risk of major depression in relatives. Bland, Newman, and Orn (1986) found the lowest risk (3.4%) for depression in relatives of patients with late onset, single-episode depression. The highest risk (17.4%) was for relatives of patients with early age at onset and recurrent depression.

There is increasing evidence that unipolar depression is causally complex. Its development is likely to involve a combination of biogenetic factors and psychosocial factors. Whatever the relative contribution of these factors, it is important to recognize and effectively intervene with depression as early as possible, because the probability of recovery from major depression steadily lessens the longer the depression lasts (Keller, Shapiro, Lavori, & Wolfe, 1982).

III. OVERVIEW OF THE BEHAVIORAL APPROACH

Currently, behavioral approaches to treatment of depression are primarily characterized by a scientific methodology rather than a specific theory or set of techniques (e.g., Kazdin, 1982). Behavioral treatments of depression tend to rely on empirical findings from general psychology, focus on current rather than historical determinants of behavior, and utilize an ongoing integration of assessment and treatment. The behavioral model suggests that unipolar depression is primarily a learned phenomenon related to negative interactions between the person and the environment (e.g., negative social relationships or low rate of reinforcement). These environmental interactions can influence and be influenced by cognitions, behaviors, and emotions, and relationships among these factors are seen as reciprocal. Behavioral strategies are designed to intervene in this system by teaching patients skills designed to interrupt a maladaptive pattern of behavior, cognition, and emotion.

Hoberman and Lewinsohn (1985) point out several commonalities associated with behavioral approaches to the treatment of depression. These treatments often begin with a collaborative redefinition of the patient's problems in a way that the patient will have a feeling of control, understanding, and hope. For example, the assessment usually involves a functional evaluation of the patterns of behavior and environmental influences contributing to the patient's experience of depression. The patient is usually asked to track mood, activities, and thoughts. Patients are encouraged to set modest, achievable goals so as to ensure early success experiences, thereby enhancing feelings of self-efficacy. Patients are encouraged to make specific agreements with themselves (e.g., contracting) and to give themselves rewards for achieving their goals. Most behavioral treatment approaches involve some systematic training designed to remedy various performance and skill deficits (e.g., assertiveness training, stress management, cognitive strategies, contingency management skills, or communication training). Finally, most of these approaches are designed to be time-limited, anywhere from 4 weeks to 12 weeks. The time limit puts pressure on the therapist and patient to set realistic treatment goals and even provides incentive for working toward their accomplishment. All behavioral approaches rely on a thorough and accurate assessment. Behavioral assessment involves both making a differential diagnosis and a functional analysis of depressive behavior.

IV. ASSESSMENT

A. Diagnosis and Functional Assessment

The assessment of depression is a complex problem. Patients usually present with a variety of symptoms that loosely fit within the same conceptual scheme. There is no identifying symptom that captures the diversity of the phenomena. Indeed, the correlation among depressive symptoms, although significant, is not sufficient to predict one symptom from another (Lewinsohn, 1975). Behaviorists have traditionally defined depression as a cluster of behaviors that are associated and can occur in varying combinations (Rehm, 1976). Unfortunately, there is little agreement regarding the nature and complexity of the various combinations observed.

Different diagnostic classifications have been developed to help organize and promote understanding of the psychopathology of depression. The most widely used classification of psychopathology in the United States is the *Diagnostic and Statistical Manual of Mental Disorders*, third edition, revised (DSM-III-R; American Psychiatric Association, 1987). DSM-III-R lists several symptoms characteristic of a major depressive disorder. These include cognitive (e.g., indecisiveness, suicidal thoughts), emotional (e.g., feelings of sadness, feelings of worthlessness, guilt), behavioral (e.g., reduced rate of behavior), and physiological (e.g., fatigue, weight loss, insomnia, psychomotor changes) signs of disturbance. In order to be diagnosed with major depression, the patient must exhibit at least five of the listed symptoms for a two-week period, and they must represent a change from a previous level of functioning. At least one of the symptoms must be depressed mood or loss of interest or pleasure.

DSM-III-R makes the further distinction between symptoms of major depression and other mood disorders of nonorganic etiology, where feelings of depression and loss of interest are cardinal features. A milder but more chronic version of major depression is dysthymia, which is similar to what was formerly called neurotic depression. For at least two years the patient must exhibit several depressive symptoms that can wax and wane, with normal moods interspersed. Dysthymia and major depression can occur simultaneously. The third DSM-III-R category of depression is adjustment disorder with depressed mood. Here the patient's depression is associated with obvious psychosocial stressors such as loss of a job, grief, or illness. While DSM-III-R helps to communicate the phenomenon of depression, it suffers from drawbacks that limit its utility. The language of the diagnostic categories is sometimes unclear, and concepts are rarely operationally defined to permit their measurement.

Other minor classification systems of depression exist, such as the typology distinguishing endogenous and reactive depression. One recent study examined depressed patients who had been exposed to upsetting life events prior to onset of their symptoms (Copeland, 1984). There were no clinical distinctions between patients diagnosed as having endogenous versus reactive depression and no differences on a 5-year follow-up assessment. Although there is only weak support for the validity of this classification, it remains popular and is still widely used. A related subtype is melancholic depression. Recent evidence suggests that DSM-III-R criteria for melancholia do not identify a qualitatively distinct subgroup, but instead simply reflect increased severity across all depressive symptoms (Zimmerman, Coryell, & Pfohl, 1986).

While the patient may present with depression, it may not be the primary problem. Depression is frequently seen in a variety of psychological disorders, such as anxiety, schizophrenia, paranoia, and the bipolar mood disorders. The accurate identification of bipolar depression is particularly important. Bipolar depression, a syndrome characterized by a distinct period of elevated, expansive, or irritable mood with other associated manic symptoms alternating with or preceding the dysphoric episode, has been shown to be a distinct disorder requiring quite different treatment (Khouri & Akiskal, 1986).

Depression is very common in patients with medical illness (Rodin & Voshart, 1986). Koranyi (1979) found, in 2,090 consecutive referrals to an outpatient psychiatric clinic where depression was a major part of the symptom picture, that 8% had an underlying organic disorder responsible for the affective disturbance. In another 22% the medical problems aggravated the psychiatric complaints. Depression can be associated with medical illness in one of several ways (Dietch & Zetin, 1983; Rodin & Voshart, 1986). The patient may present with depression in the presence of an unrelated medical condition. Treating the medical problem is unlikely to improve the depression. However, depression may be a reaction to the impairment and stress of medical illness. Alleviation of the patient's organic condition should reduce the mood disturbance. Depression of psychological origin can also frequently mimic symptoms characteristic of medical illness. For example, depressed individuals often complain of head pain, gastrointestinal distress, appetite disturbance, memory loss, fatigue, and weakness. Finally, depression may represent an underlying medical condition. Hypothyroidism, hyperthyroidism, hyperparathyroidism, pneumonia, infectious viral hepatitis, mononucleosis, arteriosclerotic cardiovascular disease, essential hypertension, hypochromic anemia, peptic ulcer, pulmonary infarction, pulmonary emboli, and diabetes mellitus can each be causative of depression (Hall, Popkin, Devaul, Fallaice, & Stickney, 1978).

Unfortunately, studies have shown that many physicians do not reliably identify organically related depression. Koranyi (1979), for instance, found that 16% of patients referred by a physician to a general mental health clinic were suffering from a medical illness directly responsible for the complaint of depression. Johnson (1968) showed that of 250 consecutive admissions to a psychiatric clinic, 12% had physical conditions judged to be etiologically related to their psychiatric symptoms. Of these, 80% were misdiagnosed by referring physicians. Understanding organic causes of depression obviously can help the clinician to work more cooperatively with the referring physician in identifying and effectively treating these depressions.

Once likely differentials are dismissed and the diagnosis of depression is made, the assessment process should shift focus by examining the relationship of the individual's depressive symptomatology to various environmental, cognitive, behavioral, and physiological events. The purpose is to establish whether or not a causal link can be drawn between the occurrence of these events and an exacerbation or triggering of the depressive symptoms. Individuals are asked to recall any patterns they have observed and are instructed to self-monitor their behavior to uncover any associations of which they were unaware or unable to report. The Pleasant Events Schedule (PES; MacPhillamy & Lewinsohn, 1982) is one example of many self-report instruments that can assist the clinician in this task. On the PES the patient is asked to produce daily mood ratings as well as track daily pleasant activities. These data can be graphed, and the relationship between certain activities and depression can be determined, thereby helping to guide treatment. At a minimum, self-monitoring involves having the patient rate mood on 0–10 scale one to four times per day and note any relevant events. Hoberman and Lewinsohn (1985) also recommend home observations, especially around mealtimes, when all family members are often present. Obviously, practical and economic considerations will limit the use of routine home visits.

B. Self-Report

Several instruments are available for assessing severity of depression and assisting the clinician in making the diagnosis of depression. Commonly used instruments showing some empirical validation are discussed below (for a complete discussion, see Gotlib & Colby, 1987; Rehm, 1976).

Minnesota Multiphasic Personality Inventory (MMPI) Depression Scale. The depression scale is one of 10 clinical scales of the MMPI (Hathaway, 1965). It was originally developed to help identify depressed patients. It is composed of 60 true-false items that were empirically derived. It is one of the most widely used instruments for measuring depression and extensive data have been generated pertaining to its use. It has been criticized for the heterogeneity of items and its complex factor structure (Gotlib & Colby, 1987). The scale has moderate test-retest reliability and better split-half reliability scores, but its concurrent and discriminant validity are only moderate (Rehm, 1976). Attempts have been made to revise the scale and address some of the test's shortcomings (e.g., Costello & Comrey, 1967), with only modest success.

Beck Depression Scale (BDI). The BDI (Beck, Ward, Mendelson, Mock, & Erbaugh, 1961) is a frequently used self-report measure of depression. It consists of 84 items arranged in 21 groups. The individual is instructed to choose one item from each group. The items are arranged in order of severity within each group. The test was constructed to measure the cognitive, behavioral, and physiological symptoms of depression. It was not designed as a diagnostic tool, but was constructed to measure the severity of depressive symptomatology across a variety of disorders (Gotlib & Colby, 1987). The BDI has demonstrated high internal consistency and strong reliability coefficients (Tanaka-Matsumi & Kameoka, 1986). There is good evidence for concurrent, construct, and discriminative validity (Beck, Steer, & Garbin, 1988). The advantages of the BDI are that it is relatively short, easy to interpret, useful for a variety of populations, and empirically sound.

Lubin Depression Adjective Check List (DACL). The DACL (Lubin, 1967) consists of several adjectives that are checked by the individual. There are negative and positive adjectives for each alternative form of the scale. The adjectives were chosen because of their synonymity to depression. There are a separate series of alternative tests for male and females. The DACL has been shown to have good reliability and the correlation between alternative forms is high. Discriminative validity for distinguishing between depressed and nondepressed is acceptable, and concurrent validity scores are moderate (Rehm, 1976). The advantages of the DACL are its short administrative time and amenability to frequent usage.

Zung Self-Rating Depression Scale (SDS). The SDS (Zung, 1965) is made up of 20 items identified in previous factor-analytic studies. The individual is required to indicate the degree of agreement for each item. Each item is grouped into three areas: pervasive affect, physiological equivalents, and psychological concomitants. The SDS correlates well with other depression instruments; however, it is not able to differentiate very well among different severity levels (Rehm, 1976). There is evidence for its good reliability and internal consistency (Tanaka-Matsumi & Kameoka, 1986).

Inventory to Diagnose Depression (IDD). A more recently developed self-report measure is the IDD (Zimmerman & Coryell, 1987), which is specifically designed to diagnose major depressive disorder according to the DSM-III criteria. It has good psychometric properties as evidenced by a reliability alpha of .92 and concordance with other depression scales (e.g., BDI or HRSD) above .80. The validity of this measure for depression awaits future research efforts.

C. Interview Rating Scales

Schedule for Affective Disorders and Schizophrenia (SADS). The SADS (Endicott & Spitzer, 1978) is an interview-based clinical rating scale that was developed to help increase the reliability of diagnoses and was intended to be used in conjunction with the Research Diagnostic Criteria (RDC; Spitzer, Endicott, & Robbins, 1978). The SADS is also designed to measure psychotic, anxiety, and personality disorders. There are several versions of the instrument. The most recent derivation, known as the SCID-P (Structured Clinical Interview for DSM-III-R—Patient Versions; Spitzer & Williams, 1985), is designed to coincide with the diagnostic criteria of DSM-III-R. The SADS has been shown to be sensitive to change in levels of depressive symptoms over time (e.g., Endicott, Cohen, Nee, Fleiss, & Sarantakos, 1981).

Hamilton Rating Scale for Depression (HRSD). The HRSD (Hamilton, 1960) is a clinical interview rating scale that consists of 17 Likert-type items. The scale was designed for use with patients who have already received the diagnosis of depression. It is useful for determining the individual's level of depression. The items require ratings of cognitive, behavioral, and physiological parameters by experienced clinicians. The scale has been shown to have good interrater reliability; however, interim correlations were found to be somewhat low and the factor structure of the scale is conceptually ambiguous (Rehm, 1976).

D. Behavioral Observation

Relatively few empirical studies have examined the overt behavior of depressed patients. The bias of earlier theories favored analyses exploring the disturbance of mood and cognition, not behavior. Moreover, practical considerations have limited the utility of gathering samples of overt behavior. Studies that have been conducted suggest that the verbal and nonverbal behavior of depressed patients may be significantly different from that of normal controls. For example, Lewinsohn and his colleagues revealed that depressed patients emit fewer verbal behaviors per hour than nondepressed subjects, emit and initiate fewer questions, are slower to respond to reactions, and elicit fewer positive reactions from others (Lewinsohn, Weinstein, & Alper, 1970; Libet & Lewinsohn, 1973). Williams, Barlow, and Agras (1972) found strong correlations between ratings of depressed patients' talking, smiling, motor activity, and time out of room to scores on the BDI and the HRSD. One study was able to demonstrate differences in activity level using telemetric monitoring between different depressed subtypes (Kupfer, Detre, Foster, Tucker, & Delgado, 1972). This method of assessment merits further empirical scrutiny.

E. Physiological Assessment

The search for biological markers to assess depression has yielded few unequivocal findings. Many researchers have been frustrated trying to identify what has become the "Holy Grail" of psychiatric diagnosis (Lehmann, 1985). For some, physiological markers represent a potential "objective" test for depression. One of the most researched topics in this area is the dexamethasone suppression test (DST). The test is used to differentiate individuals with endogenous or melancholia-like depressive disorders from normals and individuals with reactive depressions. Individuals with suppressed cortisol production after receiving dexamethasone, a potent anti-inflammatory adrenocortical steroid, are thought to have endogenous depression. Several early studies showed support for the validity of the test (see Lehmann, 1985). The DST was reported to have a sensitivity close to 50% for determining the presence of endogenous depression. Unfortunately, more recent reports have found that advanced age, weight loss, Alzheimer's disease, alcoholism, and bipolar disorder are all associated with positive DST results. One recent study found the DST was not associated with any outcome variables in a six-month prospective study (Zimmerman, Coryell, & Pfohl, 1987). The test's nonspecificity led a recent American Psychiatric Association panel of experts in depressive disorders to conclude that the clinical utility of the DST is limited (APA Task Force on Laboratory Tests in Psychiatry, 1987).

Other biological markers that have been explored include thyrotropin-releasing hormone stimulating tests, growth hormone tests, levels of neurotransmitter metabolites, affinity of imipramine and serotonin to platelets, alteration of the EEG sleep profile, and skin conductance. None of these has proven to be sensitive and specific enough to be of practical use clinically (Lehmann, 1985). Most recently, positron emission tomography (PET) has been employed in the differential diagnosis of depression. The PET provides an in vivo study of local biochemical reactions in humans and has further supported the distinction between bipolar and unipolar depression (Schwartz, Baxter, Mazziotta, Gerner, & Phelps, 1987).

F. Suicidal Risk

Assessment of suicidal risk is an important component in the assessment of depressed patients. Depressed patients are more likely to engage in suicidal behavior than patients with any other diagnosis (Miles, 1977). Suicidal behavior cannot be predicted accurately (Linehan, 1981). Even among high-risk groups, suicide is a low-base-rate behavior, making reliable prediction virtually impossible. There is no generally accepted instrument for assessing suicidal risk, although many have been proposed and developed, usually for the general population. There are likely different risk factors for the general population compared to those already at risk for suicide, making many of these instruments of questionable clinical utility (Motto, 1985). Currently, the best predictor of suicidal behavior is past suicidal behavior. From 20% to 65% of completed suicides have a prior suicide attempt (Linehan, 1981). Therefore, the best predictor is often not available to the clinician because many people kill themselves on their first documented attempt.

Murphy (1974) notes that using "high-risk" demographic criteria in one of his studies would have identified only 16% of completed suicides. Given this state of affairs, we advocate that clinicians supplement routine suicidal inquiry and clinical judgment with brief practical instruments. In a stepwise fashion, a patient should be asked about current depressed feelings, current feelings that life is not worth living, current suicidal ideation, current suicidal plans, past suicidal intent and behavior, available means for suicidal behavior, and current drug use or other self-destructive behavior. Item 9 of the Beck Depression Inventory is designed to evaluate suicidal risk. If a patient scores a 2 or a 3 on this item, the individual should be considered to be at enough risk to warrant further evaluation for hospitalization or other risk-reducing interventions.

V. BEHAVIOR THERAPIES

Once a diagnostic and functional assessment are completed, and the issue of suicidal risk addressed, a behavior therapist has a smorgasbord of interventions from which to choose for the depressed patient. The treatments outlined here are those that have been demonstrated to be effective in controlled clinical studies. Fortunately, there are many behavioral strategies that are effective in the amelioration of depression.

A. Cognitive Therapy

A wide range of stressors and negative events may serve as antecedents to depression. Yet, many ambiguous or minor events can produce profound depression. Cognitive therapies are the result of an intellectual tradition dating at least back to Stoic philosophy, and more recently empirical psychopathology, that an individual's interpretation of an event is often more important than the event itself (Bebbington, 1985).

Cognitive theories of depression emphasize that individual differences in the perception of self, others, and events influence the emotional and behavioral symptoms of depression. Although far from empirically settled (see Coyne & Gotlib, 1983), available research supports the clinical perspective that depressed individuals have negative evaluative tendencies that affect a wide range of cognitive processes, including expectancies of response-outcome contingencies, self-concept, self-referent information processing, judgments, and attributions. Furthermore, these cognitive styles have a reciprocal relation to motivational and affective responses associated with depression (Ruehlman, West, & Pasahow, 1985). For example, motivational deficits resulting from expectations that negative outcomes will occur regardless of the response help ensure the occurrence of future negative response-outcome contingencies (i.e., the so-called self-fulfilling prophecy). The attributional reformulation of the learned helplessness model (Abramson, Seligman, & Teasdale, 1978) and Beck's (Beck, Rush, Shaw, & Emery, 1979; Beck & Young, 1985) cognitive theory appear to have the most empirical support among contemporary cognitive models of depression.

The attributional reformulation of the learned helplessness model postulates that people who tend to assign causal explanations for negative events to internal, stable, and global causes are prone to depression (Abramson et al., 1978). The learned helplessness model was originally proposed to account for specific motivational, affective, and cognitive deficits that occur in response to uncontrollable negative events (Seligman, 1974, 1975). Helplessness theory, however, could not account for the paradoxical loss of self-esteem (Abramson & Sackheim, 1977) or the duration and extent to which these deficits generalized following exposure to uncontrollable events (Peterson & Seligman, 1984). The reformulation incorporated the individual's interpretation or attribution of the event as the additional variable that determines helplessness and depression. When a person is confronted with an uncontrollable negative event, the cause may be assigned to something about the person or situation (internal versus external), something that will persist across time or that is temporally limited (stable versus situational), and something that influences other events and outcomes or is limited to the current event (global versus specific). These three explanatory dimensions determine the effect on self-esteem, chronicity, and generality of helplessness and depression (Abramson et al., 1978; Peterson & Seligman, 1984).

The clinical significance of the learned helplessness reformulation theory of depression is that considerable research supports the notion that causal explanations for negative events are a risk factor for depression (Peterson & Seligman, 1984). Attributional style can be quantified (e.g., Peterson et al., 1982), which suggests that specific attributional tendencies that are theoretically related to depression can be clinically identified and targeted for intervention. Teaching individuals to change attributional styles, such as making internal, stable, and global attribution for good events and external, situational, and specific attributions for negative events has potential in the treatment and prevention of depression (Peterson, 1982; Seligman, 1981). Although attributional retraining appears promising in the areas of both achievement motivation and depression (Forsterling, 1985), treatment outcome studies have not adequately addressed this issue.

Beck's cognitive model of depression postulates that a cognitive triad of a negative view of oneself, negative interpretations of current events, and a negative view of the future are enduring cognitive styles that play a primary causal role in depressive cognitions and symptomatology (Beck et al., 1979). According to Beck, these unrealistic and distorted cognitive structures or schemas operate in an automatic fashion to produce misperceptions and misinterpretations of environmental events, resulting in depressive affective and behavioral reactions. The goal of cognitive therapy is to facilitate the evaluation and modification of the schemata that lead to recurrent negative thinking and depressive symptoms. Empirical studies have generally supported the theoretical basis of this model (Wright & Beck, 1983).

Treatment in cognitive therapy is usually limited to 20 sessions over 10 to 12 weeks (Beck et al., 1979; Wright & Beck, 1983). The individual sessions focus on discussion of previously assigned homework, relevant aspects of the patient's thinking, and a homework assignment for the next session. Beck's cognitive therapy utilizes a variety of behavioral strategies (Beck & Young, 1985), since depressed patients are often initially unable to engage in cognitive modification. Therefore, it is often useful to initiate behavioral interventions to halt or reverse the social and activity withdrawal associated with depression. Such techniques as assertion training, pleasant activities scheduling, behavioral modeling, and role playing are employed to instill a sense of self-efficacy and decrease hopelessness. Homework assignments are given on a regular basis so that the patient will practice and reinforce therapeutic interventions, and to test the validity of the patient's schemata.

As therapy progresses, more therapeutic attention is devoted to understanding and modifying the core schemata and their relationship to feelings, behaviors, and other cognitions. The patient is asked to identify and monitor upsetting events, feelings associated with those events, and automatic cognitions that are associated with dysphoria or negative feelings, and to consider alternative interpretations using concrete evidence to test the validity of the cognitions. In therapy, the point is emphasized that events can be interpreted in a variety of ways and that different interpretations lead to different affective and behavioral responses. For example, individuals who engage in "all-or-nothing thinking" may tend to refer to themselves as total failures following a mistake, which can result in a negative affective state, low self-concept, and decreased adaptive behavioral responses. Overgeneralization, disqualifying the positive, jumping to conclusions, and catastrophizing are examples of common cognitive distortions that form the basis for depression (see Burns, 1980).

Several controlled and comparative studies support the efficacy of cognitive therapy in the treatment of depression. One of the initial studies compared cognitive therapy and imipramine hydrochloride in the treatment of patients who were moderately to severely depressed according to research diagnostic criteria (Rush, Beck, Kovacs, & Hollon, 1977). Patients treated with cognitive therapy showed significantly greater improvement in depressive symptoms compared to the pharmacotherapy group. A similar study compared cognitive therapy and imipramine hydrochloride in treating 44 men and women who were at least moderately depressed (e.g., BDI score greater than 20) (Kovacs, Rush, Beck, & Hollon, 1981). Patients were treated for 12 weeks with a one-year follow-up. The results of this study indicated that cognitive therapy was superior to pharmacotherapy in symptom reduction at therapy termination and one-year follow-up. Cognitive therapy was also associated with a lower dropout rate, and patients identified as endogenomorphic versus nonendogenomorphic depressed responded equally well to cognitive therapy. Blackburn and associates report results indicating that cognitive therapy alone is as effective as pharmacotherapy or combined cognitive and pharmacotherapy in the treatment of depression (Blackburn & Bishop, 1981; Blackburn, Bishop, Glen, Whalley, & Christie, 1981).

In a controlled study, Wilson, Goldin, and Charbonneau-Pouis (1983) compared cognitive therapy, behavioral therapy, and a no-therapy control group in the treatment of 25 depressed men and women. Results of this study indicated that both cognitive and behavioral therapies were superior to the no-treatment control group and that there were no significant differences between the cognitive and behavioral therapy groups in the treatment of depression at termination or five-month follow-up. Several other studies have supported the efficacy of cognitive therapy in the treatment of depression (LaPointe & Rimm, 1980; Shaw, 1977; Zeiss, Lewinsohn, & Munoz, 1979). For example, the comparative study by Murphy, Simons, Wetzel, and Lustman (1984), discussed in more detail later in this chapter, is an outstanding example that also supports the efficacy of cognitive therapy in comparison to medication.

B. Increasing Pleasant Activities

Lewinsohn and his colleagues (e.g., Lewinsohn, Youngren, & Grosscup, 1979) have emphasized the relationship between depression and reinforcement. Depression, characterized by dysphoria and lowered rate of behavior, is seen as a consequence of a decreased rate of response-contingent positive reinforcement. The rate of reinforcement is functionally related to the availability of reinforcing events, personal skills to act on the environment, or the potency of certain types of events. There is strong evidence that depressed patients have a reduced rate of activity (particularly pleasant activities), that mood covaries with the rate of pleasant activities (Lewinsohn, 1975; Rehm, 1978), and simply keeping track of activities alone can improve mood (Harmon, Nelson, & Hayes, 1980). Lewinsohn's Pleasant Events Schedule (PES; MacPhillamy & Lewinsohn, 1982) is a particularly useful clinical device for assessing, tracking, and modifying activity level in depressed patients. Lewinsohn, Sullivan, and Grosscup (1980) demonstrated that a program of decreasing unpleasant activities, alone or in combination with a program of increasing pleasant activities, is effective in the amelioration of depression.

Around this pleasant activity therapy, Brown and Lewinsohn (1984a) developed a psychoeducational group treatment for depression titled Coping with Depression (CWD). The course consists of twelve sessions spread out over eight weeks. Skills taught in the course include generating a self-change plan, relaxation, constructive thinking strategies, stimulus control strategies for decreasing negative thoughts and increasing positive thoughts, identifying and increasing pleasant activities, social skills training, and maintenance strategies. In this particular treatment, group time is divided among lecture, review of assignments, discussion, role play, and structured tasks. A textbook (Lewinsohn, Munoz, Youngren, & Zeiss, 1978) and a workbook (Brown & Lewinsohn, 1984b) are employed to facilitate the learning and application of these coping skills. To maximize comparability of treatment across instructors, a therapist manual is employed (Lewinsohn, Antonuccio, Steinmetz-Breckenridge, & Teri, 1984) that provides detailed outlines of each unit of the course.

A total of 246 patients have been treated in three major outcome studies on the CWD course (Antonuccio, Lewinsohn, & Steinmetz, 1982; Brown & Lewinsohn, 1984; Steinmetz, Lewinsohn, & Antonuccio, 1983; Teri & Lewinsohn, 1981). Two more treatment outcome studies are currently in progress (Hoberman, Lewinsohn, & Tilson, in press; Saenz, Lewinsohn, & Hoberman, 1988). In each of these studies, course participants were carefully assessed on a wide range of variables at four points in time: pretreatment, posttreatment, one month, and six months following treatment. Among many different measures, a core assessment battery across studies included the BDI (Beck et al., 1961) and the SADS (Endicott & Spitzer, 1978) interview. Diagnoses were based on decision rules specified by the RDC (Spitzer et al., 1978).

Brown and Lewinsohn (1984a) contrasted the CWD course delivered in a group format, individual tutoring, or a minimal phone contact procedure to a delayed treatment condition. The results indicate that the active treatments were superior to the control condition, but they were not statistically different from each other. Teri and Lewinsohn (1981) found the course to be equally effective as individual behavior therapy. In a repeated measures design, Antonuccio et al. (1982) found eight different group leaders to be equally effective in the delivery of this particular treatment. In each of these studies, depressed individuals participating in the CWD course showed substantial clinical and statistical improvement at posttreatment and maintained improvement at both one-month and six-month follow-up. This was true for self-report and clinical diagnoses. On average, 79% of patients diagnosed with unipolar depression, according to RDC criteria, no longer met those criteria one month after treatment. This improvement rate is comparable to that shown by subjects in other studies.

Lewinsohn, Hoberman, Teri, and Hautzinger (1985) have recently updated the reinforcement model of depression and proposed a theoretical model that is an attempt to integrate epidemiological findings, treatment outcome research, and social psychology research on self-awareness. They propose that depression begins with stressors that disrupt substantial, important, and relatively automatic ("scripted") behavior patterns of individuals. Disruption of these scripted patterns produces a dysphoric experience, thus shifting the balance of reinforcing events in a negative direction. If the individual cannot reverse the balance of reinforcement, a heightened state of self-awareness will follow. Heightened self-awareness can lead to an increase in self-evaluation, self-criticism, self-attribution of negative outcomes, intensification of negative affect, and behavioral withdrawal. An individual's normal self-protective, self-enhancing cognitive schema breaks down under these circumstances and the person becomes more aware of his or her inability to live up to expected standards of coping. This exacerbates self-denigration and behavioral withdrawal. Finally, increasing dysphoria leads to the behavioral, cognitive, and emotional changes that have been shown to be associated with depression. These changes, then, perpetuate a vicious cycle of heightened self-awareness and dysphoria. Such a model allows for a variety of individual and environmental differences at many points in this depressogenic cycle that can increase or decrease the risk of a depressive episode.

C. Self-Control Training

Self-control training for managing depression emphasizes a combination of progressive goal attainment, self-reinforcement, contingency management, and behavioral productivity. Self-control training as developed by Rehm (1977) conceptually views depression as the result of a negative ratio of rewards to punishments. Self-control theory focuses on the individual's contribution to this negative ratio through cognitive and behavioral responses. It is theorized that depressed individuals have a tendency to be perfectionistic, set very high standards, focus on negative aspects of their environment, and administer a low number of self-reinforcements while self-punishing at a high rate. Research to support this theory has indicated that perfectionistic individuals are at a higher risk for depression following stressful life events (Hewitt & Dyck, 1986) and that positive self-evaluation is associated with goal attainment (Ward, 1989). While the theory does not attempt to minimize the role of environmental factors, it does emphasize that positive events also occur at a low rate because of dysfunctional cognitive biases and deficits in self-control skills. Through misregulation of self-expectancy and self-evaluation skills, and by selectively encoding, processing, and retrieving negative events, the depressed person is at a higher risk for self-punishment.

Fuchs and Rehm (1977) and Rehm and Kornblith (1978, 1979) have developed a treatment program based on self-control theory. The basic treatment package consists of six to twelve sessions divided into three parts. The focus is on development of adaptive self-monitoring, self-evaluation, and self-reinforcement skills. In the six-session treatment protocol, the first session involves a didactic presentation on self-control deficits relevant to depression. Patients are given the homework assignments of (1) generating a list of 20 potentially pleasurable activities, (2) maintaining a daily record of positive events during each day, and (3) rating mood after each event. Daily average mood and the number of positive daily events are graphed to provide feedback on the association between mood and positive events.

During the second session, the principles of self-monitoring are restated, with reinforcement for the appropriate application of self-control concepts. Homework assignments are reviewed to solve any problems in completing them and to reinforce compliance and skill mastery. These self-monitoring activities are continued throughout therapy, while the conceptual focus shifts to self-evaluation.

The self-evaluation phase focuses on goal-setting behavior to develop specific, discrete, overt, and attainable goals in terms of positive activities and behavioral productivity. Large goals are broken down into subgoals that are more readily achievable and reflect a realistic appraisal of current ability level. Fuchs and Rehm (1977) developed a point system for self-evaluation in which the patient is asked to assign a weight to each subgoal established. The homework assignment requires the patient to keep a tally sheet for the point values of each accomplished goal.

During the self-reinforcement phase, patients are taught to identify reinforcers and develop a "reward menu" of reinforcers that are immediately available. Based on self-monitoring and self-evaluation skills, patients are instructed to self-administer rewards as points are earned for accomplishing specific goals. At the end of treatment, patients are encouraged to continue using the self-control skills.

Fuchs and Rehm (1977) compared self-control group therapy to a nonspecific group therapy and a waiting-list control group in the treatment of 36 women diagnosed as depressed based on MMPI depression scale scores and clinical interview. The results of their study indicate that the self-control group was significantly more improved across dependent measures at termination than the nonspecific group therapy and the waiting-list control groups. This improvement was generally maintained at six-week follow-up relative to the nonspecific group treatment. In a follow-up study, Rehm, Fuchs, Roth, Kornblith, and Romano (1979) compared self-control therapy to an assertion skills training program in the treatment of 24 depressed women. The results of this study indicated that self-control therapy was more effective than assertion training in the reduction of depression levels.

Roth, Bielski, Jones, Parker, and Osborn (1982) conducted a comparative study between self-control therapy and self-control therapy plus antidepressant medication in the treatment of moderate to severely depressed men and women. Treatment lasted three months, with the subjects in the combined treatment group receiving desipramine in addition to self-control therapy. Both treatments were effective in the reduction of depression levels. At the two-month assessment the results favored the combined treatment group; however, there were no significant differences between the treatment groups at termination or three-month follow-up.

D. Social Skills Training

Behavioral theories of depression have posited that depression stems from a low rate of response-contingent positive reinforcement (e.g., Lewinsohn, 1975). The attainment of positive reinforcement is determined in part by the skillfulness of the individual in increasing the availability of and obtaining positive reinforcement. Lewinsohn contends that depression often results because individuals lack the prerequisite social skills necessary for obtaining a maximum of positive reinforcement and reducing punishment.

Poor interpersonal behavior has been shown to be associated with depressed individuals. For example, Coyne (1976) found that nondepressed individuals expressed displeasure about interacting with depressed individuals, reporting a reduction in mood after only brief conversations. In another study, Libet and Lewinsohn (1973) showed that depressed individuals had slower response times, reduced likelihood of responding positively to the initiation of others, and fewer attempts to initiate conversations compared to normal controls. Youngren and Lewinsohn (1980) also found that depressed individuals socialized less than normal controls and judged their interactions less rewarding.

These studies appear to support the need to include some element of social skills training in the treatment of unipolar depression. Several researchers and clinicians have responded by developing interventions involving multiple social skills components, such as reducing interpersonal anxiety, modifying inappropriate beliefs, and direct behavior training using role playing, modeling, coaching, role reversal, social reinforcement, feedback, and homework assignment to facilitate generalization. Social skills treatment is brief, usually not lasting more than twelve weeks (Hoberman & Lewinsohn, 1985). Individuals can be seen individually or in groups. Training begins with assessing the individual's performance in various role-playing situations in order to identify important social skills deficits. Other methods of assessment are also used, including spousal observation, self-report inventories, self-monitoring of social behaviors, and antecedents and consequences in natural and contrived situations. Since many social skills are situation dependent, treatment is aimed at improving social skills across a variety of social contexts such as work, school, and interactions with strangers, groups, and opposite-sex individuals.

Studies examining the effectiveness of social skills training for treating depression are generally favorable. Hersen, Bellack, Himmelhoch, and Thase (1984) found that improvement in social skills resulted in an improvement in self-report and therapist rating scales of depression. In this study involving 120 patients, four treatments for depression were compared; social skills plus amitriptyline, social skills plus placebo, amitriptyline alone, and dynamic psychotherapy plus placebo. Results indicated that patients in all groups benefited. Clinically relevant changes in depressive symptomatology occurred, and improvements in social skills were evident. While not statistically significant, patients in the social skills plus placebo group improved most and had the lowest dropout rate.

McLean (1981a) and his colleagues have proposed a social skills intervention that places great importance on the individual's interaction with his or her interpersonal environment. According to this view, depression results when the individual cannot interact effectively with others. Unsuccessful attempts to manage social situations cause a reduction in positive reinforcement and exposure to coercive communication patterns leading to depression. The aim of this approach is to improve social behaviors that are incompatible with depression (McLean, Ogston, & Grauer, 1973). Therapy includes components of communication training, behavioral productivity, social interaction training, assertiveness training, and decision-making and problem-solving training (McLean & Hakstian, 1979).

McLean et al. (1973) tested the effectiveness of social skills training for treating depressed married patients. The treatment group received feedback about social interactions, use of contingency contracting, and assertiveness training. Improving marital communication was the focus, with spouses playing an integral role. This group was compared to patients receiving contemporary treatment methods. The results showed that patients receiving social skills training improved on ratings of depressive symptomatology and verbal communication, while the comparison group did not improve. In a study described in detail below, McLean and Hakstian (1979) found this treatment to be superior to drug therapy, insight-oriented psychotherapy, and a relaxation placebo control group.

Unfortunately, not all studies have shown support for social skills training in treating depression. For instance, the study by Rehm et al. (1979) showed that assertiveness training produced significant changes in communication patterns, but reduction in depressive symptoms was equivocal. Other studies have also found negative results when social skills training was compared to other groups (e.g., Fagan, 1979; LaPointe, 1976). However, as Blaney (1981) points out, studies showing little support for social skills interventions in the treatment of depression have included subjects who were initially less depressed than subjects in studies with more favorable results.

E. Relaxation and Imagery-Based Treatments

The theoretical link between relaxation training and amelioration of depressive symptoms has not been developed to the same extent as other treatments. In fact, because of the lack of a clearly defined theoretical link, relaxation training has been used as a nonspecific attention treatment control (e.g., McLean & Hakstian, 1979). Relaxation and imagery-based treatments for depression may be effective because they reduce levels of tension, arousal, and reactivity that maintain a variety of depressive symptoms, such as insomnia, fatigue, and agitation, and interfere with behavioral, cognitive, and social skills resulting in decreased productivity, negative affective states, and decreased reinforcement.

There are a variety of active and passive relaxation techniques that are effective, relatively easy to learn, and adaptable to individual, group, and self-administered therapy programs. The most commonly taught relaxation procedures are versions of progressive muscle relaxation outlined by Jacobson (1938), Benson (1975), or Bernstein and Borkovec (1973). Biofeedback, imagery, and autogenic training, hypnosis, and meditation therapies provide a wide range of empirically supported techniques available to the clinician (see Woolfolk & Lehrer, 1984, for applications and implementation strategies).

While the actual technique used to induce relaxation may not be critical, there are some practical considerations in implementing the procedures that facilitate the effectiveness of training. The patient should be presented with a comprehensive rationale for the role of relaxation training in treating depression. It should also be emphasized that relaxation is a skill that can be mastered only through practice. Initially, it is beneficial for the therapist to model, coach, and pace the patient through the relaxation procedure. Therapist-assisted relaxation training is especially useful in troubleshooting problems ranging from difficulty relaxing a particular muscle group to inability to use a given technique. Also, deep states of relaxation may be associated with feelings of depersonalization or detachment, which may evoke anxiety in the individual and limit the therapy's efficacy (Borkovec et al., 1987). Discussion of these feelings prior to relaxation training and after achievement of deep relaxation seems to help prevent such paradoxical reactions. In addition to in-session relaxation training, regularly scheduled practice sessions once or twice a day at a specified time and quiet place are assigned as homework. Also, patients are typically asked to monitor mood, anxiety, and tension-producing events on a daily basis. Time is devoted in the final sessions to relaxing in situations that produce tension.

In the McLean and Hakstian (1979) study, progressive muscle relaxation training was found to be more effective than insight-oriented psychotherapy and tricyclic pharmacotherapy in the treatment of depression. Similarly, Reynolds and Coats (1986) found that relaxation training was as effective as a cognitive-behavioral treatment and both were superior to a waiting-list control group in treating moderately depressed adolescents. Relaxation training is also an important element in cognitive-behavioral treatment packages that have been shown to be effective in the treatment of depression (Brown & Lewinsohn, 1984; Steinmetz et al., 1983).

F. Exercise

Depressed individuals have also responded to exercise. Exercise as a treatment for depression seems to be a practical application of theory and empirical support for the positive effects of physical activity upon mental health (Cureton, 1963; Folkins, 1976; Folkins & Sime, 1981; Powell, 1975). Physiological, biochemical, and cognitive-behavioral theories have been offered to account for the potential benefits of exercise in the treatment of depression. The physiological theory suggests that changes in fitness mediate changes in mood, yet the studies to date have consistently found that the antidepressive effect of exercise is not mediated by fitness variables and that the change in depression scores typically occur prior to meaningful changes in fitness (Doyne, Bowman, et al., 1983; Doyne et al., 1987; Fremont & Craighead, 1984; McCann & Holmes, 1984; Sime, 1984). Biochemical theories propose that increased aminergic transmission or endorphin activity from exercise are causally linked to changes in depression levels. This theory seems plausible based on current biochemical theories of depression (see McNeal & Cimbolic, 1986; Simons, McGowan, Epstein, Kupfer, & Robertson, 1985), but has received very little empirical support thus far. Cognitive-behavioral theories generally emphasize that exercise is an affectively positive experience that helps to break the cycle of negative mood and negative thoughts in depression, and facilitates a sense of self-efficacy through skill acquisition and mastery in much the same manner as other cognitive-behavioral strategies (Simons et al., 1985).

Exercise treatments for depression typically involve three to four exercise sessions per week, with the exercise protocol following standard guide-lines such as those established by the American College of Sports Medicine (1980). Doyne, Bowman, et al. (1983) compared aerobic exercise, nonaerobic exercise, and waiting-list control groups in the treatment of 41 women diagnosed as depressed according to the RDC criteria (Spitzer et al., 1978). Subjects were randomly assigned to one of the three groups, with treatment lasting for eight weeks. Both exercise groups showed a significant reduction in BDI scores, while there was no significant change in depression scores for the waiting-list control group. Since the exercise treatment groups met four times weekly, there is the possibility of an attention-placebo confound.

McCann and Holmes (1984) compared aerobic exercise, relaxation train-ing, and no-treatment groups in the treatment of depressed college women. The results of this study indicate that the exercise treatment group pro-duced a significantly greater reduction in BDI depression scores than the relaxation or no-treatment groups. In a comparative study, Fremont and Craighead (1984) found that exercise was as effective as cognitive therapy in the treatment of mild to moderately depressed men and women. Ep-stein, Wood, and Antonuccio (1988) found aerobic exercise to be superior to delayed treatment and comparable in effectiveness to cognitive therapy in a treatment outcome study of unipolar depression.

In a recent study, Doyne et al. (1987) compared aerobic exercise (run-ning), nonaerobic exercise (weight lifting), and a waiting-list control group in the treatment of women who met RDC criteria of minor or major depression. The results of this study showed that both exercise conditions produced a significant reduction in depression and were superior to the waiting-list group at one- and twelve-month follow-up intervals.

These and other studies (Doyne, Chambless, & Beutler, 1983; Greist et al., 1979; Martinsen, 1984) establish exercise as a potentially effective treatment of depression and encourage future research in this area. Sime (1984) has suggested that exercise may have a preventive effect, which is supported by findings that exercise can help maintain improved mood (Greist, 1984). Further research on the preventive properties of exercise would be especially useful in establishing its therapeutic effects in depres-sion. Such research could also address the issue of compliance, since Dishman (1982) has indicated that the dropout rate in exercise programs may be as high as 50%. Simons et al. (1985) noted that this may confound current research, in that the low motivational states associated with severe depression may limit the applicability and generalizability of evidence sup-porting exercise as an effective treatment for mildly or moderately de-pressed subjects. While aerobic fitness per se does not seem to be impor-tant, further research must systematically address mechanisms of the antidepressive effects of exercise by measuring relevant physiological (e.g., biochemical indices) and psychological changes (e.g., self-efficacy, body image, or self-esteem) in relation to mood changes.

G. Contingency Management

Contingency management theory views depression as resulting from social reinforcement and secondary gain for depressive responses. Relevant depressive responses are conceptualized as behavioral excesses, while adaptive behavior are conceptualized as behavioral deficits. The goal of contingency management is to provide differential reinforcement to increase the frequency of the behavioral deficits and extinguish the behavioral excesses. Several early studies demonstrated antidepressive effects using within-therapy-session contingency management strategies of selective attention and differential reinforcement to increase activity levels and adaptive nondepressive behaviors (e.g., Burgess, 1969; Liberman & Raskin, 1971). Subsequent studies, however, failed to validate within-session contingency management strategies as an effective treatment of depression (see Rehm & Kornblith, 1979). Contingency management principles were also used in the form of token economies to promote nondepressive behaviors in depressed inpatients. Using single-case experimental designs, token economies produced increases in nondepressive behaviors in response to contingent reinforcement, but resulted in limited generalization beyond the treatment phase (e.g., Hanaway & Barlow, 1975; Hersen, Eisler, Alford, & Agras, 1973).

Another approach to the use of contingency management procedures that may have more clinical utility and generalization has been to teach family members of a depressed patient contingency management strategies. Liberman and Raskin (1971) report a single case study in which family members of a depressed woman were taught to attend and reinforce adaptive nondepressive behaviors selectively while selectively ignoring depressive behaviors. The results of this intervention indicated an increase in nondepressive behaviors that was maintained at the one-year follow-up. Using a multiple-baseline design across subjects, Brannon and Nelson (1987) used contingency management to treat six depressed outpatients. Patients were taught to identify behavioral excesses and deficits. The patients then selected and self-monitored one or two excesses and deficits to target for change. Significant others were trained to deliver reinforcement for the targeted behavioral deficits and ignore behavioral excesses. Training of significant others in behavioral principles and differential reinforcement involved role playing, modeling, feedback, and reinforced practice. The results of this study indicated that all subjects were judged nondepressed after treatment and at six-month follow-up according to RDC criteria.

It seems that attitudes and behaviors of significant others are especially important in depression. Family support is negatively associated with depressive episodes and positively associated with successful treatment outcome in depression (Aneshensel, 1985; Noll & Dubinsky, 1985; Steinmetz et al., 1983). To date, behavioral therapies have focused more on the individual than on the system or environment in which the depressive responses occur. From a behavioral perspective, the role of significant others in the treatment of depression has not been systematically addressed. In one sense this seems ironic, since the spirit of the behavioral revolution was to emphasize environmental influences on behavior (Winett, 1985).

VI. THE RELATIVE EFFICACY OF BEHAVIOR THERAPIES

It is clear that many behavioral treatments are effective in the amelioration of depression. However, the relative efficacy of the different types of behavioral interventions is unknown. Zeiss et al. (1979) treated 66 patients who met criteria for unipolar depression with interpersonal skills training, cognitive therapy, pleasant activities therapy, or a waiting-list control. Multiple outcome measures covering the targeted areas of the treatments were used to evaluate the selective impact of the active treatments. Results indicated that all the active treatments were more effective than the control condition, and there were no statistically significant differences among the treatments. Contrary to hypothesis, the treatments did not selectively affect the targeted outcome measures. In other words, patients improved on all measures, not just the targeted areas each treatment directly emphasized. These authors interpreted such global improvement as support of a self-efficacy perspective of depression. That is, when patients experience improvement in one area, they begin to expect improvement in other, nontargeted, areas. Taylor and Marshall (1977) and Wilson et al. (1983) also failed to find differences in treatment outcome between cognitive and behavioral treatments for depression. A more recent study compared the use of a behavioral target and a cognitive target in a self-control therapy program for depression (Rehm, Kaslow, & Rabin, 1987). The results indicated no significant differences in improvement on behavioral and cognitive targets. As in the Zeiss et al. (1979) study, subjects tended to show global improvement across measures.

Zeiss et al. (1979) suggest that effective interventions for depression include the following common elements: (1) a structured, elaborated, well-planned rationale; (2) a goal-oriented, time-limited focus; (3) self-monitoring of targeted areas; (4) training in skills; (5) independent practice of these skills outside the therapy context, usually in the form of homework assignments; and (6) attribution of patient improvement to patient skillfulness rather than to therapist skillfulness.

VII.   PHARMACOTHERAPY VERSUS BEHAVIORAL
PSYCHOTHERAPY

Antidepressant medications continue to be the most often delivered treatment for depression in this country. In an earlier thorough review of the literature, Morris and Beck (1974) found that tricyclic antidepressants were superior to a placebo in 63 out of 91 studies, offering tentative support for the efficacy of these medications. There are several outstanding studies that bear on the question of the relative efficacy of medication and cognitive-behavioral interventions in the treatment of depression.

McLean and Hakstian (1979) treated 178 depressed outpatients with ten weeks of insight-oriented psychotherapy, behavior therapy, amitriptyline, or a relaxation control condition. All patients met rigorous diagnostic criteria for primary unipolar depression and had an average pretreatment BDI score of 27. Behavior therapy involved skill training in communication, behavioral productivity, social interaction, assertiveness, decision making, problem solving, and cognitive self-control. Medication was taken in a single dose of 150 mg per day, at bedtime. In order to ensure medication compliance, unannounced blood samples were drawn on two random visits over the treatment period. Results showed behavior therapy to be superior on nine of ten measures at the end of treatment, and seven of ten measures at the three-month follow-up. The superiority of behavior therapy included symptomatic measures as well as measures of social adjustment. Behavior therapy had the lowest dropout rate, 5%, compared to 26% for insight and 36% for the drug condition. Insight-oriented psychotherapy was the least effective on most outcome measures at both evaluation periods; 30% of those patients remained in the moderate to severe range of depression, compared to 19% in the control condition. There were no significant differences between drug therapy and relaxation therapy on any outcome measure.

Another well-controlled study randomly assigned 87 moderately to severely depressed psychiatric outpatients to twelve weeks of cognitive therapy, nortriptyline, cognitive therapy plus nortriptyline, or cognitive therapy plus active placebo (G. E. Murphy et al., 1984). The placebo was designed to have mild sedative and anticholinergic effects to simulate actual medication. The therapists in this study were three psychologists and nine psychiatrists. While the 70 patients who completed treatment showed significant improvement on measures of depression, the treatment conditions were not differentially effective at treatment termination or at one-month follow-up. Inclusion of dropout patients' end-point scores did not affect these results. Thus cognitive therapy alone was as effective as medication; there was no additive effect of the combined treatment. Noteworthy about this study was the fact that the investigators drew venous blood samples every other week to ensure plasma nortriptyline levels in the therapeutic target window of 50 to 150 ng/ml. Patients were given a one-week supply of medication at a time and were asked to return any unused pills each week to measure compliance, since the plasma level, not ideal dosage, was the prescribing guide.

A one-year follow-up (Simons, Murphy, Levine, & Wetzel, 1986) was conducted for the G. E. Murphy et al. (1984) study. Of the 44 patients who had originally responded to treatment, 16 relapsed as defined by reentry into treatment or by self-reported depression scores in the moderately depressed range. Patients who relapsed had significantly more dysfunctional attitudes measured at treatment termination. Patients who had received cognitive therapy (with or without tricyclic medication) were less likely to relapse than patients who received pharmacotherapy. Conversely, patients who had received tricyclic medication (with or without cognitive therapy) were more likely to relapse than patients who received cognitive therapy.

A recent meta-analysis investigated whether combined psychotherapy and pharmacotherapy is superior to either treatment alone (Conte, Plutchik, Wild, & Karasu, 1986). The researchers reviewed fourteen controlled studies, utilizing a combined condition, of outpatients treated for unipolar depression reported between 1974 and 1984. In the analysis, studies were given different weights based on the scientific quality of the design, which were multiplied by weights based on the outcome of the study. The meta-analysis indicated that the combined active treatments (drugs plus psychotherapy) were appreciably (53%) more effective than minimal contact plus placebo, but only slightly superior to psychotherapy alone (18%), pharmacotherapy alone (29%), psychotherapy plus placebo (19%), or pharmacotherapy plus minimal contact (15%). A closer inspection of the data indicates that, of the four studies that employed a combined behavioral plus drug condition in comparison with a behavioral plus placebo medication, 97% of the evidence indicated no significant difference. Interestingly, 3% of the evidence favored the behavioral intervention when combined with the placebo rather than the tricyclic medication.

Another meta-analysis of 56 outcome studies considered the relative effectiveness of drug therapy and psychotherapy in general for treating unipolar depression in adults (Steinbreuck, Maxwell, & Howard, 1983). The evidence suggested that, when compared to a control group, psychotherapy (mean effect size = 1.22) was superior to drug therapy (mean effect size = .61). Interestingly, the data of Smith, Glass, and Miller (1980) suggest a similar result for the treatment of depression, despite an overall finding that drug therapy was more effective than psychotherapy for a wide array of other psychological disorders.

In progress at the time of this writing was an NIMH collaborative study (Elkin et al., 1986) investigating the relative effectiveness of Beck's brand of cognitive-behavior therapy (Beck et al., 1979), Klerman and Weissman's interpersonal therapy (Klerman, Rounsaville, Chevron, Neu, & Weissman,

1979), imipramine, and a pill-placebo control group. Preliminary analysis indicates that there were no significant differences between either of the psychotherapies and imipramine, or between the two psychotherapies, in reduction of depressive symptoms or in overall functioning. These data suggest that imipramine caused improvement to occur more quickly, but that the psychotherapies had caught up within sixteen weeks.

While medications may be helpful to some depressed patients, they may cause special problems for patients who are medically ill. Popkin, Callies, and Mackenzie (1985) found that use of antidepressants in medically ill patients resulted in a 60% unfavorable response rate; the antidepressant had to be discontinued in 32% of the trials due to significant side effects, the most common of which was delirium.

Based on the foregoing evidence, for moderate to severe nonpsychotic unipolar depression, pharmacologic approaches may be overrated and overused. We suggest that psychotherapeutic approaches (particularly behavioral approaches) ought to be the first line of attack for the following reasons: (1) Pharmacologic approaches do not directly affect psychosocial factors such as interpersonal, marital, family, or job-related problems; (2) behavior therapies teach skills that can be used to prevent depressive episodes; (3) medications often result in poor compliance and a high dropout rate; (4) many antidepressants are cardiotoxic and have dangerous anticholinergic side effects; (5) antidepressants can be lethal, and in one study (Kathol & Henn, 1983) they were responsible for 50% of the serious adult overdoses; and (6) the weight of the evidence suggests that the cognitive-behavioral interventions are just as effective as the tricyclic medications for symptom relief and social adjustment. Perhaps it is time to think of the behavioral "prescriptions" as the most "aggressive" treatments available for unipolar depression (Altrocchi, Antonuccio, & Miller, 1986; Antonuccio, Ward, & Tearnan, 1988), especially since they appear to be effective even with patients who have not responded to medications (Antonuccio et al., 1984).

VIII. CLINICAL ISSUES

A. Relapse

Recovering from depression is perhaps only half the battle. The issue of relapse must also be addressed. Long-term follow-up studies of patients who have recovered from depression are lacking, however. One study followed 101 unipolar patients for one year after recovery from a depressive index episode (Faravelli, Ambonetti, Pattanti, & Pazzagli, 1986). Results indicated that relapse was associated with higher levels of residual symptoms at recovery, lower social adaptation, more pathological mean personality profiles, and lower medication plasma levels despite similar doses of medication.

Gonzales, Lewinsohn, and Clarke (1985) conducted a study to examine one- to three-year outcome for patients who had completed a cognitive-behavioral intervention for depression and to identify risk factors for relapse. Using the RDC (Spitzer et al., 1978), patients were classified as having major depressive disorder, intermittent depressive disorder, or superimposed depressive disorder (i.e., both major and intermittent). Recovery rate of the major depressives (75%) was significantly higher than that of the intermittent depressives (43%) or that of the superimposed depressives (27%). About 30% of patients who had recovered (at least eight weeks symptom-free) developed another episode of depression within one year of the occurrence of the index episode. Significant predictors of relapse, accounting for 38% of the variance, included greater number of previous episodes of depression, poor health, history of depression in first-degree relatives, higher dissatisfaction with major life roles, higher depression level at entry to the study, and younger age. Results indicated that about 50% of the patients had recovered and remained symptom-free throughout the follow-up interval, considerably lower than the 75% that has typically been found immediately posttreatment. These results suggest that, although most patients are improved following cognitive-behavioral treatment, such treatment may need to be supplemented with booster sessions to help maintain improvement for many patients. Booster sessions might emphasize stress inoculation strategies and practice at generalizing the use of skills learned in treatment. However, it should be noted that booster sessions were ineffective in reducing relapse or furthering gains in one study of a cognitive-behavioral treatment for depression (Baher & Wilson, 1985). In the Baher and Wilson study, the single best predictor of relapse was initial treatment response; better response resulted in decreased risk of relapse.

B.   Compliance

Cognitive-behavioral interventions for depression require considerable effort by the patient: keeping accurate records, learning to chart and self-monitor, and home practice of various new skills. While many share the concern that the patient is just "too depressed" to carry out such assignments, in practice most depressed patients are quite capable if they believe that such activity will be helpful. In our experience (e.g., Antonuccio et al., 1982), there are at least three variables that can help to ensure homework compliance. First, it is important to present a clear and convincing rationale as to how the homework will benefit the patient's attempt to ameliorate depression. Second, the assignment should be clearly spelled out, and a behavioral sample should be taken during the session to make sure the patient has a clear understanding of what is to be done. Third, the patient's effort to do the homework must be reinforced at the next session by spending time going over his or her progress on the assignment, primarily focusing on what has been accomplished rather than on what has not. These compliance-enhancement strategies are similar to those outlined by Jacobson (1982) in his work with couples: (1) Emphasize the importance of the task, (2) give an explicit rationale, (3) exaggerate the aversiveness of the task, (4) anticipate and debunk all potential excuses for noncompliance (e.g., no time, forgot, fighting too much, everything was going well), (5) allow sufficient time (at least 5–10 minutes) at the end of the session to go over the assignment, (6) make sure the assignment is understood, (7) send the patient home with prompts (e.g., a written instruction or a structured form), (8) get an overt verbal or written commitment to do the assignment, and (9) call the patient during the week to check progress.

C. Managing Suicidal Behavior

Any clinician who has worked with depressed patients has had to manage suicidal risk. Miller (1980) proposes several strategies for use with the suicidal patient. She advises against (1) ignoring or brushing off the expression of suicidal feelings or intentions as manipulative, just threats, or not sincere; (2) disputing the patient's expressed experience; or (3) having a preconceived idea about hospitalizing the person. Positive strategies include (1) discussing the problem and possibility of suicide in a straightforward manner; (2) asking the patient for suggestions about what will help; (3) for acutely suicidal patients, letting them know that the first priority is to prevent them from killing themselves; (4) conceding that the patient ultimately has the power to kill him- or herself in order to lessen the need for the patient to assert that power; (5) telling the patient that depressive episodes tend to be time-limited; (6) involving significant others; (7) facilitating the evaluation for medications; and (8) venting and discharge of affect.

When to consider hospitalization is a practical and important matter in treating the depressed outpatient. Obviously, psychiatric hospitalization is necessary when the patient is acutely suicidal, self-destructive, or psychotic. Lacking these symptoms, hospitalization may also be indicated when psychomotor retardation, sleep disruption, weight loss, or cognitive disturbances are present to a severe degree and do not respond to outpatient intervention. It is important to note that the need for hospitalization does not contraindicate the use of behavioral interventions, as these strategies can be effective on inpatient psychiatric units (e.g., de Jong, Treiber, & Henrich, 1986; Miller, Bishop, Norman, & Keitner, 1985).

D. Matching Patients with Treatments

Genetic vulnerability, cognitive biases, social and coping skills, and stressful life demands or events all contribute in varying degrees to the clinical manifestation of depression. Ideally, it would be beneficial to target the most problematic area in a given individual. Research by Akiskal and associates suggests that individuals with a genetic vulnerability to affective disturbances (as determined by first-degree blood relatives with depressive disorders) respond favorably to tricyclic medications, while individuals with a significant social learning history of psychosocial stressors do not respond as favorably to pharmacotherapy (Akiskal, King, Rosenthal, Robinson, & Scott-Strauss, 1981; Akiskal et al., 1980). While these results encourage the exploration of genetic vulnerability as a relevant treatment decision criterion, it should be noted that Akiskal's research indicates that individuals with more disturbed social learning histories responded less favorably to any form of treatment. Currently, we know of no controlled treatment outcome study that directly addresses the issue of whether genetically vulnerable individuals respond more favorably to pharmacotherapy than to behavioral therapies.

So far, attempts to identify individual psychological and psychosocial predictors of psychotherapy outcome, including behavioral treatment for depression, have not been especially fruitful (Garfield, 1978; McLean, 1981b). Yet, continued research in this area is justified because of potential benefits in matching treatment to specific individuals or psychosocial factors. Steinmetz et al. (1983) assessed several demographic and psychological variables prior to the Coping with Depression psychoeducational group treatment of depression. They found that seven variables were significant predictors of outcome, accounting for a combined 51% of the variance in posttreatment depression level. Individuals who improved the most were initially less depressed, were younger, expected more improvement, had a greater sense of personal mastery, had higher perceptions of family support, had higher reading levels, and were not concurrently receiving another form of treatment (i.e., psychotherapy or pharmacotherapy). These variables also discriminated between the individuals who were no longer depressed and those who still met diagnostic criteria for depression at posttreatment. Hoberman, Lewinsohn, and Tilson (in press) have expanded and replicated these results. Using a similar set of predictors, plus predictors of perceived group cohesiveness, optimism regarding treatment, and quality of relationship, they were able to account for 85% of the variance in posttreatment depression level.

Whether or not these predictors are generalizable to other cognitive-behavioral treatments is uncertain. Still, these findings have some implications for the Coping with Depression group treatment approach. For example, poor readers should probably be treated with an alternative approach, and some modifications in content or structure of the treatment should be made to improve the efficacy when treating elderly patients (e.g., Thompson, Gallagher, Nies, & Epstein, 1983).

IX. SUMMARY AND FUTURE DIRECTIONS

In summary, the past decade has produced a great volume of research bearing on the effectiveness of behavioral treatments for unipolar depression. The average improvement rate for these interventions is approximately 75% (Gonzales et al., 1985). Individuals with good family support, quality relationships, perceived mastery, and positive expectations regarding treatment seem to be especially good candidates for such treatment. It is clear that many kinds of behavioral treatments are effective. It seems important that the depressed patient take *systematic* action to intervene, whether that action involves recording and changing cognitions or increasing pleasant activities or learning to be more assertive or even engaging in regular exercise. There is considerable evidence now that these treatments are as good as, and in many cases are superior to, those carried out with medications.

It should be noted that most of the treatment outcome studies reported in this chapter involved patients who did not have psychotic symptoms. Though we know of no hard data bearing on its prevalence, our experience suggests that depressed patients with significant hallucinations or delusions represent a very small percentage of unipolar depression cases. A recent study investigated the significance of psychotic features in the outcome of inpatient treatment of unipolar depression (Coryell, Zimmerman, & Pfohl, 1986). Patients with psychotic major depression were less depressed at discharge and had a longer period back to their "normal selves" during a six-month follow-up than did patients with nonpsychotic major depression. Severity ratings at discharge were better predictors of follow-up course for psychotic patients than for patients suffering nonpsychotic depression. Also, psychotic patients were more likely to show a clear outcome involving either a full syndrome or a complete absence of depressive symptoms. Although awaiting replication, this study suggests that psychotically depressed patients may have a more discrete course. Depression with psychotic symptoms may require the use of antipsychotic medications or even electroconvulsive therapy, although the relative efficacy of these treatments remains an empirical issue.

Several questions require further investigation. What is the relative contribution of the various components of the behavioral treatments? Which treatments are most effective with which types of patients? How much therapist contact is necessary to produce clinical improvement? What patient and therapist variables are predictive of treatment responders? What factors characterize the 20–25% of patients who do not respond to treatment? Will the group of nonresponders be more responsive to another kind of treatment? What alterations are required to treat depression in adolescents or the elderly effectively? Some of these questions are beginning to be addressed currently. If the progress of the past ten years continues at its current pace, we can look forward to answers to many of these questions in the not too distant future.

REFERENCES

Abramson, L. Y., & Sackheim, H. A. (1977). A paradox in depression: Uncontrollability and self-blame. *Psychological Bulletin, 84*, 838–851.

Abramson, L. Y., Seligman, M.E.P., & Teasdale, J. D. (1978). Learned helplessness in humans: Critique and reformulation. *Journal of Abnormal Psychology, 87*, 49–74.

Akiskal, H. S., King, D., Rosenthal, T. L., Robinson, D., & Scott-Strauss, A. (1981). Chronic depressions: Clinical and familial characteristics in 137 probands. *Journal of Affective Disorders, 3*, 297–315.

Akiskal, H. S., Rosenthal, T. L., Haykal, R. F., Lemmi, H., Rosenthal, R. H., & Scott-Strauss, A. (1980). Characterological depressions: Clinical features of "dysthymic" versus "character-spectrum" subtypes. *Archives of General Psychiatry, 37*, 777–783.

Altrocchi, J., Antonuccio, D. O., & Miller, G. D. (1986). Nondrug prescriptions for the depressed adult outpatient. *Postgraduate Medicine, 79*, 164–181.

Amenson, C. S., & Lewinsohn, P. M. (1981). An investigation into the observed sex difference in prevalence of unipolar depression. *Journal of Abnormal Psychology, 90*, 1–13.

American College of Sports Medicine. (1980). *Guidelines for graded exercise testing and exercise prescription* (2nd ed.). Philadelphia: Lea & Febiger.

American Psychiatric Association. (1987). *Diagnostic and statistical manual of mental disorders* (3rd ed., rev.). Washington, DC: Author.

Aneshensel, C. S. (1985). The natural history of depressive symptoms: Implications for psychiatric epidemiology. *Research in Community and Mental Health, 5*, 45–75.

Antonuccio, D. O., Akins, W. T., Chatham, P. M., Monagin, J. A., Tearnan, B. H., & Ziegler, B. L. (1984). An exploratory study: The psychoeducational group treatment of drug-refractory unipolar depression. *Journal of Behavior Therapy and Experimental Psychiatry, 15*, 309–313.

Antonuccio, D. O., Lewinsohn, P. M., & Steinmetz, J. L. (1982). Identification of therapist differences in a group treatment for depression. *Journal of Consulting and Clinical Psychology, 50*, 433–435.

Antonuccio, D. O., Ward, C., & Tearnan, B. H. (1988). Cognitive-behavior therapy vs. drugs for depression. *Psychotropics, 8*(1), 1–2.

APA Task Force on Laboratory Tests in Psychiatry. (1987). The dexamethasone suppression test: An overview of its current status in psychiatry. *American Journal of Psychiatry, 144*, 1253–1262.

Baher, A. L., & Wilson, P. H. (1985). Cognitive-behavior therapy for depression: The effects of booster sessions on relapse. *Behavior Therapy, 16*, 335–344.

Bebbington, P. (1985). Three cognitive theories of depression. *Psychological Medicine, 15*, 759–769.

Beck, A. T., Rush, A. J., Shaw, B. F., & Emery, G. (1979). *Cognitive therapy of depression.* New York: Guilford.

Beck, A. T., Steer, R. A., & Garbin (1988). Psychometric properties of the Beck Depression Inventory: Twenty-five years of evaluation. *Clinical Psychology Review, 8,* 77–100.

Beck, A. T., Ward, C. H., Mendelson, M., Mock, J., & Erbaugh, J. (1961). An inventory for measuring depression. *Archives of General Psychiatry, 4,* 561–571.

Beck, A. T., & Young, J. E. (1985). Depression. In D. H. Barlow (Ed.), *Clinical handbook of psychological disorders* (pp. 206–244). New York: Guilford.

Benson, H. (1975). *The relaxation response.* New York: William Morrow.

Bernstein, D. A., & Borkovec, T. D. (1973). *Progressive relaxation training.* Champaign, IL: Research Press.

Blackburn, I. M., & Bishop, S. (1981). Is there an alternative to drugs in the treatment of depressed ambulatory patients? *Behavioral Psychotherapy, 9,* 96–104.

Blackburn, I. M., Bishop, S., Glen, A.I.M., Whalley, L. J., & Christie, J. E. (1981). The efficacy of cognitive therapy in depression: A treatment trial using cognitive therapy and pharmacotherapy, each alone and in combination. *British Journal of Psychiatry, 139,* 181–189.

Bland, R. C., Newman, S. C., & Orn, H. (1986). Recurrent and nonrecurrent depression. *Archives of General Psychiatry, 43,* 1085–1089.

Blaney, P. H. (1981). The effectiveness of cognitive and behavioral therapies. In L. P. Rehm (Ed.), *Behavior therapy for depression: Present strategies and future directions.* New York: Academic Press.

Borkovec, T. D., Mathews, A. M., Chambers, A., Ebrahimi S., Lytle, R., & Nelson, R. (1987). The effects of relaxation training with cognitive or nondirective therapy and the role of relaxation-induced anxiety in the treatment of generalized anxiety. *Journal of Consulting and Clinical Psychology, 55,* 883–888.

Brannon, S. E., & Nelson, R. D. (1987). Contingency management treatment of outpatient unipolar depression: A comparison of reinforcement and extinction. *Journal of Consulting and Clinical Psychology, 55,* 117–119.

Brown, R. A., & Lewinsohn, P. M. (1984a). A psychoeducational approach to the treatment of depression: Comparison of group, individual, and minimal contact procedures. *Journal of Consulting and Clinical Psychology, 52,* 774–783.

Brown, R. A., & Lewinsohn, P. M. (1984b). *Participant workbook for the coping with depression course.* Eugene, OR: Castalia.

Burgess, E. P. (1969). The modification of depressive behaviors. In R. D. Rubin & C. M. Franks (Eds.), *Advances in behavior therapy, 1968.* New York: Academic Press.

Burns, D. D. (1980). *Feeling good: The new mood therapy.* New York: William Morrow.

Conte, H. R., Plutchik, R., Wild, K. V., & Karasu, T. B. (1986). Combined psychotherapy and pharmacotherapy for depression: A systematic analysis of the evidence. *Archives of General Psychiatry, 43,* 471–479.

Copeland, J.R.M. (1984). Reactive and endogenous depressive illness at five-year outcome. *Journal of Affective Disorders, 6,* 153–163.

Coryell, W., Zimmerman, M., & Pfohl, B. (1986). Outcome at discharge and six months in major depression: The significance of psychotic features. *Journal of Nervous and Mental Disease, 174,* 92–96.

Costello, C. B., & Comrey, A. L. (1967). Scales for measuring depression and anxiety. *Journal of Psychology, 66,* 303–313.

Coyne, J. C. (1976). Depression and the response of others. *Journal of Abnormal Psychology, 85,* 186–193.

Coyne, J. C., & Gotlib, I. H. (1983). The role of cognition in depression: A critical appraisal. *Psychological Bulletin, 94,* 472–505.

Cureton, T. K. (1963). Improvement of psychological states by means of exercise-fitness program. *Journal of the Association of Physical and Mental Rehabilitation, 17,* 14–26.

de Jong, R., Treiber, R., & Henrich, G. (1986). Effectiveness of two psychological treatments for inpatients with severe and chronic depressions. *Cognitive Therapy and Research, 10*, 645–663.

Dietch, J. T., & Zetin, M. (1983). Diagnosis of organic depressive disorders. *Psychosomatics, 24*, 971–979.

Dishman, R. K. (1982). Compliance/adherence in health-related exercise. *Health Psychology, 1*, 237–267.

Doyne, E. J., Bowman, E. D., Ossip-Klein, D. J., Osborn, K. M., McDougal-Wilson, I., & Neimeyer, R. A. (1983). *A comparison of aerobic and nonaerobic exercise in the treatment of depression.* Paper presented at the Seventeenth Annual Convention of the Association for the Advancement of Behavior Therapy and the World Congress on Behavior Therapy, Washington, DC.

Doyne, E. J., Chambless, D. L., & Beutler, L. E. (1983). Aerobic exercise as a treatment for depression in women. *Behavior Therapy, 14*, 434–440.

Doyne, E. J., Ossip-Klein, D. J., Bowman, E. D., Osborn, K. M., McDougal-Wilson, I. B., & Neimeyer, R. A. (1987). Running versus weight lifting in the treatment of depression. *Journal of Consulting and Clinical Psychology, 55*, 748–754.

Elkin, I., Shea, T., Imber, S., Pilkonis, P., Sotsky, S., Glass, D., Watkins, J., Leber, W., & Collins, J. (1986). *NIMH treatment of depression collaborative research program: Initial outcome findings.* Paper presented at the annual meeting of the American Association for the Advancement of Science.

Endicott, J., Cohen, J., Nee, J., Fleiss, J., & Sarantakos, S. (1981). Hamilton depression rating scale extracted from regular and change versions of the schedule for affective disorders and schizophrenia. *Archives of General Psychiatry, 38*, 98–103.

Endicott, J., & Spitzer, R. L. (1978). A diagnostic interview: The schedule for affective disorders and schizophrenia. *Archives of General Psychiatry, 38*, 98–103.

Epstein, D., Wood, Y. R., & Antonuccio, D. O. (1988). *The relative efficacy of aerobic exercise and cognitive therapy in the treatment of unipolar depression.* Paper presented at the Third World Congress on Behavior Therapy, Edinburgh, Scotland.

Fagan, M. M. (1979). Alleviated depression: The efficacy of group psychotherapy and group assertive training. *Small Group Behavior, 10*, 136–152.

Faravelli, C., Ambonetti, A., Pattanti, S., & Pazzagli, A. (1986). Depressive relapses and incomplete recovery from index episode. *American Journal of Psychiatry, 143*, 888–891.

Folkins, C. H. (1976). Effects of physical training on mood. *Journal of Clinical Psychology, 32*, 385–388.

Folkins, C. H., & Sime, W. E. (1981). Physical fitness training and mental health. *American Psychologist, 36*, 373–389.

Forsterling, F. (1985). Attributional retraining: A review. *Psychological Bulletin, 98*, 495–512.

Frank, R. G., Schulberg, H. C., Welch, W. P., Sherick, H., & Costello, A. J. (1985). Research selection bias and the prevalence of depressive disorders in psychiatric facilities. *Journal of Consulting and Clinical Psychology, 53*, 370–376.

Fremont, J., & Craighead, L. W. (1984). *Aerobic exercise and cognitive therapy for mild/ moderate depression.* Paper presented at the Eighteenth Annual Convention of the Association for the Advancement of Behavior Therapy, Philadelphia.

Fuchs, C. Z., & Rehm, L. P. (1977). A self-control behavior therapy program for depression. *Journal of Consulting and Clinical Psychology, 45*, 206–215.

Garfield, S. L. (1978). Research on client variables in psychotherapy. In S. L. Garfield & A. E. Bergin (Eds.), *Handbook of psychotherapy and behavior change: An empirical analysis.* New York: John Wiley.

Gonzales, L., Lewinsohn, P. M., & Clarke, G. (1985). Longitudinal follow-up of unipolar depressives: An investigation of predictors of relapse. *Journal of Consulting and Clinical Psychology, 53*, 461–469.

Gotlib, I. H., & Colby, C. A. (1987). *Treatment of depression: An interpersonal systems approach*. New York: Pergamon.

Greist, J. H. (1984). Exercise in the treatment of depression. In *Coping with mental stress: The potential and limits of exercise intervention*, NIMH Workshop, Washington, DC.

Greist, J. H., Klein, M. H., Eischens, R. R., Faris, J., Gurman, A. S., & Morgan, W. P. (1979). Running as treatment for depression. *Comprehensive Psychiatry, 20*, 41–54.

Hall, R. C., Popkin, M. K., Devaul, R. A., Fallaice, L. A., & Stickney, S. K. (1978). Physical illness presenting as psychiatric disease. *Archives of General Psychiatry, 35*, 1315–1320.

Hamilton, M. (1960). A rating scale for depression. *Journal of Neurology, Neurosurgery, and Psychiatry, 12*, 56–62.

Hanaway, T. P., & Barlow, D. H. (1975). Prolonged depressive behaviors in a recently blinded deaf mute: Behavioral treatment. *Journal of Behavior Therapy and Experimental Psychiatry, 6*, 43–48.

Harmon, T. M., Nelson, R. O., & Hayes, S. C. (1980). Self-monitoring of mood versus activity by depressed clients. *Journal of Consulting and Clinical Psychology, 48*, 30–38.

Hathaway, S. R. (1965). Personality inventories. In B. B. Wolman (Ed.), *Handbook of clinical psychology*. New York: McGraw-Hill.

Hersen, M., Bellack, A. S., Himmelhoch, J. M., & Thase, M. E. (1984). Effects of social skill training, amitriptyline, and psychotherapy in unipolar depressed women. *Behavior Therapy, 15*, 21–40.

Hersen, M., Eisler, R. M., Alford, G. S., & Agras, W. S. (1973). Effects of token economy on neurotic depression: An experimental analysis. *Behavior Therapy, 4*, 392–397.

Hewitt, P. L., & Dyck, D. G. (1986). Perfectionism, stress, and vulnerability to depression. *Cognitive Therapy and Research, 10*, 137–142.

Hirschfeld, R.M.A., & Cross, C. K. (1982). Epidemiology of affective disorders: Psychosocial risk factors. *Archives of General Psychiatry, 39*, 35–46.

Hoberman, H. M., & Lewinsohn, P. M. (1985). The behavioral treatment of depression. In E. E. Beckham & W. R. Leber (Eds.), *Handbook of depression: Treatment, assessment, and research*. Homewood, IL: Dorsey.

Hoberman, H., Lewinsohn, P. M., & Tilson, M. (in press). Predictors of treatment response in the Coping with Depression course. *Journal of Consulting and Clinical Psychology*.

Jacobson, E. (1938). *Progressive relaxation*. Chicago: University of Chicago Press.

Jacobson, N. S. (1982). *Clinical innovations in behavioral marital therapy*. Paper presented at the Sixteenth Annual Convention of the Association for the Advancement of Behavior Therapy, Los Angeles.

Johnson, D.A.W. (1968). The evaluation of routine physical examination in psychiatric cases. *Practitioner, 200*, 686–691.

Kathol, R. G., & Henn, F. A. (1983). Tricyclics: The most common agent used in potentially lethal overdoses. *Journal of Nervous and Mental Disease, 171*, 250–252.

Kazdin, A. E. (1982). History of behavior modification. In A. S. Bellack, M. Hersen, & A. E. Kazdin (Eds.), *International handbook of behavior modification and therapy*. New York: Plenum.

Keller, M. B., Shapiro, R. W., Lavori, P. W., & Wolfe, N. (1982). Recovery in major depressive disorder: Analysis with the life table and regression models. *Archives of General Psychiatry, 39*, 905–910.

Khouri, P. J., & Akiskal, H. S. (1986). The bipolar spectrum reconsidered. In T. Millon & G. L. Klerman (Eds.), *Contemporary directions in psychopathology* (pp. 452–471). New York: Guilford.

Klerman, G. F., Rounsaville, B., Chevron, E., Neu, C., & Weissman, M. M. (1979). *Manual for short-term interpersonal therapy (IPT) of depression*. Fourth draft preliminary, New Haven-Boston Collaborative Depression Project.

Koranyi, E. D. (1979). Morbidity and rate of undiagnosed physical illnesses in a psychiatric clinic population. *Archives of General Psychiatry, 36,* 414–419.

Kovacs, M., Rush, A. J., Beck A. T., & Hollon, S. D. (1981). Depressed outpatients treated with cognitive therapy or pharmacotherapy: A one-year follow-up. *Archives of General Psychiatry, 38,* 33–39.

Kupfer, D. J., Detre, T. P., Foster, F. G., Tucker, G. J., & Delgado, J. (1972). The application of Delgado's telemetric mobility recorder for human studies. *Behavioral Biology, 7,* 585–590.

LaPointe, K. A. (1976). Cognitive therapy versus assertiveness training in the treatment of depression (Doctoral dissertation, Southern Illinois University). *Dissertation Abstracts International, 37,* 46893. (University Microfilms No. 77–6232)

LaPointe, K. A., & Rimm, D. C. (1980). Cognitive, assertive, and insight-oriented group therapies in the treatment of reactive depression in women. *Psychotherapy: Theory, Research, and Practice, 17,* 312–321.

Lehmann, H. E. (1985). Affective disorders: Clinical features. In H. I. Kaplan & B. J. Sadock (Eds.), *Comprehensive textbook of psychiatry* (4th ed.). Baltimore: Williams & Wilkins.

Lewinsohn, P. M. (1975). The behavioral study and treatment of depression. In M. Hersen, R. M. Eisler, & P. M. Miller (Eds.), *Progress in behavior modification* (Vol. 1). New York: Academic Press.

Lewinsohn, P. M., Antonuccio, D. O., Steinmetz-Breckenridge, J. L., & Teri, L. (1984). *The Coping with Depression course: A psychoeducational intervention for unipolar depression.* Eugene, OR: Castalia.

Lewinsohn, P. M., Duncan, E. M., Stanton, A. K., & Hautzinger, M. (1986). Age at first onset for nonbipolar depression. *Journal of Abnormal Psychology, 95,* 378–383.

Lewinsohn, P. M., Hoberman, H. M., Teri, L., & Hautzinger, M. (1985). An integrative theory of depression. In S. Reiss & R. Bootzin (Eds.), *Theoretical issues in behavior therapy.* New York: Academic Press.

Lewinsohn, P. M., Munoz, R. F., Youngren, M. A., & Zeiss, A. M. (1978). *Control your depression.* Englewood Cliffs, NJ: Prentice-Hall.

Lewinsohn, P. M., Sullivan, J. M., & Grosscup, S. J. (1980). Changing reinforcing events: An approach to the treatment of depression. *Psychotherapy: Theory, Research, and Practice, 47,* 322–334.

Lewinsohn, P. M., Weinstein, M. S., & Alper, J. A. (1970). A behavioral approach to the group treatment of depressed persons: Methodological contributions. *Journal of Clinical Psychology, 26,* 525–532.

Lewinsohn, P. M., Youngren, M. A., & Grosscup, S. J. (1979). Reinforcement and depression. In R. A. Dupue (Ed.), *The psychobiology of depressive disorders: Implications for the effects of stress.* New York: Academic Press.

Liberman, R. P., & Raskin, D. E. (1971). Depression: A behavioral formulation. *Archives of General Psychiatry, 24,* 515–523.

Libet, J. M., & Lewinsohn, P. M. (1973). Concept of social skill with special reference to the behavior of depressed persons. *Journal of Consulting and Clinical Psychology, 40,* 304–312.

Linehan, M. M. (1981). A social-behavioral analysis of suicide and parasuicide: Implications for clinical assessment and treatment. In J. F. Clarkin & H. I. Glazer (Eds.), *Depression: Behavioral and directive intervention strategies.* New York: Garland STPM.

Lubin, B. (1967). *Manual for the depressive adjective checklist.* San Diego: Education and Industrial Testing Service.

MacPhillamy, D. J., & Lewinsohn, P. M. (1982). The Pleasant Events Schedule: Studies on reliability, validity, and scale intercorrelations. *Journal of Consulting and Clinical Psychology, 50,* 363–380.

Martinsen, E. W. (1984). Interaction of exercise and medication in the psychiatric patient. In *Coping with mental stress: The potential and limits of exercise intervention*, NIMH Workshop, Washington, DC.

McCann, I. L., & Holmes, D. S. (1984). Influence of aerobic exercise on depression. *Journal of Personality and Social Psychology, 46*, 1142–1147.

McLean, P. D. (1981a). Remediation of skills and performance deficits in depression: Clinical steps and research findings. In J. Clarkin & H. Glazer (Eds.), *Behavioral and directive strategies* (pp. 172–204). New York: Garland.

McLean, P. D. (1981b). Matching treatments to subject characteristics. In L. P. Rehm (Ed.), *Behavior therapy for depression: Present status and future directions* (pp. 197–207). New York: Academic Press.

McLean, P. D., & Hakstian, A. R. (1979). Clinical depression: Comparative efficacy of outpatient treatments. *Journal of Consulting and Clinical Psychology, 47*, 818–836.

McLean, P. D., Ogston, K., & Grauer, L. (1973). A behavioral approach to the treatment of depression. *Journal of Behavior Therapy and Experimental Psychiatry, 4*, 323–330.

McNeal, E. T., & Cimbolic, P. (1986). Antidepressants and biochemical theories of depression. *Psychological Bulletin, 99*, 361–374.

Miles, P. C. (1977). Condition predisposing to suicide: A review. *Journal of Nervous and Mental Disease, 164*, 231–256.

Miller, I. W., Bishop, S. B., Norman, W. H., & Keitner, G. (1985). Cognitive/behavioral therapy and pharmacotherapy with chronic drug-refractory depressed inpatients: A note of optimism. *Behavioral Psychotherapy, 13*, 320–327.

Miller, J. (1980). Helping the suicidal client: Some aspects of assessment and treatment. *Psychotherapy: Theory, Research, and Practice, 17*, 94–100.

Morris, J. B., & Beck, A. T. (1974). The efficacy of antidepressant drugs. *Archives of General Psychiatry, 30*, 667–674.

Motto, J. (1985). Paradoxes of suicide risk assessment. *Hillside Journal of Clinical Psychiatry, 7*, 109–119.

Murphy, G. E. (1974). The clinical identification of suicidal risk. In A. T. Beck, L. P. Resnik, & D. J. Lettieri (Eds.), *The prediction of suicide*. Bowie, MD: Charles.

Murphy, G. E., Simons, A. D., Wetzel, R. D., & Lustman, P. J. (1984). Cognitive therapy and pharmacotherapy: Singly and together in the treatment of depression. *Archives of General Psychiatry, 41*, 33–41.

Murphy, J. M., Sobol, A. M., Neff, R. K., Olivier, D. C., & Leighton, A. H. (1984). Stability of prevalence: Depression and anxiety disorders. *Archives of General Psychiatry, 41*, 990–997.

Myers, J. K, Weissman, M. M., Tischler, G. L., Holzer, C. E., Leaf, P. J., Orvaschel, H., Anthony, J. C., Boyd, J. H., Burke, J. D., Kramer, M., & Stoltzman, R. (1984). Six-month prevalence of psychiatric disorders in three communities: 1980 to 1982. *Archives of General Psychiatry, 41*, 959–967.

Nolen-Hoeksema, S. (1987). Sex differences in unipolar depression: Evidence and theory. *Psychological Bulletin, 101*, 259–282.

Noll, G. A., & Dubinsky, M. (1985). Prevalence and predictors of depression in a suburban county. *Journal of Community Psychology, 13*, 13–19.

Oliver, J. M., & Simmons, M. E. (1985). Affective disorders and depression as measured by the diagnostic interview schedule and the Beck Depression Inventory in an unselected adult population. *Journal of Clinical Psychology, 41*, 469–477.

Peterson, C. (1982). Learned helplessness and attributional interventions in depression. In C. Antaki & C. Brewin (Eds.), *Attributions and psychological change: A guide to the use of attribution theory in clinic and classroom*. London: Academic Press.

Peterson, C., & Seligman, M.E.P. (1984). Causal explanations as a risk factor for depression. *Psychological Review, 94*, 347–374.

Peterson, C., Semmel, A., von Baeyer, C., Abramson, L. Y., Metalsky, G. I., & Seligman, M.E.P. (1982). The Attributional Style Questionnaire. *Cognitive Therapy and Research, 6,* 287–299.

Popkin, M. K., Callies, A. L., & Mackenzie, T. B. (1985). The outcome of antidepressant use in the medically ill. *Archives of General Psychiatry, 42,* 1160–1163.

Powell, R. R. (1975). Effects of exercise on mental functioning. *Journal of Sports Medicine, 15,* 125–131.

Rehm, L. P. (1976). Assessment of depression. In M. Hersen & A. S. Bellack (Eds.), *Behavioral assessment: A practical handbook.* New York: Pergamon.

Rehm, L. P. (1977). A self-control model of depression. *Behavior Therapy, 8,* 787–804.

Rehm, L. P. (1978). Mood, pleasant events, and unpleasant events: Two pilot studies. *Journal of Consulting and Clinical Psychology, 46,* 854–859.

Rehm, L. P., Fuchs, C. Z., Roth, D. M., Kornblith, S. J., & Romano, J. M. (1979). A comparison of self-control and assertion skills treatments of depression. *Behavior Therapy, 10,* 429–442.

Rehm, L. P., Kaslow, N. J., & Rabin, A. S. (1987). Cognitive and behavioral targets in a self-control therapy program for depression. *Journal of Consulting and Clinical Psychology, 55,* 60–67.

Rehm, L. P., & Kornblith, S. J. (1978). *Self-control therapy manual, V-2 session manual.* Unpublished manuscript, University of Pittsburgh.

Rehm, L. P., & Kornblith, S. J. (1979). Behavior therapy for depression: A review of recent developments. In M. Hersen, R. M. Eisler, & P. Miller (Eds.), *Progress in behavior modification* (Vol. 7, pp. 277–318). New York: Academic Press.

Reynolds, W. M., & Coats, K. I. (1986). A comparison of cognitive-behavioral therapy and relaxation training for the treatment of depression in adolescents. *Journal of Consulting and Clinical Psychology, 54,* 653–660.

Rodin, G., & Voshart, K. (1986). Depression in the medically ill: An overview. *American Journal of Psychiatry, 143,* 696–705.

Roth, D., Bielski, R., Jones, M. J., Parker, W., & Osborn, G. (1982). A comparison of self-control therapy and combined self-control therapy and antidepressant medication in the treatment of depression. *Behavior Therapy, 13,* 133–144.

Ruehlman, L. S., West, S. G., & Pasahow, R. J. (1985). Depression and evaluative schemata. *Journal of Personality, 53,* 46–92.

Rush, A. J., Beck, A. T., Kovacs, M., & Hollon, S. (1977). Comparative efficacy of cognitive therapy and pharmacotherapy in the treatment of depressed outpatients. *Cognitive Therapy and Research, 1,* 17–37.

Saenz, M., Lewinsohn, P. M., & Hoberman, H. M. (1988). *Prediction of outcome in the Coping with Depression course.* Unpublished manuscript, University of Oregon, Eugene.

Schwartz, J. M., Baxter, L. R., Jr., Mazziotta, J. C., Gerner, R. H., & Phelps, M. E. (1987). The differential diagnosis of depression: Relevance of positron emission tomography studies of cerebral glucose metabolism to the bipolar-unipolar dichotomy. *Journal of the American Medical Association, 258,* 1368–1374.

Seligman, M.E.P. (1974). Depression and learned helplessness. In R. J. Friedman & M. M. Katz (Eds.), *The psychology of depression: Contemporary theory and research.* Washington, DC: Winston.

Seligman, M.E.P. (1975). *Helplessness: On depression, development, and death.* San Francisco: Freeman.

Seligman, M.E.P. (1981). A learned helplessness point of view. In L. P. Rehm (Ed.), *Behavior therapy for depression: Present status and future directions.* New York: Academic Press.

Shaw, B. F. (1977). Comparison of cognitive therapy and behavior therapy in the treatment of depression. *Journal of Consulting and Clinical Psychology, 45,* 543–551.

Sime, W. E. (1984). Exercise in the prevention and treatment of depression. In *Coping with mental stress: The potential and limits of exercise intervention*, NIMH Workshop, Washington, DC.

Simons, A. D., McGowan, C. R., Epstein, L. H., Kupfer, D. J., & Robertson, R. J. (1985). Exercise as a treatment for depression: An update. *Clinical Psychology Review, 5*, 553–568.

Simons, A. D., Murphy, G. E., Levine, J. L., & Wetzel, R. D. (1986). Cognitive therapy and pharmacotherapy for depression: Sustained improvement over one year. *Archives of General Psychiatry, 43*, 43–48.

Smith, M. L., Glass, G. V, & Miller, T. I. (1980). *Benefits of psychotherapy*. Baltimore: Johns Hopkins University Press.

Spitzer, R. L., Endicott, J., & Robbins, E. (1978). Research diagnostic criteria: Rationale and reliability. *Archives of General Psychiatry, 35*, 773–782.

Spitzer, R. L., & Williams, J.B.W. (1985). *Structured Clinical Interview for DSM III-R-Patient Version* (SCID-P, 7/1/85). New York: New York State Psychiatric Institute, Biometrics Research Department.

Steinbreuck, S. M., Maxwell, S. E., & Howard, G. S. (1983). A meta-analysis of psychotherapy and drug therapy in the treatment of unipolar depression with adults. *Journal of Consulting and Clinical Psychology, 51*, 856–863.

Steinmetz, J. L., Lewinsohn, P. M., & Antonuccio, D. O. (1983). Prediction of individual outcome in a group intervention for depression. *Journal of Consulting and Clinical Psychology, 51*, 331–337.

Tanaka-Matsumi, J., & Kameoka, V. A. (1986). Reliabilities and anxiety, and social desirability. *Journal of Consulting and Clinical Psychology, 54*, 328–333.

Taylor, F. G., & Marshall, W. L. (1977). Experimental analysis of a cognitive-behavioral therapy for depression. *Cognitive Therapy and Research, 1*, 59–72.

Teri, L., & Lewinsohn, P. M. (1981). *Comparative efficacy of group versus individual treatment of unipolar depression*. Paper presented at the Fifteenth Annual Convention of the Association for the Advancement of Behavior Therapy, San Francisco.

Thompson, L. W., Gallagher, D., Nies, G., & Epstein, D. (1983). Evaluation of the effectiveness of professionals and nonprofessionals as instructors of Coping with Depression classes for elders. *Gerontologist, 23*, 390–396.

Ward, C. H. (1989). *Goal systems, self-evaluation, and affective responses*. Paper presented at the 97th Annual Convention of the American Psychological Association at New Orleans, LA, August.

Weissman, M. M., Leaf, P. J., Holzer, C. E., Myers, J. K., & Tischler, G. L. (1984). The epidemiology of depression: An update on sex differences in rates. *Journal of Affective Disorders, 7*, 179–188.

Weissman, M. M., Merikangas, K. R., Wickramaratne, P., Kidd, K. K., Prusoff, B. A., Leckman, J. F., & Pauls, D. L. (1986). Understanding the clinical heterogeneity of major depression using family data. *Archives of General Psychiatry, 43*, 430–434.

Williams, J. G., Barlow, D. H., & Agras, W. S. (1972). Behavioral measurement of severe depression. *Archives of General Psychiatry, 27*, 330–333.

Wilson, P. H., Goldin, J. C., & Charbonneau-Pouis, M. (1983). Comparative efficacy of behavioral and cognitive treatments of depression. *Cognitive Therapy and Research, 7*, 11–124.

Winett, R. A. (1985). Ecobehavioral assessment in health. In P. Karoly (Ed.), *Measurement strategies in health psychology life-styles*. New York: John Wiley.

Woolfolk, R. L., & Lehrer, P. M. (Eds.). (1984). *Principles and practice of stress management*. New York: Guilford.

Wright, J. H., & Beck, A. T. (1983). Cognitive therapy of depression: Theory and practice. *Hospital and Community Psychiatry, 34*, 1119–1127.

Youngren, M., & Lewinsohn, P. M. (1980). The functional relation between depression and problematic interpersonal behavior. *Journal of Abnormal Psychology, 89*, 333–341.

Zeiss, A. M., Lewinsohn, P. M., & Munoz, R. F. (1979). Nonspecific improvement effects in depression using interpersonal, cognitive, and pleasant events focused treatments. *Journal of Consulting and Clinical Psychology, 47*, 427–439.

Zimmerman, M., & Coryell, W. (1987). The Inventory to Diagnose Depression (IDD): A self-report scale to diagnose major depressive disorder. *Journal of Consulting and Clinical Psychology, 55*, 55–59.

Zimmerman, M., Coryell, W., & Pfohl, B. (1986). Melancholic subtyping: A qualitative or quantitative distinction? *American Journal of Psychiatry, 143*, 98–100.

Zimmerman, M., Coryell, W., & Pfohl, B. (1987). Prognostic validity of the dexamethasone suppression test: Results of a six-month prospective follow-up. *American Journal of Psychiatry, 144*, 212–214.

Zung, W. (1965). A self-rating depression scale. *Archives of General Psychiatry, 12,*, 63–70.

ETIOLOGY AND TREATMENT OF PANIC DISORDERS

GEORGE A. CLUM
Virginia Polytechnic Institute and State University

JANET WOODRUFF BORDEN
Western Psychiatric Institute and Clinic

I. INTRODUCTION

Over the past ten years there has been a mushrooming of interest in the phenomena of panic attacks and panic disorders. As one index of this, the first volume of the *Journal of Anxiety Disorders* devoted 50% of all research articles to those covering some aspect of panic. The *Diagnostic and Statistical Manual of Mental Disorders*, third edition, revised (DSM-III-R; American Psychiatric Association, 1987) has recognized the primacy of panic disorder in the development of agoraphobia. While one view of the development of panic is primarily biological (Sheehan, 1984; Sheehan, Ballenger, & Jacobsen, 1980), the behavioral view has marshaled considerable evidence for panic as a complex behavioral response to stress (Faravelli, 1985; Hibbert, 1984a; Ottaviani & Beck, 1987), with important cognitive (Beck, Laude, & Bohnert, 1974; Hibbert, 1984b) and interoceptive conditioning (Barlow et al., 1985) aspects.

Likewise, early research in the pharmacological treatment of panic (e.g., Alexander & Alexander, 1986; Charney et al., 1986; Gloger, Grunhaus, Birmacher, & Troudart, 1981) has been joined by a number of studies that evaluate a variety of behavioral treatment techniques (e.g., Barlow, Cohen, et al., 1984; Borden, Clum, & Broyles, 1986). To date, however, there has been no attempt to examine the several etiological models as well as the treatments they have spawned in terms of their relative efficacy. The purpose of the present review is to address this imbalance by critically examining, first, the current status of etiological theories and, second, the various behavioral interventions for panic currently extant. We attempt to take a historical perspective in this regard, examining changes in perspective over the last decade. We then attempt to draw some general conclusions on the current status of our knowledge and to make some recommendations for research in the future.

II. SCOPE OF THE PROBLEM

A. Diagnosis

Panic attacks are sudden episodes of fear and apprehension. DSM-III-R lists the following common symptoms of an attack: "shortness of breath; dizziness; palpitations or tachychardia; trembling or shaking; sweating; choking; nausea; depersonalization; paresthesias; hot or cold flashes; chest pain; and fear of dying, going crazy, or doing something uncontrolled" (p. 238). An individual must experience at least four of these symptoms during an attack. At some point in the development of the disorder, these symptoms must occur suddenly and intensify within ten minutes. Four attacks must occur for the disorder to be diagnosed. Alternately, an individual may be diagnosed with panic disorder after experiencing one attack followed by one month of fear of having another panic attack. These criteria represent a change from previous diagnostic requirements (DSM-III; American Psychiatric Association, 1980). Previously, to receive a diagnosis of panic disorder, individuals had to experience three attacks in a three-week period. Anticipatory anxiety was not included in diagnostic decisions.

B. Epidemiology

Based on DSM-III criteria, research suggests that panic disorders are quite prevalent. The National Institute of Mental Health Epidemiological Survey found a six-month incidence of panic disorder in approximately 1% of the population (Myers et al., 1984) and a lifetime incidence of 1.5% (Robins, Helzer, Croughan, & Ratcliff, 1981). In a review of several epidemiological surveys based on the Research Diagnostic Criteria or the DSM-III, Weissman and Merikangas (1986) conclude that the one-year prevalence rates varied from 1.2% to 3.1%, while the six-month prevalence rates varied from 0.6% to 1.0%. Other estimates are higher. For example, when the criteria are expanded to include individuals who experience one or more panic attacks a year, the incidence increases to 35% of the general population (Norton, Harrison, Hauch, & Rhodes, 1985). These individuals, who likely previously failed to meet diagnostic criteria for panic disorder on the basis of the DSM-III, may meet the revised criteria for the disorder, resulting in even higher prevalence and incidence rates. Further, 80% of patients diagnosed with any anxiety disorder experience panic attacks (Barlow et al., 1985). These findings indicate that panic attacks are quite prevalent. Indeed, the prevalence may actually be underestimated given that the symptoms of panic mimic many physical ailments such as hypoglycemia, hyperthyroidism, caffeinism, and drug intoxication and withdrawal (Grant, Katon, & Beitman, 1983) and may thus be frequently misdiagnosed. Clearly, the problem of panic is prevalent and as such continues to generate tremendous amounts of research.

The demographics of panic disorder are also of interest. There has been a consistent finding of a higher prevalence rate of panic disorder among females (Barlow et al., 1985; Sheehan, Sheehan, & Minichiello, 1981; Weissman & Merikangas, 1986). This has been extended to familial studies of individuals with panic disorder (Weissman & Merikangas, 1986). Again, a review of the studies in this area reveals a disproportionate number of first-degree relatives with panic disorder who were females. Most researchers have found that panic disorder develops in young adulthood, particularly between the ages of 16 and 40 (Sheehan et al., 1981; Weissman & Merikangas, 1986). The age distribution appears to be unimodal, with the median age of onset at 24 years (Sheehan et al., 1981). Weissman and Merikangas (1986) further report that panic disorder is more prevalent among the separated and divorced, while there is no consistent relationship to race or education. These data indicate that young adult females are the group most at risk for panic disorder.

III.   ETIOLOGICAL MODELS FOR PANIC ATTACKS

Etiology has traditionally been divided into biological and psychological models. The major theories within each of these models will be reviewed, followed by recommendations for an integrated model of the etiology of the disorder.

A.   Genetic Model

Noyes et al. (1986) report that the morbidity risk for panic disorder among first-degree relatives of patients with panic disorder is 17.3%. This is significantly greater than the 2.3% risk reported for relatives of control probands (Crowe, Noyes, Pauls, & Slyman, 1983). In this same study by Noyes et al., an additional 7.4% of relatives of panic patients had panic attacks that did not meet diagnostic criteria. This, however, may not be significant given Norton et al.'s estimate of 35% of the general population having infrequent panic attacks. Torgerson (1983) examined proband-wise concordance rates for anxiety disorders between monozygotic (MZ) and dizygotic (DZ) twin pairs. For all diagnostic categories, except generalized anxiety disorder, the concordance rate for MZ twins was higher than that for DZ twins. Overall concordance for MZ twins was 34%, compared to 17% for DZ twins. However, no MZ co-twin had the same anxiety disorder as the proband. That is, co-twins and probands were more often anxious if the twin pair was MZ, but they experienced different anxiety disorders. Nonetheless, if this proband had a diagnosis of panic disorder or agoraphobia with panic attacks, their monozygotic co-twins were more likely to experience panic attacks, while their dizygotic co-twins were not. Several problems are apparent within the genetic literature on panic. First, the levels of discordance are quite high. If a strong genetic component were present, the concordance rates would presumably be higher. Further, Torgerson's (1983) results are not diagnostic-specific, though they are specific for panic attacks. Though this relationship is small, it suggests that there may be some genetic component to panic attacks. Co-twins were at higher risk for having some anxiety disorder—not the same disorder as the index case. This suggests that there is not a specific genetic transmission of the disorder. Collectively, the results argue for a genetic predisposition to develop some type of anxiety disorder. Unfortunately, there are not yet any adoption studies to address the relative role of the environmental experience in the etiology of panic.

B.   Biological Model

The question then remains as to what is genetically transmitted. Sheehan et al. (1980) speculate that panic disorder may involve a defect in the metabolism of inhibitory neurotransmitters or of receptor sensitivity to them. If this is true, individuals suffering from panic disorder should exhibit a unique sensitivity to certain substances. The most commonly used substances in producing panic attacks are adrenaline (Breggin, 1964), sodium lactate (Sheehan, Carr, Fishman, Walsh, & Peltier-Saxe, 1985), and caffeine (Charney, Heninger, & Jatlow, 1985). Another possibility is that panic disorder patients have a biological vulnerability to hyperventilation (Garssen, Van Veendaal, & Bloemink, 1983).

Breggin (1964) reports that previously anxious individuals, when injected with adrenaline, responded with physiological changes associated with anxiety attacks. Normal subjects had smaller physiological responses that were not termed attacks. Pitts and McClure (1967) propose a sodium lactate model of panic based upon research showing that patients with anxiety attacks had excessive sensitivity to lactate. The anxiety subjects responded to lactate infusions with attacks, while normals did not. Sheehan et al. (1985) report that approximately 80% of panic attack patients have attacks when infused with sodium lactate, while less than 20% of normal subjects have attacks. Further, the attacks that normal subjects experience are less severe and more transient than the panic attack population's.

Early research by Jones and Mellersh (1946) identified the connection between elevated lactic acid and anxiety. During physical exercise, normal subjects had the expected rise in lactate. However, Jones and Mellersh reported that anxiety subjects had excessive rises and also increased sensitivity to the elevated lactate level. Sodium lactate infusions are currently used for three main purposes: diagnosis, treatment, and research (Sheehan et al., 1985). Diagnostically, they are used to confirm the diagnosis of panic disorder. Since panic subjects respond uniquely to the sodium lactate challenge, the technique was conceptualized as a diagnostic tool. The infusions have also been used as an exposure-based treatment for panic attacks (e.g., Bonn, Harrison, & Fees, 1973). The rationale behind such a treatment approach involves the notion that individuals with panic attacks develop an anticipatory anxiety of having another attack, what Goldstein and Chambless (1978) term "fear of fear." In a sense, then, this anticipatory anxiety is viewed as a phobic response to the panic itself. Thus individuals are exposed to that which they fear. The Sheehan research group recommends against the routine use of sodium lactate infusions as diagnostic or treatment strategies for several reasons. First, the infusions are a rigorous and complex medical procedure that presents risks to a portion of the panic population (e.g., those with cardiovascular difficulties). Additionally, the infusions yield a false negative rate of 5–20%. Because of these problems, Sheehan and his colleagues conclude that the information to be gleaned from an infusion can more easily and with similar reliability be obtained from a quality clinical interview. A final note is that Sheehan et al. report no demonstrable treatment effects from the procedure. Accordingly, the principal usage remains at the level of basic research attempting to identify biological bases of panic.

Several issues remain unclear from the sodium lactate infusion data. The primary question of why people experience panic symptoms when infused has not been answered. Current research has ruled out a variety of hypotheses such as calcium depletion (Liebowitz et al., 1986). Additionally, Liebowitz et al. (1986) report that infusions of sodium lactate produce experiences somatically similar to panic attacks. However, these are not accompanied by the cognitive components often related to the attacks. Subjects do not report thoughts related to death, unreality, loss of control, and so on. In a comprehensive review, Margraf, Ehlers, and Roth (1986) offer four major problems with lactate and other physiological induction techniques: (1) Panic is based solely upon self-report, and recent research suggests that subjects are not very accurate concerning physiological events (Taylor, Telch, & Hawick, 1983). Thus in the Taylor et al. study, self-reported panic was accompanied by high heart rates only 58% of the time. Further, only 4 of 14 heart rate episodes identified by monitor as signifying an attack were accompanied by subjective attacks. Although only heart rate was assessed, these combined results suggest that physiological arousal is not the sole determinant of whether or not an attack occurs. (2) The research is only single-blind. (3) There are inadequate criteria for defining panic attacks. (4) Patient expectations are not controlled in these studies. In fact, some patients panic from infusions of saline. In comparing normals and panic subjects, panic subjects are often told they might experience a panic attack, whereas normal subjects are told they may experience an attack similar to one experienced when speaking in public (Clark, 1986). These different instructions may result in different expectations, potentially influencing results of infusion research. Related to this final point, Margraf et al. (1986) demonstrated that the actual increase in subjective units of distress and in physiological arousal from lactate infusion is approximately equal for panic and normal subjects. The observed differences between the two groups are dependent on the level of baseline arousal. When this is taken into account, there is little difference in degree of arousal.

Another technique for panic induction is the administration of caffeine. Recent research suggests that panic patients have increased sensitivity to the effects of caffeine (Boulenger, Uhde, Wolff, & Post, 1984; Charney et al., 1985). Such increased sensitivity includes self-reported anxiety, nervousness, nausea, and palpitations. Charney et al. (1985) report that in panic, but not normal, subjects, these symptoms are correlated with caffeine levels. In fact, 71% of panic patients reported that experiences from caffeine were similar to those during panic attacks. A variety of explanations have been provided for caffeine's effect on subjects with panic attacks. Berkowitz, Tarver, and Spector (1970) hypothesize that caffeine increases catecholamine activity. Charney et al. (1985) report that caffeine produces greater anxiety and higher blood pressures in panic subjects. They propose an abnormality in the neuronal system to account for these findings. However, this proposal remains speculative.

Panic disordered individuals may also be uniquely susceptible to the effects of hyperventilation. The most commonly occurring symptoms of a panic attack include dizziness, blurred vision, numbness, palpitations, tingling sensations, tachychardia, nausea, and breathlessness (Clark, Salkovskis, & Chalkley, 1985). These are also the most common symptoms occurring during hyperventilation (Clark et al., 1985). Hyperventilation is caused by increased respiratory ventilation, which may be produced by rapid, shallow breathing, frequent sighing, or breathing through the mouth. This activity leads to a reduction of carbon dioxide in the lungs and subsequently in the partial pressure of carbon dioxide in the blood. These bodily changes produce the unpleasant symptoms and bodily sensations common to panic attacks (van den Hout & Griez, 1984). Because of the similarity in symptomatology between hyperventilation and panic attacks, many writers have suggested that hyperventilation may produce panic attacks (Clark & Hemsley, 1982; Hibbert, 1984a; Lum, 1976).

A variety of researchers have demonstrated that a standard hyperventilation provocation can produce panic attack symptoms (Bonn, Readhead, & Timmons, 1984; Garssen et al., 1983; van den Hout & Griez, 1984). Garssen et al. (1983) report that 61% of their agoraphobic subjects experienced symptoms similar to their usual panic attacks during voluntary hyperventilation. Gorman et al. (1984) compared sodium lactate infusions and hyperventilation in the production of paniclike symptoms. They reported that 8 of their 12 subjects experienced panic symptoms with sodium lactate, while 7 of the 12 did so with carbon dioxide inhalation. The less rigorous and challenging procedure of hyperventilation produced similar results both in number of subjects experiencing symptoms and in number of symptoms experienced. Rapee (1986) compared generalized anxiety and panic disorder subjects on their responses to 90 seconds of voluntary hyperventilation. Panic disorder subjects reported greater distress and more paniclike symptoms. They also had lower resting partial pressure of carbon dioxide and higher heart rates. More anecdotally, Rapee questioned the subjects about the similarity of the experienced symptoms and their naturally occurring anxiety symptoms. Only 25% of the generalized anxiety subjects indicated that the symptoms were similar to their naturally occurring ones. Over 80% of the panic disorder subjects responded that the symptoms were similar. Importantly, even with a large majority of the panic subjects reporting that the symptoms were similar, none reported actual panic attacks. When queried, the subjects attributed this to knowledge of why the symptoms were occurring and to being in a "safe" environment.

A common finding in the induction literature is that all these procedures can produce panic-type symptoms. However, they rarely produce what subjects experience as a "panic attack." Anecdotal evidence suggests that the subjects attribute their symptoms to the experimental procedure and thus do not panic per se. The lack of subjective panic attacks in these subjects suggests that symptoms are necessary, but not sufficient, for a panic attack to occur. This issue will be addressed further in an attempt to integrate the biological and psychological models.

Additional biological markers have been reported. Jacob, Moller, Turner, and Wall (1985) examined panic patients who experienced dizziness during their panic attacks. Subjects completed a battery of vestibular and auditory tests. Results indicate that a high proportion of these patients had abnormal vestibular and audiological functioning. Although the authors appropriately caution that the results should be interpreted as preliminary, they do provide the interesting suggestion that these abnormalities may be functionally involved in the production of panic. The vestibular and auditory abnormalities may produce frightening sensations or the anxiety may result in changes in the vestibular and auditory system (Jacob et al., 1985).

Finally, cardiovascular problems have been linked to panic. Pariser, Jones, and Pinta (1979) suggest that mitral valve prolapse syndrome (MVPS) may be related to panic. They explain that MVPS is characterized by chest pain, difficulty in breathing, faintness, fatigue, and tachychardia. A quick review of the symptoms of panic confirms the potential similarity. The syndrome occurs when there is abnormal motion of one or both leaflets of the mitral valve into the left atrium of the heart (Liberthson, Sheehan, King, & Weyman, 1986). There is a wide range of reported prevalence of MVPS in normal subjects ranging from 0.4% (Liberthson et al., 1986) to 9% (Kantor, Zitrin, & Zeldis, 1980), with a consensus of approximately 5% (Shear, Devereaux, Kramer-Fox, Mann, & Frances, 1984). Researchers have reported a fairly high incidence of MVPS in panic and agoraphobia patients. The incidence ranges from 34% (Liberthson et al., 1986) to 50% (Gorman, Fyer, Glicklich, King, & Klein, 1981). However, conflicting results have also been reported. In examining 141 patients with diagnosed MVPS, Hartman, Kramer, Brown, and Devereaux (1982) found that only 16% of these patients were diagnosable as panic disordered. MVPS thus appears to be more prevalent in panic disordered individuals than in the normal population. Shear and her colleagues have identified a number of reasons for the discrepancies in rates, including differential diagnostic criteria for MVPS, with less stringent criteria resulting in higher reported proportions of panic subjects with MVPS. While MVPS occurs more frequently in panic disordered persons, it does not yet appear to have been demonstrated to have a causal role in the etiology of panic. One possible link is that a percentage of individuals with MVPS become sensitized to their bodies, especially to cardiac arrhythmias. At times this preoccupation leads to increased anxiety, with attendant catastrophizing cognitions. Such catastrophizing may then lead to a full-fledged panic attack. This possibility will be more closely examined under the cognitive hypothesis.

C. Psychological Models

Even though some biological links can be specified, they cannot completely account for the etiology of panic. For example, the course of panic waxes and wanes in terms of frequency and occurrence of attacks. Additionally, idiosyncratic stressors can often be identified for panic attack sufferers. Hibbert (1984b) reported that a large majority of his sample of panic patients (88%) had experienced significant idiosyncratic stressors within 12 months preceding the onset of their panic attacks. Ottaviani and Beck (1987) examined 30 panic disorder patients and determined that in each case, the initial panic episode was preceded by some type of stressor, either psychological or physical. Further, panic attack patients, compared to matched normal controls, experienced significantly more stressful life events such as illness or death in their families in the two months preceding their first attacks (Faravelli, 1985). Collectively, these results point to the role of some type of stressor as a potential precipitant to panic. It is not yet clear if the stressor can cause panic or provides the catalyst for a high level of anxiety to become what we see as panic.

Expanding upon a stress model, an interoceptive conditioning model has been proposed by several research groups (e.g., Craske & Barlow, 1986). This model proposes that individuals somehow susceptible to anxiety experience their initial panic attacks when under some type of stress as described above. Subsequently, these individuals develop fear of certain somatic sensations that seem to represent the initial phases of another attack (Clum & Pickett, 1984; Craske & Barlow, 1986). As Craske and Barlow argue, the difference between this interoceptive conditioning model and one of general arousal is that individuals become sensitized to specific physiological events—not to arousal in general. This is what Goldstein and Chambless (1978) term "fear of fear." In the interoceptive conditioning model, however, specific physiological events that trigger an attack may be outside of awareness, while the Goldstein and Chambless fear of fear hypothesis is much more clearly related to anticipatory anxiety of a conscious type. Individuals become sensitized to the physiological arousal during a panic attack; they then become preoccupied with a focus on these sensations, seeing them as a warning signal of another attack (Beck & Emery, 1985).

This fear of fear can also be seen in the somatization behaviors of panic patients. King, Margraf, Ehlers, and Maddock (1986) compared panic subjects and nonpanic controls. Both groups were without physical health problems. Subjects completed inventories that measured their anxiety and degree of somatization. The results indicated that panic sufferers present a pattern of significantly greater somatization, including greater focus on cardiovascular and gastrointestinal difficulties. Recent research supports the basic contention of the interoceptive conditioning model by demonstrating panic following relaxation exercises (Cohen, Barlow, & Blanchard, 1985). Subjects responded to the physiological sensations associated with relaxation with panic. As such, it would appear that these sensations were somehow frightening, perhaps due to their alteration of "normal" physiological processes. DSM-III-R reflects awareness of this model in that only one attack followed by significant fear of having another panic attack is required for diagnosis. The fear of another attack, or anticipatory fear, likely increases the somatic/physiological experiences in panic sufferers, essentially becoming conditioned stimuli for the conditioned response of a panic attack.

The cognitions of panic patients are an important element of the conditioning model. Cognitive factors have also been explored in more detailed examinations of the etiology and maintenance of panic. Beck et al. (1974) found that anxiety patients had automatic thoughts related to themes of danger, such as loss of bodily control and dying. May (1977) reports that self-regulated phobic thoughts are associated with increased physiological responding and fear. Related to panic, Hibbert (1984b) identified characteristic ideation for a group of panic patients during the panic attack itself. Thoughts tended to center on personal harm and danger, such as having a heart attack or dying. Hibbert found that subjects reported their arousal first, and then made cognitive attributions concerning reasons for the arousal. Hibbert's data can be understood as somatic symptoms followed by some kind of cognitive overreaction, resulting in a panic attack. Hibbert suggests that panic subjects systematically misconstrue somatic or physiological symptoms as more dangerous than they really are. The subjects tend to, in the term of Beck et al. (1974), "catastrophize" and subsequently panic. Additionally, Last, O'Brien, and Barlow (1985) report that in a study with a group of agoraphobic subjects with panic attacks, negative thoughts were correlated with anxiety. There was also some evidence (although not consistently significant) to support an inverse relationship between positive thoughts and anxiety. The negative thoughts were generally catastrophic, while the positive ones were related to coping.

In a series of analog studies, Wade, Malloy, and Proctor (1977) demonstrated that the content of subjects' imagery is related to their avoidance and fear. In a fearful situation, high fearful subjects reported more aversive imagery than low fearful subjects. Further, aversive imagery was positively associated with level of fear and avoidance. Imagery content was associated with fear and avoidance when subjects imagined themselves in the situations as well as when they were actually confronted with the fearful stimuli (snakes were used in this series of experiments). Finally, Ottaviani and Beck (1987) found that panic was associated with thoughts and images related to physical and mental catastrophe. The authors questioned all patients regarding their thoughts during a panic attack. All subjects showed misattribution of somatic or psychological experiences that triggered their attacks. Like other similar research, this study is retrospective and thus subject to bias or distortion. However, these studies do suggest that cognitions have some meaningful role in panic attacks.

Although the cumulative results of these studies support the notion that "negative" cognitions and anxiety reactions are related, the causal relationship remains confused. Last et al. (1985) correlated percentages of negative thought, positive thought, and self-reported anxiety during in vivo exposure. The methodology, however, did not allow for a test of causality. Hibbert (1984b) and Ottaviani and Beck (1987) relied completely on self-report of past events. Given the traumatic experience of panic, the subjects' recall of temporal sequencing of thoughts and arousal may be inaccurate. They may attempt to "make sense" of the attack by imposing a logical structure upon it after the fact.

A final psychological model of panic is an information-processing one, the best known of which is Lang's (1979) bioinformational theory of emotional imagery. Lang's theory of emotional imagery is based upon research in psychophysiology, information processing, and behavior therapy. He maintains that fear is represented as a network that includes three types of information—information about the feared stimulus, information about behavioral and physiological responses, and information about the meaning of the stimuli and responses. That is, fears are distinguished not only by individuals' responses, but also by their interpretations about the fear (Foa & Kozak, 1986). In a series of experiments, Lang, Kozak, Miller, Levin, and McLean (1980) demonstrated that subjects trained to focus on physiological cues in imaginal scenes had significantly greater physiological responding compared to both a group trained to focus upon stimulus cues and a no-instruction control group. The imaged scenes were a neutral, an action, and a feared scene. This research was extended to examine differences among subjects with different fears, social phobias, and snake phobias (Lang, Levin, Miller, & Kozak, 1983). Again, physiological-response trained subjects had greater physiological arousal than stimulus cue or control groups.

Two issues emerge from Lang's seminal work. First, cognitions and physiological arousal are intricately related. Furthermore, at least in artificial situations, specific cognitions can result in varied physiological responding. This does not provide information as to whether this would occur in a more naturalistic setting where individuals were not prompted to monitor certain cues. The second issue suggested by Lang's work concerns the relationship between a focus on somatic cues and anxiety. Subjects trained to focus upon these cues demonstrated more evidence of anxiety. Again, while subjects were trained in this focus, a somatic focus may be a relevant issue in anxiety subjects. Together with the previously discussed research suggesting an interoceptive conditioning model or, minimally, a nonadaptive focus on somatic sensations, Lang's theory suggests that just thinking about these sensations can lead to physiological changes associated with anxiety, which in turn may prompt panic attacks.

D.   Conceptual Rapprochement of the Etiology of Panic

Both types of models, biological and psychological, have received empirical support in their attempts to account for the etiology of panic. However, neither biological nor psychological accounts can explain the disorder without reference to the other. For example, the panic induction literature reveals the importance of subjects' cognitions in the experience of panic. The psychological literature requires the existence of some type of physiological sensation for a panic attack to occur. Clearly, it would be premature to argue that one model is superior to another when it is apparent that both are perhaps necessary, but perhaps not sufficient, to explain the etiology of panic. This finding is not surprising in that anxiety has been conceptualized as a multifaceted construct with cognitive, behavioral, and physiological components. Potential rapprochements have been proposed by several researchers (e.g., Clark, 1986; Clum & Pickett, 1984; Jacob & Rapport, 1984). Each of these models proposes that an initial attack occurs. The attack may be experienced as "out of the blue" or as the culmination of high levels of stress. Following this attack, the patient expectantly awaits any signs of another attack. The patient becomes preoccupied with somatic sensations and overinterprets them as the beginning of another attack. At the onset of these signs, the person is thought to become increasingly anxious, fearful, and worried, serving to exacerbate the physical sensations of anxiety, resulting in a vicious spiral of symptoms and thoughts leading to a full-blown panic attack.

These models have intuitive appeal, but require further detailed examination. However, the research to date is fairly clear that panic is not merely composed of physical sensations, nor is it the result of catastrophic thoughts alone. To attempt to explain the disorder from only one of these perspectives seems shortsighted and without adequate empirical support. Many questions remain about the etiology of panic. The fruitful avenue for exploring these questions seems to lie with the continued understanding of the dynamic and constant interplay between biological and psychological domains of the disorder.

IV. BEHAVIORAL TREATMENTS TARGETING PANIC ATTACKS

A. Introduction

In the past ten years, there has been a metamorphosis in the research literature on the treatment of agoraphobia and panic attacks. In order to understand and evaluate current treatment modalities for panic disorder, this metamorphosis must be placed in historical perspective. The most salient aspects of this transformation include the following:

(1) There has been change in the diagnostic focus vis à vis panic disorder and agoraphobia from the primacy of agoraphobia and the exclusion of panic disorder in DSM-II (American Psychiatric Association, 1968), to the listing of a separate heading for panic disorder in DSM-III (American Psychiatric Association, 1978), to the primacy of panic disorder in DSM-III-R (American Psychiatric Association, 1987). This most recent version of DSM-III recognizes the role of panic attacks as the initial and most important phase in the development of agoraphobia.

(2) Consistent with this change in diagnostic focus has been a shift in the target of therapeutic change, from a total emphasis on the avoidance behavior of agoraphobia, with little attention to panic attacks, to an emphasis on the avoidance behavior as primary target and panic attacks as a secondary target, and currently to an emphasis on panic attacks as the primary target and avoidance as the secondary target.

(3) Consistent with the above change in target focus has been a change in the treatment techniques utilized. While exposure techniques emerged as the most powerful behavioral approach for treating agoraphobia in the 1970s, the development of a variety of coping strategies for dealing with panic attacks has emerged as the focus of intervention in the 1980s.

(4) As behavioral approaches for treating panic attacks per se have been developed and tested, the type of research design has also evolved. In the 1970s and to a lesser extent in the 1980s, the most common research design compared a pharmacological agent plus exposure to another pharmacological agent plus supportive therapy or a placebo plus exposure (e.g., Telch, Agras, Taylor, Roth, & Gallen, 1985). The design typically confounded exposure with some other pharmacological treatment. The view emerging from these studies was that exposure was important for treating avoidance, but that drugs were necessary for treating panic attacks. Later studies of this genre began examining the effects of exposure on the panic attacks themselves. Only recently, however, have experimental designs shifted to an emphasis on the unconfounded analysis of behavioral interventions on panic attacks.

In keeping with these shifts in focus, the present review is concerned solely with behavioral intervention techniques as they affect panic attacks and panic disorders. Studies were included in this review if they met one of the following criteria: (1) the study directly targeted individuals with panic disorder as opposed to agoraphobia; (2) agoraphobia patients were the principal target group, but the impact of the interventions on panic attacks was also assessed; and (3) the study assessed factors predictive of response to interventions for either of the above groups.

In our review we attempted to follow this historical development to the extent feasible while keeping a logical order to the studies reviewed. Accordingly, we first review exposure techniques for those studies with data on the effects of exposure on panic attacks. The examination of exposure techniques is followed by an analysis of the effectiveness of relaxation and breathing retraining techniques, cognitive therapies, and combination therapies (i.e., therapies that combine several different treatment approaches). Finally, we deal with the issue of factors predictive of response to behavioral therapies.

B. Exposure Techniques

Exposure treatments are based on Mowrer's (1939) two-factor theory of anxiety. This theory posits that two learning paradigms, classical and operant conditioning, are required to explain the development and maintenance of anxiety disorders. In agoraphobia, situational cues, such as driving or restaurants, become conditioned stimuli that can elicit anxiety attacks. The avoidance of the situational cues that follows is reinforced by the reduction in anxiety. Exposure techniques place the anxiety sufferer in the anxiety-producing situation until the cues inherent in the situation fail to elicit the anxiety response. Thus extinction has been attempted with exposure techniques that place the anxiety sufferer in the actual physical situation (in vivo) or require the individual to imagine the eliciting cues vividly (imaginal flooding). While exposure techniques were known to reduce avoidance behavior, the possible effects of exposure on panic attacks were suggested by studies (Mavissakalian & Michelson, 1983, 1986) in which exposure was equally as effective as imipramine plus self-directed exposure in reducing agoraphobic avoidance behavior and the anxiety typically accompanying exposure. Perhaps the exposure was also serving to reduce the panic attacks that were typically experienced in the phobic situations.

Because antidepressant medications emerged from the 1970s as an important vehicle for treating panic attacks, it was natural for exposure techniques to be compared to antidepressant medications in the treatment of panic. In a study representative of this approach, the effects of therapist-aided exposure were compared to relaxation in agoraphobics receiving either imipramine (a tricyclic antidepressant) or placebo (Marks et al., 1983). The assumption in this study and others like it is that the comparison of exposure plus placebo to imipramine plus relaxation allows conclusions about the relative efficacy of exposure and imipramine. In this study, individuals treated with exposure had significantly fewer spontaneous panic

attacks than individuals treated with relaxation. This effect disappeared by
the end of the 52-week assessment period. There was, on the other hand,
no superiority of imipramine-treated patients over placebo-treated patients
on the panic measure. Marks et al. argue that imipramine had an antipanic
effect only on those individuals also suffering from depression. In a separate analysis, the authors conclude that exposure was the most significant
therapeutic agent, with imipramine adding little to the effect of placebo.
The problem with these conclusions is that exposure is always confounded
with either imipramine or placebo.

In contrast to the confounded study of Marks et al. (1983), a direct test
of whether exposure added anything to the treatment of panic and phobic
avoidance when treated with imipramine was provided by Mavissakalian,
Michelson, and Dealy (1983), who compared exposure plus imipramine to
imipramine only. Of three panic measures, only one, mean panic score,
was significantly more improved in the imipramine plus exposure group
when compared to the imipramine-only group. Further, comparing the two
treatment groups on the proportion of patients experiencing greater than
50% pre-post improvement favored the drug plus exposure group on only
one of four measures. On phobic anxiety and avoidance, however, the
imipramine plus exposure treatment was clearly superior to imipramine
alone. These results indicate that exposure, when combined with
antidepressants, has the primary effect of reducing avoidance and anxiety
in the phobic situation and a lesser effect on panic itself.

These conclusions, however, were partially contradicted by another
study (Telch et al., 1985) that compared three groups: (1) imipramine-no
exposure, (2) imipramine plus exposure, and (3) placebo plus exposure. A
measure of panic obtained from daily diaries served as the primary dependent measure of interest. Avoidance behavior in this sample of agoraphobics was also measured. As with the study by Mavissakalian et al. (1983),
the two exposure groups were superior to the imipramine treatment without exposure. However, the imipramine plus exposure group was significantly more improved on the panic frequency measure than the
imipramine-no exposure group. This finding stresses the importance of
combining the two treatments as the placebo plus exposure group did not
show a reduction in panic attacks. Again, avoidance behavior appears to be
the principal target of exposure, though exposure combined with
imipramine clearly results in fewer panic attacks than imipramine alone.

Mavissakalian and Michelson (1986) conducted a study that permitted
an analysis of the relative effects of imipramine plus exposure, imipramine
plus programmed practice, placebo plus exposure, and placebo plus programmed practice. A panic attack measure that combined severity and
frequency of panic over a three-day period prior to the evaluation point
was the primary dependent measure. A second measure of panic—
spontaneous attacks while at home—was also used. No differences among

the four treatments were found for either of the panic measures. Interestingly, while imipramine dose was related to degree of improvement on most other dependent measures, there was no differential effect of treatment dose on the panic measures. While this study seems to contradict the conclusions of Marks et al. (1983), it is possible that the programmed practice approach, utilized in the imipramine and placebo groups, was itself a powerful exposure technique. Clearly, however, exposure in vivo was not shown to be superior to the programmed practice technique.

In addition to exposure techniques applied in vivo, several researchers have examined the relative effectiveness of imaginal exposure. The effects of imaginal flooding have been examined in both sedated and unsedated agoraphobics. The question being addressed in these studies was whether sedation attenuates the effects of exposure. In the first study designed to address this question, the authors report that a drug that produced sedation (methohexitone sodium) reduced the effectiveness of imaginal flooding by reducing anxiety across flooding sessions (Chambless, Foa, Groves, & Goldstein, 1979). While improvements occurred with imaginal flooding on measures of phobic avoidance, there were no effects of this procedure on frequency of panic attacks.

In the second study, 21 agoraphobics with panic attacks were separated into nondrug flooding (N = 8), drug flooding (N = 7), and an attention-control group (N = 6) (Chambless, Foa, Groves, & Goldstein, 1982). Only imaginal flooding was used throughout the treatment and follow-up periods. All clients received eight two-hour treatment sessions. The flooding sessions consisted of 90 minutes of imagined exposure to the avoided situations and the fantasized disastrous consequences of panic. Subjects in the attention control group received 90 minutes of supportive therapy and functional analysis of panic attacks followed by 30 minutes of progressive relaxation. In a second phase of the study, nondrug flooding subjects received treatment sessions aimed at teaching them self-monitoring of anxiety levels, the identification of interpersonal events that led to anxiety attacks, and techniques for handling these events productively. Drug-flooding and control group subjects received further treatment in dealing with fear and avoidance behavior and in the use of paradoxical self-instruction to manage panic attacks. This was an extremely convoluted design, since even the control group received exposure in the second phase and learned coping strategies for dealing with panic in the first phase. The results, however, are instructive. There were no treatment group differences or treatment by time interaction effects for either client or therapist ratings of panic attacks. There was an effect for occasions, however, as all treatment groups experienced significant reductions in panic over time. Identical results were found for a "fear of fear" measure, with no differences between treatments. These studies indicate that when the target symptom is panic attacks, whether or not the client is receiving sedating drugs makes no difference with regard to the outcome for flooding treatment. It also points to the possibility that, where panic attacks are the target behaviors, coping strategies may be comparable in effectiveness to exposure strategies.

C. Relaxation and Breathing Retraining

A number of studies have examined relaxation training and breathing retraining in reducing panic attacks. Studies of the effects of relaxation training have been of two types: (1) attempts to teach relaxation with the apparent hope of producing a general reduction in the level of anxiety and thus indirectly affecting panic attacks, and (2) attempts to teach relaxation as a coping technique during panic attacks or at their incipient stage.

A single-case design was employed by Frame, Turner, Jacob, and Szekely (1984) to assess the effectiveness of progressive muscle relaxation training plus self-directed exposure in an agoraphobic woman with panic attacks. In a 35-day baseline period she experienced three panic attacks. During treatment, which extended over a 60-day period, her panic attacks dropped to zero. A follow-up period of 18 months continued to reveal that she was panic-free. Several problems exist with this study. First, three panic attacks in a 30-day period is inadequate to establish a connection between their disappearance and the onset of therapy. One would almost have to conclude that it was beginning treatment rather than the completion of treatment that led to a cessation of attacks. More important for our purposes is the fact that the effects of relaxation training are confounded with self-directed exposure.

As indicated in the above section, Marks et al. (1983) found relaxation not as effective as exposure in reducing spontaneous panic attacks. Marks et al.'s conclusions with regard to the noneffectiveness of imipramine were challenged in a study comparing imipramine plus supportive therapy to behavior therapy plus placebo (Zitrin, Klein, Woerner, & Ross, 1983). In this study, the behavioral intervention combined desensitization in fantasy and assertiveness training. On three of four panic measures, including ratings of frequency and severity, imipramine plus support was superior to desensitization and assertiveness plus placebo. Interestingly, although not significant, lower relapse rates (16%) existed in individuals treated with behavior therapy than in individuals treated with imipramine plus support (31%).

Similar conclusions were reached in another study designed to compare alprazolam to placebo in a group of panic disordered individuals (Chouinard, Annable, Fontaine, & Solyom, 1982). In this study, relaxation plus desensitization was added to half the patients' treatment in both the placebo and drug groups after four weeks of treatment. No treatment effects for this behavioral intervention were found on the total Hamilton

Anxiety Rating Scale within either the placebo or alprazolam groups. While these results might be interpreted as indicating no additional effect for relaxation training, another conclusion is possible. The differences between placebo and alprazolam evident at the end of week four had disappeared by the end of week eight, the first assessment point subsequent to the institution of relaxation and desensitization. This analysis suggests that the behavioral intervention had allowed the placebo group to catch up to the alprazolam group.

The behavioral intervention utilized in these studies was not the treatment of choice for agoraphobia, a fact alluded to by the authors of the first study (Zitrin et al., 1983). A comparison of exposure and desensitization had in fact previously been carried out (Zitrin, Klein, & Woerner, 1980), with exposure producing much more rapid improvement but desensitization catching up at the end of six months. In none of these three studies was relaxation training or desensitization expected to be the most powerful treatment. Accordingly, they were examined within the experimental design in ways least likely to demonstrate their effectiveness.

In a direct examination of the effects of relaxation training (RT), Taylor, Kenigsberg, and Robinson (1982) compared RT to diazepam, placebo, and a control in a group of panic disordered individuals. No direct measures of panic were taken. Brief relaxation training consisting of five half hour sessions was found to be the most effective treatment on self-report measures of general anxiety. Diazepam plus support proved to be the most effective treatment on a physiological measure consisting of heart rate measured at baseline and during stress. Again, 2-½ hours of relaxation training is not a powerful treatment approach in the amelioration of panic disorders.

Michelson and Marchione (1986) compared relaxation training to a cognitive treatment—paradoxical intention and graduated exposure. Two measures of panic were utilized—self-rating of panic attacks and severity of spontaneous attacks. There were no significant differences among the three treatments at mid- and posttreatment or three-month follow-up. All three treatments improved significantly from pre- to posttreatment and maintained these gains at follow-up. Unlike the previous studies examining relaxation, the study by Michelson and Marchione was specifically designed to test the effectiveness of relaxation training.

In all of the previous studies, relaxation training was employed as a vehicle for reducing anxiety in general. It was not taught as a coping skill per se, to be utilized when a panic attack was imminent or in progress. Relaxation as a coping strategy was, however, taught in a study conducted by Craske and Barlow (1986). These researchers report that this relaxation training procedure significantly reduced panic attacks from pre- to posttreatment. When compared to a wait list control group, however, there were no significant differences at posttreatment.

Unlike most of the studies examining relaxation training as a treatment for panic attacks, breathing retraining sprang directly from a theoretical model and was designed specifically for dealing with panic attacks. Breathing retraining is an outgrowth of studies (e.g., Bonn et al., 1984; Garssen et al., 1983) demonstrating that hyperventilation can produce panic attacks in panic disordered individuals. If hyperventilation can produce panic attacks in panic disordered individuals, then, the reasoning goes, it is possible that it does produce panic attacks. Teach appropriate breathing techniques and you may reduce or eliminate the attacks. The technique is simple and straightforward. Breathing retraining focuses on teaching slowed, diaphragmatic breathing techniques in seeking to restore a normal level of blood carbon dioxide and consequently reduce symptoms of panic attacks. In a single case study of breathing retraining in an individual with panic disorder, Rapee (1985) reported a marked decrease in the frequency and severity of these attacks within a three-week treatment period. At a six-month follow-up, this subject was no longer experiencing panic attacks. While of interest as a demonstration, this study leaves unanswered the question of whether breathing retraining was the essential ingredient of change in the treatment of panic attacks, especially in light of the fact that smoking and caffeine were both eliminated and an exercise program instituted as part of the treatment package. Since caffeine sensitivity is common in panic disordered individuals, its elimination could by itself have accounted for the change.

Two studies were conducted by Clark and his associates on the effects of breathing retraining on panic attacks (Clark et al., 1985; Salkovskis, Jones, & Clark, 1986). In the first study, patients were preselected on the basis of whether they perceived a marked similarity between their attacks and the effects of overbreathing or hyperventilation (Clark et al., 1985). All were suffering from panic attacks, although they were not diagnosed as having a panic disorder. They were encouraged to avoid increasing their exposure to feared situations during the first two weeks of treatment but were told to expose themselves to avoided situations for the next phase of treatment (average number of additional sessions = 9.7). Eighteen patients completed the study. An A-B single case design was utilized. No difference in number of attacks was found between the two pretreatment assessment periods, while there was a significant decline in the number of attacks from pre- to posttreatment, that is, at the conclusion of breathing retraining. Likewise, for a subgroup of individuals who experienced panic in specific situations, anxiety in those situations did not change pretreatment but was significantly reduced from pre- to posttreatment. The number of attacks continued to decline from the third to the thirteenth treatment week, an effect maintained at six-month and two-year follow-ups.

In one of the few controlled studies examining the effect of breathing retraining, Bonn et al. (1984) compared breathing retraining plus exposure

(N = 7) to exposure only (N = 5) in a group of agoraphobics with panic attacks. Those individuals in the first group had two sessions of breathing retraining followed by seven two-hour in vivo exposure sessions. The second group had nine two-hour in vivo exposure sessions. The two groups did not differ at the end of treatment on mean resting breathing rate, global phobia score, somatic symptom score, or agoraphobia score, though both groups improved significantly on these measures. Frequency of panic attacks was significantly lower at the end of treatment in the breathing retraining group. At six-month follow-up, all dependent measures were significantly lower in the breathing retraining group but not in the exposure-only group. The failure of the exposure-only group to continue its general improvement in the follow-up period occurred as the result of worsening of symptoms in general. This is one of the few studies comparing the most common behavioral treatment of agoraphobia—namely, exposure—to a treatment primarily aimed at panic attacks but including exposure. The results indicate the importance of eliminating panic attacks via breathing retraining in reducing the rate of relapse in this population.

D. Cognitive Approaches

Cognitive treatment approaches in dealing with panic are an outgrowth of a model discussed in an earlier section that ties cognitions to the recurrence and exacerbation of panic attacks. Elimination or reduction of cognitive errors associated with attacks or introduction of adaptive cognitive coping strategies are accordingly employed to manage panic attacks.

A variety of cognitive techniques, including relaxation, implosion, systematic desensitization, respiratory control, and cognitive restructuring, were utilized in individually tailored treatment programs for a group of agoraphobics with panic attacks (Cottraux, Mollard, Duinat, & Riviere, 1986). No comparison group was utilized. The treated group experienced a significant reduction in both the number of panic attacks and the number of psychotropic medications taken. These treatment effects were maintained for a subgroup of individuals available at six-month follow-up.

The use of coping self-statements was employed in a sample of twelve individuals with free-floating anxiety, "usually also with panic attacks" (Ramm, Marks, Yuksel, & Stern, 1981, p. 367). Half of the subjects received positive coping statements and half received negative statements. While there were between-group differences on the frequency of panic attacks at the end of treatment, these differences disappeared by follow-up. No between-treatments differences were manifested on either severity or duration of panic attacks. Further, there were no differences across time for any of the panic measures. This study suggests that coping self-statements are ineffective in reducing panic attacks. However, these treatment failures were likely a function of the decision to utilize coping statements that were not individually tailored to the problems and preferences of each patient.

Coping self-statements (SST) as a treatment modality was the subject of another study in which it was compared to paradoxical intention (PI) (Mavissakalian, Michelson, Greenwald, Kornbluth, & Greenwald, 1983). All patients (N = 24) were told of the importance of confronting phobic situations and were in fact encouraged to enter such situations as treatment progressed. The PI condition was superior to the SST condition on the panic attack measure at the end and midpoint of therapy. It was also the only treatment to evidence a significant improvement in panic attacks from pre- to posttreatment. By the end of the six-month follow-up period, however, the SST condition had caught up to the PI condition on all dependent measures, including the frequency of panic attacks. The assessed effects of treatment on both coping and self-defeating cognitions revealed across-the-board decreases in the latter, with an interesting effect for coping statements. Coping statements decreased in the PI groups and remained unchanged with the SST group. These findings could not be resolved by the authors, who were unable to attribute the improvement from therapy to improvements in cognitive coping ability.

Another recently developed cognitive strategy for treating panic attacks is guided imaginal coping (GIC; Clum, 1985). This technique trains individuals in a variety of coping strategies under conditions of imagining situational, cognitive, and symptom response cues associated with panic attacks. Coping strategies include breathing retraining, self-coping statements, restructuring cognitions, and various forms of distraction. In a preliminary analysis of the GIC technique, Borden et al. (1986) compared GIC to imaginal flooding and a no-treatment control. While all three groups experienced a drop in number of attacks, subjects receiving the GIC treatment reported no panic attacks at four-month follow-up. In comparison, 40% of the flooding group and 78% of the wait list control experienced at least a 50% drop in the frequency of attacks. Severity of attacks as measured by the number and duration of catastrophic thoughts was significantly less in the GIC group at posttreatment, while neither the flooding nor control groups evidenced such change. Symptom reduction during attacks was also significantly less in the GIC group by posttreatment, while no change was evident in the two other groups. As we shall see, GIC bears a close resemblance to several other newly developed strategies for dealing with panic attacks.

A cognitive coping strategy (plus one session of breathing retraining) was also utilized as one of the treatment approaches by Craske and Barlow (1986). On two measures of panic, frequency of attacks and proportion of patients with no attacks, the cognitive restructuring group was superior to a wait list control group. Further, it was the only treatment group in which all of the members experienced no panic attacks posttreatment. An important component of this treatment, similar to GIC, is the induction of paniclike symptoms utilized in order to practice the cognitive techniques.

E. Combined Treatments

A number of studies have combined several different treatment approaches in dealing with the diverse aspects of panic and its sequelae. One recent study targeting agoraphobics with panic (Chambless, Goldstein, Gallagher, & Bright, 1986) describes a multimodal treatment package compressed into an intensive treatment period (10 days of 7–9 hours of intensive treatment). The keystone of this program is a five-hour group experience emphasizing in vivo exposure plus psychotherapy. During the in vivo experience, subjects are taught coping strategies for dealing with panic, including thought stopping, focused attention, cognitive restructuring, and calming breathing techniques. Accepted for the study were 35 clients who were not on drugs, with the exception of mild tranquilizers. Using a criterion of at least 50% improvement on measures of both avoidance and panic, 58% of the clients were found to be improved at six months after the conclusion of treatment.

Beck (1988) describes a primarily cognitive-reorientation approach to individuals with panic disorder. Also incorporated into the treatment was training in relaxation, breathing, and distraction techniques. The last essentially involved coping strategies to be used in the early stages of a panic attack or during the attack itself. Length of therapy varied depending on the needs of the patients, a luxury permitted because this was an uncontrolled clinical trial. Results were impressive. By the conclusion of treatment, the number of panic attacks had dropped to zero. Further, this improvement was maintained through three follow-up periods up to one year. The follow-up data were, however, of questionable reliability, as the number of subjects available to follow up was reduced by 4, 6, and 19 individuals at 3, 6, and 12 months, respectively. As with the approaches of Borden et al. (1986) and Craske and Barlow (1986), Beck induced panic symptoms as a vehicle for practicing coping techniques.

The question of whether behavioral treatments can specifically target panic attacks was examined in a multiple, single-case design for three individuals with panic disorder (Waddell, Barlow, & O'Brien, 1984). Each of the subjects was assessed over baselines of four, six, or eight weeks. This was followed by a cognitive therapy phase and a cognitive therapy plus relaxation therapy phase. The frequency and severity of these episodes of intense anxiety decreased during both phases of treatment. This is in contrast to changes in background levels of anxiety, which were much more sporadic and in some cases actually exhibited an increase while high-anxiety episodes were decreasing. These data suggest that it is possible to treat panic attacks specifically even when background anxiety remains unchanged.

In one of the first controlled studies specifically targeting panic disordered patients, five patients who were treated with a combination of EMG biofeedback, relaxation, and a cognitive treatment were compared to six in a no-treatment control (Barlow, Cohen, et al., 1984). Psychophysiological assessments of EMG and heart rate during relaxation and stressor tasks, self-ratings of panic attacks, and clinical ratings of level of disturbance were used as dependent measures. The treated and control groups were divided into patients with panic disorder (PD) and patients with generalized anxiety disorders (GAD). The treated groups were improved from pre- to posttreatment when compared to the untreated group. While the pattern of improvement was the same for both PD and GAD diagnostic groups, no separate analyses were completed for either of these groups. Number of diagnosed panic attacks was not monitored, nor were the effects of treatment assessed formally for the follow-up period.

In one controlled comparison of the effects of including spouses in the treatment group, 28 agoraphobic women (14 with spouses and 14 without) were treated using cognitive-restructuring and self-initiated exposure (Barlow, O'Brien, & Last, 1984). While the spouse group evidenced more improvement than the nonspouse group on a number of measures, including a clinical rating of global improvement, there were no differences between the two groups on a measure of frequency, duration, and intensity of spontaneous panic attacks measured over a posttreatment three-day period. Only 6 of the 28 clients rated themselves as having no panic attacks at the end of treatment.

Several studies exist that permit direct comparisons of different behavioral interventions in terms of their effect on panic attacks. In a study previously discussed, 95 severe and chronic agoraphobics were treated with cognitive treatment (paradoxical intention; PI), graduated exposure (GE), or progressive deep muscle relaxation (PMR) (Michelson & Marchione, 1986). All groups received instructions to confront situations previously avoided. Differential but not significant dropout rates were found, with 25% dropping from the PI treatment and 27% from the GE treatment, but only 17% from the RT treatment. A standard rating of panic attacks on a 0–8 scale as well as the number and severity of spontaneous attacks were the principal dependent measures. These measures were evaluated at pre- and posttreatment and at a three-month follow-up period. While no differences were found between treatments at posttreatment and follow-up periods, treatment differences emerged when finer-grained analyses were conducted. Thus the effect of RT was achieved faster and more lastingly than the other two treatments. The improvement from PI was slower, with some loss of effectiveness from posttreatment to follow-up. GE was the slowest and least potent of the three treatments. Severity of panic attacks was reduced best by the PI and RT treatments. These results seem to indicate that panic attacks are ameliorated more effectively by psychological treatments that provide a means of coping with them, as opposed to simple exposure approaches.

Data analyses from an earlier version of this study (Michelson, Mavissakalian, & Marchione, 1985) (N = 36) reported no significant between-treatment differences on spontaneous panic attacks (SPAs). All three treatment groups changed significantly on this measure. For PI there was a 50% reduction in the number of subjects with SPAs from pre- to posttreatment, and a 67% reduction from pretreatment to follow-up. Less dramatic results were in evidence for the two other treatment groups.

In a reported study that examined in part the sections on relaxation and cognitive approaches, Craske and Barlow (1986) utilized a treatment approach combining cognitive restructuring, relaxation training, breathing retraining, and the use of interoceptive conditioning cues in treating panic disordered individuals. This combined treatment proved to be superior on measures of reduced frequency of panic attacks and proportion of individuals with zero attacks to a wait list control. It was not, however, superior to either the relaxation training or cognitive restructuring approaches. It may be, therefore, that the cognitive component of the combined treatment is the most important ingredient in this combined approach.

F. Prognosis

With very few exceptions (see, e.g., Beck, 1988), treatment studies of panic attacks produce less than 100% improvement. Studies of factors that predict outcome, therefore, offer the possibility of clarifying why some patients fail to respond to treatment and thereby provide hypotheses for further treatment refinements. Poorer outcome has been associated with higher levels of depression (Watson, Mullet, & Pillay, 1973; Zitrin et al., 1980), trait anxiety (Mathews, Johnston, Shaw, & Gelder, 1974; Watson et al., 1973), social anxiety (Doctor, Gaer, & Wright, 1983), and marital dissatisfaction (Bland & Hallam, 1981; Milton & Hafner, 1979). However, in the Chambless et al. (1986) study, no relationship was found between improvement and age, social class, duration or severity of agoraphobia, level of depression, trait anxiety, social anxiety, or marital dissatisfaction. Chambless et al. observed that treatment failures (14% of the treatment sample who had not improved at all) were similar in that they were in extremely trapped or conflicted family/marital relationships; or that they were wealthy and able to achieve a comfortable life-style in spite of agoraphobic fears.

Barlow, Cohen, et al. (1984) also report that there was no relationship of outcome to level of depression. On the basis of clinical judgments, Barlow et al. suggest that clients who exhibited overvalued ideations, a belief that their phobic fears were realistic, had the worst outcomes.

In a study specifically designed to assess prognostic factors, outcome in a group of agoraphobic women (N = 33) was predicted from a number of pretreatment variables (Hafner & Ross, 1983). When assessed prior to treatment, level of disability and extrapunitiveness (hostility directed outward) were both related to a negative outcome.

Mavissakalian and Michelson (1986) examined the effects of several personal and treatment variables on a measure of global outcome in a sample of agoraphobics with panic treated by imipramine plus exposure, flooding, flooding plus imipramine, or exposure alone. Imipramine dose and being female predicted better outcome, while duration of illness, a behavior measure of avoidance, self-rating of phobias, and the presence of spontaneous panic predicted a negative outcome.

In a separate study, a locus of control (LOC) measure was used to predict response to treatment (Michelson, 1983). Agoraphobics who were more external showed a greater degree of improvement than agoraphobics who were more internal. The author speculates that individuals with high externality may be more susceptible to behavioral interventions that are very directive in nature.

In an earlier version of the above study, synchrony-desynchrony effects on outcome and maintenance of positive treatment response were studied (Michelson et al., 1985). Synchrony was defined as concordance of behavioral, subjective anxiety, and physiological measures of anxiety, while desynchrony was defined as falling in the top third on one or two measures and the bottom third on at least one other measure. Posttreatment desynchrony was related to lower levels of improvement at both posttreatment and three-month follow-up.

V. SUMMARY AND CONCLUSIONS

At this point in time, what do we know concerning the etiology and treatment of panic disorders? First, it appears that panic disorder is reached through multiple paths. Genetic vulnerability manifested through biological vulnerability appears to be a factor in at least some instances of this disorder. Environmental factors, such as interpersonal and other forms of stress, as well as various cognitive processing errors, also likely play a part in the development of panic. Whether these factors are additive or not or whether they combine in some other way to increase the probability that panic will develop is simply unknown at this time.

A number of behavioral treatment techniques have developed within the past ten years as ways of ameliorating panic disorder. These techniques have been tied conceptually to etiological models of panic. In addition to exposure techniques, various physiologically based approaches (e.g., breathing retraining) and cognitively based approaches have been studied. These approaches target not only the avoidance behavior of agoraphobia, but also the panic attacks themselves. It appears safe to say that these techniques currently provide a viable alternative to pharmacological agents. Nonetheless, controlled studies that directly assess the relative merits of behavioral and pharmacological techniques are vitally needed.

The present review uncovered a number of research questions and methodological issues. Unresolved etiological issues requiring clarification in the near future include the following: (1) Are stressful events important in the development of panic, or are they more incidentally related? Important in answering this question will be studies comparing panic disordered individuals with others suffering from such disorders as dysthymic reaction as well as other anxiety disorders. Also important will be longitudinal studies of individuals found to be suffering from panic disorder in order to determine whether exacerbations are stress related. (2) Are catastrophic thinking and other cognitive errors primary or secondary to panic disorder? That is, are such cognitive problems stable characteristics of panic disordered persons, or do they develop secondarily to panic disorders? (3) What determines whether an individual who develops panic disorder will also develop avoidance behavior? Along these same lines, will treatment approaches that successfully reduce panic have the secondary effect of reducing the prevalence of agoraphobia? (4) Are the behavioral techniques currently being developed to treat panic disorders viable with more severe types of agoraphobia, and will they add significantly to improvement rates when paired with exposure techniques?

REFERENCES

Alexander, P. E., & Alexander, D. D. (1986). Alprazolam treatment for panic disorders. *Journal of Clinical Psychiatry, 47*(6), 301–304.

American Psychiatric Association. (1968). *Diagnostic and statistical manual of mental disorders* (2nd ed.). Washington, DC: Author.

American Psychiatric Association. (1980). *Diagnostic and statistical manual of mental disorders* (3rd ed.). Washington, DC: Author.

American Psychiatric Association. (1987). *Diagnostic and statistical manual of mental disorders* (3rd ed., rev.). Washington, DC: Author.

Barlow, D. H., Cohen, A. S., Waddell, M. T., Vermilyea, B. B., Klosko, J. S., Blanchard, E. B., & DiNardo, P. A. (1984). Panic and generalized anxiety disorders: Nature and treatment. *Behavior Therapy, 15*, 431–449.

Barlow, D. H., O'Brien, G. T., & Last, C. G. (1984). Couples treatment of agoraphobia. *Behavior Therapy, 15*, 41–58.

Barlow, D. H., Vermilyea, J., Blanchard, E. B., Vermilyea, B. B., DiNardo, P. A., & Cerny, J. A. (1985). The phenomenon of panic. *Journal of Abnormal Psychology, 94,* 320–328.

Beck, A. T. (1988). Cognitive approaches to panic disorder: Theory and therapy. In S. Rachman & J. Maser (Eds.), *Panic: Psychological perspectives* (pp. 91–109). Hillsdale, NJ: Erlbaum.

Beck, A. T., & Emery, G. D. (1985). *Anxiety disorders and phobias: A cognitive perspective.* New York: Basic Books.

Beck, A. T., Laude, R., & Bohnert, M. (1974). Ideational components of anxiety neurosis. *Archives of General Psychiatry, 31,* 319–325.

Berkowitz, B. A., Tarver, J. H., & Spector, S. (1970). Release of norepinephrine in the central nervous system by theophylline and caffeine. *European Journal of Pharmacology, 10,* 64–71.

Bland, K., & Hallam, R. S. (1981). Relationship between response to graded exposure and marital satisfaction in agoraphobics. *Behaviour Research and Therapy, 19,* 335–338.

Bonn, J. A., Harrison, J., & Fees, W. (1973). Lactate infusion in the treatment of "free-floating anxiety." *Canadian Psychiatric Association Journal, 18,* 41–45.

Bonn, J. A., Readhead, C.P.A., & Timmons, B. H. (1984, September 22). Enhanced adaptive behavioral response in agoraphobic patients pretreated with breathing retraining. *Lancet,* pp. 665–669.

Borden, J., Clum, G. A., & Broyles, S. (1986, August). *Imaginal coping and flooding as treatments of panic attacks.* Paper presented at the annual meeting of the American Psychological Association, Washington, DC.

Boulenger, J., Uhde, T. W., Wolff, E. A., & Post, R. M. (1984). Increased sensitivity to caffeine in patients with panic disorders. *Archives of General Psychiatry, 41,* 1067–1071.

Breggin, P. R. (1964). The psychophysiology of anxiety: With a review of the literature concerning adrenaline. *Journal of Nervous and Mental Disease, 139,* 559–569.

Chambless, D. L., Foa, E. B., Groves, G. A., & Goldstein, A. J. (1979). Brevital in flooding with agoraphobics. *Behaviour Research and Therapy, 17,* 243–251.

Chambless, D. L., Foa, E. B., Groves, G. A., & Goldstein, A. J. (1982). Exposure and communications training in the treatment of agoraphobia. *Behaviour Research and Therapy, 20,* 219–231.

Chambless, D. L., Goldstein, A. J., Gallagher, R., & Bright, P. (1986). Integrating behavior therapy and psychotherapy in the treatment of agoraphobia. *Psychotherapy: Theory, Research, and Practice, 23*(1), 150–159.

Charney, D. S., Heninger, G. R., & Jatlow, P. I. (1985). Increased anxiogenic effects of caffeine in panic disorder. *Archives of General Psychiatry, 42,* 233–243.

Charney, D. S., Woods, S. W., Goodman, W. K., Rifkin, B., Kench, M., Aiken, B., Quadrino, L. M., & Heninger, G. R. (1986). Drug treatment of panic disorder: The comparative efficacy of imipramine, alprazolam, and trazodone. *Journal of Clinical Psychiatry, 47*(12), 580–586.

Chouinard, G., Annable, L., Fontaine, R., & Solyom, L. (1982). Alprazolam in the treatment of generalized anxiety and panic disorders: A double-blind placebo-controlled study. *Psychopharmacology, 77,* 299–233.

Clark, D. M. (1986). A cognitive approach to panic. *Behaviour Research and Therapy, 24,* 461–470.

Clark, D. M., & Hemsley, D. R. (1982). Effects of hyperventilation: Individual variability and its relation to personality. *Journal of Behavior Therapy and Experimental Psychiatry, 13,* 41–47.

Clark, D. M., Salkovskis, P. M., & Chalkley, A. J. (1985). Respiratory control as a treatment for panic attacks. *Journal of Behavior Therapy and Experimental Psychiatry, 16,* 23–30.

Clum, G. A. (1985). *Guided imaginal coping: A treatment manual for treating panic attacks.* Unpublished manuscript.

Clum, G. A., & Pickett, C. (1984). Panic disorders and generalized anxiety disorders. In H. E. Adams & P. B. Sutker (Eds.), *Comprehensive handbook of psychopathology.* New York: Plenum.

Cohen, A. S., Barlow, D. H., & Blanchard, E. B. (1985). Psychophysiology of relaxation-associated panic attacks. *Journal of Abnormal Psychology, 94,* 96–101.

Cottraux, J., Mollard, E., Duinat, A., & Riviere, B. (1986, November). *Psychotropic medication suppression or reduction after behavior therapy in 81 agoraphobics with panic attacks.* Paper presented at the annual meeting of the Association for Advancement of Behavior Therapy, Chicago.

Craske, M. G., & Barlow, D. H. (1986, November). *Behavioral treatment of panic: A controlled study.* Paper presented at the annual meeting of the Association for Advancement of Behavior Therapy, Boston.

Crowe, R. R., Noyes, R., Pauls, D. L., & Slyman, D. (1983). A family study of panic disorder. *Archives of General Psychiatry, 40,* 1065–1069.

Doctor, R. M., Gaer, T., & Wright, M. (1983, May). *Success at one-year follow-up for agoraphobia treatment.* Paper presented at the Fourth Annual Conference of the Phobia Society of America, White Plains, NY.

Faravelli, C. (1985). Life events preceding the onset of panic disorder. *Journal of Affective Disorders, 9,* 103–105.

Foa, E. B., & Kozak, M. J. (1986). Emotional processing of fear: Exposure to corrective information. *Psychological Bulletin, 99,* 20–35.

Frame, C. L., Turner, S. M., Jacob, R. G., & Szekely, B. (1984). Self-exposure treatment of agoraphobia. *Behavior Modification, 8*(1), 115–122.

Garssen, B., Van Veendaal, W., & Bloemink, R. (1983). Agoraphobia and hyperventilation syndrome. *Behaviour Research and Therapy, 21,* 643–649.

Gloger, S., Grunhaus, L., Birmacher, B., & Troudart, T. (1981). Treatment of spontaneous panic attacks with chlomipramine. *American Journal of Psychiatry, 138*(9), 1215–1217.

Goldstein, A. J., & Chambless, D. L. (1978). A reanalysis of agoraphobia. *Behavior Therapy, 9,* 47–59.

Gorman, J. M., Askanazi, J., Liebowitz, M. R., Fyer, A. J., Stein, J., Kinney, J. M., & Klein, D. F. (1984). Response to hyperventilation in a group of patients with panic disorder. *American Journal of Psychiatry, 141,* 857–861.

Gorman, J. M., Fyer, A. F., Glicklich, J., King, M. E., & Klein, D. F. (1981). Mitral valve prolapse and panic disorders: Effect of imipramine. In D. F. Klein & J. Rabkin (Eds.), *Anxiety: New research and changing concepts.* New York: Raven.

Grant, B., Katon, W., & Beitman, B. (1983). Panic disorder. *Journal of Family Practice, 17,* 907–914.

Hafner, R. J., & Ross, G. W. (1983). Predicting the outcome of behaviour therapy for agoraphobia. *Behaviour Research and Therapy, 21*(4), 375–382.

Hartman, N., Kramer, R., Brown, W. T., & Devereaux, R. B. (1982). Panic disorder in patients with mitral valve prolapse. *American Journal of Psychiatry, 139,* 669–970.

Hibbert, G. A. (1984a). Hyperventilation as a cause of panic attacks. *British Medical Journal, 288,* 263–264.

Hibbert, G. A. (1984b). Ideational components of anxiety: Their origin and content. *British Journal of Psychiatry, 144,* 618–624.

Jacob, R. G., Moller, M. B., Turner, S. M., & Wall, C. (1985). Otoneurological examination in panic disorder and agoraphobia with panic attacks: A pilot study. *American Journal of Psychiatry, 142,* 715–720.

Jacob, R. G., & Rapport, M. D. (1984). Panic disorder: Medical and psychological parameters. In S. M. Turner (Ed.), *Behavioral theories and treatment of anxiety.* New York: Plenum.

Jones, M., & Mellersh, V. (1946). Comparison of exercise response in anxiety states and normal controls. *Psychosomatic Medicine, 8,* 180–187.

Kantor, J. S., Zitrin, C. M., & Zeldis, S. M. (1980). Mitral valve prolapse syndrome in agoraphobic patients. *American Journal of Psychiatry, 137,* 467–469.

King, R., Margraf, J., Ehlers, A., & Maddock, R. J. (1986). Panic disorder: Overlap with symptoms of somatization disorder. In I. Hand & H. V. Wittchen (Eds.), *Panic and phobias: Empirical evidence of theoretical models and long-term effects of behavioral treatments.* Berlin: Springer-Verlag.

Klein, D. F., Zitrin, C. M., Woerner, M. G., & Ross, D. C. (1983). Treatment of phobias II: Behavior therapy and supportive psychotherapy: Are there any specific ingredients? *Archives of General Psychiatry, 40,* 139–145.

Lang, P. J. (1979). A bio-informational theory of emotional imagery. *Psychophysiology, 16,* 495–512.

Lang, P. J., Kozak, M. J., Miller, G. A., Levin, D. N., & McLean, A. (1980). Emotional imagery: Conceptual structure and pattern of somato-visceral response. *Psychophysiology, 17,* 179–192.

Lang, P. J., Levin, D. N., Miller, G. A., & Kozak, M. J. (1983). Fear behavior, fear imagery, and the psychophysiology of emotion: The problem of affective response integration. *Journal of Abnormal Psychology, 92,* 276–306.

Last, C. G., O'Brien, G. T., & Barlow, D. H. (1985). The relationship between cognitions and anxiety. *Behavior Modification, 9,* 235–241.

Liberthson, R., Sheehan, D. V., King, M. E., & Weyman, A. E. (1986). The prevalence of mitral valve prolapse with panic disorders. *American Journal of Psychiatry, 143,* 511–515.

Liebowitz, M. R., Gorman, J. M., Fyer, A., Dillon, D., Levitt, M., & Klein, D. F. (1986). Possible mechanisms for lactate's induction of panic. *American Journal of Psychiatry, 143,* 495–502.

Lum, L. C. (1976). The syndrome of habitual chronic hyperventilation. In O. W. Hill (Ed.), *Modern trends in psychosomatic medicine* (Vol. 3, pp. 196–230). London: Butterworth.

Margraf, J., Ehlers, A., & Roth, W. T. (1986). Sodium lactate infusions and panic attacks: A review and critique. *Psychosomatic Medicine, 48,* 23–51.

Marks, I. M., Gray, S., Cohen, D., Hill, R., Dawson, D., Ramm, E., & Stern, R. S. (1983). Imipramine and brief therapist-aided exposure in agoraphobics having self-exposure homework. *Archives of General Psychiatry, 40,* 153–162.

Mathews, A. M., Johnston, D. W., Shaw, P. M., & Gelder, M. G. (1974). Process variables and the prediction of outcome in behavior therapy. *British Journal of Psychiatry, 125,* 256–264.

Mavissakalian, M., & Michelson, L. (1983). Self-directed in vivo exposure practice in behavioral and pharmacologic treatments of agoraphobia. *Behavior Therapy, 14,* 506–519.

Mavissakalian, M., & Michelson, L. (1986). Agoraphobia: Relative and combined effectiveness of therapist-assisted in vivo exposure and imipramine. *Journal of Clinical Psychiatry, 47*(3), 117–122.

Mavissakalian, M., Michelson, L., & Dealy, R. S. (1983). Pharmacological treatment of agoraphobia: Imipramine versus imipramine with programmed practice. *British Journal of Psychiatry, 143,* 348–355.

Mavissakalian, M., Michelson, L., Greenwald, D., Kornbluth, S., & Greenwald, M. (1984). Cognitive-behavioral treatment of agoraphobia: Paradoxical intention vs self-statement training. *Behaviour Research and Therapy, 21*(1), 75–86.

May, J. R. (1977). Psychophysiology of self-regulated phobic thoughts. *Behavior Therapy, 8,* 150–159.

Michelson, L. (1983). Prognostic utility of locus of control in treatment of agoraphobia. *Behaviour Research and Therapy, 21*(3), 309–313.

Michelson, L. (1984). The role of individual differences, response profiles, and treatment consonance in anxiety disorders. *Journal of Behavioral Assessment, 6*(4), 349–368.

Michelson, L., & Marchione, K. (1986, August). *Cognitive-behavioral treatments of panic.* Paper presented at the annual meeting of the American Psychological Association, Washington, DC.

Michelson, L., Mavissakalian, M., & Marchione, K. (1985). Cognitive and behavioral treatments of agoraphobia: Clinical, behavioral, and psychophysiological outcomes. *Journal of Consulting and Clinical Psychology, 53*(6), 913–925.

Michelson, L., Mavissakalian, M., & Meninger, S. (1983). Prognostic utility of locus of control in treatment of agoraphobia. *Behaviour Research and Therapy, 21*(3), 309–313.

Milton, F., & Hafner, J. (1979). The outcome of behavior therapy for agoraphobia in relation to marital adjustment. *Archives of General Psychiatry, 36*, 307–311.

Mowrer, D. H. (1939). A stimulus-response analysis of anxiety and its role as a reinforcing agent. *Psychological Review, 46*, 553–565.

Myers, J. K., Weissman, M. M., Tischler, G. L., Holzer, C. E., Leaf, P. J., Orvaschel, H., Anthony, J. C., Boyd, J. H., Burke, J. D., Kramer, M., & Stolzman, R. (1984). Six-month prevalence of psychiatric disorders in three communities. *Archives of General Psychiatry, 41*, 959–967.

Norton, G. R., Harrison, B., Hauch, J., & Rhodes, L. (1985). Characteristics of people with infrequent panic attacks. *Journal of Abnormal Psychology, 94*, 216–221.

Noyes, R., Crowe, R. R., Harris, E. L., Hamra, B. J., McChesney, C. M., & Chaudhry, D. R. (1986). Relationship between panic disorder and agoraphobia: A family study. *Archives of General Psychiatry, 43*, 227–232.

Ottaviani, R., & Beck, A. T. (1987). Cognitive aspects of panic disorder. *Journal of Anxiety Disorders, 1*, 15–28.

Pariser, S. F., Jones, B. A., & Pinta, E. R. (1979). Panic attacks: Diagnostic evaluations of 17 patients. *American Journal of Psychiatry, 136*, 105–106.

Pitts, F. N., & McClure, J. N. (1967). Lactate metabolism in anxiety neurosis. *New England Journal of Medicine, 277*, 1329–1337.

Ramm, E., Marks, I. M., Yuksel, S., & Stern, R. S. (1981). Anxiety management training for anxiety states: Positive compared with negative self-statements. *British Journal of Psychiatry, 140*, 367–373.

Rapee, R. (1985). A case of panic disorder treated with breathing retraining. *Journal of Behavior Therapy and Experimental Psychiatry, 16*(1), 63–65.

Rapee, R. (1986). Differential response to hyperventilation in panic disorder and generalized anxiety disorder. *Journal of Abnormal Psychology, 95*, 24–28.

Robins, L. M., Helzer, J. E., Croughan, J., & Ratcliff, K. S. (1981). National Institute of Mental Health Diagnostic Interview Schedule: Its history, characteristics, and validity. *Archives of General Psychiatry, 38*, 318–389.

Salkovskis, P. M., Jones, D.R.O., & Clark, D. M. (1986). Respiratory control in the treatment of panic attacks: Replication and extension with concurrent measurement of behavior and pc02. *British Journal of Psychiatry, 148*, 526–532.

Shear, M. K., Devereaux, R. B., Kramer-Fox, R., Mann, J. J., & Frances, A. (1984). Low prevalence of mitral valve prolapse in patients with panic disorder. *American Journal of Psychiatry, 141*, 302–303.

Sheehan, D. V. (1984). *The anxiety disease.* New York: Charles Schribner's Sons.

Sheehan, D. V., Ballenger, J., & Jacobsen, G. (1980). Treatment of endogenous anxiety with phobic, hysterical, and hypochondriacal symptoms. *Archives of General Psychiatry, 37*, 51–59.

Sheehan, D. V., Carr, D. B., Fishman, S. M., Walsh, M. M., & Peltier-Saxe, D. (1985). Lactate infusion in anxiety research: Its evolution and practice. *Journal of Clinical Psychiatry, 46*, 158–165.

Sheehan, D. V., Sheehan, K. F., & Minichiello, W. E. (1981). Age of onset of phobic disorders: A reevaluation. *Comprehensive Psychiatry, 22*, 544.

Taylor, C. B., Kenigsberg, M. L., & Robinson, J. M. (1982). A controlled comparison of relaxation and diazepam in panic disorder. *Journal of Clinical Psychiatry, 43*(10), 423–425.

Taylor, C. B., Telch, M. J., & Hawick, D. (1983). Ambulatory heart rate changes during panic attacks. *Journal of Psychiatry Research, 143*, 478–482.

Telch, M. J., Agras, W. S., Taylor, C. B., Roth, W. T., & Gallen, C. C. (1985). Combined pharmacological and behavioral treatment for agoraphobia. *Behaviour Research and Therapy, 23*, 325–336.

Torgerson, S. (1983). Genetic factors in anxiety disorders. *Archives of General Psychiatry, 40*, 1085–1089.

Uhde, T. W., Boulenger, J. P., Roy-Byrne, P. P., Garaci, M. F., Vittone, B. J., & Post, R. M. (1985). Longitudinal course of panic disorder: Clinical and biological considerations. *Progress in Neuro-Psychopharmacology and Biological Psychiatry, 9*, 39–51.

van den Hout, M. A., & Griez, E. (1984). Panic symptoms after inhalation of carbon dioxide. *British Journal of Psychiatry, 144*, 503–507.

Waddell, M. T., Barlow, D. H., & O'Brien, G. T. (1984). A preliminary investigation of cognitive and relaxation treatment of panic disorder: Effects of intense anxiety vs "background" anxiety. *Behaviour Research and Therapy, 22*(4), 393–402.

Wade, T. C., Malloy, T. E., & Proctor, S. (1977). Imaginal correlates of self-reported fear and avoidance behavior. *Behaviour Research and Therapy, 15*, 17–22.

Watson, J. P., Mullet, C. E., & Pillay, H. (1973). The effects of prolonged exposure to phobic situations upon agoraphobic patients treated in groups. *Behaviour Research and Therapy, 11*, 531–545.

Weissman, M. M., & Merikangas, K. R. (1986). The epidemiology of anxiety and panic disorders: An update. *Journal of Clinical Psychiatry, 47*(6), 11–17.

Zitrin, C. M., Klein, D. F., & Woerner, M. G. (1978). Behavior therapy, supportive psychotherapy, imipramine and phobia. *Archives of General Psychiatry, 35*, 307–316.

Zitrin, C. M., Klein, D. F., & Woerner, M. G. (1980). Treatment of agoraphobia with group exposure in vivo and imipramine. *Archives of General Psychiatry, 37*, 63–72.

Zitrin, C. M., Klein, D. F., Woerner, M. G., & Ross, D. C. (1983). Treatment of phobias I: Comparison of imipramine hydrochloride and placebo. *Archives of General Psychiatry, 40*, 125–138.

THE ROLE OF COGNITIVE VARIABLES IN THE ASSESSMENT AND TREATMENT OF MARITAL DISCORD

DONALD H. BAUCOM
University of North Carolina, Chapel Hill

NORMAN EPSTEIN
University of Maryland, College Park

I. INTRODUCTION

Behavioral theoreticians, researchers, and clinicians have increasingly espoused the importance of investigating couples' cognitions in order to provide a more complete understanding of marital distress and to develop effective treatment interventions. Perhaps surprisingly, then, only limited research and no comprehensive behaviorally based theories of marital discord or treatment interventions for distressed couples have been developed and evaluated that give a primary role to cognitive variables. In addition, the research that has been conducted has had a rather narrow focus, primarily investigating spouses' attributions or explanations for various marital events. Even this area of cognitive research has provided little direction in developing more comprehensive theory and treatment strategies. As noted elsewhere, this lack of progress likely has resulted from several factors: (a) The important cognitive variables to be considered in marital interaction and distress have not been elucidated clearly; (b) there are numerous methodological problems still unresolved in attempting to assess cognitions, resulting in few well-validated assessment measures; (c) with the important variables poorly delineated and with limited assessment strategies available, existing theories of marital distress have been hampered in attempts to incorporate cognitive variables; (d) considering the aforementioned problems, attempts to integrate spouses' cognitions systematically into intervention strategies are only at the beginning stages (Baucom, Epstein, Sayers, & Sher, 1989). The current chapter will address these issues, reviewing the existing data regarding cognitions and marital distress/interventions, discussing unresolved conceptual and methodological problems in the field along with unexplored assumptions of researchers and theoreticians, and offering suggestions for future directions in the field.

II. THEORETICAL AND EMPIRICAL STATUS OF COGNITIONS IN MARRIAGE

At least five classes of cognitive variables are likely to be of importance in understanding marital functioning and spouses' satisfaction with their relationships. Although any given marital event or stimulus does not necessarily evoke all of these cognitive processes, it is certainly possible for all five classes of cognitive activity to be called into play when a couple interacts or reflects on past interactions. When a couple interacts, there is some selection of what is attended to, such that a spouse's awareness of what the marital relationship involves is, in part, a function of the perceptual process of *selective attention*. Given that a specific behavior or interaction is noted by a spouse, that individual at times is likely to try to explain why that behavior or interaction occurred. That is, the spouse makes *attributions* or explanations for what takes place in the marriage. In order to maintain desired behavior and alter undesirable behavior, the spouse also is likely to focus on the future, to consider the outcomes of certain behaviors or behavioral sequences. More specifically, the spouse develops *expectancies* for how the partner and self are likely to behave under certain circumstances and what the outcome of such behavior is likely to be.

The above processes could be very time- and energy-consuming if the individual had no context to provide guidance or ways of organizing each separate experience. However, individuals do seem to organize their experiences around certain *assumptions* about people's characteristics and the way that the world operates. Thus when new events occur, the individual interprets these new experiences according to existing schemata, which serve as somewhat stable templates for categorizing information. Phrased differently, assumptions deal with the individual's cognitions about the way relationships *are*. In addition, spouses evaluate the acceptability of behaviors in which they and their partners engage. All persons develop *beliefs* or *standards* regarding how they think relationships *should be*. Regarding marriage, spouses appear to develop standards for relationships per se as well as standards for individual behavior. Just as with assumptions, many beliefs or standards seem to be rather stable. However, it is critical to differentiate between assumptions and standards, as defined here, because often major discrepancies exist between spouses' assumptions regarding the way they think their partners are and their standards for how their partners should be. Such disparity might, in fact, be a major source of distress for many couples.

In summary, various cognitive variables appear to play a role when a behavior or event relevant to the marriage is processed. Through selective attention, the spouse focuses on certain events, whereas other behaviors and events are ignored. When a given marital event is perceived, the spouse often makes attributions for why that event occurred. In addition, the spouse develops expectancies or attempts to predict future behavior in order to maximize rewarding aspects of the relationship, while minimizing other more aversive relationship events. These cognitive processes are facilitated through the development of assumptions regarding how the individual thinks the world and people operate, thus providing an organizational framework for incoming stimuli and cognitions. Finally, the events and behaviors are evaluated according to standards for how people should behave and how relationships should be.

A. Selective Attention

The term *selective attention* (or *selective abstraction*) refers to a cognitive bias on an individual's part that involves attending to certain aspects of an environment while ignoring other relevant aspects (Beck, Rush, Shaw, & Emery, 1979). This process can have an important impact on a relationship because it appears that the individual who is selectively attending typically is unaware that this is occurring. Therefore, to the individual, his or her perceptions constitute a reasonable representation of reality, without the awareness that important information is being ignored. Thus should one spouse selectively attend to the negative behaviors of the partner without being aware of the partner's more positive behaviors, the spouse is likely to become disenchanted with the relationship. Similarly, once the individual becomes unhappy with the relationship, continued selective attention to negative behaviors from the partner can make the person unaware of positive changes on the partner's part. Therefore, efforts to improve the relationship may go unnoticed.

The issue of selective attention has not been directly addressed in empirical investigations of married couples, but two types of related behavioral investigations have implications for the issue. First, the extent to which the two members of a married couple share a common perception of what has occurred in their relationship provides information regarding the selective abstraction of information. Sullaway and Christensen (1983) provide an excellent analysis of the findings to date in this arena. In order to minimize the likelihood that differential reporting of behavioral events in the relationship is largely a function of memory, only investigations that asked couples to report on recent behaviors (typically occurring within the past 24 hours) will be considered here. Most of these studies were based on the Spouse Observation Checklist (SOC; Patterson, 1976; Weiss & Margolin, 1977) or some variant of it. Using this procedure, each person is given a list of 400 or fewer behaviors that the spouse or couple might engage in during a 24-hour period. By having each person complete this inventory regarding the partner's behavior and his or her own behavior, it is possible to evaluate the extent to which the spouses agree on what marital events and behaviors have occurred on a daily basis. Several investigators have reached similar conclusions regarding spouses' discrepancies in perceptions (Christensen & Nies, 1980; Christensen, Sullaway, & King, 1983; Jacobson & Moore, 1981). All of these investigations demonstrated that married partners have relatively different perceptions of what behaviors have occurred in their marriages during a given 24-hour period; the kappas calculated between the husbands' and wives' reports of behavior average approximately .50. Calculated differently, Jacobson and Moore (1981) concluded that two partners in a marriage agreed less than half of the time whether or not a certain event had occurred during the past day. This level of agreement is far below what is typically considered acceptable for interrater agreement, pointing out that the spouses have meaningfully different perceptions of what has occurred.

Of particular importance for the issue of selective attention, there is considerable variability in the extent of agreement across couples. For example, Jacobson and Moore (1981) found that the rate of agreement ranged from a high of 79% for one couple to a low of 31% for another couple. In addition, all three of the investigations mentioned above as well as a study by Christensen and Wallace (1976) indicate that more satisfied couples evidence a higher rate of perceptual agreement than more distressed couples. Thus, whereas a certain degree of differential perception of marital events appears to be a way of life for most, if not all, couples, more distressed spouses seem to show greater selective attention than nondistressed couples.

The cause-effect status of this empirical relationship is unclear. For example, attending to different marital events could create very different perceptions of the marriage, which could serve as the basis of discord. On the other hand, once couples become distressed they may be invested in viewing the relationship in certain ways to protect themselves as individuals and to continue to justify their negative feelings toward their spouses (Baucom, 1987). Selectively attending to certain behaviors can help one to maintain one's view of the marital relationship. Third, both the marital distress and selective attending might result from a host of other factors and may not be causally related. The causal relationship may vary from couple to couple, which in turn would lead to differential treatment interventions.

Whereas a low rate of agreement between married partners provides evidence supportive of selective attention, a high level of agreement does not mean that selective attention is not occurring. That is, it is possible for both partners to attend selectively in the same way, resulting in agreement regarding the events that have occurred. For example, both a husband and wife might come to view the wife as inadequate and focus on her negative behavior while ignoring her more positive acts. Therefore, a second source of information relevant to selective attention is important. Instead of assessing the agreement between the two spouses in terms of what marital behaviors have occurred, other investigators have compared a spouse's report of marital events with a trained rater's reporting of the couple's behavior. The logic underlying such investigations is that a trained rater will have less reason to be motivated to ignore certain events and will be sensitized to the full range of behaviors under investigation. For example, Robinson and Price (1980) trained observers to rate the behaviors of both distressed and nondistressed couples in their own homes. Using a modified version of the SOC, the couples also rated their own behaviors. Comparing the raters' observations with the couples' observations, the results are consistent with the above findings. First, the level of overall agreement between raters and spouses was low, with correlations of approximately .50. Also, there was greater agreement among raters and nondistressed couples than among the raters and distressed couples. In fact, distressed couples underestimated the frequency of pleasurable events by 50%.

Thus data exist that are consistent with the notion of selective attention among married couples. Furthermore, findings indicate that more distressed couples have an increased tendency to abstract information selectively, such that their perceptions of what occurs in their marriages is less likely to coincide with the observations of others, whether partners or trained observers. Whereas these investigations indicate that this process does occur in marriage, very little else is known about the phenomenon. What is the cause of selective attention among couples? Are there certain situational determinants that increase the likelihood of this process? Are certain types of events likely to be distorted? Sullaway and Christensen

(1983) conclude that specific events lead to less distortion than more general events; it may be possible to isolate other characteristics of the events that are selectively attended to or ignored as well.

B. Causal Attributions

Of the five classes of cognitive variables currently being discussed, attributions or causal explanations have by far captured the great bulk of attention from marital researchers and theoreticians (see Thompson & Snyder, 1986, for a recent critical review). Whereas there seems to be no theoretical basis for the supremacy given to attributional research among marital investigators, the focus given to attributions likely stems from two sources. First, attribution theory (Heider, 1958; Jones & Davis, 1965; Kelley, 1967) has gained widespread attention as a context for studying interpersonal relationships within social psychology, with a focus primarily on stranger dyads. It was but a short leap to extend the investigation into the study of intimate interpersonal relationships, such as marriage. Second, learned helplessness theory, which has served as a popular analog model for understanding certain types of depression, was reformulated within the context of attribution theory (Abramson, Seligman, & Teasdale, 1978). As Epstein (1985) has noted, there are many points of overlapping symptoms between depression and marital distress; therefore, an extension of learned helplessness theory into the study of marital distress was understandable.

Based on learned helplessness theory, many investigators have sought to understand how positive and negative marital events are explained along certain preconceived dimensions. A major focus of almost all investigations is the locus of the attribution; that is, whether the event or behavior is attributed to the self, the partner, outside circumstances, or some combination of the above. Whereas investigations in other domains have studied this question in terms of a single internal/external locus dimension, this strategy is problematic when studying marital relationships. That is, in a marital relationship, factors external to oneself include the partner as well as factors outside of the marriage. Recognizing that these distinctions are likely to be important, investigators typically ask respondents to evaluate separately the extent to which each factor is a cause of a given event. A second dimension focused upon is whether the cause is viewed as global or specific. A global cause is one that is likely to affect many aspects of the marriage, whereas a specific cause is likely to affect few marital domains. Third, causes can be viewed as stable (likely to continue into the future) or unstable (having an increased possibility of change in the future). Thus if a husband attributes his wife's late return home as due to her self-centered nature, he would likely rate this cause (a) as due to characteristics of his wife (rather than to characteristics of himself or factors outside the relationship), (b) as stable, and (c) as global.

A number of studies have been conducted to investigate the extent to which level of marital adjustment is correlated with different attributions. Investigators have hypothesized that more satisfied couples will view the causes of positive marital events as more stable and global, whereas negative marital events would be viewed as unstable and specific. Distressed couples would make attributions in the opposite direction. The hypotheses regarding the locus ratings have been less consistent, but investigators typically have expected distressed couples to blame their partners for negative marital events.

Some studies have asked spouses to rate the causes of hypothetical marital events (e.g., Baucom, Bell, & Duhe, 1982; Fincham, Beach, & Baucom, 1987, Study 1; Fincham, Beach, & Nelson, 1987; Fincham & O'Leary, 1983; Kyle & Falbo, 1985); others have asked couples to rate the causes for actual events in their marriages (e.g., Fichten, 1984; Fincham, 1985; Fincham, Beach, & Baucom, 1987; Holtzworth-Munroe & Jacobson, 1985; Jacobson, McDonald, Follette, & Berley, 1985). Although the results are not totally consistent, overall they support the hypotheses described above. That is, compared to nondistressed couples, distressed couples tend to rate the causes of negative behaviors by their partners as more global and stable. Nondistressed spouses rate causes of positive partner behaviors as more global and stable than do distressed spouses. Also, distressed spouses tend to blame their partners for marital problems more than do nondistressed spouses. From a clinical perspective, changing these attributional patterns would seem to be quite important. That is, if a spouse views the partner as the basis for the marital problems and believes that these causes are global and stable, there is likely to be little motivation for this individual to attempt to improve the marriage.

While great energy has been expended to validate the relationship between causal attributions and marital distress, the research thus far has provided little coherent direction for future investigations, comprehensive theories of marital functioning, or intervention. For example, with the exception of a study by Fincham and Bradbury (1987a), little attention has been devoted to examining the cause-effect relationship between these variables. A number of other specific issues have been addressed, such as various ways to assess attributions from couples (Holtzworth-Munroe & Jacobson, 1985), the importance of attributions made to the self relative to attributions made to the partner (Fincham, Beach, & Baucom, 1987), and whether or not spouses evidence an attributional style across marital situations (Baucom & Sayers, 1987). Also, several theoretical papers have been written that propose the functions served by attributions in marital relationships, but thus far little systematic research has attempted to evaluate these theoretical notions (Baucom, 1987; Berley & Jacobson, 1984; Fincham & Bradbury, 1987b). Attempts have been made to alter dysfunctional attributions in marital therapy outcome studies. The number of investigations are few and are at an early stage in terms of understanding how to translate basic research findings regarding attributions into useful clinical intervention strategies (Baucom, 1985; Baucom & Lester, 1986; Emmelkamp et al., 1988; Epstein, Pretzer, & Fleming, 1982; Huber & Milstein, 1985).

C. Expectancies

Married partners tend to focus on the past and attempt to explain events that have occurred. They also try to predict what events are likely to transpire in the future. Just as with forming attributions, this cognitive process serves the important functions of helping to maintain a sense of control over one's life and providing guidance as to where and how to expend energy and effort. Developing predictions about the future course of the marriage and each spouse's behavior is not maladaptive in itself. However, expectancies become a source of concern when they are based on incomplete or distorted data, or when appropriate data are used in an illogical manner to make predictions. Therefore, if a spouse has selectively attended to the negative aspects of a partner's behavior, then a potentially inaccurate prediction about future negative behavior by the partner might be made. Similarly, if one spouse remains aware of the various pieces of pertinent information needed to make a prediction but puts that information together in an illogical way, then the spouse still might make improbable predictions. These predictions are important because they likely influence the individual's behavior and emotional response. For example, a wife who believes that no matter what she does her husband will not want to spend time talking to her is unlikely to make efforts to accomplish that goal and might feel angry and/or depressed. Her actions or inaction can then serve as a self-fulfilling prophesy in demonstrating that her husband does not change.

The simplest expectancies involve straightforward predictions of behavior (e.g., a wife may predict that her husband will come home late). However, there are more complex forms of predictions. Bandura (1977) has made a distinction between two types of expectancies that focus on the consequences of predicted behavior. That is, they are conditional "if/then" statements. First, an *outcome expectancy* is a person's estimate that a particular action will lead to certain consequences in a given situation. Thus when a therapist presents a treatment plan to a couple and recommends that they focus on communication skills, each spouse likely will make some prediction as to whether or not such an approach will improve their marriage. One spouse might conclude that improved communication is exactly what they need to improve their relationship. However, the partner might believe that their disordered communication is but a symptom of their basic incompatibility; consequently, this person might view communication training as a cosmetic procedure that does not address more fundamental issues that determine marital satisfaction. The clinician must address such expectancies, or the spouse who lacks confidence in the communication training is unlikely to put forth great effort. Listening to the spouse with a negative outcome expectancy also is important because this individual might be aware of factors that the clinician does not know about or has inappropriately minimized.

The second type of expectancy discussed by Bandura is *efficacy expectancy*. This involves a person's estimate of the probability that he, she, or the couple will be able to carry out the action that would result in certain consequences. For example, if the clinician has conceptualized a couple's problems clearly, both spouses might agree that improved communication is a key to improving their marriage. Using the current terminology, both partners have a positive outcome expectancy regarding the value of improved communication for their marriage. However, the two partners' efficacy expectancies—that is, the extent to which they believe that they can learn to communicate differently—might be quite disparate. One partner might believe, "If we work at it, we can learn to communicate," whereas the other might conclude, "Whether we try or not, there is little chance we can ever learn to communicate with each other."

Another system for categorizing expectancies, orthogonal to Bandura's, has been provided by Rotter (1954), who distinguishes between *specific expectancies*, which are particular to a given situation (e.g., "I bet he will forget to pick up the groceries"), and *generalized expectancies*, which are more stable and global (e.g., "Our relationship is never really going to change. Twenty years from now we will be arguing about the same issues"). Thus far, few investigations have focused on spouses' expectancies about each other's behavior or the relationship. However, most studies that have been conducted have focused on generalized efficacy and outcome expectancies. For example, Pretzer, Epstein, and Fleming (1985) used a self-report inventory to assess spouses' outcome expectancies (e.g., "I think that our relationship will improve"), efficacy expectations (e.g., "I don't think it's possible for us to handle problems that come up better than we do now"), and attributions for marital events. They found that compared to more distressed couples, more satisfied couples reported that they believed that they could improve their relationships. Spouses who believed they could improve their relationships in the future also attributed more of their marital problems to themselves rather than to their partners, and they were less depressed.

Notarius and Vanzetti's (1983) Marital Agendas Protocol (MAP) elicits more specific expectancies that spouses have about their abilities as a couple to resolve disagreements in each of ten areas of their relationship (e.g., money, communication, in-laws). For each of the ten marital issues, each spouse is asked to indicate how many such disagreements out of ten they resolve as a couple. Notarius and Vanzetti report that scores on this index of "relational efficacy" (with efficacy ratings on the ten issues summed to produce an overall efficacy measure) had a significant positive correlation with a measure of marital adjustment, negative correlations with spouses' perceptions of negative partner behaviors for both husbands and wives, and a positive correlation with wives' perceptions of pleasing behaviors by their husbands. It is not clear that the MAP's instructions, "Out of every ten disagreements in each marital area below, how many do you believe you and your spouse resolve to your mutual satisfaction?" elicits expectancies of efficacy in *future* marital interactions as opposed to summaries of past events. Although the scale's implicit assumption that an individual's prediction of future efficacy is based on his or her past experiences, it remains for future research with the MAP to clarify the nature of the cognitions assessed. Furthermore, it seems that summing the efficacy ratings for the ten marital issues produces an index of more generalized than specific expectancies, and it would be interesting to investigate whether a low efficacy rating for even one relationship issue can lower marital satisfaction.

Clearly, the investigation of the role of expectancies in marital distress has just begun. Combining Rotter's and Bandura's categorization schemes produces a four-category conceptualization of expectancies: (a) specific outcome expectancies (e.g., "If I express my anger to my partner concerning his/her criticism about my weight, my partner will be more tactful"); (b) generalized outcome expectancies (e.g., "If I communicate my feeling to my partner, he/she will be more likely to meet my needs"); (c) specific efficacy expectancies (e.g., "There is little chance that I can relax enough to express anger directly to my partner"); and (d) generalized efficacy expectancies (e.g., "I lack the ability to learn to express feelings to my partner"). Pretzer et al. (1985) have begun to focus on generalized efficacy and outcome expectancies, but little attention has yet been paid by marital researchers to specific expectancies. As noted earlier, Notarius and Vanzetti's (1983) MAP has potential to elicit data regarding expectancies concerning conflict resolution in particular areas of marriage, but use of a summary score across marital areas produces an index of generalized expectancies. It would seem that in clinical practice and research, the level of assessment of specific expectancies may need to be more molecular, focusing on predictions that a spouse makes about particular outcomes under specific sets of circumstances.

Unfortunately, due to the limited research on marital expectancies, at present it is unknown which type of expectancies are most highly correlated with marital distress. Furthermore, there has been no research investigating how the four types of expectancies are related to one another. For example, one might investigate the degree to which spouses can hold optimistic outcome expectancies (e.g., "We can resolve the basic conflicts between our life-style priorities") in spite of holding specific negative efficacy expectancies (e.g., "We just can't listen to each other in a more open-minded way when we hear each other expressing values that we do not accept").

Understanding the four different types of expectancies is not only important from a basic science perspective, but also is critical for identifying the most effective means for clinically altering different types of expectancies. For example, although there are no data bearing on the issue, changing distorted generalized expectancies might be more difficult than altering distorted specific expectancies. Frequently, the cognitive therapist approaches distorted expectancies by helping the individual to focus on information that has been overlooked or minimized and that is contrary to the prediction. When the individual is making a specific prediction, previously neglected evidence focal to that particular prediction might successfully alter the prediction. However, when a generalized prediction is made, the client may discard the same contradictory information as an exception to the broader pattern. Generalized predictions would appear to be more difficult to change because they are often based on a large yet ill-defined data base, such that knowing exactly what to challenge is difficult, and specific examples are not adequate to alter a prediction based on years of previous experience.

Most marital therapists acknowledge that realistic positive expectancies are very important in motivating clients to make efforts to engage in the therapy process initially and to maintain their continued efforts when problems arise during treatment. Whereas this is an important issue in all types of psychotherapy, it is particularly important and complex in marital therapy because in addition to the self, the partner and the relationship are central foci. Consequently, negative expectancies in any of these domains—self, partner, or the relationship—can decrease motivation for treatment and a willingness to expend effort to change. Again, separate assessments of expectancies regarding the self, partner, and marital relationship have not been conducted but are vital to a clear understanding of the role of expectancies in marital distress and marital therapy.

D. Cognitive Schemata

In order to organize their experiences, observations, and information provided by others, individuals develop cognitive structures or schemata. Seiler (1984) suggests that cognitive structures are the internalized representations that an individual has for categorizing things and events, for solving problems, and for taking action. For example, Bem (1981) has suggested that most people develop gender schemata and process interpersonal and social events in terms of a male versus female dichotomy. In addition, cognitive structures include an appraisal component in which the individual evaluates whether some event or object meets the individual's subjective standards. In essence, cognitive structures or schemata involve templates or organizational strategies for making sense of the world. Although cognitive theorists use varied terminology in describing these phenomena, the current discussion will differentiate between two major related classes of schemata: (a) *assumptions* and (b) *standards* or *beliefs*. Whereas assumptions are an individual's cognitions about the way the world and people actually *are*, beliefs or standards are the individual's cognitions about the way the world and people *should be*.

Assumptions. Individuals develop assumptions about the nature of the world, events, and people. Such assumptions are necessary because they help to organize the vast flood of incoming stimuli and help the individual to process information efficiently. Thus the development of assumptions per se is not of concern; instead, the existence of inaccurate or distorted assumptions is what may lead to marital discord. For example, Nisbett and Ross (1980) have categorized assumptions into person assumptions or "personae" and event assumptions or "scripts." Certain personae, such as the assumptions that some people hold that males and females can never hope to understand one another due to their genetically based different ways of thinking or that people never really change, could certainly lead to a sense of futility and lack of effort to improve a marital relationship. Along this line, Epstein and Eidelson (1981) found that when distressed spouses believed that partners could not change a relationship and that overt disagreement was destructive, they preferred individual over marital therapy and were less optimistic that their own marital relationships could change.

The above assumptions are quite general, but other assumptions might be specific to a particular individual. For example, a wife might conclude about her husband, "Your mother always babied you as you were growing up. Now you see me as having taken her place, and you want me to continue to baby you. You are not really looking for a wife; you are looking for a mother." However, even this particular specific assumption might be based on the broader assumption that the type of relationship one develops with one's opposite-sexed parent determines how one behaves toward one's spouse. As can be seen from the above example, assumptions are not limited to a description of a single attribute of an individual or relationship but can include a set of assumed correlations; in the above example, a certain type of interaction with the husband's mother is assumed to be correlated with the husband's later relationship with his wife.

In order to help an individual challenge his or her distorted assumptions, it can be useful to understand the way in which those assumptions developed. Helping the individual to see how the assumption arose and how it does not apply to the current situation can often be of assistance to the individual challenging the assumption. There are likely at least three ways in which faulty assumptions develop. First, individuals might be exposed to other persons who are not representative of most married couples or members of the opposite sex. For example, a woman who is lied to in several important relationships with men might develop the assumption that you cannot trust men. These conclusions about the nature of men based on a few painful experiences are a particular instance of overgeneralization. For some individuals, it appears that a few painful experiences are sufficient to lead to an overgeneralized assumption that tends to serve the function of minimizing any further possibility of hurt or disappointment.

Second, maladaptive assumptions can result from inappropriate processing or selectively attending to portions of events in one's life. For example, a child who is overly concerned with the stability of the family might selectively focus on his or her parent's arguments that result in alienation and not attend to the large number of instances when the parents disagreed but successfully resolved their problems. As a result, that person might develop the assumption that disagreement is destructive.

Third, "illusory correlations" based on the semantic association between two characteristics or events can lead to inappropriate assumptions (Chapman & Chapman, 1969). For example, a man gradually began to have difficulty attaining erections during sex with his wife. Not only did the wife become distressed about this change, but she increasingly gave her husband advice about how to deal with his boss at work. The pressure that she exerted regarding his work was due to an assumption she made that sexual virility is an indicator of a man's overall "manliness" (i.e., aggressiveness, strength) and that her husband now was likely to be unassertive at work. The semantic connection that she had made between sexual "potency" and force of personality in fact was inaccurate, and her husband resented her intruding into his work life.

At present, other than the beginning work by Epstein and Eidelson (1981), the area of assumptions in marital relationships is unexplored. As in the area of expectancies, there is little knowledge regarding whether certain assumptions are particularly detrimental to marital functioning. Also, the relative importance of rather broad, general assumptions versus specific assumptions is unknown. Understanding people's assumptions about the ways that relationships work, their assumptions about the nature of individuals, and their views about the nature of the world is likely to benefit considerably our understanding of their marital relationships; therefore, increased attention to this class of cognitive variables is needed.

Standards or beliefs. Whereas assumptions reflect an individual's cognitions about the way the world and people are, standards or beliefs reflect an individual's cognitions about how the world and people *should be.* Whereas some cognitive therapists seem to want individuals to eschew the word *should,* as with the other cognitions there is nothing inappropriate about the development of standards per se. They are necessary for an individual to evaluate the appropriateness of his or her own behavior, as well as the behavior of others. These standards may be based on moral beliefs about what is right and wrong (e.g., "You should not abuse other people physically") or on more pragmatic bases of what is adaptive and maladaptive for the individual, the couple, and society. However, standards can become problematic in several ways: (a) if the standard is too extreme or unattainable, or, if attainable, it actually leads to misery rather than happiness; (b) if distinctions between standards and mere preferences are not recognized, such that an individual's desires are translated into moral issues; (c) if the standards are held too rigidly, such that a violation of even minor standards is seen as catastrophic or awful. For example, a wife might believe that married partners should meet all of each other's emotional needs; this standard is probably unattainable for most, if not all, couples. Second, the belief that we should have a right to go on vacation for two weeks each summer is more appropriately viewed as a preference and likely could be more fruitfully discussed from that perspective rather than engaging in a debate over one's moral rights to vacation. Finally, an evaluation that it is *awful* if you do not agree with me is a rather extreme evaluation of a violation of a standard.

A major impetus for the study of extreme standards has come from rational emotional therapy (RET) (Ellis, 1962), which emphasizes extreme standards for individual behavior. More recently, Eidelson and Epstein (1982) developed the Relationship Belief Inventory (RBI), which focuses on extreme standards about intimate relationships per se. Thus RET has dealt primarily with beliefs such as "I must be perfect," whereas Eidelson and Epstein have considered such relationship beliefs as "In a good relationship, partners should be able to mind read each other's needs and preferences." Epstein and Eidelson (1981) found that marital distress is more closely correlated with extreme beliefs about intimate relationships than it is with individual beliefs derived from RET. Also, Jordan and McCormick (1987) conclude that marital distress is more highly correlated with extreme beliefs about relationships than with beliefs about sexual relationships. Both of these findings point out that the content of the standards assessed is important, and extreme standards focal to marital relationships are most likely to be related to marital distress. Whereas the RBI has demonstrated that marital distress is related to extreme relationship beliefs, little more is known about this class of cognitions from an empirical perspective. Thus far, only a very few extreme relationship standards have been investigated, yet there are likely to be an almost infinite set of extreme beliefs about the ways that relationships "should be" that can conceivably interfere with successful marital functioning.

The discussion thus far has focused solely on extreme or unrealistic relationship standards and how they can contribute to marital distress. In addition, clinical observation suggests that discord can result when each spouse has a set of standards that appears reasonable, but the two sets of standards are incompatible. For example, a husband might believe that in dealing with finances, each person should contribute a certain amount to the family fund to meet ongoing expenses, but beyond that, each person should control the money that he or she makes. This may not be merely a preference, but a belief concerning personal rights and freedoms in a relationship. On the other hand, the wife might believe that they should pool their finances totally and make joint decisions about how to spend their money. She believes that the couple should function as a single unit in this domain. Many couples appear to manage their finances successfully with each of these types of strategies; the difficulty arises when these two sets of standards clash. For the couple with this conflicting set of standards, the issue is not merely how to pay the bills successfully. Instead, it involves more fundamental sets of beliefs about what it should mean to be married. What is really at stake are basic standards about the extent to which they should maintain a sense of individuality versus the extent to which they should function jointly as a couple. At present, the role of incompatible yet realistic standards has not been addressed in the empirical literature.

III.   METHODS OF ASSESSING COGNITIONS

As noted above, the investigation of a number of cognitions believed to be relevant to marital functioning is only beginning. Consequently, strategies for assessing these same cognitions are in the early stages of development. Some of the assessment approaches described below have been used almost entirely for research purposes, whereas others have been used in clinical contexts without basic research to validate the results obtained from such strategies.

A.   Self-Report Measures

Self-report measures exist that allow for at least some assessment of each of the five types of cognitions addressed in this chapter. Although not developed for that specific purpose, as described previously, the Spouse Observation Checklist can be employed such that comparing reports between the two partners or between one spouse and an outside observer can provide information about the extent to which the partners are selectively attending to certain types of information. Whereas such data typically have been summarized in terms of frequency of overall positive and negative behaviors in research contexts, for clinical purposes it might be quite useful to consider the data on a more detailed level, taking into account the actual content of the behaviors that have been emphasized and overlooked. For example, it might become quite apparent to a clinician that the partners differ considerably on the amount of affection that they believe has been expressed during a given period. The clinician might then train the couple to monitor those specific behaviors.

A number of self-report measures have been developed to assess couples' causal attributions. These measures have differed in two major ways: (a) whether actual or hypothetical events have been used as the stimuli for which attributions are made, and (b) whether the content of the attribution is focused upon in the response or whether ratings on attributional dimensions are gleaned from the attributions. Two inventories have been modeled after the Attributional Style Questionnaire (Seligman, Abramson, Semmel, & von Baeyer, 1979), which was developed for use in learned helplessness investigations. Both inventories present hypothetical positive and negative marital situations and ask the respondent to supply an attribution for why the partner might behave as described (Baucom & Sayers, 1987; Fincham & O'Leary, 1983). Then the attribution is rated on three dimensions: locus, global-specific, and stable-unstable. The scores on these dimensions then become the foci of study. Thus a distressed spouse might respond that he or she views the partner as responsible for negative marital events and views the cause as stable and global.

By altering the SOC, Baucom, Wheeler, and Bell (1984) developed a self-report measure that assesses attributions for behaviors that occur on a daily basis. That is, spouses complete a shortened SOC and provide attributions for the behaviors that have occurred; the attributions are then rated on the three dimensions discussed above. Most studies have relied upon either (a) hypothetical events or (b) actual events only, and the findings from these investigations have been similar. Fincham and Beach (in press) have directly compared the two types of stimuli and concluded that with minor exceptions, spouses respond similarly to the two types of stimuli.

In the development of the Marital Attitude Survey (MAS), Pretzer et al. (1985) took a different approach to assessing cognitions. Rather than focusing on attributional dimensions, they emphasized the content of the attributions. Thus they asked respondents whether marital events were attributed to one's own behavior, partner's behavior, one's own personality, partner's personality, partner's malicious intent, or partner's lack of love. Both strategies, assessing attributional dimensions and the content of the attributions, have resulted in findings that indicate that attributions are related to level of marital discord. It has been found most consistently that greater marital distress is associated with blaming one's partner for marital problems, as well as attributing the problems to stable and global traits of the partner (e.g., personality), and negative motives, feelings, and intentions (e.g., Epstein, Pretzer, & Fleming, 1987; Fincham, Beach, & Nelson, 1987; Fincham & Bradbury, 1988; Holtzworth-Munroe & Jacobson, 1985; Pretzer et al., 1985). However, the relative merits of assessing attributional dimensions versus content have yet to be investigated.

The MAS contains an additional subscale that focuses on an important expectancy—the extent to which the respondent believes that the couple will improve their relationship. As predicted, a negative expectancy on this subscale is related to marital distress and depression (Pretzer et al., 1985). However, the multitude of additional expectancies that are involved in a marital relationship have not been assessed with self-report measures. The Areas-of-Change Questionnaire (AC; Weiss, Hops, & Patterson, 1973) could be adapted for this purpose. The AC lists 34 specific behavioral aspects of a marital relationship. The respondent is asked to describe the degree of change desired from the partner in each of these areas. It would be a simple task to have the respondent also indicate the extent to which he or she believes the partner will change in each of those areas. Although this would broaden the domain on which expectancies could be assessed, it still would not allow for an evaluation of the moment-to-moment expectancies that guide behavior toward one's partner.

Three subscales on the Relationship Belief Inventory (Eidelson & Epstein, 1982) focus on assumptions about individuals and members of the opposite sex. One subscale assesses the extent to which an individual assumes that partners can change. Another subscale, sex-role rigidity, assesses the extent to which the respondent assumes that the two sexes can hope to understand each other, and the extent to which their needs and desires are assumed to be different. The third subscale addresses the assumption that disagreement between spouses is destructive. Endorsing these assumptions is negatively correlated with level of marital adjustment (Eidelson & Epstein, 1982). These assumptions were selected for assessment because of their apparent pervasive impact on the relationship. Again, however, the many other assumptions that spouses might hold about people and relationships have not been incorporated into self-report measures.

Finally, there are two published self-report inventories that focus on standards or beliefs about how individuals and relationships should be. Jones (1968) developed the Irrational Beliefs Test (IBT) to assess ten irrational beliefs focal to rational emotive therapy. As noted above, these beliefs focus on individuals, not relationships, and they do not seem to be strongly related to level of marital adjustment. However, the RBI, also discussed above, focuses on cognitions relevant to intimate relationships. Two subscales deal with relationship standards: (a) that a partner should know what the other person wants and is thinking, and (b) that sexual encounters should always be wonderful. As expected, both subscales correlate negatively with marital adjustment. As with expectancies and assumptions, the many other specific standards that couples might have about relationships and that might prove to be problematic have yet to be explored with self-report measures.

Another self-report measure, which is not a questionnaire, is Beck's Daily Record of Dysfunctional Thoughts (DRDT; Beck et al., 1979). As the name implies, this is a recording form for listing one's own dysfunctional thoughts, along with their associated emotions, and the context within which the cognitions arose. This general recording form can be used to focus on the various categories of cognitions relevant to intimate relationships. Because the respondent must be trained in the principles and procedures of cognitive therapy in order to monitor him- or herself and record useful cognitions, the DRDT is most often used during therapy rather than as an initial assessment device.

B. Clinical Interviews

During the initial clinical interviews with a couple and throughout therapy, the clinician has an opportunity to observe each spouse's expressions of his or her cognitions. Often the clients will volunteer information pertinent to these cognitions. For example, frequently one spouse will complain that the partner rarely engages in certain behaviors, such as helping in the kitchen, whereas that partner claims to help frequently, thus providing information perhaps relevant to selective attention. Similarly, spouses often will provide their explanations or attributions for the problems they are having, for example: "The reason we have problems with your mother is because you start acting like her good little girl, always trying to please her every time we go home. You become a totally different person from what you are like when you are with just me and the kids." Likewise, clients offer their expectancies: "You know, all those complaints he just made about me. Even if I make all the changes he asked for, it won't do any good. He will just have new complaints because he needs somebody to complain about, so he doesn't have to look at himself."

At times, the individual cognitions offered by a spouse have no particular utility in understanding cognitive themes operating within the couple, but frequently the various specific cognitions fit into a broader pattern that the clinician can discern. For example, a number of complaints from one spouse might lead the clinician to believe that the spouse clings to the standard that the partner should know what the person wants without the person having to state it, and that it shows a lack of love and concern if the partner does not know. Rarely do the spouses express such broad, general standards directly, although they might offer their specific standards for a particular situation. Similarly, spouses rarely offer some of their more general assumptions about people and relationships. These rather basic schemata about people and relationships might guide much behavior and emotion, yet they appear to go unnoticed or at least are not spontaneously verbalized by the spouses. This view that the person's schemata operate in a rather automatic manner or without purposeful thought and that they may not even be fully in the person's awareness is an assumption of cognitive therapy (see Beck et al., 1979) that is yet to be empirically investigated.

When spouses do not offer cognitions spontaneously, the clinician can probe for cognitions with questions. Thus if a spouse mentions an area of discord within the couple, the clinician can ask each person for his or her understanding of why that problem occurs, thus eliciting attributions. Also, when discussing specific problems in a couple's relationship, the clinician can ask directly about the extent to which each person believes change in that area is likely to occur, resulting in a discussion of expectancies. Again, the individuals' schemata at times are more difficult to evoke, and a series of questions is often needed. Burns (1980) describes the "downward arrow" technique, which involves a series of questions that continue to probe for why a particular behavior or situation is upsetting to an individual, with the aim of elucidating the person's schemata.

At times, directly asking a client what he or she is thinking does not result in the classes of cognitions described in this chapter. Instead, asking the client what *emotions* he or she is experiencing can serve as a meaningful first step. For example, after a woman clarifies that she is angry with her husband, the clinician then can ask, "What are the angry thoughts you are having that go along with that feeling?" Therefore, one very effective way to elicit cognitions is through an initial discussion of related emotions. Consequently, it often is fruitful to probe for cognitions when one spouse appears to be having an emotional response during the interview. Dysfunctional thoughts often underlie an emotional reaction (a) when it is not apparent from what is being discussed in the session that such an emotional response would be expected, (b) when the emotional response appears to be far out of proportion to the content being discussed, and (c) when there is an unpredictable shift in emotional tone from one of the spouses.

Although the above strategies for a clinical interview appear to have utility, they have not been evaluated empirically. Therefore, the validity of cognitions obtained through these approaches is unclear. In studying attributions, Holtzworth-Munroe and Jacobson (1985) found that different approaches for eliciting attributions resulted in rather different information; thus more investigation is needed to clarify how the findings from these different assessment strategies interrelate.

C.   Behavioral Observation

Finally, cognitions can be assessed from directly observing the spouses interacting with each other, because they often express important dysfunctional cognitions to each other. Most cognitive-behavioral marital therapists provide an opportunity for couples to communicate directly with each other during the initial assessment without intervention from the clinician. One major goal of this interaction is to give the therapist the chance to observe the couple's communication and problem-solving skills. In order to assess the couple's problem-solving skills, the clinician might ask them to select a problem of moderate severity in their relationship and attempt to resolve it. To assess the couple's ability to express emotions, the clinician might ask each person to share with his or her partner (a) emotions about something he or she likes about the partner or their relationship and (b) emotions about something he or she would like to see changed in the partner or their relationship. In addition to providing information about communication skills, such interactions offer much insight into the spouses' cognitions. Just as when talking to the clinician, the spouses often are explicit with each other about many of their cognitions related to the marriage. In addition to the content of the cognitions, the amount of time spent discussing cognitions can provide useful information to the clinician. For example, some couples when asked to resolve a problem become focused on attributions for the problem, attempting to decide who is to blame. Regardless of the content of the attributions, such an extended discussion of attributions can interfere with reaching an acceptable solution to the problem.

Evaluating the cognitions obtained from direct behavioral observations of a couple's interaction is important. Unfortunately, there have been few coding systems developed for rating the cognitions provided. However, Holtzworth-Munroe and Jacobson (1985) have developed a coding system for rating unsolicited attributions. Although this system was developed for coding written statements provided by couples, it also can be used to code verbal statements from direct interaction. This system provides guidelines for determining whether a statement involves an attribution and ratings on the following attributional dimensions: locus, trait/state, stability, globality, positive or negative intentionality, and voluntariness. The findings indicate that raters can reliably conclude whether a statement includes an attribution, and the resulting attributions can be reliably classified as either distress-maintaining or relationship-enhancing. As with most observational coding systems, this one requires a great deal of time to apply and is not feasible for routine clinical use.

IV.   FUTURE DIRECTIONS IN ASSESSMENT

There are two major directions that are important for future research in assessing cognitions relevant to marital functioning. First and most basic, there is a great need for well-constructed, validated assessment instruments. In terms of self-report measures, only a few of the potentially important cognitions (mostly attributions, and to a much lesser degree assumptions, standards, and expectancies) have been included among the items on existing questionnaires. To some extent, this lack of measures has resulted because the categories of cognitions have not been clearly elucidated. In addition, developing inventories to assess these cognitions involves a number of difficult conceptual and methodological issues (Baucom et al., in press). For example, in assessing attributions, it is unclear whether it is more important to focus on (a) the content of the attributions or (b) where those attributions lie on various dimensions (e.g., stable-unstable, global-specific) believed to be of theoretical importance (e.g., Doherty, 1981a).

Additional effort also is needed in developing strategies to assess cognitions from direct observation or other contexts in which the attributions are emitted spontaneously, without direction from an inventory or clinician. This, also, is a difficult task because often spouses do not offer cognitions in a clear manner that meet the definitions provided above. Thus raters are in the position of either making subjective judgments as to whether a particular cognition (e.g., standard) was emitted or using guidelines for deciding that a particular cognition has occurred that are so concrete that many meaningful cognitions are not coded because they do not meet the guidelines. Providing appropriate delimiting rules for category formation is an important task of any coding system, but this is particularly difficult in assessing cognitions because, by definition, the constructs are quite subjective in nature and may be expressed in varying ways by different spouses.

Once these two different approaches to assessment of cognitions (structured inventories and systems for coding spontaneous expression of attributions, expectancies, assumptions, and standards) have been developed further, the second major direction for research is to compare these two strategies. Asking a person to provide an explanation for why a marital event has occurred directs that individual to think about explanations for the event; without that instruction, the person might not have thought about why the event occurred (Pyszcynski & Greenberg, 1981). Although there are more indirect ways to probe for cognitions using self-report measures, almost all current self-report measures direct the respondent to consider certain cognitions. This methodological approach could result in cognitions that are not typical of the person's thoughts in everyday life when the person is not directed toward certain cognitions. Obtaining cognitions without instructions to the couple to provide certain types of cognitions is less directive. Whether or not cognitions gleaned from these two different approaches are comparable is unclear. For example, Holtzworth-Munroe and Jacobson (1985) probed for attributions about marital events both directly and indirectly. Although the results from these two different approaches were statistically related, the correlations between the resulting attributions were small in size. Thus it appears that the manner in which one probes for or elicits marital cognitions might influence the findings, and the relative merits of the different methodological approaches are unclear.

V. COGNITIVE TREATMENT OF MARITAL DISCORD

A. Varieties of Cognitive Therapy

The terms *cognitive therapy* and *cognitive restructuring* are summary labels that indicate that in some way the clinician is focusing on the couple's thoughts. However, within that broad domain, there is room for extreme variability in clinical application in at least three different ways. First, as noted throughout this chapter, there are at least five different categories of cognitions that might be focused upon in treatment. Some clinicians might focus on one or more of these categories to the exclusion of other types of cognitions. This might result because of the particular couple's needs or because a clear model concerning the roles of different types of cognitions in marriage has been lacking until this time. Focusing on different categories of cognitions is likely to influence the results of a treatment outcome investigation or the progress with a particular couple significantly.

Second, there are a large number of specific therapeutic techniques or strategies available for dealing with these various cognitions, such that knowing that a clinician or outcome investigator focused on attributions or expectancies does not clarify exactly what intervention strategies were employed. For example, some of the major strategies employed in cognitive therapy with couples include (a) conducting a logical analysis of the spouse's cognition to clarify whether it seems appropriate; (b) searching for alternative cognitions that appear more likely to fit the current situation; (c) searching for confirming or disconfirming evidence from a variety of contexts, such as from planned behavioral experiments; and (d) weighing the pros and cons of maintaining certain cognitions, such as specific standards. A discussion of these various techniques is beyond the scope of this chapter, but it should be clear that the various strategies might be differentially effective. Additionally, certain intervention techniques might be particularly useful with specific couples. (For descriptions of the clinical implementation of various treatment techniques, see Epstein & Baucom, in press; Epstein, Schlesinger, & Dryden, 1988.)

Third, the context or format for presenting cognitive restructuring techniques can vary. For example, cognitive therapy can be presented alone, as an entire treatment without other treatment techniques (e.g., Emmelkamp et al., 1988; Epstein et al., 1982; Huber & Milstein, 1985). Alternatively, cognitive restructuring techniques can be presented as a module, along with other treatment modules (such as various behavioral interventions) in a sequential manner (e.g. Baucom, 1985; Baucom & Lester, 1986). Finally, cognitive restructuring techniques can be integrated with other treatment strategies such as behavioral interventions, employing a treatment approach in which the clinician shifts back and forth among cognitions, behavior, and affect as is appropriate within the session (e.g., Epstein &

Baucom, in press). At present, only the first two formats have been explored empirically, and they have not been compared directly with each other.

B. Cognitive-Behavioral Treatment Outcome Investigations

At present, five empirical investigations have been conducted exploring the effectiveness of cognitive restructuring with distressed couples. Three of those investigations employed cognitive restructuring as the sole treatment (Emmelkamp et al., 1988; Epstein et al., 1982; Huber & Milstein, 1985). Two other investigations have been conducted based upon a different rationale. A large number of outcome investigations have demonstrated the effectiveness of behavioral marital therapy (BMT) in working with distressed couples (see Baucom & Hoffman, 1986, for a recent review). Still, there is a substantial minority of couples who do not benefit from BMT or benefit only to a limited extent (Jacobson et al., 1984). Consequently, cognitive restructuring was employed along with BMT strategies in order to determine whether this combined treatment would bolster the effectiveness of behavioral techniques (Baucom, 1985; Baucom & Lester, 1986).

The cognitive foci of these investigations have varied somewhat and have not systematically included attention to all five categories of cognitions discussed here. For example, three studies have focused almost exclusively on altering dysfunctional attributions and standards (Baucom, 1985; Baucom & Lester, 1986; Emmelkamp et al., 1988). Epstein et al.'s (1982) approach has been somewhat broader, dealing with any upsetting cognitions that the spouses were having about the relationship; again, the primary focus of treatment was attributions and standards. Huber and Milstein (1985) provided a brief cognitive restructuring component aimed at altering dysfunctional standards, as well as the assumption that partners and relationships cannot change in the positive direction. Consequently, the outcome studies conducted thus far have focused largely on attributions and standards, with very little attention given to selective attention, expectancies, and assumptions.

All of these investigations indicate that the cognitive restructuring techniques employed significantly reduced dysfunctional relationship standards (as measured by the RBI). Epstein et al. also found that cognitive restructuring was effective in reducing spouses' tendencies to attribute relationship problems to the malice of their partners. In addition, Huber and Milstein conclude that their cognitive restructuring intervention increased the couples' expectancy that marital therapy would benefit them, as well as their desire to improve their relationships. However, when the effects of cognitive restructuring are compared with behavioral interventions in terms of promoting cognitive changes, the findings are unclear. Of the four studies employing a BMT comparison group, three (Baucom, 1985; Baucom & Lester, 1986; Emmelkamp et al., 1988) found no significant differences between the cognitive and behavioral groups on the RBI. That is, Emmelkamp et al. found that cognitive restructuring alone did not differ from BMT alone in promoting cognitive changes. Baucom found in both of his studies that cognitive restructuring plus BMT did not differ from BMT alone in producing cognitive changes. Epstein et al. did find that cognitive restructuring was more effective than BMT (communication training) in altering one relationship standard—that mind reading is effective and desirable. Similarly, in both of Baucom's studies and Emmelkamp's investigation, both treatments effectively reduced presenting complaints of specific behaviors, with no significant differences between the two groups.

Most marital investigators employ cognitive and behavioral interventions for the purpose of improving the quality of the couple's relationships. Therefore, it is important to determine not only whether cognitions and behaviors have changed, but also whether marital adjustment has improved with treatment. Here again, the results are mixed. Baucom's studies indicate that cognitive restructuring plus BMT and BMT alone were equally effective in significantly increasing marital adjustment for both husbands and wives. Huber and Milstein also found that cognitive restructuring significantly improved marital adjustment relative to a wait list condition. However, Emmelkamp found that cognitive restructuring increased marital adjustment for males only, whereas BMT did not result in significant improvement for either sex. Epstein et al. found that neither BMT nor cognitive restructuring increased marital adjustment; however, the changes were of the magnitude typically found in other outcome investigations, and the small sample sizes might have accounted for the lack of statistically significant change.

In summary, the results of the investigations are most consistent in demonstrating that cognitive restructuring as defined in these studies can produce the types of cognitive changes assessed on the RBI, primarily unrealistic relationship standards. Unfortunately, due to the lack of measures for assessing couples' attributions when these investigations were undertaken, their effectiveness in altering attributions is unclear, even though attributions were a major focus of all studies. Also, there is a lack of evidence that cognitive restructuring as employed in these initial investigations is more effective than BMT in producing cognitive changes or increasing marital adjustment.

Clearly, investigation into the effectiveness of cognitive restructuring is just beginning. The above investigations should be viewed only as initial efforts for several reasons. First, almost all of the investigations focus solely on attributions and relationship standards to the exclusion of selective attention, expectancies, and assumptions about relationships. Therefore, the scope of variables assessed in cognitive restructuring needs to be broadened. Second, the lack of a broad range of validated cognitive measures has compromised the ability to discern the effects of these treatments clearly. Third, no studies have attempted to investigate the effectiveness of an integrated cognitive/behavioral approach, which likely is practiced by a number of clinicians in applied settings. Fourth, the number of sessions focusing on cognitive restructuring has been rather limited. For example, in both of Baucom's studies and Huber and Milstein's investigation only six weeks were devoted to cognitive restructuring. Our clinical impression is that this is too brief a time period for couples to learn the cognitive model, isolate their own dysfunctional cognitions, and meaningfully alter cognitions that would benefit the relationship.

Finally, in all five of the above investigations, as well as all other marital therapy outcome investigations, the couples were randomly assigned to treatment without any attempt to match couples with treatment. Baucom and Lester (1986) and Emmelkamp et al. (1988) note that in their investigations there were couples who seemingly would have benefited from the alternative treatment. Some couples who were assigned to BMT alone evidenced a number of distorted cognitions; similarly, other couples who spent a number of weeks focusing on cognitions could have spent their time more fruitfully making behavioral changes. An integrated cognitive/ behavioral approach that provides the flexibility to focus on cognitions or behaviors when appropriate circumvents this difficulty. As mentioned above, the effectiveness of such an approach is unknown. When couples are not matched optimally to treatments, there is wide variability in response within each treatment condition, which results in a lack of significant differences between groups. Thus the particular research designs used thus far might mask any differential effectiveness that does exist between treatment conditions. As a result, both Emmelkamp and Baucom have called for a halt to outcome investigations that randomly assign couples to inflexible treatments, because more than a decade of outcome studies using this design in marital therapy provide consistent findings of no significant differences among active treatment conditions (Baucom & Hoffman, 1986).

VI.   CONCLUSIONS

It is hard to refute that the ways that spouses think about their relationships are an important component of marital distress. Yet translating this general statement into specifics in such a way as to advance our understanding of marital discord is a significant challenge. In this chapter we have delineated what we believe to be the important cognitive variables in marital adjustment. Because so little empirical investigation has been devoted to several of these variables, a first step is to conduct basic research to come to a better understanding of marital expectancies, assumptions, and standards. This task will be accomplished more easily if theories of marital functioning are developed that take cognitions into account (Fincham & Bradbury, 1988; Doherty, 1981a, 1981b). These theories must consider how the various categories of cognitions relate to each other, and how they interact with important behaviors and emotions within the marital context. Such theories should provide guidance in operationalizing the cognitive variables and assist in the development of well-validated assessment tools. Additional investigations should examine the relative importance of these variables in understanding marital discord. What has become apparent is that up to this point attention has been focused too narrowly on causal attributions, without any direction for future research. This chapter's delineation of cognitive variables and methodological issues for investigating them is intended to give new direction to the study of cognitive factors in marriage.

Additional basic research and well-formulated theories can be of great service in developing effective treatment interventions for distressed couples. In that regard, a number of important questions remain. What cognitive variables should be focused on in treatment? If treatment is to be matched to a particular couple's needs, how does that matching occur? If a couple needs more than one type of intervention—such as cognitive restructuring and behavioral techniques—how are those interventions to be integrated or sequenced? Even if the couple presents with significant cognitive distortions, are there particular behavioral techniques that are effective in reducing these distortions, while also producing behavioral changes? And, if so, is this a more parsimonious way to produce both cognitive and behavioral changes? In addition, are there particular cognitive interventions that are effective in reducing impediments to effective therapy, such as a sense of hopelessness and a lack of collaboration between the spouses? The next decade should be a time of great excitement as theoreticians along with basic and clinical researchers attempt to unravel the answers to these complex yet compelling questions, which have the potential to take us one step closer to understanding the intricate nature of intimate interpersonal relationships.

REFERENCES

Abramson, L. Y., Seligman, M.E.P., & Teasdale, J. D. (1978). Learned helplessness in humans: Critique and reformulation. *Journal of Abnormal Psychology, 87*, 49–74.

Bandura, A. (1977). *Social learning theory*. Englewood Cliffs, NJ: Prentice-Hall.

Baucom, D. H. (1985, November). *Enhancing behavioral marital therapy with cognitive restructuring and emotional expressiveness training*. Paper presented at the Nineteenth Annual Convention of the Association for the Advancement of Behavior Therapy, Houston.

Baucom, D. H. (1987). Attributions in distressed relations: How can we explain them? In S.

Duck & D. Perlman (Eds.), *Heterosexual relations, marriage and divorce* (pp. 177–206). London: Sage.

Baucom, D. H., Bell, W. G., & Duhe, A. (1982, August). *The measurement of couples' attributions for positive and negative dyadic interactions.* Paper presented at the annual meeting of the Association for the Advancement of Behavior Therapy, Los Angeles.

Baucom, D. H., Epstein, N., Sayers, S., & Sher, T. G. (1989). The role of cognitions in marital relationships: Definitional, methodological, and conceptual issues. *Journal of Consulting and Clinical Psychology, 57,* 31–38.

Baucom, D. H., & Hoffman, J. A. (1986). The effectiveness of marital therapy: Current status and application to the clinical setting. In N. S. Jacobson & A. Guzman (Eds.), *Clinical handbook of marital therapy.* New York: Guilford.

Baucom, D. H., & Lester, G. W. (1986). The usefulness of cognitive restructuring as an adjunct to behavioral marital therapy. *Behavior Therapy, 17,* 385–403.

Baucom, D. H., & Sayers, S. L. (1987, November). *Attributional style and attributional patterns among married couples.* Paper presented at the Twenty-first Annual Convention of the Association for the Advancement of Behavior Therapy, Boston.

Baucom, D. H., Wheeler, C. M., & Bell, G. (1984, November). *Assessing the role of attributions in marital distress.* Paper presented at the Eighteenth Annual Convention of the Association for the Advancement of Behavior Therapy, Philadelphia.

Beck, A. T., Rush, A. J., Shaw, B. F., & Emery, G. (1979). *Cognitive therapy of depression.* New York: Guilford.

Bem, S. L. (1981). Gender schema theory: A cognitive account of sex typing. *Psychological Review, 88,* 354–364.

Berley, R. A., & Jacobson, N. S. (1984). Causal attributions in intimate relationships: Toward a model of cognitive behavioral marital therapy. In P. Kendall (Ed.), *Advances in cognitive-behavioral research and therapy* (Vol. 3, pp. 1–60). New York: Academic Press.

Burns, D. D. (1980). *Feeling good.* New York: William Morrow.

Chapman, L. J., & Chapman, J. P. (1969). Illusory correlation as an obstacle to the use of valid psychodiagnostic signs. *Journal of Abnormal Psychology, 74,* 271–280.

Christensen, A., & Nies, D. C. (1980). The Spouse Observation Checklist: Empirical analysis and critique. *American Journal of Family Therapy, 8,* 69–79.

Christensen, A., Sullaway, M., & King, C. E. (1983). Systematic error in behavioral reports of dyadic interaction: Egocentric bias and content effects. *Behavioral Assessment, 5,* 129–140.

Christensen, A., & Wallace, L. (1976). Perceptual accuracy as a variable in marital adjustment. *Journal of Sex and Marital Therapy, 2,* 130–136.

Doherty, W. J. (1981a). Cognitive processes in intimate conflict: I. Extending attribution theory. *American Journal of Family Therapy, 9*(1), 5–13.

Doherty, W. J. (1981b). Cognitive processes in intimate conflict: II. Efficacy and learned helplessness. *American Journal of Family Therapy, 9*(2), 35–44.

Eidelson, R. J., & Epstein, N. (1982). Cognition and relationship maladjustment: Development of a measure of dysfunctional relationship beliefs. *Journal of Consulting and Clinical Psychology, 50,* 715–720.

Ellis, A. (1962). *Reason and emotion in psychoterapy.* New York: Lyle Stuart.

Emmelkamp, P. M. G., van Linden van den Heuvell, C., Ruphan, M., Sanderman R., Scholing, A., & Stroink, F. (1988). Cognitive and behavioral interventions: A comparative evaluation with clinically distressed couples. *Journal of Family Psychology,* 365–377.

Epstein, N. (1985). Depression and marital dysfunction: Cognitive and behavioral linkages. *International Journal of Mental Health, 13*(3–4), 86–104.

Epstein, N., & Baucom, D. H. (in press). Cognitive-behavioral marital therapy. In A. Freeman, K. M. Simon, H. Arkowitz, & L. Butler (Eds.), *Handbook of cognitive therapy,* New York: Plenum.

Epstein, N., & Eidelson, R. J. (1981). Unrealistic beliefs of clinical couples: Their relationship to expectations, goals and satisfaction. *American Journal of Family Therapy, 9*(4), 13–22.

Epstein, N., Pretzer, J., & Fleming, B. (1982, November). *Cognitive therapy and communication training: Comparisons of effects with distressed couples.* Paper presented at the Sixteenth Annual Convention of the Association for the Advancement of Behavior Therapy, Los Angeles.

Epstein, N., Pretzer, J. L., & Fleming, B. (1987). The role of cognitive appraisal in self-reports of marital communication. *Behavior Therapy, 18*, 51–69.

Epstein, N., Schlesinger, S. E., & Dryden, W. (1988). *Cognitive behavioral therapy with families.* New York: Brunner/Mazel.

Fichten, C. F. (1984). See it from my point of view: Videotape and attributions in happy and distressed couples. *Journal of Social and Clinical Psychology, 2*, 125–142.

Fincham, F. (1985). Attributions in close relationships. In J. Harvey & G. Weary (Eds.), *Attribution: Basic and applied issues.* New York: Academic Press.

Fincham, F. D., & Beach, S. (in press). Attribution processes in distressed and nondistressed couples: 5. Real versus hypothetical events. *Cognitive Therapy and Research.*

Fincham, F. D., Beach, S., & Baucom, D. H. (1987). Attribution processing in distressed and nondistressed couples: 4. Self-partner attribution differences. *Journal of Personality and Social Psychology, 52*, 739–748.

Fincham, F. D., Beach, S., & Nelson, G. (1987). Attribution processes in distressed and nondistressed couples: 3. Causal and responsibility attributions for spouse behavior. *Cognitive Therapy and Research, 11*, 71–86.

Fincham, F. D., & Bradbury, T. (1987a). The impact of attributions in marriage: A longitudinal analysis. *Journal of Personality and Social Psychology, 53*, 510–517.

Fincham, F. D., & Bradbury, T. (1987b). Cognitive processes and conflict in close relationships: An attribution-efficacy mode. *Journal of Personality and Social Psychology, 53*, 1106–1118.

Fincham, F. D., & Bradbury, T. (1988). The impact of attributions in marriage: Empirical and conceptual foundations. *British Journal of Clinical Psychology, 27*, 77–90.

Fincham, F. D., & Bradbury, T. (in press). The impact of attributions in marriage: An experimental analysis. *Journal of Social and Clinical Psychology.*

Fincham, F. D., & O'Leary, K. D. (1983). Causal inferences for spouse behavior in maritally distressed and nondistressed couples. *Journal of Social and Clinical Psychology, 1*, 42–57.

Heider, F. (1958). *The psychology of interpersonal relations.* New York: John Wiley.

Holtzworth-Munroe, A., & Jacobson, N. S. (1985). Causal attributions of married couples: When do they search for causes? What do they conclude when they do? *Journal of Personality and Social Psychology, 48*, 1398–1412.

Huber, C. H., & Milstein, B. (1985). Cognitive restructuring and a collaborative set in couples' work. *American Journal of Family Therapy, 13*(2), 17–27.

Jacobson, N. S., Follette, W. C., Revenstorf, D., Baucom, D. H., Hahlweg, K., & Margolin, G. (1984). Variability in outcome and clinical significance of behavioral marital therapy: A reanalysis of outcome data. *Journal of Consulting and Clinical Psychology, 52*, 497–504.

Jacobson, N. S., McDonald, D. W., Follette, W. C., & Berley, R. A. (1985). Attributional processes in distressed and nondistressed married couples. *Cognitive Therapy and Research, 9*, 35–50.

Jacobson, N. S., & Moore, D. (1981). Spouses as observers of the events in their relationships. *Journal of Consulting and Clinical Psychology, 49*, 269–277.

Jones, E. E., & Davis, K. E. (1965). From acts to dispositions: The attribution process in person perception. *Advances in Experimental Social Psychology, 2*, 219–266.

Jones, R. G. (1968). *A factored measure of Ellis' irrational belief system, with personality and maladjustment correlates.* Unpublished doctoral dissertation, Texas Technological College. (University Microfilms No. 69–6443)

Jordan, T. J., & McCormick, N. B. (1987, April). *The role of sex beliefs in intimate relationships*. Paper presented at the annual meeting of the American Association of Sex Educators, Counselors and Therapists, New York.

Kelley, H. H. (1967). Attribution theory in social psychology. *Nebraska Symposium on Motivation, 15*, 192–238.

Kyle, S. O., & Falbo, T. (1985). Relationships between marital stress and attributional preferences for own and spouse behavior. *Journal of Social and Clinical Psychology, 3*, 339–351.

Nisbett, R., & Ross, L. (1980). *Human inference: Strategies and shortcomings of social judgment*. Englewood Cliffs, NJ: Prentice-Hall.

Notarius, C. I., & Vanzetti, N. A. (1983). The Marital Agendas Protocol. In E. E. Filsinger (Ed.), *Marriage and family assessment: A sourcebook for family therapy* (pp. 209–277). Beverly Hills, CA: Sage.

Patterson, G. R. (1976). Some procedures of assessing changes in marital interaction patterns. *Oregon Research Institute Research Bulletin, 16*(7).

Pretzer, J. L., Epstein, N., & Fleming, B. (1985). *The Marital Attitude Survey: A measure of dysfunctional attributions and expectancies*. Unpublished manuscript.

Pyszcynski, T. A., & Greenberg, J. (1981). Role of disconfirmed expectancies in the instigation of attributional processing. *Journal of Personality and Social Psychology, 40*, 31–38.

Robinson, E. A., & Price, M. G. (1980) Pleasurable behavior in marital interaction: An observational study. *Journal of Consulting and Clinical Psychology, 48*, 117–118.

Rotter, J. B. (1954). *Social learning and clinical psychology*. Englewood Cliffs, NJ: Prentice-Hall.

Seiler, T. B. (1984). Development of cognitive theory, personality, and therapy. In N. Hoffmann (Ed.), *Foundations of cognitive therapy: Theoretical methods and practical applications* (pp. 11–49). New York: Plenum.

Seligman, M., Abramson, L. Y., Semmel, A., von Baeyer, C. (1979). Depressive attributional style. *Journal of Abnormal Psychology, 88*, 242–247.

Sullaway, M., & Christensen, A. (1983). Couples and families as participant observers of their interaction. In J. P. Vincent (Ed.), *Advances in family intervention, assessment and theory* (Vol. 3, pp. 119–160). Greenwich, CT: JAI.

Thompson, J. S., & Snyder, D. K. (1986). Attribution theory in intimate relationships: A methodological review. *American Journal of Family Therapy, 14*, 123–138.

Weiss, R. L., Hops, H., & Patterson, G. R. (1973). A framework for conceptualizing marital conflict, a technology for altering it, some data for evaluating it. In L. A. Hamerlynck, L. C. Handy, & E. J. Mash (Eds.), *Behavior change: Methodology, concepts, and practice* (pp. 309–342). Champaign, IL: Research Press.

Weiss, R. L., & Margolin, G. (1977). Marital conflict and accord. In A. R. Ciminero, K. S. Calhoun, & H. E. Adams (Eds.), *Handbook for behavioral assessment*. New York: John Wiley.

INDEX